Computer Science Workbench

Editor: Tosiyasu L. Kunii

Computer Science Workbench

N. Magnenat Thalmann, D. Thalmann: Image Synthesis. Theory and Practice. XV, 400 pp., 223 figs., including 80 in color. 1987

B.A. Barsky: Computer Graphics and Geometric Modeling Using Beta-splines. IX, 156 pp., 85 figs., including 31 in color. 1987

H. Kitagawa, T.L. Kunii: The Unnormalized Relational Data Model. For Office Form Processor Design. XIII, 164 pp., 78 figs. 1989

N. Magnenat Thalmann, D. Thalmann: Computer Animation. Theory and Practice. Second Revised Edition. XIII, 245 pp., 156 figs., including 73 in color. 1990

N. Magnenat Thalmann, D. Thalmann: Synthetic Actors in Computer-Generated 3D Films. X, 129 pp., 133 figs., including 83 in color. 1990

K. Fujimura: Motion Planning in Dynamic Environments. XIII, 178 pp., 85 figs. 1991

M. Suk, S.M. Bhandarkar: Three-Dimensional Object Recognition from Range Images. XXII, 308 pp., 107 figs. 1992

Minsoo Suk · Suchendra M. Bhandarkar

Three-Dimensional Object Recognition from Range Images

With 107 Figures

Springer-Verlag Tokyo Berlin Heidelberg New York
London Paris Hong Kong Barcelona Budapest

Prof. Minsoo Suk
Department of Electrical and Computer Engineering
Syracuse University
121 Link Hall
Syracuse, New York 13244-1240, USA

Prof. Suchendra M. Bhandarkar
Department of Computer Science
University of Georgia
415 Boyd Graduate Studies Research Center
Athens, Georgia 30602-7404, USA

Series   Editor:
Prof. Dr. Tosiyasu L. Kunii
Department of Information Science
Faculty of Science
The University of Tokyo
7-3-1 Hongo, Bunkyo-ku
Tokyo, 113 Japan

ISBN-13:978-4-431-68215-8   e-ISBN-13:978-4-431-68213-4
DOI: 10.1007/978-4-431-68213-4

Printed on acid-free paper
© Springer-Verlag Tokyo 1992
Softcover reprint of the hardcover 1st edition 1992

SERIES PREFACE

Computer Science Workbench is a monograph series which will provide you with an in-depth working knowledge of current developments in computer technology. Every volume in this series will deal with a topic of importance in computer science and elaborate on how you yourself can build systems related to the main theme. You will be able to develop a variety of systems, including computer software tools, computer graphics, computer animation, database management systems, and computer-aided design and manufacturing systems. Computer Science Workbench represents an important new contribution in the field of practical computer technology.

Tosiyasu L. Kunii

PREFACE

The primary aim of this book is to present a coherent and self-contained description of recent advances in three-dimensional object recognition from range images. Three-dimensional object recognition concerns recognition and localization of objects of interest in a scene from input images. This problem is one of both theoretical and practical importance. On the theoretical side, it is an ideal vehicle for the study of the general area of *computer vision* since it deals with several important issues encountered in computer vision—for example, issues such as feature extraction, acquisition, representation and proper use of knowledge, employment of efficient control strategies, coupling numerical and symbolic computations, and parallel implementation of algorithms. On the practical side, it has a wide range of applications in areas such as robot vision, autonomous navigation, automated inspection of industrial parts, and automated assembly.

The major research emphasis in computer vision during the last few decades has been primarily on the extraction and analysis of information in intensity images. This was partly due to the lack of reliable range sensors. Today, range sensing technology has progressed to a point where fast, reliable, and economical range sensors are readily available. This has prompted a recent surge in research dealing with the processing and analysis of range data. The book intends to identify important issues in 3-D object recognition from range images and to describe recent advances on those issues. We have tried to present the material in the broader context of computer vision wherever possible.

Computer vision draws from the rich and vast body of knowledge accumulated in the areas of image processing and artificial intelligence over the past several decades. Image processing algorithms such as edge detection, segmentation, and feature extraction and representation form the basis of low- and intermediate-level vision. *Artificial Intelligence* concepts and methodologies that deal with knowledge representation and problem solving via constraint propagation and constraint satisfaction provide the bases for high-level vision. Low- and intermediate-level vision algorithms deal largely with numerical, pixel-level data, whereas high-level techniques deal largely with symbolic entities. A typical vision system, such as one dealing with 3-D object recognition from range images, can therefore be considered to be a *coupled system* where numerical and symbolic computation need to be closely and synergestically coupled in order to solve a given problem efficiently. Our discussion of the 3-D object recognition emphasizes this aspect of computer vision, namely the interaction between numerical and symbolic processing.

The two most significant problems encountered during the process of 3-D object recognition, especially when dealing with multiple-object scenes with partial occlusion, are the *combinatorial explosion* of the search space of scene interpretations and the generation of *spurious scene interpretations*. We present a novel concept of using *qualitative features* to tackle these problems. The idea is to use qualitative features (symbolic) to control the combinatorial explosion (numerical) in a coupled system. We integrate all these components into an object recognition system that can recognize objects from multiple-object scenes with partial occlusion. Scenes containing polyhedral objects as well as complex curved objects are used for experiments.

The magnitude of computation required in a typical computer vision system is huge. Fortunately, *massively parallel computers* are now widely available. Today, parallel computation is not only a topic for theoretical research, but also one with a wide range of practical applications. Keeping this in mind, the book describes in detail the parallel implementation of our 3-D object recognition algorithms on the Connection Machine and hypercube computers.

The book consists of three parts that develop the subject matter in a natural and logical sequence. Part I describes the basic issues and concepts underlying computer vision, and 3-D object recognition in particular. The terminology is outlined, along with definitions of the basic ideas developed in the book. Range sensors and sensing technology, range image segmentation, feature extraction, and representation of features and models are reviewed. Popular recognition and localization techniques, including interpretation tree search, generalized Hough transform, matching of relational structures, and geometric hashing are then described. The shortcomings of existing vision systems that use these techniques are pointed out. Part II deals with the use of qualitative features in object recognition. We show how the use of qualitative features enables us not only to prune the search space, but also to improve the accuracy of recognition. This concept is demonstrated by experiments using multiple-object scenes of increasing complexity—polyhedral objects, objects made up of curved surfaces, and complex curved objects. Part III deals with performance and implementation issues. We present the sensitivity analysis of recognition and localization techniques and parallel implementation of our algorithms.

This book is meant to address a fairly wide and diverse audience. It is suitable for a one-semester or a two-quarter graduate-level course in electrical engineering, computer engineering, or computer science. It could also be used as supplementary material for a graduate-level course in mechanical/aerospace engineering dealing with sensor-based or intelligent robotics. The book would provide excellent reference material for researchers in computer vision, pattern recognition, image processing, robotics, and artificial intelligence. Certain graduate students and researchers in biomedical imaging, remote-sensing and cartography may find some of the basic material herein very helpful.

We owe a debt of gratitude to many people for their help in preparing this book. We wish to extend our appreciation to Professor Tosiyasu Kunii, the Series Editor, for his encouragement, and Miss Yuka Hirahara of Springer-Verlag for her editorial help on numerous occasions and her patience. We are very grateful to R. Shankar, G. Ramamoorthy, M. Yang, Z. Xu, S. Choi, J. Koh, D. Kim, and A. Siebert. M. Suk gratefully acknowledges H. J. Lee for his help in using LaTeXand Ms. E. Weinman for her careful reading of the manuscript. Finally, special appreciation to our family, Younghee, Eugene, Brian, and Swati.

August 1992

Minsoo Suk
Syracuse, New York

S. Bhandarkar
Athens, Georgia

Contents

SERIES PREFACE   v
PREFACE   vii
Credits for Copyrighted Material   xv

1   Introduction   1
   1.1   Computer Vision   1
   1.2   Three-Dimensional Object Recognition   4
       1.2.1   Representation   8
       1.2.2   Indexing   8
       1.2.3   Constraint Propagation and Constraint Satisfaction   . . .   9
   1.3   Common Goals of Three-Dimensional Object Recognition Systems   10
   1.4   Qualitative Features   11
       1.4.1   Study of Qualitative Properties in Low-level Vision Processes   11
       1.4.2   Qualitative Features in Object Recognition   12
   1.5   The Scope and Outline of the Book   13

I   Fundamentals of Range Image Processing and Three-Dimensional Object Recognition   15

2   Range Image Sensors and Sensing Techniques   17
   2.1   Range Image Forms   17
   2.2   Classification of Range Sensors   20
       2.2.1   Radar Sensors   20
       2.2.2   Triangulation Sensors   25
       2.2.3   Sensors based on Optical Interferometry   30
       2.2.4   Sensors Based on Focusing Techniques   32
       2.2.5   Sensors Based on Fresnel Diffraction   33
       2.2.6   Tactile Range Sensors   34

3   Range Image Segmentation   39
   3.1   Mathematical Formulation of Range Image Segmentation   40
   3.2   Fundamentals of Surface Differential Geometry   41
   3.3   Surface Curvatures   44
   3.4   Range Image Segmentation Techniques   50

	3.4.1	Edge-based Segmentation Techniques	50
	3.4.2	Region-based Segmentation Techniques	58
	3.4.3	Hybrid Segmentation Techniques	69
3.5	Summary	75

4 Representation   **77**
	4.1	Formal Properties of Geometric Representations	77
	4.2	Wire-Frame Representation	79
	4.3	Constructive Solid Geometry (CSG) Representation	80
	4.4	Qualitative Representation using Geons	83
	4.5	Aspect Graph Representation	84
	4.6	EGI Representation	86
	4.7	Representation Using Generalized Cylinders	89
	4.8	Superquadric Representation	94
	4.9	Octree Representation	98
	4.10	Summary	101

5 Recognition and Localization Techniques   **103**
	5.1	Recognition and Localization Techniques—An Overview	103
	5.2	Interpretation Tree Search	105
	5.3	Hough Clustering	110
	5.4	Matching of Relational Structures	116
	5.5	Geometric Hashing	124
	5.6	Iterative Model Fitting	127
	5.7	Indexing and Qualitative Features	130
	5.8	Vision Systems as Coupled Systems	135
	5.8.1	Object-Oriented Representation for Coupled Systems . .	136
	5.8.2	Object-Oriented Representation for 3-D Object Recognition	137
	5.8.3	Embedding Parallelism in an Object-Oriented Coupled System	140
	5.9	Summary	141

II Three-Dimensional Object Recognition Using Qualitative Features   **143**

6 Polyhedral Object Recognition   **145**
	6.1	Preprocessing and Segmentation	145
	6.1.1	Plane Fitting to Pixel Data	147
	6.1.2	Clustering in Parameter Space	148
	6.1.3	Post Processing of Clustering Results	149
	6.1.4	Contour Extraction and Classification	150
	6.1.5	Computation of Edge Parameters	151
	6.2	Feature Extraction	157
	6.3	Interpretation Tree Search	160
	6.3.1	Pose Determination	162

      6.3.2 Scene Interpretation Hypothesis Verification 165

  6.4 Generalized Hough Transform 169

      6.4.1 Feature Matching 170

      6.4.2 Computation of the Transform 171

      6.4.3 Pose Clustering 173

      6.4.4 Verification of the Pose Hypothesis 173

  6.5 Experimental Results 174

  6.6 Summary 180

7 Recognition of Curved Objects 183

  7.1 Representation of Curved Surfaces 184

      7.1.1 Extraction of Surface Curvature Features from Range Images 186

  7.2 Recognition Using a Point-Wise Curvature Description 188

      7.2.1 Object Recognition Using Point-Wise Surface Matching . 192

  7.3 Recognition Using Qualitative Features 196

      7.3.1 Cylindrical and Conical Surfaces 197

      7.3.2 The Recognition Process Using Qualitative Features . . . 198

      7.3.3 Localization of a Cylindrical Surface 200

      7.3.4 Localization of a Conical Surface 201

      7.3.5 Localization of a Spherical Surface 201

      7.3.6 An Experimental Comparison 202

  7.4 Recognition of Complex Curved Objects 206

  7.5 Dihedral Feature Junctions 207

      7.5.1 Types of Dihedral Feature Junctions 207

      7.5.2 Matching of Dihedral Feature Junctions 207

      7.5.3 Pose Determination 210

      7.5.4 Pose Clustering 213

  7.6 Experimental Results 213

  7.7 Summary 214

III Sensitivity Analysis and Parallel Implementation 221

8 Sensitivity Analysis 223

  8.1 Junction Matching and Pose Determination 224

  8.2 Sensitivity Analysis 227

  8.3 Qualitative Features 235

  8.4 The Generalized Hough Transform 236

      8.4.1 The Generalized Hough Transform in the Absence of Occlusion and Sensor Error 236

      8.4.2 The Generalized Hough Transform in Presence of Occlusion and Sensor Error 237

      8.4.3 Probability of Spurious Peaks in the Generalized Hough Transform 239

  8.5 The Use of Qualitative Features in the Generalized Hough Transform 241

8.5.1 Reduction in the Search Space of Scene Interpretations due to Qualitative Features 242

8.5.2 Reducing the Effect of Smearing in Parameter Space using Qualitative Features 243

8.5.3 The Probability of Random Peaks in the Weighted Generalized Hough Transform 244

8.5.4 Determination of $\mu_k(x)$, $p_k(x)$ and $P(k)$ 245

8.6 Weighted Generalized Hough Transform 249

9 Parallel Implementations of Recognition Techniques   257

9.1 Parallel Processing in Computer Vision 257

9.1.1 Parallel Architectures 257

9.1.2 Parallel Algorithms 259

9.2 The Connection Machine 260

9.2.1 System Organization 260

9.2.2 Performance Specifications 263

9.3 Object Recognition on the Connection Machine 264

9.3.1 Feature Extraction 265

9.3.2 Localization of Curved Surfaces 265

9.3.3 Computation of Dihedral Feature Junctions 266

9.3.4 Matching and Pose Computation 266

9.3.5 Pose Clustering 266

9.4 Object Recognition on the Hypercube 266

9.4.1 Scene Description 267

9.4.2 Model Data 268

9.4.3 Scene Feature Data 269

9.4.4 Pruning Constraints 269

9.4.5 Localization 270

9.5 Mapping the Interpretation Tree on the Hypercube 271

9.5.1 Breadth-First Mapping of the Interpretation Tree 271

9.5.2 Depth-First Mapping of the Interpretation Tree 272

9.5.3 Depth-First Mapping of the Interpretation Tree with Load Sharing 273

9.5.4 Experimental Results 273

BIBLIOGRAPHY 279

Index 300

Credits for Copyrighted Material

Figure 2.1 Reprinted from: Besl, P.J. "Active Optical Range Imaging Sensors," in *Advances in Machine Vision*, Ed. Jorge L. C. Sanz, Springer-Verlag, New York, 1989, pp. 1-63, (Figure 1.5, adapted). Copyright: 1989 Springer-Verlag.

Figure 2.2 Reprinted from: Besl, P.J. "Active Optical Range Imaging Sensors," in *Advances in Machine Vision*, Ed. Jorge L. C. Sanz, Springer-Verlag, New York, 1989, pp. 1-63, (Figure 1.5, adapted). Copyright: 1989 Springer-Verlag.

Figure 2.3 Reprinted from: Jarvis, R.A. "A Perspective on Range Finding Techniques for Computer Vision, in *IEEE Trans. Pattern Analysis and Machine Intelligence*, Vol. PAMI-5, No. 2, March 1988, pp. 122-139, (Figure 15, adapted). Copyright: 1988 IEEE.

Figure 2.4 Reprinted from: Besl, P.J. "Active Optical Range Imaging Sensors," in *Advances in Machine Vision*, Ed. Jorge L. C. Sanz, Springer-Verlag, New York, 1989, pp. 1-63, (Figure 1.8). Copyright: 1989 Springer-Verlag.

Figure 2.8 Reprinted from: Besl, P.J. "Active Optical Range Imaging Sensors," in *Advances in Machine Vision*, Ed. Jorge L. C. Sanz, Springer-Verlag, New York, 1989, pp. 1-63, (Figure 1.9). Copyright: 1989 Springer-Verlag.

Figure 2.9 Reprinted from: Inokuchi, S., Sato, K., and Matsuda, F., "Range Imaging System for 3D Object Recognition," in *Proc. IEEE Intl. Conf. on Pattern Recognition*, Montreal, Canada, 1984, pp. 806-808, (Figure 2). Copyright: 1984 IEEE.

Figure 2.10 Reprinted from: Besl, P.J. "Active Optical Range Imaging Sensors," in *Advances in Machine Vision*, Ed. Jorge L. C. Sanz, Springer-Verlag, New York, 1989, pp. 1-63, (Figure 1.14). Copyright: 1989 Springer-Verlag.

Figure 2.11 Reprinted from: Leger, J.R. and Snyder, M.A., "Real Time Depth Measurement and Display Using Fresnel Diffraction and White Light Processing," in *Applied Optics*, Vol. 23, No. 10, May 15, 1984, pp. 1655-1670, (Figure 1). Copyright: 1984 Optical Society of America.

Figure 3.1 Reprinted from: Besl, P.J., and Jain, R.C., "Invariant Surface Characteristics for 3D Object Recognition in Range Images", in *Computer Vision Graphics and Image Processing*, Vol. 33, 1986, pp. 33-80, (Figure 4). Copyright 1986 Academic Press.

Figure 5.4 Reprinted from: Dhome. M. and Kasvand, T., "Polyhedra Recognition by Hypothesis Accumulation," in *IEEE Trans. Pattern Analysis and Machine Intelligence*, Vol. 9. No. 3, May 1987, pp. 429-433, (Figure 4). Copyright: 1987 IEEE.

Figure 5.5 Reprinted from: Krishnapuram, R. and Casasent, D., "Determination of Three-Dimensional Object Location and Orientation from Range Images, in *IEEE Trans. Pattern Analysis and Machine Intelligence*, Vol. 11, No. 11, November 1989, pp. 1158-1167, (Figure 1). Copyright: 1989 IEEE.

Figure 5.8 Reprinted from: Wong, A.K.C., Lu, S.W. and Rioux, M., "Recognition and Shape Synthesis of 3-D Objects based on Attributed Hypergraphs," in *IEEE Trans. Pattern Analysis and Machine Intelligence*, Vol. 11, No. 3, March 1989, pp. 279-290, (Figure 3). Copyright: 1989 IEEE.

Figure 5.9 Reprinted from: Stein, F. and Medioni, G., "Structural Indexing; Efficient 3-D Object Recognition" in *IEEE Trans. PAMI*, Vol. 14, No.2, Feb. 1992, pp. 125-145, (Figure 5 (a) and (b), adapted). Copyright: 1992 IEEE.

Figure 5.10 Reprinted from: Bhandarkar, S.M. and Suk, M., "Recognition and Localization of Objects with Curved Surfaces," in *Machine Vision and Applications*, Vol. 4, 1991, pp. 15-31, (Figure 5). Copyright: 1991 Springer-Verlag.

Figure 6.1 Reprinted from: Bhandarkar, S.M. and Siebert, A., "Integrating Edge and Surface Information for Range Image Segmentation", to appear in *Pattern Recognition*, (Figure 1). Copyright: Pergamon Press.

Figure 6.2 Reprinted from: Bhandarkar, S.M. and Siebert, A., "Integrating Edge and Surface Information for Range Image Segmentation", to appear in *Pattern Recognition*, (Figure 2). Copyright: Pergamon Press.

Figure 6.3 Reprinted from: Bhandarkar, S.M. and Siebert, A., "Integrating Edge and Surface Information for Range Image Segmentation", to appear in *Pattern Recognition*, (Figure 3). Copyright: Pergamon Press.

Figure 6.4 Reprinted from: Bhandarkar, S.M. and Siebert, A., "Integrating Edge and Surface Information for Range Image Segmentation", to appear in *Pattern Recognition*, (Figure 4). Copyright: Pergamon Press.

Figure 6.5 Reprinted from: Bhandarkar, S.M. and Siebert, A., "Integrating Edge and Surface Information for Range Image Segmentation", to appear in *Pattern Recognition*, (Figure 5). Copyright: Pergamon Press.

Figure 6.6 Reprinted from: Bhandarkar, S.M. and Siebert, A., "Integrating Edge and Surface Information for Range Image Segmentation", to appear in *Pattern Recognition*, (Figure 6). Copyright: Pergamon Press.

Figure 7.10 Reprinted from: Bhandarkar, S.M. and Suk, M., "Recognition and Localization of Objects with Curved Surfaces," in *Machine Vision and Applications*, Vol. 4, 1991, pp. 15-31, (Figure 8). Copyright: 1991 Springer-Verlag.

Figure 7.11 Reprinted from: Bhandarkar, S.M. and Suk, M., "Recognition and Localization of Objects with Curved Surfaces," in *Machine Vision and Applications*, Vol. 4, 1991, pp. 15-31, (Figure 9). Copyright: 1991 Springer-Verlag.

Figure 7.12 Reprinted from: Bhandarkar, S.M. and Suk, M., "Recognition and Localization of Objects with Curved Surfaces," in *Machine Vision and Applications*, Vol. 4, 1991, pp. 15-31, (Figure 10). Copyright: 1991 Springer-Verlag.

Figure 7.13 Reprinted from: Bhandarkar, S.M. and Suk, M., "Recognition and Localization of Objects with Curved Surfaces," in *Machine Vision and Applications*, Vol. 4, 1991, pp. 15-31, (Figure 11). Copyright: 1991 Springer-Verlag.

Figure 7.14 Reprinted from: Bhandarkar, S.M. and Suk, M., "Recognition and Localization of Objects with Curved Surfaces," in *Machine Vision and Applications*, Vol. 4, 1991, pp. 15-31, (Figure 12). Copyright: 1991 Springer-Verlag.

Figure 7.15 Reprinted from: Bhandarkar, S.M. and Suk, M., "Recognition and Localization of Objects with Curved Surfaces," in *Machine Vision and Applications*, Vol. 4, 1991, pp. 15-31, (Figure 13). Copyright: 1991 Springer-Verlag.

Figure 7.16 Reprinted from: Bhandarkar, S.M. and Suk, M., "Recognition and Localization of Objects with Curved Surfaces," in *Machine Vision and Applications*, Vol. 4, 1991, pp. 15-31, (Figure 14). Copyright: 1991 Springer-Verlag.

Figure 7.17 Reprinted from: Bhandarkar, S.M. and Suk, M., "Recognition and Localization of Objects with Curved Surfaces," in *Machine Vision and Applications*, Vol. 4, 1991, pp. 15-31, (Figure 15). Copyright: 1991 Springer-Verlag.

Figure 7.18 Reprinted from: Bhandarkar, S.M. and Suk, M., "Recognition and Localization of Objects with Curved Surfaces," in *Machine Vision and Applications*, Vol. 4, 1991, pp. 15-31, (Figure 16). Copyright: 1991 Springer-Verlag.

Table 7.6 Reprinted from: Bhandarkar, S.M. and Suk, M., "Recognition and Localization of Objects with Curved Surfaces," in *Machine Vision and Applications*, Vol. 4, 1991, pp. 15-31, (Table 2). Copyright: 1991 Springer-Verlag.

Table 8.4 Reprinted from: Bhandarkar, S.M. and Suk, M., "Qualitative Features and the Generalized Hough Transform," to appear in *Pattern Recognition*, (Table 4). Copyright: Pergamon Press.

Figure 8.6 Reprinted from: Bhandarkar, S.M. and Suk, M., "Qualitative Features and the Generalized Hough Transform," to appear in *Pattern Recognition*, (Figure 9). Copyright: Pergamon Press.

Table 8.5 Reprinted from: Bhandarkar, S.M. and Suk, M., "Qualitative Features and the Generalized Hough Transform," to appear in *Pattern Recognition*, (Table 5). Copyright: Pergamon Press.

Figure 9.1 Reprinted from: Tucker, L.W. and Robertson, G.G., "Architecture and Applications of the Connection Machine," in *IEEE Computer*, pp. 26-38, August 1988, (Figure 1). Copyright: 1988 IEEE.

Figure 9.2 Reprinted from: Bhandarkar, S.M., "Parallelizing Object Recognition on the Hypercube", in *Pattern Recognition Letters*, Vol 13, No. 6, June 1992, pp. 433-441, (Figure 1). Copyright: 1992 Elsevier Science Publishers.

Figure 9.3 Reprinted from: Bhandarkar, S.M., "Parallelizing Object Recognition on the Hypercube", in *Pattern Recognition Letters*, Vol 13, No. 6, June 1992, pp. 433-441, (Figure 2). Copyright: 1992 Elsevier Science Publishers.

Figure 9.4 Reprinted from: Bhandarkar, S.M., "Parallelizing Object Recognition on the Hypercube", in *Pattern Recognition Letters*, Vol 13, No. 6, June 1992, pp. 433-441, (Figure 3). Copyright: 1992 Elsevier Science Publishers.

Figure 9.5 Reprinted from: Bhandarkar, S.M., "Parallelizing Object Recognition on the Hypercube", in *Pattern Recognition Letters*, Vol 13, No. 6, June 1992, pp. 433-441, (Figure 4). Copyright: 1992 Elsevier Science Publishers.

Figure 9.6 Reprinted from: Bhandarkar, S.M., "Parallelizing Object Recognition on the Hypercube", in *Pattern Recognition Letters*, Vol 13, No. 6, June 1992, pp. 433-441, (Figure 5). Copyright: 1992 Elsevier Science Publishers.

Table 9.1 Reprinted from: Bhandarkar, S.M., "Parallelizing Object Recognition on the Hypercube", in *Pattern Recognition Letters*, Vol 13, No. 6, June 1992, pp. 433-441, (Table 1). Copyright: 1992 Elsevier Science Publishers.

Table 9.2 Reprinted from: Bhandarkar, S.M., "Parallelizing Object Recognition on the Hypercube", in *Pattern Recognition Letters*, Vol 13, No. 6, June 1992, pp. 433-441, (Table 2). Copyright: 1992 Elsevier Science Publishers.

Chapter 1

Introduction

Three-dimensional object recognition, the subject of this book, is an important topic in computer vision. It concerns the recognition and localization of objects of interest in a scene from an image of the scene. The input image can be an intensity image (included in this category are color and multi-spectral images) or a range image. This problem is encountered in scenarios such as robot bin-picking, automated industrial inspection, autonomous navigation, to name just a few. In addition to the practical interest, three-dimensional object recognition is of considerable theoretical interest as well. It is an ideal vehicle for the study of the general area of computer vision. It involves typical issues encountered in computer vision—for example, issues such as feature extraction, acquisition, representation and proper use of knowledge, employment of efficient control strategies, coupling numerical and symbolic computations, and parallel implementation of algorithms. The intention of this book is to provide a detailed discussion of these and other important issues in three-dimensional object recognition, and to present some recent advances. The emphases are given to the dual issues of representation and control, and to the use of qualitative features to combat the combinatorial explosion of the search space of scene interpretations.

1.1 Computer Vision

The goal of *image processing* is to transform an input image to another image to facilitate human interpretation and/or further analysis by machine (Figure 1.1). The transformation from input to output images aims to expose certain properties of the input image more explicitly. Note that the transformation makes information already present in the input image more explicit without necessarily adding any new information. Typical tasks in image processing include enhancement, restoration, compression, segmentation, feature extraction, and description. These are also the foundations of computer vision.

Computer vision, according to Ballard and Brown [1982], is "the construction of explicit, meaningful description of physical objects from images." A

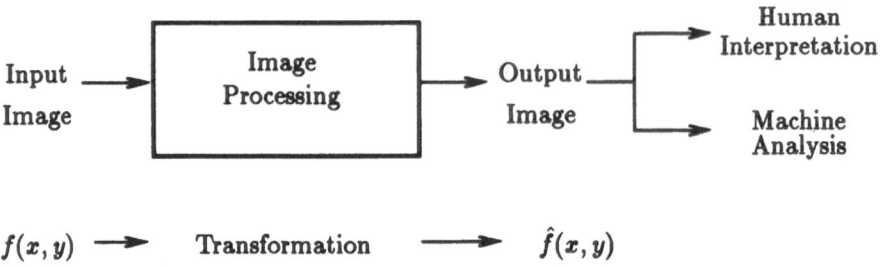

$$f(x,y) \longrightarrow \quad \text{Transformation} \quad \longrightarrow \quad \hat{f}(x,y)$$

Figure 1.1: The goal of image processing is to expose certain characteristics of the input image more explicitly for human interpretation or further machine analysis.

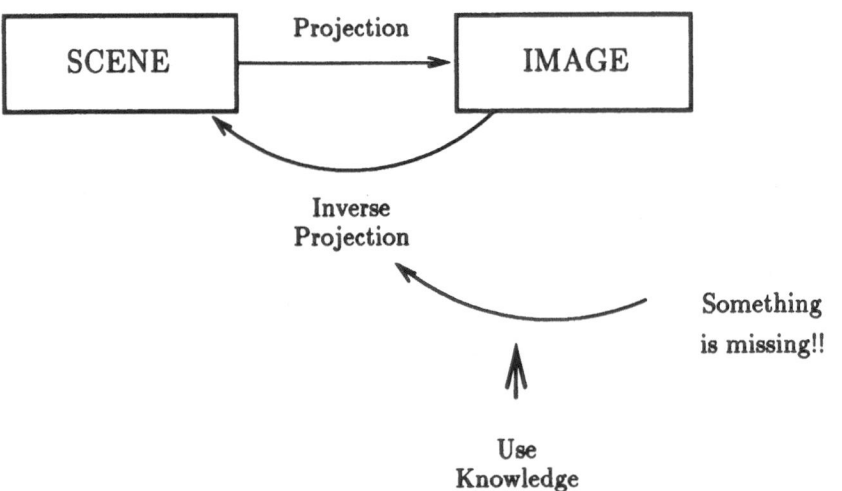

Figure 1.2: Many problems in computer vision are ill-posed and the use of knowledge is essential.

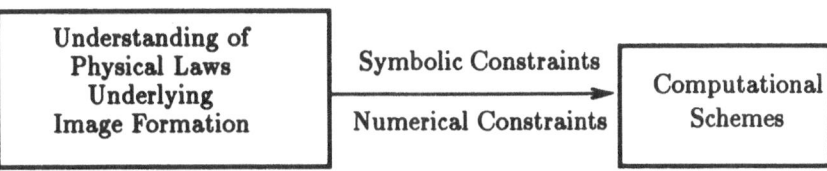

Figure 1.3: Knowledge in low-level vision provides symbolic and numerical constraints for vision algorithms.

(two-dimensional) image is a projection of a (three-dimensional) scene. Thus the inverse mapping from an image to a scene is inherently ill-posed (Figure 1.2). The ultimate goal of computer vision, however, is to construct a description of a scene from its image. So how can this goal be achieved? The key to this question is the use of *knowledge*! In low-level vision, the knowledge is derived from the physical laws that underlie the image formation. The knowledge is translated into symbolic and numerical constraints which are incorporated into computational schemes (Figure 1.3). For example, the *shape-from-shading* scheme [Horn 1977] [Ikeuchi and Horn 1981] utilizes the physical laws governing reflected light from the surface of an object. The physical laws model reflected energy as a function of the physical properties of the surface, and the geometry of the source, camera, and surface orientation. The inherently ill-posed problem is regularized by using the constraints derived from the smoothness assumption. In high-level vision, domain-specific knowledge , common sense knowledge, and meta-knowledge are used to prune the search space in order to come up with consistent and valid scene descriptions quickly (Figure 1.4). For example, geometric reasoning based on three-dimensional object models and projections is used in ACRONYM [Brooks 1981].

Marr's paradigm [Marr 1982], which provides a computational theory of computer vision, has dominated research in computer vision for over a decade. The paradigm is referred to as a *computational paradigm*, and it views computer vision as an *information processing* activity. The basis of information processing is arriving at representations at various abstraction levels. Visual processing, then, consists of successive transformations between these representations in order to discover "what is present in the world, and where it is." (Figure 1.5). Abstraction levels include generalized images, segmented images, geometric structures, and relational structures. Each representation must be a useful description of the visible environment.

Generalized images are analogous representations of input data. Some iconic representations, such as edge elements that are useful in the next level of processing, can be produced by domain-independent processing. Intrinsic images produced at this level show physical properties of the image such as surface orientation or surface reflection. Segmented images are produced from generalized

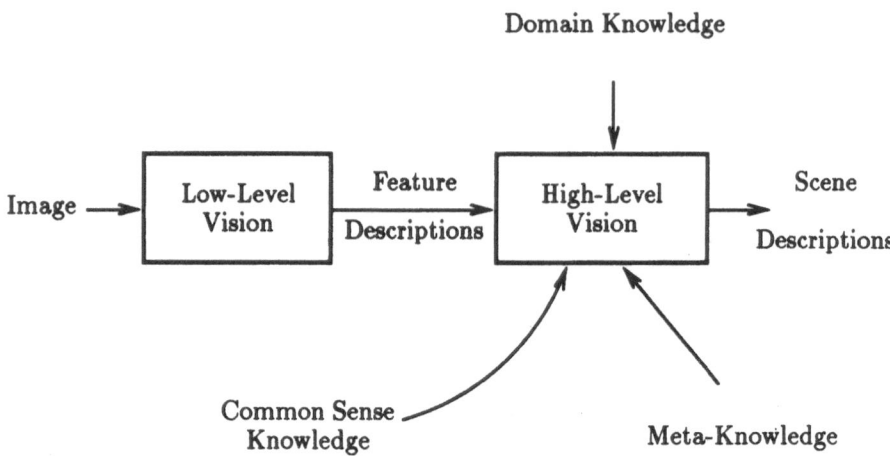

Figure 1.4: Domain knowledge, common sense knowledge, and meta-knowledge are used in interpreting the image features.

images by grouping their elements into meaningful objects. Segmentation is the highest domain-independent abstraction of input data. In high-level vision, domain-specific knowledge is used in conjunction with the segmented image, resulting in the subsequent levels of abstraction. Geometric representations are used to capture two- and three-dimensional shapes of objects. Relational structures are the highest-level abstractions of input describing the relations among many objects in the scene.

Processes in computer vision are grouped into two broad and overlapping levels: *low-level vision* and *high-level vision*. Low-level vision concerns the recovery of three-dimensional scene features from two-dimensional images. The outcome of this process is called a *full 2 1/2-D sketche* that makes explicit the orientation and rough depth of visible surfaces and contours of discontinuities. Also considered as low-level vision are preprocessing, segmentation, and feature extraction. High-level vision concerns the cognitive use of domain-specific knowledge and deals with the interpretation of the scene.

1.2   Three-Dimensional Object Recognition

Consider a three-dimensional object recognition problem where there are K three-dimensional objects of interest. After choosing a representation scheme, a library containing the descriptions of K objects is created. An image, either an intensity image or a range image, of a scene is given. The task of object recognition, then, is to determine whether any of these objects are present in

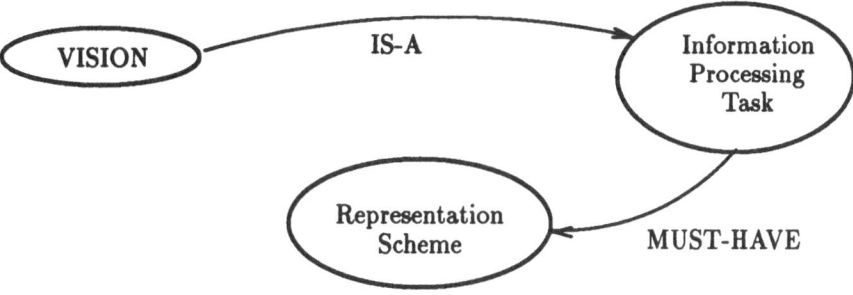

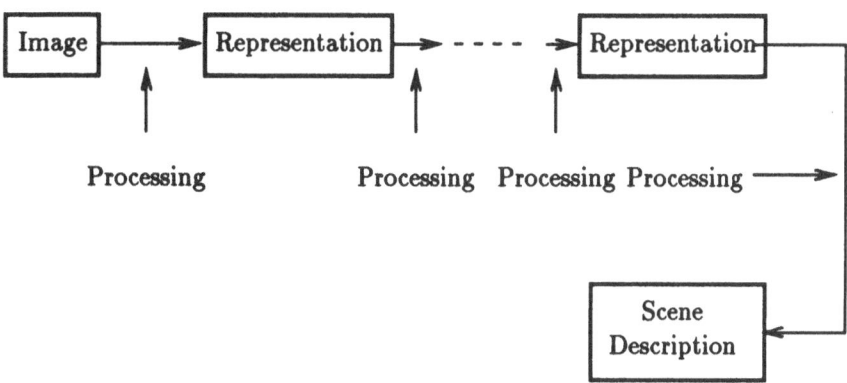

Figure 1.5: The computational paradigm views vision as an information processing task constructing successively higher level abstractions of the data.

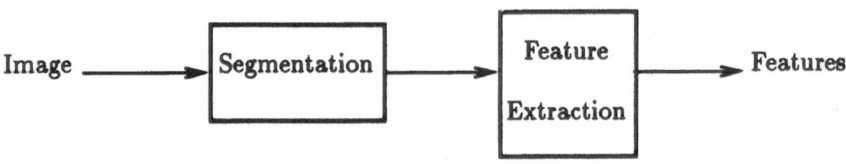

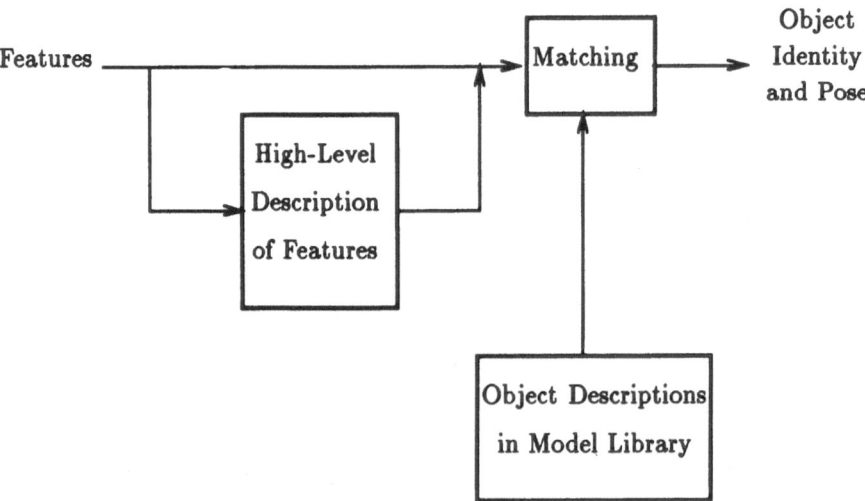

Figure 1.6: Block diagram of a typical object recognition system.

the scene, and if they are, to determine their locations and orientations. Object recognition involves surface feature extraction followed by recognition and localization (Figure 1.6). Features are usually local features, and their choice is greatly influenced by the representation and recognition schemes. For recognition, either: (1) a higher-order description of features extracted from input is derived and is matched against the object descriptions in the library; or (2) the input features are matched directly against the object descriptions. The basic idea behind the latter approach is that features belonging to a valid object form a coherent peak in a parameter space, thus signifying global consistency.

The two distinct approaches to object recognition are called: (1) *recognition-followed-by-localization,* and (2) *recognition-via-localization.* In the recognition-followed-by-localization approach, higher-order relational descriptions or global features of input are matched to similar descriptions of objects. Typical control strategies used are graph-theoretic constraint propagation techniques such as maximal clique detection and subgraph isomorphism. Alternatively, we can match the primitive geometric features extracted from input directly to the object models. The typical control strategy used is based on the propagation of geometric constraints that arise from the matching of these primitive geometric features until a consistent interpretation is found. This is the recognition-via-localization approach to object recognition.

The recognition-followed-by-localization approach calls for extensive segmentation, but the recognition and localization process is fast and efficient. It is not always robust to occlusion, especially if global shape descriptions are used, and is thus not suitable for multiple-object recognition. The recognition-via-localization approach involves minimal effort in segmentation; however, the combinatorial complexity of the geometric constraint propagation proves prohibitive, especially in the case of multiple-object recognition with partial occlusion. In addition, we have to deal with the problem of spurious scene interpretations for a multiple-object scene. Therefore, this approach can be used for multiple-object recognition only when it is coupled with an efficient control strategy that can neutralize the combinatorial explosion and prune spurious interpretations. In Part II we will show how the use of qualitative features can provide a good solution to these requirements.

In a three-dimensional object recognition problem, the representation scheme and control strategy are closely interrelated. In general, a complex representation scheme allows the use of a simpler control strategy, and vice versa. The dual issues of representation and control are crucial to the problem of three-dimensional object recognition and to other problems in computer vision as well. Different approaches to three-dimensional object recognition could be looked upon as different ways of making a trade-off between the complexity of representation and the complexity of control. We now discuss representation and control (in terms of indexing and constraint propagation) in detail.

1.2.1   Representation

The issue of representation deals with the choice of image features and the choice of model features. The choice of image features is often attuned to the nature of the application domain and the nature of the sensor used. The choice of representation for the object models is also dependent on the application domain. To facilitate matching, the representation of the object models is closely tied to the representation chosen for the image features.

The representation of object models is given in terms of surface descriptions or volumetric descriptions. Surface descriptions are used extensively in constrained environments where it is possible to extract surface features from active range sensors, stereo imaging, or photometric stereo. Volumetric descriptions based on generalized cylinders were first used by Brooks [1981] in ACRONYM.

Surface and volumetric descriptions could be either local or global. Local surface descriptions are typically based on local curvature properties of the surface. Besl and Jain [1986], Fan et al. [1987], Brady et al. [1985], and Vemuri and Aggarwal [1986] have described segmentation schemes based on surface curvature properties. Faugeras and Herbert [1986] describe segmentation of the surface into planar and quadric surface patches and an associated surface matching scheme. Global surface descriptors are based on a few global parameters such as superquadrics [Barr 1981]. Bajcsy and Solina [1987] describe an iterative surface-fitting technique for extracting global shape parameters for superquadrics. Surface normal distribution such as the extended Gaussian image (EGI) has also been used [Horn 1984] as a global surface descriptor. Generalized cylinders are examples of global volumetric descriptors, whereas voxel-based oct-tree representations [Chien et al. 1988] are local volumetric descriptions. Local features are well suited for recognition in the presence of occlusion, whereas global features enable rapid recognition in those situations where the image data is unoccluded.

Features may also be classified as generic or distinctive. Generic features cover a broad range of objects under the domain of interest. Distinctive features, on the other hand, make specific assumptions about the objects in question such as in the 3-DPO vision system [Bolles and Horaud 1986]. Distinctive features sacrifice generality for recognition speed, whereas generic features sacrifice recognition speed for generality.

1.2.2   Indexing

In building a large scale vision system, the object models in the library must be organized effectively so that a linear search of all the object models can be avoided. The general consensus is that the model library should be structured along multiple hierarchies, i.e., class/subclass, part/subpart, and multiple scale hierarchies.

Turney et al. [1985] describe a system that builds a library by finding salient features that uniquely identify each object relative to all other models in the library. Knoll and Jain [1985] developed the feature-indexed-hypothesis method to perform model library indexing using the features common to several objects. The system constructs the library automatically by finding all the objects that contain each feature. Assuming that the cost of matching a feature is equal to the cost of verifying the resulting hypothesis, it can be shown that the ideal number of matches per feature in the library is proportional to the square root of the total number of objects.

The system by Connell [1985] uses analogies between instances of similar objects to infer the important shape cues common to a whole set of objects, and detailed shape cues that differentiate between related models. Ettinger [1987] shows how decomposition of object models along part/subpart hierarchies and feature scale hierarchies results in significant improvement in performance. The design of indexing techniques for large-scale vision systems remains a challenging issue on account of its combinatorial complexity.

1.2.3 Constraint Propagation and Constraint Satisfaction

A scene interpretation can be looked upon as a solution to a constraint satisfaction problem. The process of arriving at a consistent scene interpretation is therefore a constraint-directed search through the space of possible scene interpretations. Three-dimensional object recognition systems can be classified into four groups according to the search strategy employed.

1. *Top-down or model-driven search.* This is commonly used in the recognition-via-localization approach to object recognition. The features used are primitive, and matching takes place very early in the recognition process. Primitive geometric features are matched against similar features in the object model. Matches are checked for local consistency by using simple geometric constraints such as distance and angle measurements. A set of locally consistent matches is used to compute a global transformation from the model coordinate system to the scene coordinate system. The interpretation tree (IT) approach [Grimson and Lozano-Perez 1987] matches a scene feature with a model feature at every stage in the recognition/localization process. Locally consistent matches are represented by a path in the interpretation tree. Local geometric constraints are used to prune paths in the interpretation tree, thereby restricting the possible interpretations. When a path of sufficient length is found, a global transformation is computed. The control structure of the algorithm is that of sequential hypothesize-and-test with backtracking. The Hough (pose) clustering approach [Stockman 1987] matches each scene feature to each model feature. The matches are constrained by local geometric constraints based on angle and distance measurements. Each match is mapped to a point in the Hough (parameter) space. Clustering of points in the Hough space yields a globally consistent hypothesis regarding the pose of the object. Model-driven approaches are useful when noisy or occluded data precludes a higher level abstraction of data.

2. *Bottom-up or data-driven search.* In this approach, higher level semantic descriptions are used. Matching takes place fairly late in the recognition process. A high-level semantic description of the image is matched against a high-level semantic description of the object. The recognition phase is typically based on paradigms such as graph-matching, subgraph isomorphism, and maximal clique detection. Recognition is followed by localization, for which highly object-specific shape descriptors are used. Since a higher level description of data is used, the number of hypotheses generated in the matching phase is small in number. The disadvantage is that this approach requires extensive preprocessing of image data, requiring that the quality of the data be good, i.e., unoccluded and unambiguous.

3. *Interpretive search.* An interpretive search strategy uses object models interpretively. Knowledge extracted from the model is transformed into an execution strategy to be used at run time. The system relies on a generic reasoning mechanism such as numerical optimization of some matching criterion, constraint satisfaction by symbolic reasoning, or tree search by hypothesize-and-test. An interpretive system sacrifices speed for generality and flexibility. Thus when the aim is to recognize specific objects in the scene, the approach may not be the most efficient one. ACRONYM is an example of an interpretive system.

4. *Precompiled search* . In a precompiled search strategy, relevant control knowledge is embedded in the object model and compiled into a recognition strategy off line. As a result, little computation is done during the process of recognition. The work by Goad [1983] and Ikeuchi [1987] are examples of this approach. The advantage of precompilation is that recognition is fast, but at the cost of loss of generality.

It is possible to further categorize search strategies into distributed vs. centralized search strategies. In distributed search, several processes cooperate to come up with an interpretation, whereas in centralized search the control strategy is located within a centralized control module. Most of the three-dimensional object recognition systems to date employ a centralized search strategy.

1.3   Common Goals of Three-Dimensional Object Recognition Systems

In spite of the variety of representation and control schemes used, most model-based three-dimensional object recognition systems address common goals:

1. *Robustness of the recognition process.* The object recognition system must be capable of coping with occlusion, noise, and ambiguous or incomplete data. It should be capable of handling changes in viewpoint of the objects as they appear in the scene.

2. *Generality of representation.* The representation scheme should be capable of handling a wide variety of objects. The features used for recognition should satisfy the conditions of global scalability and richness of local support.

3. *Flexibility in control strategy.* The control strategy should be capable of changing with the state of the problem-solving process. Constraint propagation techniques should be able to tune themselves to the appropriate granularity of representation.

4. *Speed and efficiency.* Effective pruning of the search space of possible interpretations needs to be developed. Object models need to be organized into libraries to support fast and effective indexing. Parallelism needs to be exploited, and symbolic and numerical processing need to be effectively integrated.

The above goals often pose conflicting requirements. Most existing three-dimensional object recognition systems therefore represent a good compromise among these goals.

1.4 Qualitative Features

Human vision, for the most part, aims at a *qualitative* interpretation of the scene rather than relying on precise *quantitative* measurement. There has been some successful use of the qualitative nature of features and knowledge in computer vision problems. It is also widely recognized that the coupling of symbolic and numerical methods is an effective means of solving many complex problems in science, engineering, and business [Kowalik 1986] [Kowalik and Kitzmiller 1988], where both insight and precision are frequently needed.

The importance of studying the qualitative properties of the underlying problem domain has been brought out in recent studies of low-level vision processes. The use of qualitative features for matching and localization, however, has not received as much attention. The use of qualitative features for object recognition is one of the themes of this book.

1.4.1 Study of Qualitative Properties in Low-level Vision Processes

The role of qualitative properties in perceptual grouping has been studied by both psychologists and computer vision researchers. Lowe [1985] and Walters [1987] show that grouping of intensity discontinuities based on the qualitative Gestalt properties of proximity, continuity parallelism, smoothness, simplicity, containment, etc., serves as an excellent indexing mechanism into a database of object models. These Gestalt properties could also be used to group primitive patterns called textons for texture-based segmentation as shown by Julesz and

Bergen [1983]. Hoffman and Richards [1985] use minima of curvature for a similar grouping of space curves.

Qualitative description of shape has been considered by Guzman [1968], Huffman [1971], Cloves [1971], Waltz [1975], and, more recently, by Malik [1987]. The work of Guzman, Huffman, Cloves, and Waltz deals with junction-labeling of trihedral solids, whereas Malik deals with the labeling of junctions of curved solids. The qualitative information conveyed by junctions and boundaries is used in shape-from-XYZ algorithms. Horn's shape-from-shading algorithm [Horn 1977] [Ikeuchi and Horn 1981] and Witkin's[1981] shape-from-texture algorithm use the occluding boundary as a boundary condition. Shape-from-stereo [Barnard and Fischler 1982] uses the presence of intensity discontinuities as a means of limiting the search for correspondence. Malik [1989], in his recent work, uses the shape-from-shading algorithm in conjunction with his junction-labeling algorithm to come up with a quantitative description of shape. Verri and Poggio [1989] have shown how the smoothed optical flow and motion field can be interpreted as vector fields tangent to the flows of planar dynamical systems. Using the theory of structural stability of dynamical systems, stable qualitative properties of the motion field that give useful information about the three-dimensional velocity field and the three-dimensional structure of the scene can be obtained from the optical flow. Weinshall [1987] shows how qualitative depth information can be obtained from stereo disparities with almost no computation. The algorithm orders the matched points in a depth-consistent fashion from image coordinates only. The results are in accordance with psychological evidence.

1.4.2   Qualitative Features in Object Recognition

Since there are K object descriptions and a large number of local features extracted from the input image, the number of matches produced in recognition-via-localization is very large. In many cases, this number is prohibitive, and the problem is known as *combinatorial explosion* in artificial intelligence literature. Further, for the problem of multiple-object recognition with partial occlusion, we need to be concerned with the presence of many spurious scene interpretations. The reduction in the combinatorial complexity of searching and the robustness of the recognition process can be achieved by employing an efficient control strategy. In the context of Hough clustering this translates to being able to suppress spurious peaks in the parameter space, which are inherent to the Hough clustering technique. Since the technique relies on the accumulation of local evidence to come up with a global hypothesis, spurious accumulation of evidence may result from false matches of scene features to model features. In single-object scenes, spurious hypotheses tend to be insignificant in comparison to the true peak, which corresponds to a globally consistent pose. In multiple-object scenes with partial occlusion, the spurious accumulation of evidence from false matches may be reinforced, causing spurious hypotheses to be greater or comparable in magnitude to the true pose hypotheses. The role of qualitative features is to restrict the number of false matches and thereby suppress the false peaks in the Hough space. Part II of this book shows that the use of qualitative features in object recognition enhances the robustness, accuracy, and efficiency of the recognition and localization process.

1.5   The Scope and Outline of the Book

The material in this book is organized into three parts. Part I provides a thorough review of the areas of range image processing and three-dimensional object recognition. Range sensors, segmentation, feature extraction, representation, and several successful approaches to recognition are described. Particular attention is given to exposing the dual issues of representation and control.

Part II describes an advanced topic, the use of qualitative features in object recognition from a *range image*. The input scenes contain multiple objects with objects partially occluding each other. As discussed earlier, recognition-via-localization is preferred for this case, and Hough clustering and interpretation tree search are chosen as the constraint propagation/satisfaction mechanisms because of their conceptual simplicity and potential ease of parallelization. Three problem scenarios of increasing complexity are examined:

1. Multiple polyhedral objects with partial occlusion.

2. Objects with curved surfaces such as conical, cylindrical and spherical surfaces with surfaces partially occluding each other.

3. Objects composed of piecewise combinations of curved surfaces such as conical, cylindrical, spherical, and planar surfaces with objects partially occluding each other.

We show how the use of qualitative features enables us not only to prune the search space, but also to improve the accuracy of recognition. For each problem scenario, the recognition/localization technique was evaluated in terms of efficiency, robustness, and accuracy.

Part III deals with performance and implementation issues such as sensitivity analysis and parallel implementation.

Part I

Fundamentals of Range Image Processing and Three-Dimensional Object Recognition

Chapter 2

Range Image Sensors and Sensing Techniques

Range imaging sensors collect three-dimensional coordinate data from visible surfaces of objects in the scene. The output of a range sensor is termed a *range image*. Range images are unique in that the image pixels explicitly represent scene surface geometry in a sampled form. Since three-dimensional information is directly available in a range image, the problem of recognizing and localizing three-dimensional objects in a range image is to a great extent simplified. This is in contrast to a video sensor wherein the extraction of three-dimensional scene geometry from the pixel intensity values involves imposing specific constraints on the geometrical and physical properties of the objects in the scene, as is done in shape-from-shading, shape-from-texture, shape-from-shadows, etc. Range images are used in a wide variety of applications such as automated inspection, robot bin-picking, automated assembly, autonomous navigation, and medical diagnosis.

2.1 Range Image Forms

A range image is a collection of distance measurements from a known reference coordinate system to surface points on objects in a scene. If distance measurements are listed relative to three orthogonal coordinate axes, the range image is said to be in the xyz form. Since there is no ordering of points in a range image in the xyz form, it could be considered to be the most general form. However, efficient processing of range images in the xyz form proves very difficult. If measurements are made on sampling points uniformly spaced in the horizontal and vertical directions on the surface, then the range image in the xyz form can be represented in a more specialized form as a matrix with rows and columns of scaled and quantized range values r_{ij} where the indices i and j represent sampling intervals along the x- and y-directions, respectively. If r_{ij} is the value at the ith row and j^{th} column, then the xyz coordinate values of the corresponding point are given by

$$
\begin{aligned}
x &= a_x + s_x i \\
y &= a_y + s_y j \\
z &= a_z + s_z r_{ij}
\end{aligned}
\tag{2.1}
$$

where $\mathbf{a} = (a_x, a_y, a_z)$ is the translational offset and $\mathbf{s} = (s_x, s_y, s_z)$ represents the sampling increments (or scale factors). Thus, a range image given in a matrix form can be converted to the xyz form using the scene parameter $\mathbf{a}$ and the sensor parameter $\mathbf{s}$. Mathematically, the r_{ij} matrix represents a sampled version of a surface of the form $z = f(x, y)$, which is termed a *Monge Patch*. This is analogous to the representation of a conventional intensity image p_{ij}, which is a sampled version of a two-dimensional intensity function of the form $I = f(x, y)$. In fact, the matrix r_{ij} can be displayed on a video monitor in the same manner as an intensity image except that each pixel (matrix element) represents a distance rather than an intensity value.

The form of the range image represented by the set of Eq. (2.1) is said to be *orthographic* where the term orthographic signifies that the depths are measured along parallel rays perpendicular to the xy plane. Eq. (2.1) also assumes that the sampling is linear and uniform in x- and y-directions. In most sensing systems, however, sampling is *equiangular* in the horizontal and vertical directions. In spherical coordinates the indices i and j correspond to angular increments in steps of s_ϕ and s_θ in the vertical and horizontal directions, respectively (Figure 2.1). The angle ϕ is referred to as the elevation angle and the angle θ as the azimuthal angle in spherical coordinates. In the case of equiangular sampling, the transformation of the r_{ij} matrix to the xyz form is given by the equations

$$
\begin{aligned}
x &= a_x + s_r r_{ij} \cos(i s_\phi) \sin(j s_\theta) \\
y &= a_y + s_r r_{ij} \sin(i s_\phi) \\
z &= a_z + s_r r_{ij} \cos(i s_\phi) \cos(j s_\theta)
\end{aligned}
\tag{2.2}
$$

where s_r, s_ϕ, and s_θ, are the range, elevation, and the azimuthal increments (or scale factors), and $\mathbf{a} = (a_x, a_y, a_z)$ is the translational offset.

Alternatively, the elevation angle ϕ can be defined as shown in Figure 2.2. In this case, the transformation of the r_{ij} matrix to the xyz form is given by the equations

$$
\begin{aligned}
x &= a_x + s_r r_{ij} \frac{\tan(j s_\theta)}{\sqrt{1 + \tan^2(i s_\theta) + \tan^2(j s_\phi)}} \\
y &= a_y + s_r r_{ij} \frac{\tan(i s_\phi)}{\sqrt{1 + \tan^2(i s_\theta) + \tan^2(j s_\phi)}} \\
z &= a_z + s_r r_{ij} \frac{1}{\sqrt{1 + \tan^2(i s_\theta) + \tan^2(j s_\phi)}}
\end{aligned}
\tag{2.3}
$$

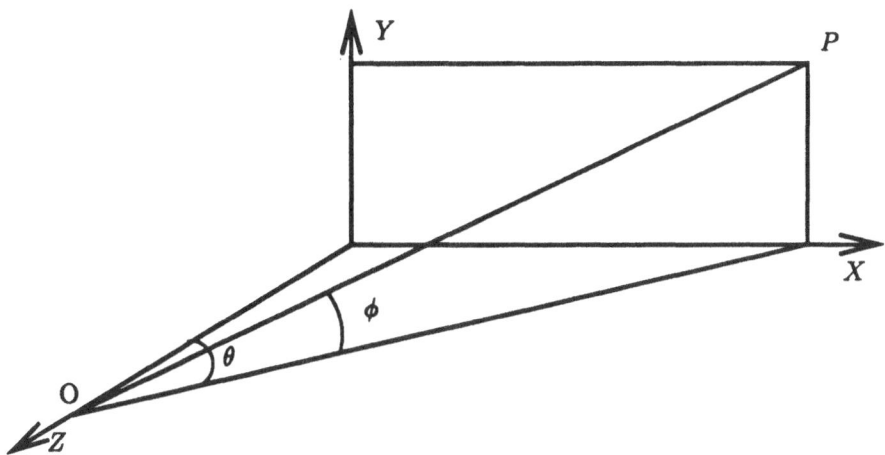

Figure 2.1: Cartesian and spherical coordinates in range sensing.

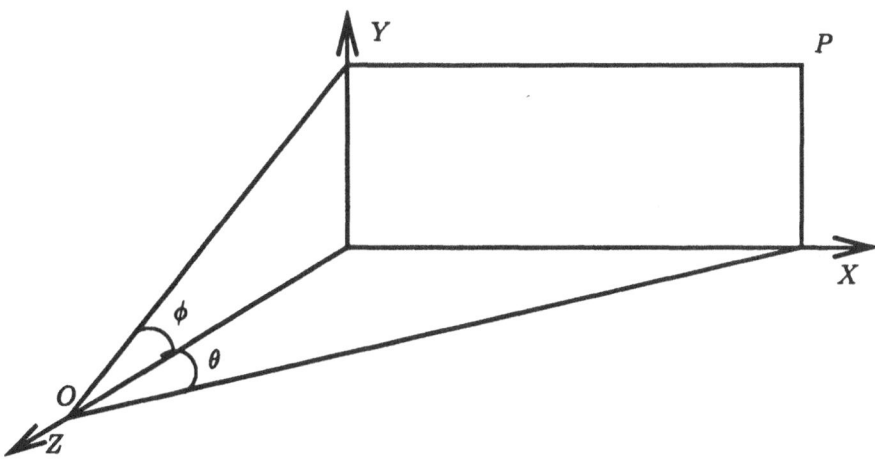

Figure 2.2: Another spherical coordinate system used in range sensing.

If the distance of the object in the scene from the sensor is sufficiently large, the equiangular sampling can be approximated by linear uniform sampling with small error.

2.2   Classification of Range Sensors

Range imaging sensors are classified as either *active* or *passive*. Active sensors project energy (typically optical or sonic energy) on the objects in the scene and detect the reflected portion of the energy. Passive sensors, on the other hand, use ambient environmental conditions during the process of data acquisition. Sensors can also be classified as contact or non-contact sensors. Contact sensors need to be in contact or close proximity of the object being sensed, which is not the case with non-contact sensors. Sensors can be classified into six broad categories based on the physical range-imaging principles involved (i.e., sensor physics) as follows:

1. Radar sensors that are active and of the non-contact type.

2. Triangulation sensors that are either active or passive and of the non-contact type.

3. Sensors based on optical interferometry that are active and of the non-contact type.

4. Sensors based on lens focusing that are either active or passive and of the non-contact type.

5. Sensors based on Fresnel diffraction that are active and of the non-contact type.

6. Tactile sensors that are passive and of the contact type.

An extensive review of optical sensors can be found in Jarvis [1983a], Besl [1988a], Nitzan [1988], and Jain and Jain [1989]. Fearing [1990] and Nicholls and Lee [1989] have written excellent survey articles reviewing the state-of-the-art in tactile-sensing technology. In the following subsections we briefly describe each of the sensor categories and discuss their advantages and shortcomings.

2.2.1   Radar Sensors

Historically, radar sensors were used primarily for military applications such as target detection and localization. A radar sensor in a broad sense can be defined as any sensor that emits time-varying signal energy, detects time-varying signal energy reflected from an object, and determines the range of an object from the difference between the transmitted and received signal. The basic time/range proportionality equation that governs the operation of all radar sensors is given by the equation [Skolnick 1962]

$$v\tau = 2r \qquad\qquad (2.4)$$

where v is the velocity of signal propagation in the given medium, τ is the time delay between the transmitted and the reflected signal, and r is the measured range of the object. Traditional radar sensors used for detecting aircraft use electromagnetic signals at radio frequencies. Radar sensors for computer vision applications use laser signals at optical or infrared frequencies. The lateral resolution of a radar sensor is measured in terms of the azimuthal angle θ (Figures 2.1 and 2.2). From the Rayleigh criterion, the minimum angular separation θ_{min} measured in radians between two points required for successful resolution is given by

$$\theta_{min} = 1.22\frac{\lambda}{D} \tag{2.5}$$

where λ is the wavelength of the signal and D is the diameter of the aperture of the receiver. Thus for a specified size of the receiver aperture, the lateral resolution θ_{min} of the sensor is directly proportional to the signal wavelength or inversely proportional to the signal frequency.

Time-of-Flight Radar Sensor

Radar sensors can be classified based on how the time delay τ is actually measured. Time-of-flight (TOF) radar sensors measure the time delay directly. A typical TOF radar sensor sends a sequence of narrow pulses (typically in the sub-nanosecond pulse-width range). The reflected pulse stream is fed through a constant fraction discriminator circuit to remove amplitude variations in the return signal. The incident and the original pulse stream are fed through a time-to-pulse height converter to produce pulses whose height varies with the time delay, which is proportional to the measured range. The pulses are averaged to yield the final distance measurement for that pixel. The schematic diagram of the TOF radar sensor is depicted in Figure 2.3. The sensors designed by Jarvis [1983b], Ahola et al. [1985], Heikkinen et al. [1986], and Lewis and Johnston [1977] are examples of TOF radar sensors.

Amplitude Modulated (AM) Radar Sensor

Instead of measuring the time-of-flight directly, the transmitted signal can be amplitude-modulated with an appropriately chosen modulating signal. The transmitted signal is reflected from the target back to the detector. The detector low-pass filters the reflected signal so as to pass only the amplitude-modulating signal frequency f_{mod}. The transmitted signal and the output of the detector are fed to a phase detector, which measures the phase difference $\delta\phi$ between the two. Since the phase difference $\delta\phi$ is proportional to the time delay τ, the measured phase difference is proportional to the range r. The range r is given by

$$r(\delta\phi) = \frac{c}{4\pi f_{mod}}\delta\phi = \frac{\lambda_{mod}}{4\pi}\delta\phi \tag{2.6}$$

where λ_{mod} is the wavelength of the modulating signal and c is the velocity of light (electromagnetic signals) in the given medium. Since the phase angle is

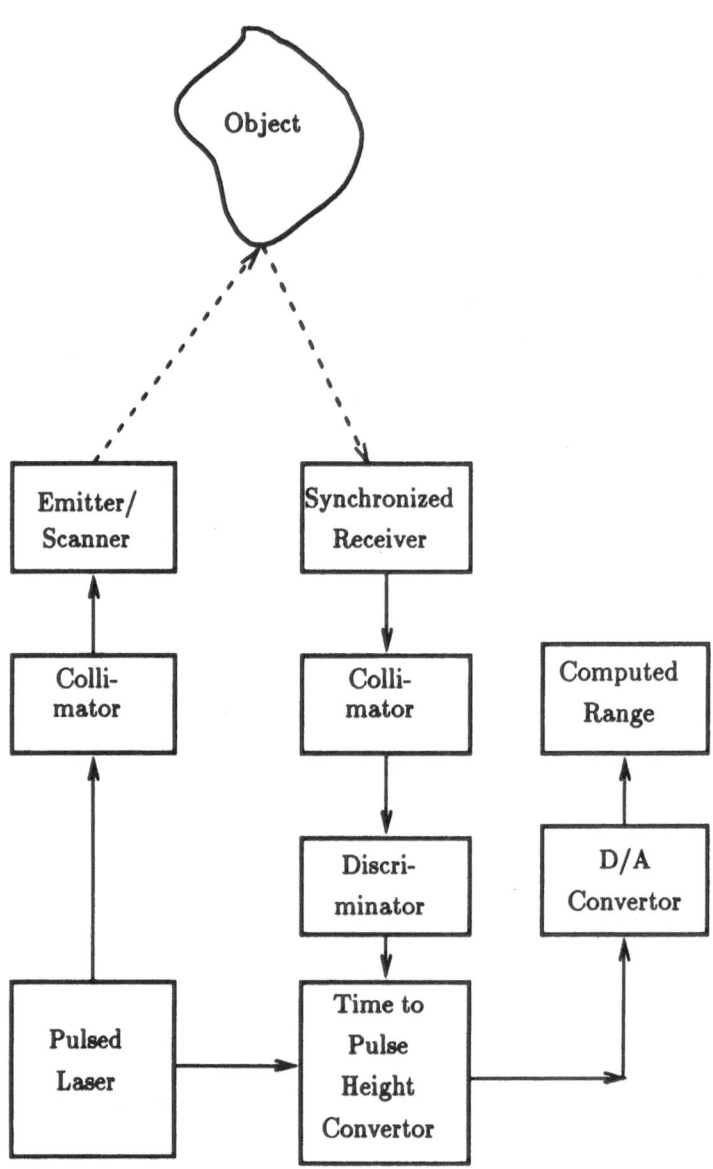

Figure 2.3: A schematic diagram of a TOF radar sensor.

only measured modulo 2π, there is an inherent ambiguity in the measured range. Therefore, the depth of field for this range sensor is limited by the interval $[0, 2\pi]$ for the phase difference. The depth of field for this sensor is given by

$$D = \frac{c}{2f_{mod}} = \frac{\lambda_{mod}}{2} \qquad (2.7)$$

The Environmental Research Institute of Michigan (ERIM) at Ann Arbor, Michigan, has developed AM radar range sensors for a variety of applications. Sampson [1987] describes the ERIM ALV sensor designed for the Autonomous Land Vehicle system. Svetkoff [1986] describes the ERIM ITA sensor developed for their Intelligent Task Automation system. A commercially available AM laser range sensor built by Odetics, Inc., in Anaheim, California, has been described by Binger and Harris [1987].

Frequency Modulated Radar Sensor

It is also possible for the transmitted signal to be frequency modulated. In a frequency modulated (FM) radar, the transmitted optical frequency is linearly swept in the interval $f \pm \delta f$ to create a total frequency deviation of δf in the time interval $1/f_{mod}$ where f_{mod} is the linear sweep modulating frequency (Figure 2.4). The reflected signal is mixed with the transmitted signal in a heterodyne receiver to create a beat frequency f_b that is proportional to the range r and is given by

$$r(f_b) = \frac{c}{4f_m\delta f}f_b \qquad (2.8)$$

In order to measure the beat frequency f_b, we can measure the number of zero crossings, N_b, of the beat signal during one ramp of the linear sweep frequency modulation. N_b is given by the equation

$$N_b = \left\lfloor \frac{f_b}{f_{mod}} \right\rfloor \qquad (2.9)$$

From Eq. (2.8) and Eq. (2.9) we can say that

$$r(N_b) \approx \frac{c}{2\delta f}N_b \qquad (2.10)$$

where the error in the computed range is $\pm c/(4\delta f)$ since N_b is constrained to be an integer.

An FM laser radar sensor manufactured by Digital Optronics has been described by Hersman et al. [1987] and used in their vision system for meteorological applications. Beheim and Fritsch [1986] have designed a range sensor based on similar principles.

Sonar Sensors

As an alternative to electromagnetic signals at radio or optical frequencies, it is possible to construct ranging devices that use ultrasonic signals. Range devices that use ultrasonic signals are called *sonars*. Sonars are based on identical

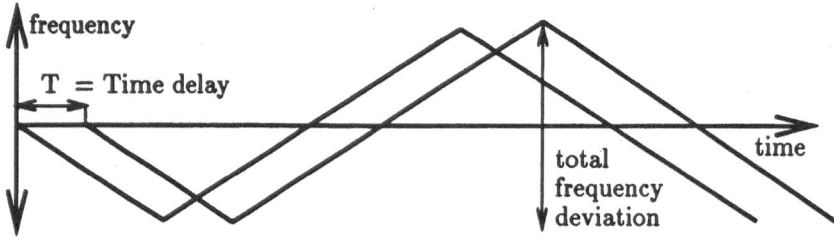

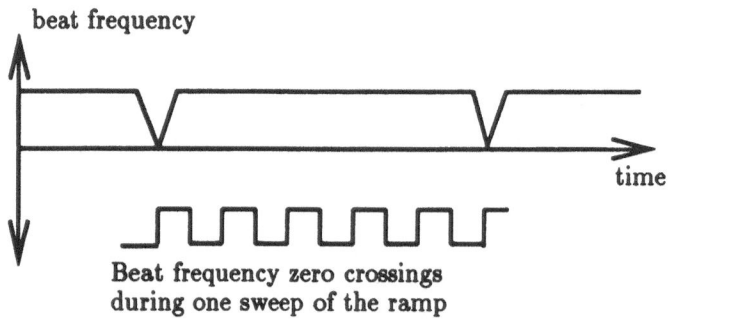

Figure 2.4: The principle of FM radar range sensing.

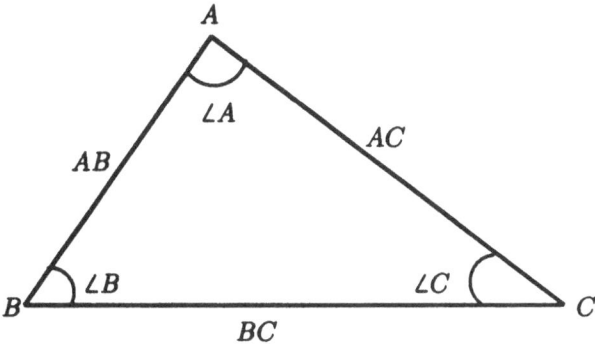

Figure 2.5: Triangulation sensors use the law of sines.

ranging principles as radars. Sonars have a cost advantage over optical ranging systems because acoustic transducers and detectors are cheaper than their optical counterparts, and the associated electronic circuitry operates at far lower speeds. Sonars based on the time-of-flight principle are in common use. Since the time delays associated with ultrasonic signals are orders of magnitude larger than those associated with electromagnetic signals, the time delay can be measured with greater accuracy and with far less expensive electronic devices. The sensors designed by Campbell [1986], Crowley [1985], Acampora and Winters [1989], and Barshan and Kuc [1990] are examples of sonar range sensors.

2.2.2 Triangulation Sensors

The principle of triangulation for the measurement of depth is one of the earliest known ranging techniques since the days of Euclid and Pythagoras. The basis of triangulation sensors is the law of sines as expressed by the equation (Figure 2.5)

$$\frac{\sin(\angle A)}{BC} = \frac{\sin(\angle B)}{AC} = \frac{\sin(\angle C)}{AB} \tag{2.11}$$

If the length of the baseline AB of triangle ABC is known, and if the two included angles $\angle A$ and $\angle B$ are known, then the remaining angle $\angle C$ and the lengths of sides AC and BC can be computed (Figure 2.5).

Triangulation systems can be active or passive. All triangulation systems suffer from the problem of *missing parts* or *shadows* when occlusion prevents the measurement of the second side, because the point in question is visible along one side of the triangle only.

Binocular Stereo

Among passive triangulation techniques, binocular stereo is the most commonly used technique and has been the topic of extensive computer vision research

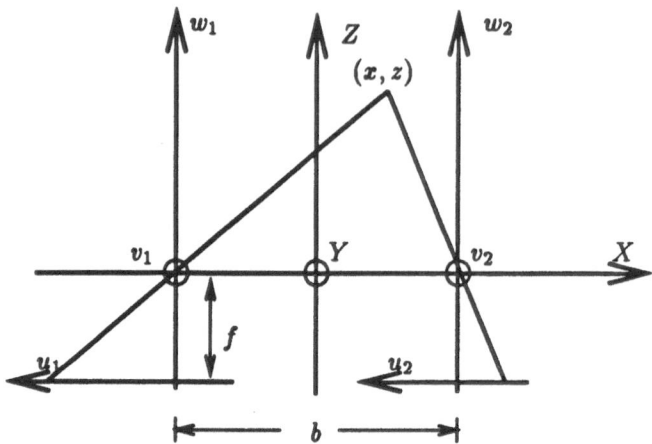

Figure 2.6: Camera geometry for binocular stereo.

over the past few years. Ganapathy [1975], Marr and Poggio [1976], Barnard and Fischler [1982], Grimson [1985], Kak [1985], and Barnard[1986] have studied binocular stereo extensively.

Binocular stereo with parallel camera axes is the most commonly used configuration. A left-handed world coordinate system with axes labeled X, Y, and Z is positioned at the midpoint between two cameras with parallel optical axes (Figure 2.6). The cameras are separated by a distance of b, which is the stereo baseline distance. The focal length of each camera is f and the focal plane of each camera is spanned by the u and v axes such that the Y and the v axes are parallel and the u and X axes are antiparallel. The two cameras are so configured that their corresponding v axes are aligned. The aligned axes are referred to as the *epipolar* line. A visible point on a 3-D surface is given by the position vector $\mathbf{p} = [x, y, z]^T$ in the world coordinate frame of reference. The corresponding projection in the focal plane of the camera is given by the position vector $\mathbf{q} = [u, v]^T$. If the cameras are modeled as *pinhole* cameras with focal length measured in the same units as u and v, then the perspective projection that maps the point $\mathbf{p} = [x, y, z]^T$ on to the point $\mathbf{q} = [u, v]^T$ in the focal plane of the camera is given by the equations

$$u = \frac{fx}{z} \quad \text{and} \quad v = \frac{fy}{z} \tag{2.12}$$

If the pixel $\mathbf{q}_1 = [u_1, v_1]^T$ in the left image and the pixel $\mathbf{q}_2 = [u_2, v_2]^T$ in the right image are determined to be mappings of a same point P, then $v_1 = v_2 = v$ and the disparity $d(u_1, u_2)$ is given by the equation

$$d(u_1, u_2) = u_1 - u_2 = \frac{f}{z} \cdot \left(x + \frac{b}{2}\right) - \frac{f}{z} \cdot \left(x - \frac{b}{2}\right) = \frac{fb}{z} \tag{2.13}$$

Once the correspondence between the pixels in the left and right images is established and the disparity d computed, the 3-D coordinates x, y, and z are
recovered from the observed 2-D quantities u_1, u_2 and v as follows:

$$x(u_1, u_2) = \frac{b}{d} \cdot \left(\frac{u_1 + u_2}{2} \right)$$

$$y(v, d) = \frac{b}{d} \cdot v$$

$$z(d) = \frac{b}{d} \cdot f \qquad (2.14)$$

The spatial resolution of a triangulation sensor depends on the distance of a
point from the sensor baseline. It is limited by the accuracy of the measurement
of the disparity d. If the disparity d is measured to only $\pm\frac{1}{2}$ pixel accuracy, then
the resolution of the sensor is given by

$$\Delta z = z \left(d - \frac{1}{2} \right) - z \left(d + \frac{1}{2} \right) = \frac{fb}{d^2 - \frac{1}{4}} = \frac{4fbz^2}{4f^2b^2 - z^2} \qquad (2.15)$$

The problem of deciding which pixel in the right image is to be matched to
a given pixel in the left image (or vice versa) for the measurement of disparity
is termed the *correspondence problem* in computer vision literature. Because
the correspondence problem is very difficult, several approaches for its solution
have been proposed [Barnard and Fischler 1982] [Barnard and Thompson 1980]
[Grimson 1985].

Motion Stereo

In binocular stereo we use the disparity between the projections of a point in the
scene on the focal planes of two cameras to compute the range. In motion stereo,
on the other hand, we use the displacement due to relative motion between a
single camera and a point in the scene to measure the range. If the relative
motion is along the optical axis of the camera, then the ranging technique is
termed *axial motion stereo*.

Consider a coordinate system (Figure 2.7) attached to the moving camera
such that the camera is constrained to move in the z-direction (along the optical
axis). Let (x_1, y_1, z_1) be the location of the scene point at time t_1, and let
(x_2, y_2, z_2) be the location at time t_2. Since the motion is along the z axis,
$x_1 = x_2 = x$ and $y_1 = y_2 = y$. Moreover, if the focal length of the camera is f
and we assume perspective projection on the focal plane of the camera, then at
time t_1 the point (x, y, z_1) is projected onto the point (u_1, v_1) where

$$u_1 = \frac{fx}{z_1} \quad \text{and} \quad v_1 = \frac{fy}{z_1} \qquad (2.16)$$

Similarly, at time t_2 the point (x, y, z_2) is projected onto the point (u_2, v_2) where

$$u_2 = \frac{fx}{z_2} \quad \text{and} \quad v_2 = \frac{fy}{z_2} \qquad (2.17)$$

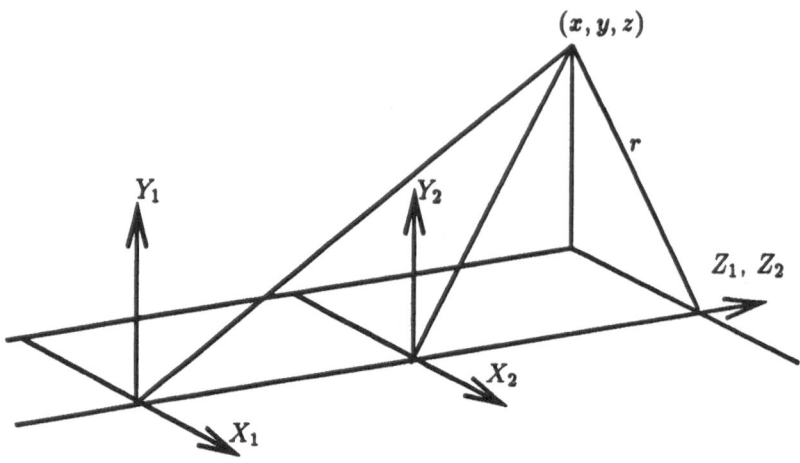

Figure 2.7: Geometry for axial motion stereo.

Let $q_1{}^2 = u_1{}^2 + v_1{}^2$, $q_2{}^2 = u_2{}^2 + v_2{}^2$ and $r^2 = x^2 + y^2$. Then, due to the radial symmetry about the z axis, $z_1 = fr/q_1$ and $z_2 = fr/q_2$. Therefore, the distance traveled during the point in the time interval $t_2 - t_1$ is given by

$$b = z_1 - z_2 = fr \left(\frac{1}{q_1} - \frac{1}{q_2} \right) \tag{2.18}$$

The x, y, z coordinates of the point can be computed by

$$x = \frac{bu_2(q_2 - d)}{fd}$$

$$y = \frac{bv_2(q_2 - d)}{fd}$$

$$z = \frac{b(q_2 - d)}{d} \tag{2.19}$$

where $d = q_2 - q_1$ is the radial disparity. The range of points along the z axis, i.e., $(0, 0, z)$ cannot be determined, since they always project to the point $u = 0, v = 0$ on the focal plane of the camera. The point $u = 0$, $v = 0$ is said to be the *focus of expansion* for the relative motion between the camera and the scene. Motion stereo has been studied by a large number of researchers, including Baker and Bolles [1985], Jain et al. [1987], and Ullman [1979]. However, there has been no known commercially available sensor based on the principles of motion stereo.

Active Triangulation Systems

Both binocular and motion stereo suffer from the correspondence problem. Solutions to the correspondence problem prove not only computationally expensive,

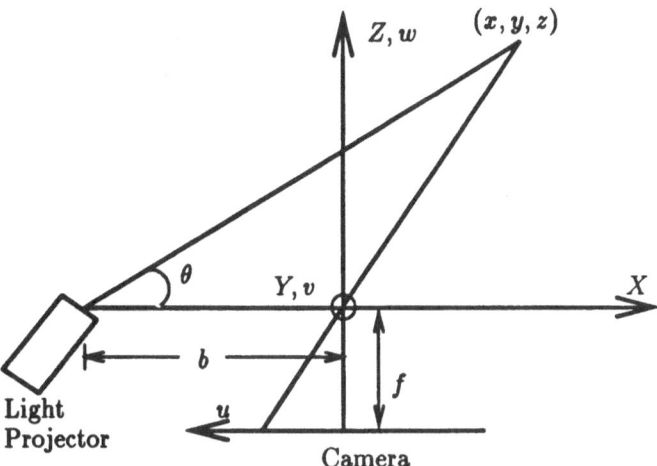

Figure 2.8: Geometry for active triangulation.

but also subject to error that for most applications may not be admissible. In active triangulation systems, a narrow beam of light is projected on the scene so as to light up a small point-like area on the object surface (Figure 2.8). The image of the illuminated point is formed on the focal plane of the camera. We can show that (Figure 2.8)

$$x = \frac{b}{f \cot \theta - u} \cdot u$$

$$y = \frac{b}{f \cot \theta - u} \cdot v$$

$$z = \frac{b}{f \cot \theta - u} \cdot f \qquad (2.20)$$

The disadvantage of shining a point-light source on the scene is that the scene must be scanned both horizontally and vertically. Instead, if a vertical light stripe is projected on the scene, then the range can be computed using Eq. (2.20) for each point on the vertical stripe independently and, with suitable hardware, the process can be easily parallelized. With a vertical stripe of light , the scene needs to be scanned only horizontally. Rioux [1984] designed a range sensor based on a single point-light source with synchronized scanners. Yang and Kak [1986], Smith and Kanade [1986], and Asada et al. [1988] have used striped light in their experiments on object recognition from range imagery. This technique has also been used in a commercial sensor called White Scanner developed by Technical Arts Corporation, Seattle, Washington [Technical Arts Corporation 1990].

It is also possible to project a regular grid on the scene and extract range

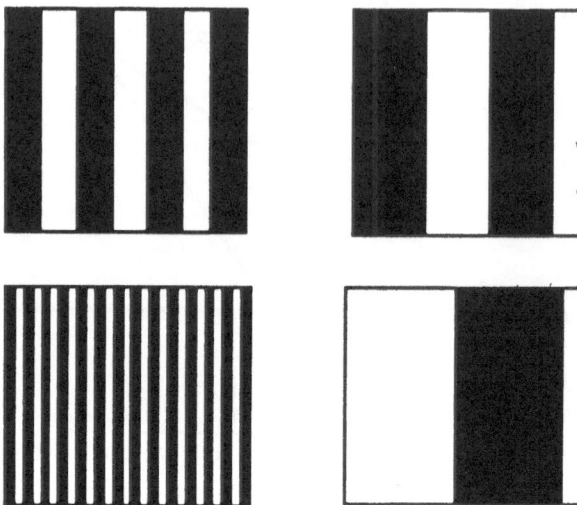

Figure 2.9: Binary patterns used in range sensing based on coded pattern triangulation.

measurements from the deformation of the grid formed on the object surface. Hu and Stockman [1989], Shrikhande and Stockman [1989], Harrison and Weir [1990], Will and Pennington [1971, 1972], and Wang et al. [1987] discuss techniques for obtaining depth and surface orientation from the projection of a regular grid pattern on the scene using a combination of constraint formulation and constraint propagation.

Rather than scanning a light stripe over a scene and processing several images, or dealing with the ambiguities that could result from a multi-stripe image, it is possible to obtain the same amount of information from $\lceil \log_2 N \rceil$ (where N is the number of bits used in the range quantization) images where the scene is illuminated with a series of binary patterns (Figure 2.9). The first pattern with the smallest pitch establishes the least significant bit in the computed range. The next pattern having twice the pitch establishes the next significant bit, and so on. This technique is relatively fast and inexpensive and has been used by Inokuchi et al. [1984], Sato and Inokuchi [1985], Yamamoto et al. [1986], Vuylsteke and Oosterlinck [1990], and Boyer and Kak [1987] in their experiments.

2.2.3 Sensors based on Optical Interferometry

When two monochromatic (of the same wavelength) waves traveling in a medium meet, they interfere with each other, thus forming a *standing* wave with an amplitude $\phi_1(x) - \phi_2(x)$. $\phi_1(x)$ and $\phi_2(x)$ are the individual phase functions of the two waves, and, typically, they are slowly varying functions of the distance

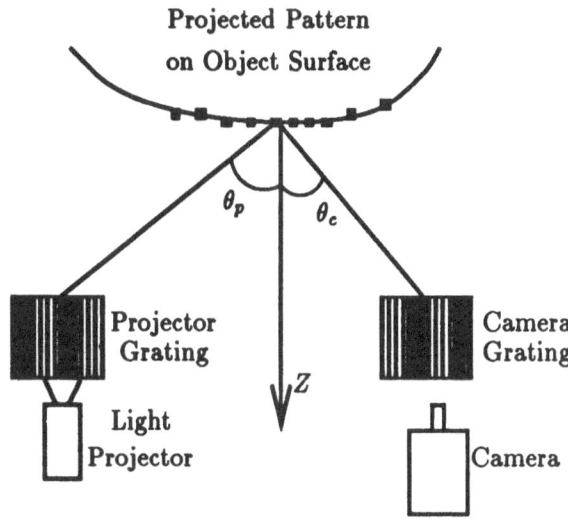

Figure 2.10: Configuration for Moire interferometry-based ranging.

x. Optical interference is used in two types of range sensing techniques: Moire interferometry and holographic interferometry.

Moire Interferometry

Moire interferometry technique uses line gratings of alternating opaque and transparent lines of equal width. The pitch P of the grating is the number of transparent or opaque lines per unit distance, which defines the spatial frequency of the grating The period $p = 1/P$ of the grating is the distance between the centers of two consecutive transparent or opaque lines. A Moire pattern is a low frequency interference pattern created when two gratings of slightly different spatial frequendies are superimposed.

In a Moire interferometer a precisely matched pair of gratings is used. The projection grating is placed in front of a focused light source called a projector, and the camera grating is placed in front of the camera. The projector is located at an angle θ_p relative to the z axis, and the viewing camera is kept at an angle of θ_c relative to the z axis (Figure 2.10). The fringe pattern from the projection grating undergoes deformation when projected upon the object surface. The nature of the deformation is dependent on local surface orientations. The projected fringe pattern, when viewed from the camera grating, results in a Moire interference pattern. If the spacing between two consecutive fringes as observed by the camera is p_0, then the depth spacing between the corresponding surface points is given by the equation

$$\Delta z = \frac{p_0}{\tan(\theta_c) + \tan(\theta_p)} \qquad (2.21)$$

The resolution of the Moire interferometer is directly proportional to the pitch of the grating used. Range sensing techniques based on Moire interferometry have been described by Reid [1986], Gasvik [1983], and Pirodda [1982]. More recently, Srinivasan and Lumia [1989] have designed a laser range finder based on Moire interferometry and have demonstrated its use for robotics applications. A commercial sensor based on Moire interferometry is manufactured by Electro-Optical Information Systems, Inc., (EOIS) of Santa Monica, California [Electro-Optical Information Systems 1990].

Holographic Interferometry

In a holographic interferometer, coherent light from a laser source is used to produce interference patterns. These interference patterns are created by the optical phase differences that resulted from path differences among the light sources. In a Moire interferometer the spacing of interference fringes is proportional to the pitch of the grating, whereas in a holographic interferometer the spacing of interference fringes is proportional to the wavelength being used. Holographic interferometers can have a finer resolution than the Moire interferometers, whose resolution is limited due to the physical and technological limitations on the pitch of an interference grating. The advantage of using Moire interferometry is that the light sources do not have to be coherent. Range sensors based on holographic interferometry have been described by Tozer et al. [1985], Mader [1985], and Sasaki and Okazaki [1986a, 1986b]. A commercial sensor based on holographic interferometry is manufactured by Newport Corporation in Fountain Valley, California [Newport Corporation 1990].

2.2.4 Sensors Based on Focusing Techniques

According to the Gauss law for thin lenses, a thin lens of focal length f will focus a point source in a scene at a distance z from the center of the lens onto a focal plane behind the lens at a distance w from the center of the lens such that

$$\frac{1}{f} = \frac{1}{z} + \frac{1}{w} \qquad (2.22)$$

which can be alternatively written as

$$z(w) = \frac{wf}{w - f} \qquad (2.23)$$

As w is varied from its minimum value of f to some physically determined maximum value w_{max}, points from $z = \infty$ to $z = z_{min} = w_{max}f/(w_{max} - f)$ are brought into focus. To determine whether a point has been brought into focus or not, most sensors mechanically adjust w until some measure of focus has been optimized. A typical measure of focus is the high frequency energy content in the video signal.

Eq. (2.23) can be used as a basis for range sensing. In an actual range sensor using lens with finite aperture of diameter D, a point source is not imaged as a point, but is blurred. This blurring is referred to as *diffraction blurring*. The diffraction blurring caused by a lens can be modeled as a point spread function of the form of a circularly symmetric 2-D Gaussian intensity distribution of diameter σ. The blurring causes an uncertainty in the measured range of a point. The range of the point can be determined only within an interval $[z_+(w, \sigma), z_-(w, \sigma)]$ where

$$z_{\pm}(w, \sigma) = \frac{wf}{w - f \pm \sigma F} \tag{2.24}$$

and where $F = f/D$ is the f-number of the lens aperture. Both active and passive focusing techniques are in common use. Passive focusing techniques use ambient lighting conditions, whereas active focusing techniques use structured light, typically in the form of stripes or a grid. Krotov and Martin [1986], Grossman [1987], and Pentland [1987] have described passive depth-from-focus techniques that optimize a simple focus measure in order to extract range information. Rioux and Blais [1986] have used two active focusing techniques, one using a grid of point sources, and the other using multi-stripe structured light to design a compact range imaging sensor.

2.2.5 Sensors Based on Fresnel Diffraction

Any wave passing through a finite aperture is subject to diffraction. It was observed by Talbot [1836] that when a periodic optical grating $T(x, y) = T(x + p, y)$ with period p is illuminated with coherent light, exact in-focus images of the grating are formed at intervals of D. These images are referred to as *Talbot images*. The value of D is given by the equation deduced by Raleigh,

$$D = \frac{2p^2}{\lambda} \text{ when } p \gg \lambda \tag{2.25}$$

If a grating is illuminated by a monochromatic plane wave of wavelength λ and a screen is placed at a distance z from the grating, the diffraction pattern on the screen will have a periodic modulation whose fundamental frequency is that of the grating (Figure 2.11). If we define a contrast ratio as the ratio of the power in the fundamental frequency to the power in the zero frequency component, then the contrast ratio is a periodic function with a period D, as given in Eq. (2.25). Leger and Snyder [1984], and Chavel and Strand [1984] have computed the functional dependence of the contrast ratio to the range for a variety of grating geometries such as regularly spaced (square wave) gratings and cosine gratings. The spatial intensity modulation can be converted to a temporal modulation of a video signal by raster-scanning the fringe pattern. The temporal modulation, and thereby the contrast ratio, can be recovered by analog or digital low-pass filtering or demodulation techniques.

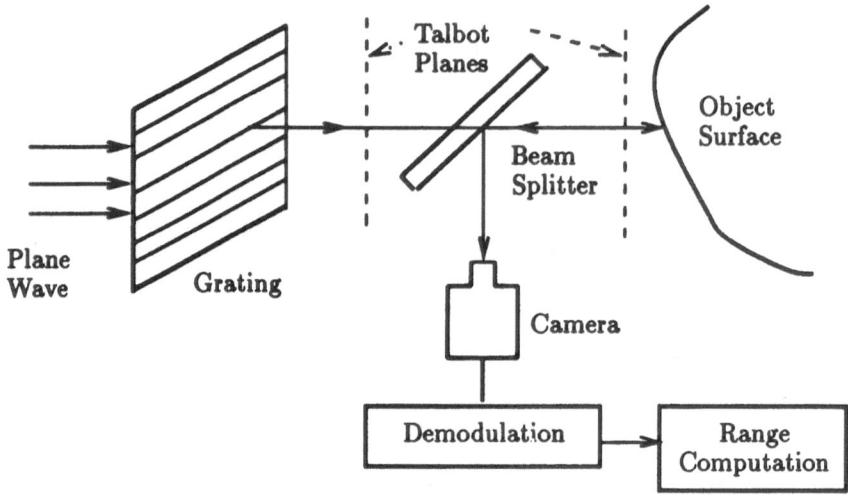

Figure 2.11: Configuration for range measurement using Fresnel diffraction.

2.2.6   Tactile Range Sensors

A tactile sensor is a device that measures the parameters of contact interaction between the device and a physical stimulus. The interaction is limited to a touch-sensitive region of the device's surface. Tactile sensing differs from other passive sensing modalities in that a robot with multiple tactile sensors can probe, move, and change its environment. Tactile sensors are *proximity* sensors producing sparse data, in contrast to other sensor types. Tactile sensing is in a stage of infancy compared to other range-sensing techniques, largely due to the relative paucity of robust, reliable, and accurate high-resolution sensors. For a detailed description of various tactile sensors, the interested reader is referred to the excellent survey articles by Fearing [1990], and Nicholls and Lee [1989].

Tactile sensors can be categorized based on their *dimensionality*. A zero-dimensional sensor relies on a point contact, whereas in a one-dimensional sensor the sensing sites are arranged collinearly. In a two-dimensional sensor, which is the current state of art, the sensing sites are arranged as a grid. Each element of such a grid is called a *tactel*, which stands for tactile element just as a *pixel* denotes a picture element. Tactile sensors are more commonly categorized based on the way in which the interaction between the contacting stimulus and the tactile sensor is transduced into a form suitable for subsequent computer analysis.

Tactile Sensors Based on Resistive and Conductive Transducers

Tactile sensors based on resistive and conductive transducers measure change in resistance or conductance of a resistive or conductive *elastomer* (elastic polymer) when an external force is applied. The pressure exerted by an external stimulus results in the deformation of the elastomer, altering the local particle density within it and thereby changing its resistivity or conductivity. This type of tactile sensor has been widely used in industry on account of its durability, wide dynamic range, good overload tolerance, and compatibility with VLSI integrated circuits. However, these sensors do suffer from problems stemming from hysteresis, limited spatial resolution, non-linear response characteristics, and difficulty of synthesizing good elastomer materials. The designs of Robertson and Walkden [1986] and Raibert [1984] are good examples of such a sensor type.

Tactile Sensors Based on Piezoelectric and Pyroelectric Transducers

Tactile sensors based on piezoelectric transducers generate voltage across the sensing element when pressure is applied to it. The generated voltage is proportional to the applied pressure. No external voltage is required and continuous analog output is available. Pyroelectric transducers, on the other hand, generate a voltage when the sensing element is either heated or cooled. Tactile sensors based on piezoelectric and pyroelectric transducers are inherently dynamic. If pressure is applied and maintained at a constant value, or if the temperature is maintained at a constant value, then the sensor output decays to zero. Thus, these sensors are most suitable for measurement of change in pressure or temperature. The materials used in these sensors are polymers with piezoelectric or pyroelectric properties. These sensors have a wide dynamic range, are fairly durable, and are capable of both force and temperature sensing. However, the difficulty of separating the piezoelectric and pyroelectric effects from the sensor materials, and the complexity of sensor design, have limited the use of these sensors. The sensors designed by Dario and De Rossi [1985] and Dario et al. [1987] are typical examples of such a sensor type.

Tactile Sensors Based on Capacitive Transducers

Tactile sensors based on capacitive transducers measure capacitance, which varies under applied loads. An elastomer with dielectric properties is sandwiched between the plates of a capacitor. External pressure applied to the plates of the capacitor causes physical deformation of the elastomer, resulting in a change of capacitance that is proportional to the external pressure. Some tactile sensors cause external pressure to result in relative displacement of the dielectric with respect to the capacitor plates, which in turn results in a change in capacitance. These sensors have a wide dynamic range, a fairly linear response, and are fairly robust. However, they are susceptible to noise, and their spatial resolution is limited since capacitance decreases with physical size. Also, the fact that dielectrics are generally temperature sensitive complicates the design of the sensor. The sensor designed by Siegel et al. [1987] is a typical example of such a sensor type.

Tactile Sensors Based on Magnetic Transducers

Tactile sensors based on magnetic transducers are divided into two major categories. The first category uses mechanical movement to produce a change in magnetic flux. The second category uses magnetoelastic materials that exhibit a change in the magnetic field when subjected to mechanical stress. Sensors that rely on mechanical moving parts are simple to design, have a wide dynamic range, and allow large displacements. However, they suffer from poor spatial resolution. On the other hand, sensors that use magnetoelastic materials have not only the advantages of a wide dynamic range, linear response, and robustness, but also have the capability to sense normal force, torque, and shear force. However, magnetoelastic materials are susceptible to noise, and stray electromagnetic fields need special AC noise shielding circuits to protect them. The sensor designed by Sato et al. [1986] uses a magnetic transducer based on mechanical movement, whereas the sensors designed by Hackwood et al. [1986] and Vranish [1986a, 1986b] use magnetoelastic materials.

Tactile Sensors Based on Mechanical Transducers

Tactile sensors based on mechanical transducers measure the mechanical displacement caused by an applied force. A common example is a spring-loaded switch that gives on/off contact readings. Another example is a linear potentiometer with a graded scale of deflection whose output can be treated as a measure of the applied force or the traversed displacement. Other devices measuring angular displacement include devices such as optical shaft encoders, angular potentiometers, etc. Mechanical transducers represent a well-understood and well-exploited technology; however, sensors based on mechanical transduction generally tend to be bulky and consequently suffer from very limited spatial resolution. The sensor designed by Russel [1985] is a typical example of a mechanical transducer-based tactile sensor.

Tactile Sensors Based on Optical Transducers

This category of tactile sensors uses optomechanical transduction coupled with mechanical displacement. The sensor surface is made up of a compliant material that has on its underside a grid of elongated pins. When external pressure is exerted on the compliant surface, the pins on the underside undergo a mechanical displacement normal to the surface. Each pin is moved into the light path of a photoemitter-receiver pair. The amount of movement determines the amount of light reaching the photoreceiver that, when digitized, represents the amount of pressure applied on the sensor surface. Optical transducers have very high spatial resolution, do not suffer from electrical interference problems, and can be interfaced with other vision-based sensing modalities quite easily. Optical technology has not yet advanced to a point where such sensors could prove cost-effective, but it holds future promise. The sensors designed by King and White [1985] and Mott et al. [1986] are examples of tactile sensors that use optomechanical transduction coupled with mechanical displacement.

Recently, the integration of tactile sensing with other visual sensing modalities has been receiving much attention. Allen [1988] deserves much credit for pioneering research in integrating vision and touch for object-recognition tasks. Allen describes a robotics system for object recognition that uses passive stereo vision in conjunction with active exploratory tactile sensing. It has been shown how the complementary natures of visual and tactile sensing can be synergetically exploited to discover the underlying 3-D structure of the objects to be recognized. In particular, it has been shown how tactile sensing can overcome the problems of occlusion encountered in the case of visual sensors. A hierarchical object recognition procedure that integrates visual and tactile data into three-dimensional surface features has been described. First, the zero-crossings are detected in a pair of stereo images using the Marr-Hildreth edge operator and are subsequently grouped to form region contours. The stereo-matching algorithm determines the depth at the pixels on the region contours from the disparity, resulting in sparse three-dimensional data. The sparse three-dimensional data is inadequate for generating a rich surface description that would enable object recognition. Tactile sensing is then used to explore regions isolated by the processing of visual data to build a richer surface description. Regions are characterized as either continuous surface patches, holes, or cavities. A *Coons* patch is fitted for each continuous surface patch using a process of hierarchical refinement. The three-dimensional contours from the visual sensing form the initial Coons patch grid from which the description is refined by tactile sensing in the interior of the region. Features such as cavities and holes are discovered by tactile sensing and are characterized by attributes such as length and diameter of the hole, depth and diameter of the cavity, etc. A three-dimensional moment-based matching technique is used to match sensed features to model features and to generate an interpretation hypothesis. A feature-based verification technique is used for hypothesis verification. More recently, the work has been extended to the recognition of objects that can be modeled as superquadrics [Allen and Michelman 1990].

Chapter 3

Range Image Segmentation

The output of a range image sensor is the scene surface geometry in sampled form. It is most commonly represented as an image that is, a two-dimensional array of pixels, each pixel conveying the range of a sampled point on the surface from a reference point. This representation, though voluminous, conveys very little *geometric* or *semantic* information about the visible surfaces in the scene. The role of segmentation is to extract geometric primitives relevant to higher level cognitive processes from the pixel-level representation of a range image. The segmentation process partitions a range image into geometric primitives so that all the image pixels are grouped into clusters with a common geometric representation or property.

Segmentation is the first and most crucial step toward the interpretation of the range image. It is largely *data-driven*, that is, it makes no assumption regarding the semantic content of the scene through knowledge of the presence or absence of objects in the scene and their spatial inter-relationships. Being data-driven, segmentation should incorporate only generic constraints on scene surface geometry, imaging geometry, and the physical and optical properties of the sensing devices. Also, the geometric primitives to be extracted by the initial segmentation algorithm should be simple and generic so as to avoid making any constraining assumptions about the application-specific higher level processes involved. In the context of range image segmentation, the simplest possible geometric primitives are continuous surface patches and surface discontinuities.

Although the purpose of the initial segmentation seems simple, it has proved to be the most difficult stumbling block in computer vision. Human vision, on the other hand, is remarkably adept at detecting surface discontinuities, surface regularities, smoothness, and spatial coherence even in noisy images without any *a priori* knowledge about the objects in the scene. Yet, this aspect of human vision known as *perceptual organization* has proved very difficult to emulate in computer vision systems.

Segmentation algorithms for range images need to incorporate scene surface properties that satisfy the following criteria:

1. Properties should be *generic* so that they have applicability over a wide

spectrum of application domains.

2. Properties should fully characterize the surface.

3. Properties should provide a rich description so as to be of use to higher
   level vision processes.

4. Properties should have local support, that is, they should be computable
   in a local window centered around a range image pixel of interest.

5. Properties should be invariant to changes in viewpoint and scale.

The mean, Gaussian, and principal surface curvatures satisfy the above properties.

3.1 Mathematical Formulation of Range Image Segmentation

The output of a range sensor can be treated as a digital geometric signal [Besl
1990], which is defined as a collection of N discrete samples of an underlying
function $\mathbf{F} : \mathcal{R}^m \rightarrow \mathcal{R}^n$

$$\mathbf{x}_i = \mathbf{F}(\mathbf{u}_i) \tag{3.1}$$

where $\mathbf{u}_i \in \mathcal{R}^m$ and $\mathbf{x}_i \in \mathcal{R}^n$ and $i = 1, \ldots N$.

$\mathcal{R}^n$ is an n-dimensional Euclidean space that constitutes the scene domain,
and $\mathcal{R}^m$ is an m-dimensional parameter space in which the geometrical signal is
represented. For a static range image, the domain space has dimension $n = 3$,
that is, $\mathbf{x}_i = (x_i, y_i, z_i)$, and the parameter space has dimension $m = 2$, that
is, $\mathbf{u}_i = (u_i, v_i)$. Thus $\mathbf{x}_i = \mathbf{F}(\mathbf{u}_i) = (x_i(u_i, v_i), y_i(u_i, v_i), z_i(u_i, v_i))$. For a
time-varying image, the time variable t constitutes an additional dimension,
thus $n = 4$, $\mathbf{x}_i = (x_i, y_i, z_i, t_i)$, $m = 3$, $\mathbf{u}_i = (u_i, v_i, t_i)$, and $\mathbf{x}_i = \mathbf{F}(\mathbf{u}_i) =
(x_i(u_i, v_i, t_i), y_i(u_i, v_i, t_i), z_i(u_i, v_i, t_i), t_i)$.

A scene can be considered to consist of a finite number of smooth or textured
surface patches. These surface patches intersect at a finite number of edges
forming surface discontinuities. The function $\mathbf{F}$ can therefore be considered to be
piecewise smooth and can be partitioned into a finite number of partitions, each
partition corresponding to a smooth surface without discontinuities. Therefore

$$\mathbf{x} = \mathbf{F}(\mathbf{u}) = \sum_{j=1}^{K} [\mathbf{g}_j(\mathbf{u}) + \mathbf{t}_j(\mathbf{u}) + \mathbf{n}_j(\mathbf{u})]C_j(\mathbf{u}) \tag{3.2}$$

where K is the number of partitions; $\mathbf{g}_j(\mathbf{u})$ is a smooth C^2 function (a function
with continuous second-order derivatives) defined over a closed bounded subset
P_j of $\mathcal{R}^n$; $\mathbf{t}_j(\mathbf{u})$ is a texture function with zero first-order moment and finite
second moment defined over P_j describing the physical texture of the surface;
$\mathbf{n}_j(\mathbf{u})$ is a zero-mean stochastic noise process which, in general, is dependent on

the scene sensing geometry and the physical and optical properties of the sensor; and $C_j(\mathbf{u})$ is the characteristic function of the subset P_j defined by

$$C_j(\mathbf{u}) = \begin{cases} 1 & \mathbf{u} \in P_j \subset \mathcal{R}^n \\ 0 & \text{otherwise} \end{cases} \tag{3.3}$$

The subsets $\{P_j\}$ are chosen such that each P_j is the largest subset possible with $g_j(\mathbf{u})$ still a C^2 function. A region label $\mathbf{L}(\mathbf{u})$ can be defined as

$$\mathbf{L}(\mathbf{u}) = \sum_{j=1}^{K} j \cdot C_j(\mathbf{u}) \tag{3.4}$$

with each partition P_j assigned a unique label from among $\{1, \cdots K\}$ by $\mathbf{L}(\mathbf{u})$.
Now, formally, the segmentation problem can be stated as follows:

Given a geometric signal specified by the data set $(\mathbf{u}_i, \mathbf{x}_i)$ which is denoted symbolically as observed function $\mathbf{F}$, find $\hat{K}$ approximating functions $\hat{g}_j(\mathbf{u})$ and $\hat{t}_j(\mathbf{u})$ defined over the $\hat{K}$ partitioning subsets P_j such that ϵ and $\hat{K}$ are minimized simultaneously subject to the constraints on $\hat{g}_j(\mathbf{u})$ and $\hat{t}_j(\mathbf{u})$, which are the same as those for $g_j(\mathbf{u})$ and $t_j(\mathbf{u})$, respectively. $\epsilon = \|\mathbf{F} - \hat{\mathbf{F}}\|$ is the total geometric error between the estimate $\hat{\mathbf{F}}(\mathbf{u}) = \sum_{j=1}^{\hat{K}}[\hat{g}_j(\mathbf{u}) + \hat{t}_j(\mathbf{u})]C_j(\mathbf{u})$ and the observed function $\mathbf{F}$.

The partition $\mathcal{P} = \{P_j \,|\, 1 \leq j \leq \hat{K}\}$ is said to constitute the segmentation of the range image. The crux of the segmentation problem, therefore, is to come up with the approximating functions $\hat{g}_j(\mathbf{u})$, $\hat{t}_j(\mathbf{u})$ and the appropriate value of $\hat{K}$. A good segmentation algorithm should partition a range image into subsets or regions that can be directly associated with meaningful physical entities in the scene.

3.2 Fundamentals of Surface Differential Geometry

A C^2 surface can be written in the following parametric form [Faux and Pratt 1979]:

$$\mathbf{x}(\mathbf{u}) = \mathbf{x}(u, v) = (x(u, v), y(u, v), z(u, v)) \tag{3.5}$$

Two important mathematical entities associated with a C^2 surface are the two surface fundamental forms.

The *first fundamental form* of the surface is given by

$$\begin{aligned} \mathbf{I}(u, v, du, dv) &= d\mathbf{x} \cdot d\mathbf{x} = E\,du^2 + 2F\,du\,dv + G\,dv^2 \\ &= [du\ dv]\begin{bmatrix} g_{11} & g_{12} \\ g_{21} & g_{22} \end{bmatrix}\begin{bmatrix} du \\ dv \end{bmatrix} \\ &= d\mathbf{u}^T \mathbf{G}\, d\mathbf{u} \end{aligned} \tag{3.6}$$

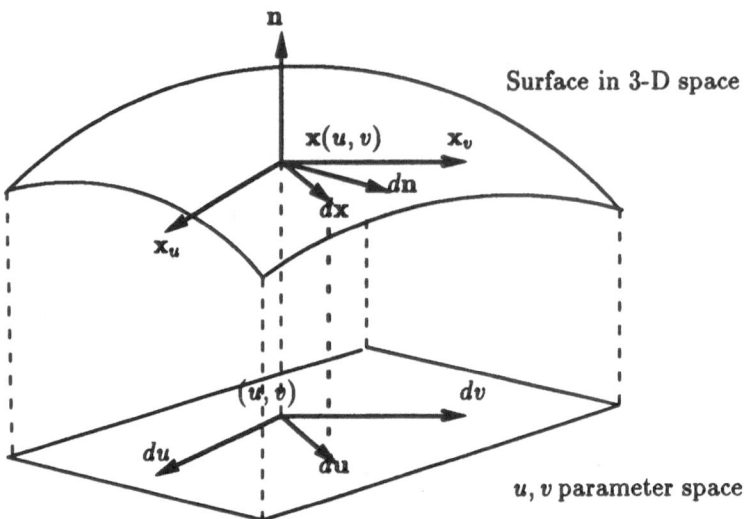

Figure 3.1: Local coordinate frame at a surface point x for computing the first and second fundamental forms of the surface.

where G is the first fundamental form matrix of a surface whose elements are given as

$$g_{11} \quad = \quad E = \mathbf{x}_u \cdot \mathbf{x}_u \tag{3.7}$$
$$g_{12} \quad = \quad g_{21} = F = \mathbf{x}_u \cdot \mathbf{x}_v \tag{3.8}$$
$$g_{22} \quad = \quad G = \mathbf{x}_v \cdot \mathbf{x}_v \tag{3.9}$$

where

$$\mathbf{x}_u(u, v) \quad = \quad \frac{\partial \mathbf{x}(u, v)}{\partial u} \tag{3.10}$$
$$\mathbf{x}_v(u, v) \quad = \quad \frac{\partial \mathbf{x}(u, v)}{\partial v} \tag{3.11}$$

The first fundamental form $I(u, v, du, dv)$ of a surface measures the movement $\|d\mathbf{x}\|^2$ on the surface at a point (u, v) corresponding to a given small movement $d\mathbf{u} = (du, dv)$ (Figure 3.1). The first fundamental form of a surface depends entirely on the surface itself, and not on how the surface is embedded in 3-D space, i.e., it is an *intrinsic* characteristic of the surface.

The *second fundamental form* of the surface is given by

$$\mathrm{II}(u, v, du, dv) \quad = \quad -d\mathbf{x} \cdot d\mathbf{n} = L\,du^2 + 2M\,du\,dv + N\,dv^2$$
$$= \quad [du \ dv] \begin{bmatrix} b_{11} & b_{12} \\ b_{21} & b_{22} \end{bmatrix} \begin{bmatrix} du \\ dv \end{bmatrix}$$

$$= du^T B\, du \tag{3.12}$$

where B is the second fundamental form matrix of a surface whose elements are given by

$$b_{11} = L = \mathbf{x}_{uu} \cdot \mathbf{n} \tag{3.13}$$
$$b_{12} = b_{21} = M = \mathbf{x}_{uv} \cdot \mathbf{n} \tag{3.14}$$
$$b_{22} = N = \mathbf{x}_{vv} \cdot \mathbf{n} \tag{3.15}$$

where

$$\mathbf{x}_{uu}(u, v) = \frac{\partial^2 \mathbf{x}(u, v)}{\partial u^2} \tag{3.16}$$

$$\mathbf{x}_{uv}(u, v) = \frac{\partial^2 \mathbf{x}(u, v)}{\partial u \partial v} \tag{3.17}$$

$$\mathbf{x}_{vv}(u, v) = \frac{\partial^2 \mathbf{x}(u, v)}{\partial v^2} \tag{3.18}$$

and $\mathbf{n}(u, v)$ is the unit surface normal vector given by

$$\mathbf{n}(u, v) = \frac{\mathbf{x}_u(u, v) \times \mathbf{x}_v(u, v)}{\|\mathbf{x}_u(u, v) \times \mathbf{x}_v(u, v)\|} \tag{3.19}$$

where $\times$ denotes the vector cross product.

The second fundamental form $\mathbf{II}(u, v, du, dv)$ measures the correlation between $d\mathbf{n}$, the change in surface normal vector and $d\mathbf{x}$, the change in surface position at a surface point $\mathbf{u} = (u, v)$ corresponding to a small movement $du = (du, dv)$ in the parameter space (Figure 3.1). The second fundamental form is an *extrinsic* property of the surface in that it depends on how the surface is embedded in 3-D space.

The *Existence and Uniqueness Theorem* for 3-D surfaces of type C^2 states that:

1. **Existence:** Let $g_{11}(u, v)$, $g_{12}(u, v)$, and $g_{22}(u, v)$ be continuous functions with continuous second partial derivatives. Let $b_{11}(u, v)$, $b_{12}(u, v)$ and $b_{22}(u, v)$ be continuous functions with continuous first partial derivatives. Assume that all six functions are defined on an open set D containing the point (u_0, v_0). If all six functions satisfy the compatibility equations and sign restrictions, then there exists a unique surface patch defined in the neighborhood of (u_0, v_0) such that $G = [g_{ij}]$ and $B = [b_{ij}]$ are its first and second fundamental form matrices, respectively. Uniqueness is determined up to translation and rotation in three-dimensional Euclidean space. The sign restrictions are as follows:

$$g_{11} > 0, \ g_{22} > 0 \text{ and } \det G = g_{11}g_{12} - g_{12}^2 > 0 \tag{3.20}$$

The compatibility equations are as follows:

$$(b_{11})_v - (b_{12})_u = b_{11}\Gamma_{12}^1 + b_{12}(\Gamma_{12}^2 - \Gamma_{11}^1) - b_{22}\Gamma_{11}^2$$

$$(b_{12})_v - (b_{22})_u = b_{11}\Gamma_{22}^1 + b_{12}(\Gamma_{22}^2 - \Gamma_{21}^1) - b_{22}\Gamma_{21}^2$$
$$b_{11}b_{22} - b_{12}^2 = g_{12}[(\Gamma_{22}^2)_u - (\Gamma_{12}^2)_v + \Gamma_{22}^1\Gamma_{11}^2 - \Gamma_{12}^1\Gamma_{12}^2] +$$
$$g_{11}[(\Gamma_{22}^1)_u - (\Gamma_{12}^1)_v + \Gamma_{22}^1\Gamma_{11}^1 + \Gamma_{22}^2\Gamma_{12}^1 -$$
$$\Gamma_{12}^1\Gamma_{12}^1 - \Gamma_{12}^2\Gamma_{22}^1] \qquad (3.21)$$

where

$$\Gamma_{ij}^k(u,v) = \frac{1}{2}\sum_{m=1}^{m=2} g^{km}\left[\frac{\partial g_{jm}}{\partial u^i} + \frac{\partial g_{mi}}{\partial u^j} - \frac{\partial g_{ij}}{\partial u^m}\right] \qquad (3.22)$$

where $u^1 = u$ and $u^2 = v$ and g^{km} is the inverse matrix of g_{km}, which is the tensor notation for **G**. $\Gamma_{ij}^k = \Gamma_{ji}^k$ since **G** is a symmetric matrix.

2. **Uniqueness**: If two surfaces S and S^* possess the fundamental form matrices **G**, **B**, **G*** and **B***, respectively, where **G** = **G*** and **B** = **B***, then there exists an appropriate translation and rotation such that S and S^* coincide exactly.

Thus the six functions g_{11}, g_{12}, g_{22}, b_{11}, b_{12} and b_{22} (or, alternatively, E, F, G, L, M, N) are necessary and sufficient to uniquely specify any C^2 surface modulo rigid body motion in three-dimensional Euclidean space. Since the two fundamental forms of a surface are invariant to rigid body motion in Euclidean space, they form the basis for *invariant surface features*, i.e., surface features that are invariant to viewpoint.

3.3   Surface Curvatures

A space curve C is a one-dimensional entity embedded in three-dimensional Euclidean space. C can be represented in a parametric form by the equation:

$$C = \{\mathbf{x}(t) = (x(t), y(t), z(t)) \mid \mathbf{x} = (x, y, z) \in \mathcal{R}^3, t \in [a,b] \subset \mathcal{R}\} \subset \mathcal{R}^3 \quad (3.23)$$

The speed function $s(t)$ of a space curve C is given by the equation

$$s(t) = \|\mathbf{x}_t(t)\| = \left\|\frac{d\mathbf{x}(t)}{dt}\right\| = \sqrt{\left(\frac{dx(t)}{dt}\right)^2 + \left(\frac{dy(t)}{dt}\right)^2 + \left(\frac{dz(t)}{dt}\right)^2} \quad (3.24)$$

The unit tangent vector function $\mathbf{t}(t)$ to the curve is given by the equation:

$$\mathbf{t}(t) = \frac{\mathbf{x}_t(t)}{s(t)} = \frac{1}{s(t)}\frac{d\mathbf{x}(t)}{dt} = \frac{\frac{d\mathbf{x}(t)}{dt}}{\left\|\frac{d\mathbf{x}(t)}{dt}\right\|} = \frac{(\frac{dx(t)}{dt}, \frac{dy(t)}{dt}, \frac{dz(t)}{dt})}{\left\|(\frac{dx(t)}{dt}, \frac{dy(t)}{dt}, \frac{dz(t)}{dt})\right\|} \quad (3.25)$$

The curvature function $\kappa(t)$ is given by the equation:

$$\kappa(t) = \frac{\|\mathbf{t}_t(t)\|}{s(t)} = \frac{1}{s(t)}\left\|\frac{d\mathbf{t}(t)}{dt}\right\| = \frac{\|\mathbf{x}_t(t) \times \mathbf{x}_{tt}(t)\|}{s^3(t)} \quad (3.26)$$

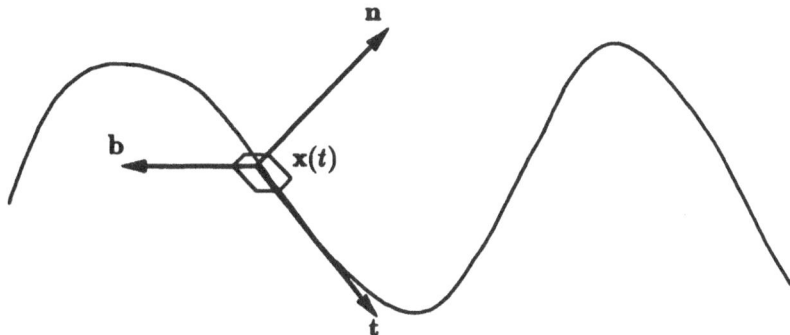

Figure 3.2: The Frenet frame, a local orthogonal coordinate frame consisting of
$\mathbf{b}, \mathbf{t}$, and $\mathbf{n}$, defined at each point on a space curve where the speed and curvature
functions are non-zero.

The curvature function $\kappa(t)$ is proportional to the rate of change $\mathbf{t}_t(t)$ of the
tangent function $\mathbf{t}(t)$, and is undefined wherever the speed function $s(t)$ is zero.
Points where $s(t) = 0$ represent points of singularities for the curvature function
$\kappa(t)$. Computation of the curvature function involves the computation of second-
order derivatives.

The unit normal vector function $\mathbf{n}(t)$ is also a measure of the rate of change
of the unit tangent vector function and is given by

$$\mathbf{n}(t) = \frac{\mathbf{t}_t(t)}{\|\mathbf{t}_t(t)\|} = \frac{\mathbf{t}_t(t)}{\kappa(t)s(t)} = \frac{s^2(t)\mathbf{x}_{tt}(t) - (\mathbf{x}_{tt}(t) \cdot \mathbf{x}_t(t))\mathbf{x}_t(t)}{\kappa(t)s^4(t)} \qquad (3.27)$$

The unit binomial vector function $\mathbf{b}(t)$ is normal to both $\mathbf{n}(t)$ and $\mathbf{t}(t)$ and is
given by

$$\mathbf{b}(t) = \mathbf{t}(t) \times \mathbf{n}(t) = \frac{\mathbf{x}_t(t) \times \mathbf{x}_{tt}(t)}{\|\mathbf{x}_t(t) \times \mathbf{x}_{tt}(t)\|} = \frac{\mathbf{x}_t(t) \times \mathbf{x}_{tt}(t)}{\kappa(t)s^3(t)} \qquad (3.28)$$

The vectors $\mathbf{b}(t)$, $\mathbf{t}(t)$ and $\mathbf{n}(t)$ define a local orthogonal coordinate frame at each
point where the speed and the curvature functions are non-zero. This frame of
reference is referred to as the Frenet frame (Figure 3.2). The torsion function
$\tau(t)$ is proportional to the third derivative of C and is given by

$$\tau(t) = \frac{\mathbf{n}(t) \cdot \mathbf{b}(t)}{s(t)} = \frac{\mathbf{x}_{ttt}(t) \cdot (\mathbf{x}_t(t) \times \mathbf{x}_{tt}(t))}{\|\mathbf{x}_t(t) \times \mathbf{x}_{tt}(t)\|^2} = \frac{\mathbf{x}_{ttt}(t) \cdot (\mathbf{x}_t(t) \times \mathbf{x}_{tt}(t))}{\kappa^2(t)s^6(t)} \qquad (3.29)$$

The three unit-vector functions $\mathbf{t}(t)$, $\mathbf{n}(t)$, and $\mathbf{b}(t)$, and the three scalar functions $\kappa(t)$, $s(t)$, and $\tau(t)$, completely describe a space curve that is free of singularities.

Now consider a space curve C on a given surface S. C is parametrically
represented by the equation $\mathbf{u} = \mathbf{u}(t) = (u(t), v(t))$, and S is represented in

parametric form $\mathbf{x}(\mathbf{u}) = \mathbf{x}(u, v) = (x(u, v), y(u, v), z(u, v))$. Whereas $\mathbf{x}(u, v)$ denotes a general point on the surface S, $\mathbf{x}(t)$ denotes a point on C. The tangent vector function is given by

$$\mathbf{x}_t(t) = \frac{\mathbf{x}(t)}{dt} = \frac{\partial \mathbf{x}}{\partial u} u_t(t) + \frac{\partial \mathbf{x}}{\partial v} v_t(t) = \mathbf{A} \mathbf{u}_t \qquad (3.30)$$

where $\mathbf{u}(t) = [u(t), v(t)]^T$, and $\mathbf{u}_t(t) = [u_t(t), v_t(t)]^T$, and $\mathbf{A}$ is given by

$$\mathbf{A} = \begin{bmatrix} \frac{\partial x}{\partial u} & \frac{\partial x}{\partial v} \\ \frac{\partial y}{\partial u} & \frac{\partial y}{\partial v} \\ \frac{\partial z}{\partial u} & \frac{\partial z}{\partial v} \end{bmatrix} = [\mathbf{x}_u \ \mathbf{x}_v] \qquad (3.31)$$

The speed function $s(t)$ of C is given by the equation

$$s^2(t) = \|\mathbf{x}_t(t)\|^2 = \mathbf{x}_t^T \mathbf{x}_t = \mathbf{u}_t^T \mathbf{A}^T \mathbf{A} \, \mathbf{u}_t = \mathbf{u}_t^T \mathbf{G} \, \mathbf{u}_t \qquad (3.32)$$

where

$$\mathbf{G} = \mathbf{A}^T \mathbf{A} = \begin{bmatrix} \mathbf{x}_u \cdot \mathbf{x}_u & \mathbf{x}_u \cdot \mathbf{x}_v \\ \mathbf{x}_u \cdot \mathbf{x}_v & \mathbf{x}_v \cdot \mathbf{x}_v \end{bmatrix} \qquad (3.33)$$

is the first fundamental form matrix of S. The unit tangent vector function for C is then given by the equation

$$\mathbf{t}(t) = \frac{\mathbf{x}_t(t)}{s(t)} = \frac{\mathbf{A} \mathbf{u}_t}{\sqrt{\mathbf{u}_t^T \mathbf{G} \, \mathbf{u}_t}} \qquad (3.34)$$

Using Eq. (3.25) and Eq. (3.27), we can show that

$$\mathbf{x}_t(t) = s(t) \mathbf{t}(t) \qquad (3.35)$$

and

$$\mathbf{x}_{tt}(t) = s_t(t) \mathbf{t}(t) + s^2(t) \kappa(t) \mathbf{n}(t) \qquad (3.36)$$

Let $\mathbf{n}_C$ denote the unit normal vector function of C and $\mathbf{n}_S$ the unit surface normal to S. Then

$$\begin{aligned} \mathbf{x}_{tt}(t) &= s_t(t) \mathbf{t}(t) + s^2(t) \kappa(t) \mathbf{n}_C(t) \\ &= \frac{\partial^2 \mathbf{x}}{\partial u^2} u_t^2 + 2 \frac{\partial^2 \mathbf{x}}{\partial u \partial v} u_t v_t + \frac{\partial^2 \mathbf{x}}{\partial v^2} v_t^2 + \frac{\partial \mathbf{x}}{\partial u} u_{tt} + \frac{\partial \mathbf{x}}{\partial v} v_{tt} \\ &= \mathbf{x}_{uu} u_t^2 + 2 \mathbf{x}_{uv} u_t v_t + \mathbf{x}_{vv} v_t^2 + \mathbf{x}_u u_{tt} + \mathbf{x}_v v_{tt} \end{aligned} \qquad (3.37)$$

From Eq. (3.19) and Eq. (3.27), $\mathbf{n}_S$ can be seen to be perpendicular to $\mathbf{x}_u$, $\mathbf{x}_v$, and $\mathbf{t}$. Therefore, the component of $\mathbf{x}_{tt}$ along the direction of the surface normal $\mathbf{n}_S$ is given by

$$\begin{aligned} \mathbf{x}_{tt} \cdot \mathbf{n}_S &= s^2 \kappa \, \mathbf{n}_C \cdot \mathbf{n}_S \\ &= \mathbf{n}_S \cdot \frac{\partial^2 \mathbf{x}}{\partial u^2} u_t^2 + 2 \mathbf{n}_S \cdot \frac{\partial^2 \mathbf{x}}{\partial u \partial v} u_t v_t + \mathbf{n}_S \cdot \frac{\partial^2 \mathbf{x}}{\partial v^2} v_t^2 \\ &= \mathbf{n}_S \cdot \mathbf{x}_{uu} u_t^2 + 2 \mathbf{n}_S \cdot \mathbf{x}_{uv} u_t v_t + \mathbf{n}_S \cdot \mathbf{x}_{vv} v_t^2 \end{aligned} \qquad (3.38)$$

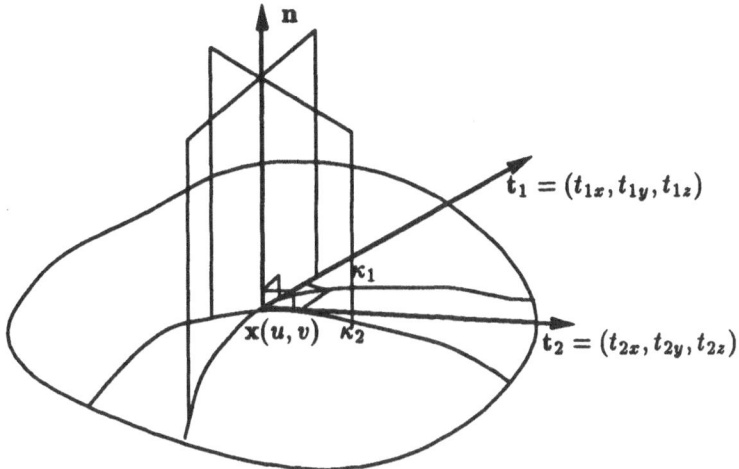

Figure 3.3: Principal curvatures κ_1 and κ_2 at a surface point $\mathbf{x}$, and a local coordinate frame $(\mathbf{n}, \mathbf{t}_1, \mathbf{t}_2)$.

We can express the curvature in matrix notation as

$$s^2 \kappa \, \mathbf{n}_C \cdot \mathbf{n}_S = \mathbf{u}_t^T \mathbf{B} \, \mathbf{u}_t \qquad (3.39)$$

where

$$\mathbf{B} = \begin{bmatrix} \mathbf{n}_S \cdot \frac{\partial^2 \mathbf{x}}{\partial u^2} & \mathbf{n}_S \cdot \frac{\partial^2 \mathbf{x}}{\partial u \partial v} \\ \mathbf{n}_S \cdot \frac{\partial^2 \mathbf{x}}{\partial u \partial v} & \mathbf{n}_S \cdot \frac{\partial^2 \mathbf{x}}{\partial v^2} \end{bmatrix} = \begin{bmatrix} \mathbf{n}_S \cdot \mathbf{x}_{uu} & \mathbf{n}_S \cdot \mathbf{x}_{uv} \\ \mathbf{n}_S \cdot \mathbf{x}_{uv} & \mathbf{n}_S \cdot \mathbf{x}_{vv} \end{bmatrix} \qquad (3.40)$$

is the second fundamental matrix of the surface S.

Consider a surface S defined by $\mathbf{x}(u, v) = \{(x(u, v), y(u, v), z(u, v)) | (x, y, z) \in \mathcal{R}^3, (u, v) \in \mathcal{R}^2\}$. Let C_x be the space curve formed by the intersection of S and a plane P containing the surface normal $\mathbf{n}_S(u, v)$ at a given point $\mathbf{x}$ on the surface S. The curvature κ of C_x at point $\mathbf{x}$ is referred to as the *normal curvature* of S at $\mathbf{x}$ and is denoted by κ_n. The normal curvature κ_n is a function of the orientation of the plane P and has a maximum and a minimum value for two distinct orientations of P (Figure 3.3). The extremal values of κ_n denoted by κ_1 and κ_2 are referred to as the *principal surface curvatures* of S at point $\mathbf{x}$. The unit tangent vectors, at point $\mathbf{x}$, to the space curves of intersection C_1 and C_2 corresponding to κ_1 and κ_2 (denoted by $\mathbf{t}_1$ and $\mathbf{t}_2$, respectively) are referred to as the *principal directions* of the surface curvatures at point $\mathbf{x}$. The vectors $\mathbf{n}_S$, $\mathbf{t}_1$ and $\mathbf{t}_2$ can be shown to constitute a local orthogonal coordinate frame of reference at point $\mathbf{x}$ on S.

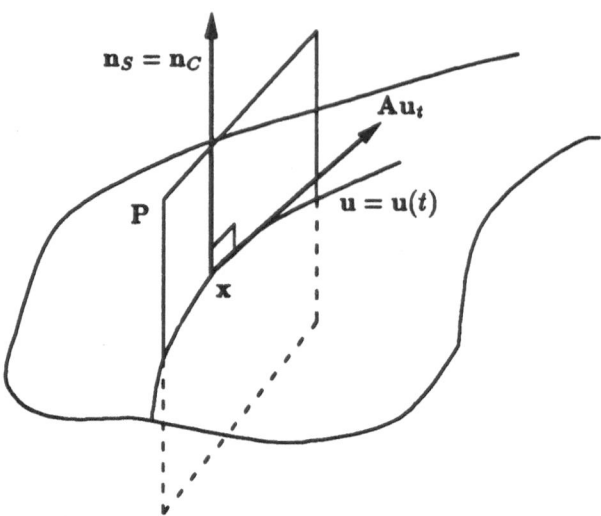

Figure 3.4: The plane defining the normal curvature at a point $\mathbf{x}$.

The plane P defining the normal curvature κ_n of the surface S at point $\mathbf{x}$ in the direction of $\mathbf{A}\mathbf{u}_t$ also contains the unit tangent vector $\mathbf{t}$ to curve C at point $\mathbf{x}$ (Figure 3.4). For such a curve $\mathbf{n}_S = \mathbf{n}_C$ and the normal curvature, using Eq. (3.39), can be shown to be

$$\kappa_n = \frac{\mathbf{u}_t^T \mathbf{B} \, \mathbf{u}_t}{s^2} = \frac{\mathbf{u}_t^T \mathbf{B} \, \mathbf{u}_t}{\mathbf{u}_t^T \mathbf{G} \, \mathbf{u}_t} \tag{3.41}$$

With this definition, the curvature κ_n is positive when the curve is turning toward the positive direction of the surface normal.

Differentiating Eq. (3.41) with respect to $\mathbf{u}_t$, the extremal values of κ_n can be shown to occur when

$$(\mathbf{B} - \kappa_n \mathbf{G})\mathbf{u}_t = 0 \tag{3.42}$$

which gives the scalar equations

$$
\begin{aligned}
(b_{11} - \kappa_n g_{11})u_t + (b_{12} - \kappa_n g_{12})v_t &= 0 \\
(b_{21} - \kappa_n g_{21})u_t + (b_{22} - \kappa_n g_{22})v_t &= 0
\end{aligned}
\tag{3.43}
$$

Eliminating u_t and v_t from Eq. (3.43)

$$\|\mathbf{G}\|\kappa_n^2 - (g_{11}b_{22} + d_{11}g_{22} - 2g_{12}d_{12})\kappa_n + \|\mathbf{B}\| = 0 \tag{3.44}$$

where $\|\mathbf{G}\| = det\,\mathbf{G}$ and $\|\mathbf{B}\| = det\,\mathbf{B}$. The two roots of Eq. (3.44) are the maximum and the minimum principal curvatures κ_1 and κ_2, respectively. From Eq.

(3.43), the corresponding principal curvature directions in the (u, v) parameter space can be shown to be

$$(b_{11} - \kappa_n g_{11}) + (b_{12} - \kappa_n g_{12})\frac{dv}{du} = 0$$

$$(b_{21} - \kappa_n g_{21}) + (b_{22} - \kappa_n g_{22})\frac{dv}{du} = 0 \tag{3.45}$$

or, alternatively

$$(b_{11} - \kappa_n g_{11})\frac{du}{dv} + (b_{12} - \kappa_n g_{12}) = 0$$

$$(b_{21} - \kappa_n g_{21})\frac{du}{dv} + (b_{22} - \kappa_n g_{22}) = 0 \tag{3.46}$$

where $n = 1, 2$.

The mean curvature H and the Gaussian curvature K at a point are defined to be

$$H = \frac{\kappa_1 + \kappa_2}{2} \tag{3.47}$$

$$K = \kappa_1 \kappa_2 \tag{3.48}$$

or, alternatively,

$$H = \frac{1}{2}[trace(\mathbf{G}^{-1}\mathbf{B})] \tag{3.49}$$

$$K = \frac{\|\mathbf{B}\|}{\|\mathbf{G}\|} \tag{3.50}$$

The surfaces encountered most often when dealing with range imagery are of the form $z = f(x, y)$, which is referred to as a *Monge patch*. In parametric form the surface can be represented by $x = u$, $y = v$ and $z = f(u, v)$. Hence

$$\begin{align}
\mathbf{x}(u, v) &= (u, v, f(u, v)) \tag{3.51} \\
\mathbf{x}_u(u, v) &= (1, 0, f_u(u, v)) \tag{3.52} \\
\mathbf{x}_v(u, v) &= (0, 1, f_v(u, v)) \tag{3.53} \\
\mathbf{x}_{uu}(u, v) &= (0, 0, f_{uu}(u, v)) \tag{3.54} \\
\mathbf{x}_{vv}(u, v) &= (0, 0, f_{vv}(u, v)) \tag{3.55} \\
\mathbf{n}(u, v) &= \frac{\mathbf{x}_u(u, v) \times \mathbf{x}_v(u, v)}{\|\mathbf{x}_u(u, v) \times \mathbf{x}_v(u, v)\|} = \frac{(-f_u, -f_v, 1)}{\sqrt{1 + f_u^2 + f_v^2}} \tag{3.56}
\end{align}$$

Using Eq. (3.45), Eq. (3.46) and Eq. (3.51) through Eq. (3.56), the directions of the normal curvature can be shown to be

$$t_n = \frac{(1, \lambda_n, f_u + \lambda_n f_v)}{\sqrt{1 + \lambda_n^2 + (f_u + \lambda_n f_v)^2}} \tag{3.57}$$

where $\lambda_n = dv/du$ evaluated for κ_n, $n = 1, 2$, or, alternatively,

$$t_n = \frac{(\gamma_n, 1, f_v + \gamma_n f_u)}{\sqrt{1 + \gamma_n^2 + (f_v + \gamma_n f_u)^2}} \tag{3.58}$$

where $\gamma_n = du/dv$ evaluated for κ_n, $n = 1, 2$.

Since H, K, κ_1, and κ_2 are functions solely of the first and second fundamental forms of the surface, it follows directly from the Existence and Uniqueness Theorem for C^2 surfaces that H, K, κ_1, and κ_2 are invariant to rotation and translation in three-dimensional Euclidean space. These surface curvatures form the basis of most of the surface segmentation algorithms described in the next section.

3.4   Range Image Segmentation Techniques

The crux of a segmentation technique is to detect surface discontinuities and smooth surface regions in a range image. Likewise, most surface segmentation techniques can be classified as either edge-based or region-based, depending on whether they emphasize the detection of surface discontinuities or the detection of smooth surface regions, respectively.

3.4.1   Edge-based Segmentation Techniques

The basic idea behind edge-based range image segmentation techniques is to detect significant surface discontinuities and classify them as one of:

1. *Jump edges* (Figure 3.5a) signify discontinuities in range. For planar surfaces, jump edges are also called step edges.

2. *Crease edges* (Figure 3.5b) signify continuity in range, but a discontinuity in the surface normal. For planar surfaces, crease edges are also called roof edges. Crease edges can be classified as concave or convex roof edges.

3. *Curvature edges* (Figure 3.5c) signify a continuity in range and surface normal, but discontinuity in curvature.

Jump edges can be detected using standard edge operators designed for intensity images such as the gradient, Sobel, Kirsch, Laplacian-of-Gaussian, and Canny edge operators.   Detection of crease and curvature edges, however, requires specialized operators that do not have direct counterparts for intensity images. Once edge pixels have been detected and classified, they are linked together to form surface discontinuity contours or boundaries. Continuous surface patches are those regions that are bounded by surface discontinuity contours.

Langridge [1984] describes the problem of detecting and locating discontinuities in the first derivatives of surfaces determined by arbitrarily spaced data.

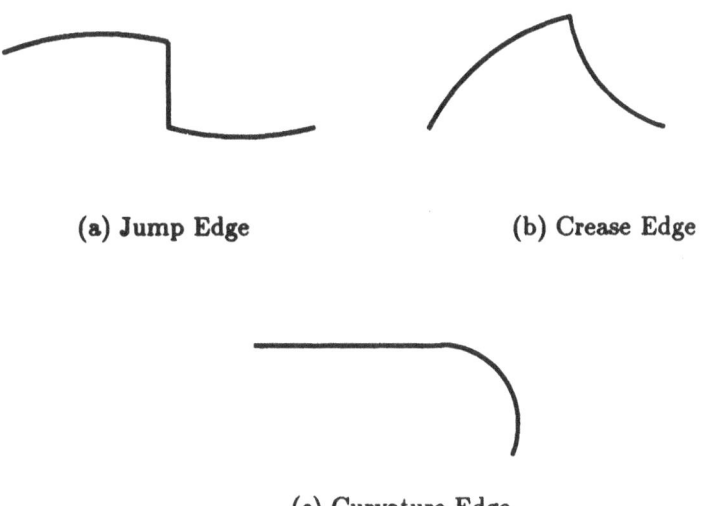

(a) Jump Edge　　　　　　　　　　(b) Crease Edge

(c) Curvature Edge

Figure 3.5: The types of edges encountered in a range image.

The biharmonic or the bilaplacian operator is used as a measure of smoothness for a surface of the form $z = f(x, y)$

$$\nabla^4 f(x, y) = \frac{\partial^4 f(x, y)}{\partial x^4} + \frac{\partial^2 f(x, y)}{\partial x^2}\frac{\partial^2 f(x, y)}{\partial y^2} + \frac{\partial^4 f(x, y)}{\partial y^4} \qquad (3.59)$$

To obtain a discrete approximation to the ∇^4 operator, a biquartic polynomial (i.e., a polynomial where the highest order terms are in $x^2 y^2$, x^4 and y^4) is used,

$$f(x, y) \cong a_0 x^2 y^2 + a_1 x^4 + a_2 y^4 + r(x, y) \qquad (3.60)$$

where

$$r(x, y) = a_3 x^3 + a_4 x^2 y + \cdots + a_{10} x + a_{11} y + a_{12} \qquad (3.61)$$

represents the 10 lower order terms. The approximated function f has 13 unknown coefficients and thus at least 13 points are needed to evaluate them— usually, a point p_0 and its 12 neighbors, p_i (Figure 3.6). Let $P = \{p_i : 0 \leq i \leq 12\}$. The coefficients $a_0 \ldots a_{12}$ can then be solved for using the equation

$$\mathbf{F a} = \mathbf{z} \qquad (3.62)$$

where $\mathbf{F}$ is the matrix of powers of x and y, $\mathbf{a}$ is the column vector of coefficients $[a_0, a_1, \ldots a_{12}]^T$, and $\mathbf{z}$ is the column vector $[z_0, z_1, \ldots z_{12}]^T$ of the z values at each of the 13 points. If $\mathbf{r}_i$ is the ith row of $\mathbf{F}^{-1}$, then $a_i = \mathbf{r}_{i+1}\mathbf{z}$. Since $\nabla^4 f = 8 a_0 + 24 a_1 + 24 a_2 = (8\mathbf{r}_1 + 24\mathbf{r}_2 + 24\mathbf{r}_3)\mathbf{z}$, the discrete $\nabla^4 f$ operator is given by $8\mathbf{r}_1 + 24\mathbf{r}_2 + 24\mathbf{r}_3$. If the $\nabla^4 f$ operator is denoted by the row vector

		10		
	5	2	6	
9	1	0	3	11
	8	4	7	
		12		

Figure 3.6: The 12 neighboring points used for approximating $f(x, y)$.

$b = [b_0, b_1, \ldots b_{12}]$, then $v = bz$ is the value of the biharmonic at point p_0. This technique applies to general spacing of data points. For points on a cartesian grid, with the point indices as shown in Figure 3.6, the value of the biharmonic at point p_0 is given by

$$v = bz = 20z_0 - 8(z_1 + z_2 + z_3 + z_4) + 2(z_5 + z_6 + z_7 + z_8) + z_9 + z_{10} + z_{11} + z_{12} \quad (3.63)$$

The value at p_0 that makes Eq. (3.60) zero is denoted as g_0 and is given by

$$g_0 = (8(z_1 + z_2 + z_3 + z_4) - 2(z_5 + z_6 + z_7 + z_8) - z_9 - z_{10} - z_{11} - z_{12})/20 \quad (3.64)$$

The value g_0 represents the value of the local biharmonic surface $g(x, y)$ at p_0 interpolated from the 12 neighbors of p_0. Alternatively, g_0 can be obtained by substituting for $f(x, y)$ from Eq. (3.60) into Eq. (3.59), which gives

$$a_0 + 3a_1 + 3a_2 = 0 \qquad (3.65)$$

Eliminating a_0 from Eq. (3.60) using Eq. (3.65)

$$g(x, y) = a_1 x^2 (x^2 - 3y^2) + a_2 y^2 (y^2 - 3x^2) + r(x, y) \qquad (3.66)$$

To obtain g_0, the 12 neighbors of p_0 are used to solve the matrix equation $Ga = z$ where G is the matrix of powers of x and y, a is the column vector $[a_1, a_2, \ldots a_{12}]^T$, and z is the column vector $[z_1, z_2, \ldots z_{12}]^T$. As $g_0 = g(0, 0)$, then the last row of G^{-1} determines the value of g_0. It can be shown that $g_0 = r_{12}z$, where r_{12} is the row corresponding to the coefficient a_{12}. The deviation $d_0 = |z_0 - g_0|$ is a measure of the local surface smoothness at p_0. The matrix equation is solved iteratively using the equation

$$z_i^{p+1} = z_i^p - d_i^p/2 \qquad (3.67)$$

where p denotes the iteration count. Eq. (3.67) is subject to the constraint

$$z_i^0 - \epsilon \leq z_i^{p+1} \leq z_i^0 + \epsilon \qquad (3.68)$$

where ϵ_i is the maximum allowable shift in p_i. For points on a cartesian grid, $\epsilon_i = \epsilon = $ constant.

On a cartesian grid (Figure 3.6) the neighbors of p_0 can be divided into three groups:

$$G_1 = (p_1, p_2, p_3, p_4), \quad G_2 = (p_5, p_6, p_7, p_8), \quad G_3 = (p_9, p_{10}, p_{11}, p_{12}) \qquad (3.69)$$

The groups G_1, G_2, and G_3 are referred to as the immediate, inner, and outer points, respectively, of p_0. To detect a surface discontinuity in the neighborhood of p_0, the following procedure is applied:

1. An outer point is removed.

2. Using the function g, a biharmonic surface patch is fitted to the remaining 12 points.

3. The matrix G^i is inverted to obtain the first-derivative operators g_x^i and g_y^i at p_0.

The superscript i denotes the outer point, which has been removed from the neighborhood. Let

$$\gamma_x = \frac{max(g_x^i - g_x^j)}{b} \qquad (3.70)$$

then γ_x denotes the maximum difference in the g_x values obtained by dropping different outer points; γ_y is defined in the same manner. Let $\gamma_m = max(\gamma_x, \gamma_y)$. A point p_0 is determined to be a surface discontinuity if, (1) it satisfies the constraints in Eq. (3.68), (2) the value of v increases with each successive iteration (i.e., $v^i \geq v^{i-1}$), and (3) $\gamma_m v^i \geq \tau$ where τ is a predefined threshold. This technique need not be restricted to points on a cartesian grid. For arbitrarily spaced points, neighbors are defined in terms of Voronoi neighborhoods. Langridge has demonstrated his segmentation technique on two synthetic range images.

Inokuchi et al.[1982] present an edge-region segmentation operator for range images. A ring operator extracts a one-dimensional periodic function of depth values that surround a given pixel. This function is transformed into the frequency domain using an FFT algorithm for either 8 or 16 values, depending on the window size. Planar regions, step edge pixels, convex roof edge pixels, and concave roof edge pixels are distinguished by examining the 0th, 1st, 2nd, and 3rd components of the resulting FFT spectrum. However, this technique has the disadvantage of requiring that the FFT be computed at every pixel in the image and is therefore computationally feasible only with dedicated FFT hardware. The operator has been demonstrated on synthetic range images of polyhedral objects.

Mitiche and Aggarwal [1983] describe a range edge detection technique based on Bayesian optimization. They consider the detection of step and roof edges

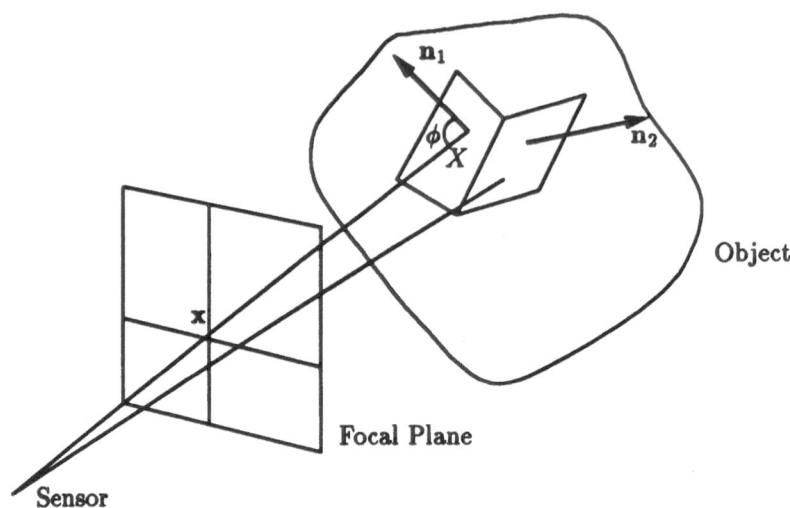

Figure 3.7: Partitioning the neighborhood of a point for fitting surfaces in Mitiche and Aggarwal's approach.

in range images containing polyhedral objects. For a given point x in the range image (Figure 3.7) a suitable neighborhood N around x is defined. Planes are fitted to the range points in the neighborhood N such that the squared error is minimized. The collection of points in N, together with the surface normals $\mathbf{n}_i$ of the best fitting planes, is referred to as a partition Γ of N. For a set of partitions, Γ_i, $i = 1 \ldots n$, of an appropriately sized neighborhood N, with S being the sample points in N, the conditional probability of Γ_i given S can be written as

$$p(\Gamma_i|S) = \frac{p(S|\Gamma_i)p(\Gamma_i)}{p(S)} \tag{3.71}$$

where

$$p(S) = \sum_{i=1}^{n} p(S|\Gamma_i)p(\Gamma_i) \tag{3.72}$$

$p(\Gamma_i)$ is the *a priori* probability of the partition Γ_i and

$$p(S|\Gamma_i) = \prod_{X \in S} p(r_X|\Gamma_i) \text{ where } i = 1 \ldots n \tag{3.73}$$

where X is a point in the sample S and r_X is the random variable denoting the range measurement at point X. For a given partition Γ_i, r_X can be considered to be a Gaussian random variable with mean $\mu_X = R_X$ (where R_X is the nominally measured range at X) and variance $\sigma_X = \sigma_X(R_X, \rho, \phi)$ (where ρ is the surface reflectance and ϕ is the orientation of the appropriate plane in Γ_i).

The edge extraction procedure proceeds as follows:

1. All jump (step) edges are extracted using a gradient operator.

2. The partitions Γ_i are computed; the angles Θ_i between the planes in the partition are computed.

3. All points for which $\Theta_i < \tau$ (where τ is a predefined threshold) are discarded as points in the interior of the planes.

4. The best partition Γ is selected for the remaining points; all points for which $\Theta < \tau$ (where Θ is the angle associated with the best partition) are discarded.

5. The previous step generates a set of points that are candidate edge points. However, it includes true edge points surrounded by non-edge points. For all the candidate edge points, $p(\Gamma)$ (where Γ is the best partition) is evaluated. All points for which $p(\Gamma)$ is not a local maximum in an interval orthogonal to the edge are discarded. This is referred to as *non-maxima suppression*.

Mitiche and Aggarwal have demonstrated their segmentation technique on synthetic range data artificially corrupted by additive Gaussian noise. Their technique, however, needs to be tested on real range data.

Fan et al. [1987] describe an edge detection technique that is based on the computation of the principal surface curvatures. Two edge-based segmentation techniques have been described, one suited for noisy range images and the other for relatively noise-free images. Jump edges are treated as zero-crossings of principal curvatures in a direction normal to the boundary direction. Crease edges are treated as local extrema (minima or maxima) of the curvature function.

For the first technique, for noisy images, the range image is convolved with a Gaussian mask $g(x, y) = \exp\{-(x^2 + y^2)/2\sigma^2\}$, where σ is the width of the filter. First- and second-order differences are used to approximate first- and second-order derivatives, respectively. First-order differences are computed by using directional masks in four different orientations 45° apart. Second-order differences are computed by convolving the first-order differences in each of the four different orientations with the directional masks mentioned previously. The surface curvature along each of the four directions is computed as

$$\kappa_\psi = \frac{f_{\psi\psi}}{\sqrt{1 + f_x^2 + f_y^2}} \tag{3.74}$$

where $f_{\psi\psi}$ is the second-order difference in the direction ψ, f_x and f_y are the first-order differences in the x and y directions, respectively, and κ_ψ is the curvature measured in the direction ψ. Computation of the surface curvature in four directions 45° apart is shown to be equivalent to computing the principal curvatures κ_1 and κ_2. In fact, if the directions chosen are 0°, 45°, 90° and 135°

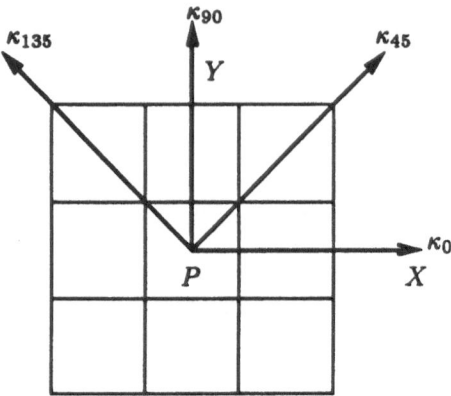

Figure 3.8: The surface curvatures in four directions used in computing the mean and Gaussian curvatures H and K.

(Figure 3.8), then the mean and the Gaussian curvatures H and K are given by

$$H = \frac{1}{4}(\kappa_0 + \kappa_{45} + \kappa_{90} + \kappa_{135})$$
$$K = \kappa_0\kappa_{90} + \kappa_{45}\kappa_{135} - H^2 \qquad (3.75)$$

Surface curvature is computed at different scales by varying the parameter σ in the Gaussian mask. For each of the four directional curvatures computed at a certain scale, zero-crossings and local extrema are determined. The use of multiple scales permits the detection of features without loss in localization accuracy. The features are detected at a coarse scale corresponding to the range image smoothed with the widest Gaussian filter. The features are then localized at the finest scale corresponding to the range image smoothed with the narrowest Gaussian filter. Correspondence is established between features at different scales by predicting their shift (based on the value of σ) in the image space for different scales. The extrema and zero crossings are tracked independently, and only the features present at the coarsest level are used in the final description. When tracking an extremum, if there is a *fork* that is a choice between two extrema at the next finer scale, then the extremum with the higher curvature value is chosen. If there is a *fork* for a zero-crossing, then the tracking is halted at that level and the position at the lowest unambiguous level is marked. The four tracked images in each direction are then merged into a single image using a logical OR operation. The final image contains pixel locations marked as curvature extrema or curvature zero-crossings. The second technique, on the other hand, determines the extrema and zero-crossings of only the larger principal curvature κ_1 on a range image smoothed at a particular scale. Since only one curvature value is computed for each pixel and there is no inter-scale tracking, the second technique is considerably faster than the first, but not as robust. The value of σ chosen to smooth the range image is a critical parameter, and thus this technique can be used only for relatively noise-free images that will allow a small value of σ to be chosen, thereby permitting sufficient localization accuracy.

After having extracted the zero-crossings and extrema of the surface curvature by either of the two techniques, the segmentation process proceeds to identify jump and crease boundaries by determining associations between the zero-crossings and extrema. Associations are made by examining a window, whose size depends on σ, around each significant zero-crossing or extremum and observing the group of features that occur therein. Each group of features can then be labeled as one of the following types:

1. *Type 1.* Isolated positive extremum (+)

2. *Type 2.* Isolated negative extremum (−)

3. *Type 3.* Associated positive extremum and zero-crossing (+0)

4. *Type 4.* Associated negative extremum and zero-crossing (−0)

5. *Type 5.* Associated positive extremum, zero-crossing, and negative extremum (+0−).

Each of the above groups is labeled at the appropriate pixel location. For feature groups belonging to types 1 and 2, the label is localized at the location of the curvature extremum, whereas for types 3, 4, and 5 the label is localized at the location of the zero-crossing. Feature groups with identical labels are spatially linked if their orientations are compatible, i.e., within 45° of each other. One-pixel gaps between feature groups are filled. Jump boundaries are identified as those feature groups corresponding to type 5 labels, whereas crease boundaries are identified as belonging to type 3, type 4, or *steep* type 1 or type 2 labels. A curvature extremum is deemed steep if it has high curvature slope on both sides. At the end of the spatial linking phase, the result is an image with closed boundaries enclosing surface patches. Each surface patch is then approximated by a biquadratic bivariate polynomial

$$g(x, y) = a_0 + a_1 x + a_2 y + a_3 x^2 + a_4 y^2 + a_5 xy$$

This technique has been demonstrated on several synthetic and real range images with satisfactory results.

Nackman [1984] and Ponce and Brady [1985] have also proposed edge-based segmentation schemes based on surface curvature properties. Nackman's approach extracts local maxima, local minima, and saddle points of a surface, and connects these features to obtain a graphical representation that describes the smooth variations of the surface. Ponce and Brady's approach determines the surface curvature at each point on the range image. The magnitudes and the directions of the principal curvatures at each pixel are used to link compatible pixels to form curves of principal curvature on the range surface. The curves of principal curvature are shown to provide a rich representation of the range surface. Curves with significant curvature values are used to infer surface boundaries.

A primary drawback of edge-based segmentation techniques is the inevitable fragmentation of the edges in noisy images. If the edges are fragmented or discontinuous, they must be linked using a heuristic technique. For this reason, edge-based segmentation techniques have proved to be less popular than region-based segmentation techniques.

3.4.2   Region-based Segmentation Techniques

The key idea behind region-based range image segmentation is to estimate the surface curvature at each range pixel and cluster range pixels with homogeneous surface curvature properties to form smooth surface regions. A feature vector can be associated with each range pixel where the components of the feature vector are surface curvature parameters. Clustering can then be performed in feature space using standard clustering techniques from pattern recognition literature. Alternatively, clustering can be done in the image domain using region growing techniques. In many cases, a combination of feature clustering and region-growing is used. Region-based segmentation techniques can be broadly classified as analytical or numerical based on the method used to estimate surface curvature.

1. *Analytical Techniques.* Analytical techniques fit a surface $f(u,v)$ to the range values in a neighborhood centered around a pixel where the surface curvature needs to be computed. The analytical expression for the function $f(u,v)$ is then used to compute the partial derivatives f_u, f_v, f_{uv}, f_{uu} and f_{vv}. The mean, Gaussian, and principal curvature values are computed from the surface derivatives.

2. *Numerical Techniques:* Numerical techniques estimate the surface derivatives by approximating them by differences. Directional derivatives of the surface are approximated by differences in the appropriate directions. Specialized operators that operate on a local window centered around the pixel of interest can be devised. These operators are similar to the directional edge detectors for intensity images. The directional derivatives can then be used to determine the mean, Gaussian, and principal curvature values. It is to be noted that numerical techniques operate on the range values directly. This is in contrast to analytical techniques that use the parameters of the fitted surface for curvature computation.

Analytical techniques can be further classified based on the nature of the surface fitting function $f(u,v)$.

Surface Fitting Using Orthogonal Polynomials

Besl and Jain [1986] and Haralick et al. [1983] have proposed surface fitting techniques that use discrete biorthogonal polynomials as basis functions. The digital range surface in a local $N \times N$ (where N is odd) window centered about the point of interest is approximated by using discrete biorthogonal Chebychev polynomials as basis functions. The orthogonality of the basis functions enables efficient computation of the coefficients of the functional approximation. The first four orthogonal polynomials are:

$$
\begin{aligned}
\phi_0 &= 1 \\
\phi_1 &= u \\
\phi_2 &= u^2 - \frac{\mu_2}{\mu_0} \\
\phi_3 &= u^3 - \left(\frac{\mu_4}{\mu_2}\right)u \\
\text{where } \mu_k &= \sum_{u=-M}^{i=+M} u^k \\
\text{and } M &= \frac{(N-1)}{2}
\end{aligned}
\tag{3.76}
$$

A discrete two-dimensional biorthogonal basis is created from the $\phi_i's$

$$
\phi_{i,j}(u,v) = \phi_i(u)\phi_j(v)
\tag{3.77}
$$

The best approximation that minimizes the sum of squared surface fitting error within the window is given by

$$
\hat{f}(u,v) = \sum_{i,j=0}^{3} a_{i,j}\phi_i(u)\phi_j(v)
\tag{3.78}
$$

The coefficients of the functional approximation are given by

$$
a_{i,j} = \sum_{(u,v)=(-M,-M)}^{(u,v)=(+M,+M)} f(u,v)b_i(u)b_j(v)
\tag{3.79}
$$

where the $b_i(u)$ are the normalized versions of the polynomials $\phi_i(u)$ given by

$$
b_i(u) = \frac{1}{\sum_{i=-M}^{i=+M} \phi_i^2(u)}\phi_i(u)
\tag{3.80}
$$

The estimates of the first- and second-order derivatives of the surface are given by :

$$
\begin{aligned}
f_u &= a_{10} - \frac{\mu_2}{\mu_0}a_{12} - \frac{\mu_4}{\mu_2}a_{30} + \frac{\mu_4}{\mu_0}a_{32} \\
f_v &= a_{01} - \frac{\mu_2}{\mu_0}a_{21} - \frac{\mu_4}{\mu_2}a_{03} + \frac{\mu_4}{\mu_0}a_{23} \\
f_{uu} &= 2a_{20} - 2\frac{\mu_2}{\mu_0}a_{22}
\end{aligned}
$$

Table 3.1: Eight qualitative surface types based on the HK signs.

	$H < 0$	$H = 0$	$H > 0$
$K < 0$	 Saddle Ridge	 Minimal Surface	 Saddle Valley
$K = 0$	 Ridge Surface	 Flat Surface	 Valley Surface
$K > 0$	 Peak Surface	None	 Pit Surface

$$f_{vv} = 2a_{02} - 2\frac{\mu_2}{\mu_0}a_{22}$$

$$f_{uv} = a_{11} - \frac{\mu_4}{\mu_2}a_{31} - \frac{\mu_4}{\mu_2}a_{13} + \frac{\mu_4^2}{\mu_0}a_{33} \qquad (3.81)$$

Estimates of partial derivatives are used to compute coefficients of the first and second fundamental forms of the surface and the mean, Gaussian and principal surface curvatures.

Besl and Jain [1988] use curvature estimates from the surface fitting technique to classify a range surface patch into one of the eight qualitative surface types based on the signs of the mean and Gaussian curvature (Table 3.1). The resulting description is called an HK sign map. The initial segmentation and classification of the range image is used to form seed regions for the subsequent stage, which attempts to refine the initial segmentation. Besl and Jain describe an iterative region-growing algorithm based on variable-order bivariate polynomial surface fitting. Polynomials of successive order such as planar, biquadratic, bicubic, and biquartic are used. The order of the surface shape hypotheses is automatically controlled by fitting surfaces to the image data and testing the surface fits. A surface of a certain order is fitted to a group of pixels. The surface is then expanded to fit neighboring pixels using a region growing algorithm. The decision whether to consider the surface of the next higher order is made by examining the spatial distribution of the signs of the residual surface fitting errors and comparing the mean square residual error of the fit to a threshold proportional to an estimate of the noise variance. In this iterative procedure the images are not only segmented into regions of arbitrary shape, but the image data in those regions is also approximated with flexible bivariate functions such that it is possible to compute a complete noiseless image reconstruction based on the extracted functions and regions.

Haralick et al. [1983] have also used orthogonal Chebyshev polynomials to compute a local surface fit $f(u,v)$ to a range surface. Partial derivatives computed from the surface fit are used to compute the Hessian matrix

$$H = \begin{bmatrix} \frac{\partial^2 f}{\partial u^2} & \frac{\partial^2 f}{\partial u \partial v} \\ \frac{\partial^2 f}{\partial v \partial u} & \frac{\partial^2 f}{\partial u^2} \end{bmatrix}$$

The eigenvalues of H, denoted as λ_1 and λ_2, are values of the extrema of the second directional derivative of $f(u,v)$, and their associated eigenvectors v_1 and v_2 are the directions in which the second directional derivative is extremized. Using the gradient ∇f and the values of λ_1 and λ_2, the pixels on the range surface can be classified as one of the following:

1. *Peak*, characterized by $||\nabla f|| = 0$, $\lambda_1 < 0$, $\lambda_2 < 0$

2. *Pit*, characterized by $||\nabla f|| = 0$, $\lambda_1 > 0$, $\lambda_2 > 0$

3. *Ridge*, characterized by any one of the following conditions:

    (a) $||\nabla f| \neq 0$, $\lambda_1 < 0$, $\nabla f \cdot v_1 = 0$
    (b) $||\nabla f|| \neq 0$, $\lambda_2 < 0$, $\nabla f \cdot v_2 = 0$
    (c) $||\nabla f|| = 0$, $\lambda_1 < 0$, $\lambda_2 = 0$

4. *Ravine*, characterized by any one of the following conditions:

    (a) $||\nabla f|| \neq 0$, $\lambda_1 > 0$, $\nabla f \cdot v_1 = 0$
    (b) $||\nabla f|| \neq 0$, $\lambda_2 > 0$, $\nabla f \cdot v_2 = 0$
    (c) $||\nabla f|| = 0$, $\lambda_1 > 0$, $\lambda_2 = 0$

5. *Saddle*, characterized by $||\nabla f|| = 0$, $\lambda_1 \cdot \lambda_2 < 0$

6. *Flat* characterized by $||\nabla f|| = 0$, $\lambda_1 = 0$, $\lambda_2 = 0$

7. *Hillside*, if it cannot be classified as any of the above six categories. Hillside pixels can be further classified as

(a) *Slope* if $\lambda_1 = \lambda_2 = 0$

(b) *Convex* if $\lambda_1 \geq \lambda_2 \geq 0$ and $\lambda_1 \neq 0$

(c) *Concave* if $\lambda_1 \leq \lambda_2 \leq 0$ and $\lambda_1 \neq 0$

(d) *Saddle Hill* if $\lambda_1 \cdot \lambda_2 < 0$.

Range pixel classification in the above manner is used to derive a dense description, called a *topographic primal sketch* that encodes the variations in the range surface.

Regression-based techniques

Instead of fitting a product of orthogonal polynomials to the local neighborhood of each point, the local surface fitting problem could be looked upon as a linear regression problem. A biquadratic, bicubic, or biquartic polynomial could be fitted to a group of pixels in an $N \times N$ window centered around the pixel of interest. For example, in the case of a biquartic polynomial,

$$
\begin{aligned}
f(u, v) \;=\; & b_0 + b_1 u + b_2 v + b_3 u^2 + b_4 v^2 \\
+ \; & b_5 uv + b_6 u^3 + b_7 v^3 + b_8 u^2 v + b_9 uv^2 \\
+ \; & b_{10} u^4 + b_{11} v^4 + b_{12} u^2 v^2 + b_{13} u^3 v + b_{14} uv^3
\end{aligned}
$$

If $N^2 > 15$, then we must solve an over-constrained set of equations in $b_0 \ldots b_{14}$ to obtain the surface parameters. Standard linear regression techniques can be used to determine the values of $b_0 \ldots b_{14}$ [Flynn and Jain 1988, 1989]. Surface curvature values can then be computed from the surface parameter values. More reliable curvature estimates can be expected with bigger window size. Flynn and Jain [1991b] in their vision system BONSAI use bicubic and biquadratic polynomials to compute the curvature values of the range surface.

Spline-Based Surface Fitting

Bicubic splines are used extensively in surface segmentation and description because bicubic spline functions ensure overall continuity of gradient and curvature [Naik and Jain 1988]. Moreover, B-splines are local in nature in that the effect of changing a single spline coefficient is localized to a small portion of the surface, which is not true of other surface fitting functions.

If we consider a closed rectangular domain, $D = [a, b] \times [c, d]$ and the strictly increasing sequence of real numbers

$$
a = \lambda_0 < \lambda_1 < \cdots < \lambda_g < \lambda_{g+1} = b
$$

and

$$
c = \mu_0 < \mu_1 < \cdots < \mu_h < \mu_{h+1} = d
$$

then the function $s(x, y)$ is called a bicubic spline on D with knots λ_i, $i = 1, \ldots g$ in the x-direction, and μ_j, $j = 1, \ldots h$ in the y-direction if the following two conditions are satisfied:

1. On any sub-rectangle $D_{ij} = [\lambda_i, \lambda_{i+1}] \times [\mu_j, \mu_{j+1}]$ where $i = 0, \ldots g$, $j = 0 \ldots h$, $s(x, y)$ is a bicubic polynomial in x and y.

2. All partial derivatives $\partial^{i+j} s(x, y)/\partial x^i \partial y^j$ for $0 \le i \le 2$ and $0 \le j \le 2$ are continuous everywhere in D.

It is to be noted that continuity of the zeroth-, first- and second-order derivatives is all that is needed for curvature computation. Bicubic splines are the lowest order of spline functions that satisfy this criteria.

A set of basis functions representing the general bicubic spline can be constructed from the tensor product of two one-dimensional sets of normalized cubic B-splines. Let

$$x_+^{n-1} = \begin{cases} x^{n-1}, & x \ge 0 \\ 0, & x < 0 \end{cases} \tag{3.82}$$

and $M(x, y) = (y - x)_+^3$. Consider the points $x_{i-4}, x_{i-3}, \ldots, x_i$. Let $w_i(x) = (x - x_{i-4})(x - x_{i-3}) \ldots (x - x_i)$, then one can define

$$M_i(x) = \sum_{k=i-4}^{i} \frac{(x_k - x)_+^3}{w_i'(x_k)} \tag{3.83}$$

where

$$w_i'(x) = \frac{\partial w_i(x)}{\partial x}$$

$M_i(x)$ is termed a B-spline of order 3 (i.e., a cubic B-spline) based on the knot points $x_{i-4}, x_{i-3}, \ldots, x_i$. $M_i(x)$ has the property that

$$\begin{aligned} M_i(x) &> 0, \quad x \in (x_{i-4}, x_i) \\ &= 0 \quad \text{otherwise} \end{aligned} \tag{3.84}$$

If we introduce additional knots

$$\begin{aligned} \lambda_{-3} = \lambda_{-2} = \lambda_{-1} = \lambda_0 &= a \\ \mu_{-3} = \mu_{-2} = \mu_{-1} = \mu_0 &= c \\ \lambda_{g+1} = \lambda_{g+2} = \lambda_{g+3} = \lambda_{g+4} &= b \\ \mu_{h+1} = \mu_{h+2} = \mu_{h+3} = \mu_{h+4} &= d \end{aligned}$$

then every bicubic spline $s(x, y)$ on D with knots λ_i, $i = 1, \ldots g$ in the x-direction, and μ_j, $j = 1, \ldots h$ in the y-direction can be written as a linear combination of the cross products of the B-splines $M_i(x)$, $i = 1, \ldots, g + 4$ and $N_j(y)$, $j = 1, \ldots, h + 4$, i.e.,

$$s(x, y) = \sum_{i=1}^{g+4} \sum_{j=1}^{h+4} c_{ij} M_i(x) N_j(y) \tag{3.85}$$

Given depth values f_{ij} specified at (x_i, y_j), $i = 1, \ldots, m$, $j = 1, \ldots n$ on a rectangular grid defining the range image plane, the objective is to determine a bicubic spline function $s(x, y)$ that minimizes the squared error

$$\sum_{i=1}^{m} \sum_{j=1}^{n} [f_{ij} - s(x_i, y_j)]^2 \tag{3.86}$$

This can be alternatively expressed as a problem in determining the coefficients c_{ij} of the bicubic function as a least-squares solution to the observation equations

$$\sum_{i=1}^{g+4} \sum_{j=1}^{h+4} c_{ij} M_i(x_k) N_j(y_l) = f_{kl} \tag{3.87}$$

where x_k, $k = 1, \ldots, m$ and y_l, $l = 1, \ldots, n$ are the pixel locations, and f_{kl} is the range at those pixel locations. The equations can be written in matrix notation as

$$\mathbf{G}\,\mathbf{c} = \mathbf{F} \tag{3.88}$$

where $\mathbf{G}$ is an $mn \times (g+4)(h+4)$ matrix with elements $\mathbf{G}_{pq} = M_i(x_k)N_j(y_l)$, $\mathbf{c}$ is a $(g+4)(h+4)$ length column vector with elements $c_q = c_{ij}$, and $\mathbf{F}$ is an mn-length column vector with elements $\mathbf{F}_p = f_{k,l}$. The matrix $\mathbf{G}$ can be written as the Kronecker product of the matrices $\mathbf{B}$ and $\mathbf{A}$, which are the observation matrices of the one-dimensional least-squares problem in the y- and x-directions, respectively, i.e.,

$$\mathbf{B} \quad : \quad n \times (h+4) \text{ matrix, } \mathbf{B}_{lj} = N_j(y_l) \tag{3.89}$$

$$\mathbf{A} \quad : \quad m \times (g+4) \text{ matrix, } \mathbf{A}_{ki} = M_i(x_k) \tag{3.90}$$

and $\mathbf{G} = \mathbf{B} \otimes \mathbf{A} = [\mathbf{B}a_{ij}]$. The locality of the B-splines can be exploited by arranging the values of x_k and y_i in increasing order whereby the matrices $\mathbf{A}$ and $\mathbf{B}$ will have a band structure of bandwidth four. The Kronecker product can then be computed efficiently using specialized algorithms.

Tension splines have also been used for surface fitting. Tension splines are similar to B-splines except that they possess a parameter σ, referred to as a *tension* parameter that permits greater control over the surface shape. In order to fit a tension-spline curve to a set of $m + 1$ points $P_0, P_1, \ldots, P_m$, $m \geq 3$, in the x-y plane, we need to determine a set of polynomial curve segments $Q_3, Q_4, \ldots, Q_m$. Each of these polynomial curve segments is represented in the parametric form $(x(t), y(t))$ such that each Q_i is defined over the parameter range $t_i \leq t \leq t_{i+1}$ for $3 \leq i \leq m$. If we define the row vector $\mathbf{T}_i = [(t - t_i)^3, (t - t_i)^2, (t - t_i), 1]$, the tension spline basis matrix

$$\mathbf{M}_\sigma = \begin{bmatrix} 0 & 2\sigma & -2\sigma & 2 \\ 0 & -\sigma & 3\sigma & 0 \\ 0 & 0 & 0 & 0 \\ 0 & \sigma & 2 & 0 \end{bmatrix} \quad \sigma \geq 0$$

and the column vector $G_i = [P_{i-3}, P_{i-2}, P_{i-1}, P_i]^T$ of control points in the x-y plane, then the ith tension spline segment $Q_i(t)$ that passes through the control points $P_{i-3}, P_{i-2}, \ldots, P_i$ is given by the equation

$$Q_i(t) = T_i M_\sigma G_i \quad t_i \leq t \leq t_{i+1} \tag{3.91}$$

The corresponding equation for a tension-spline surface can be written as

$$Q_{i,j}(s,t) = S_i M_{\sigma_1} G_{i,j} M_{\sigma_2}^T T_j^T \quad s_i \leq s < s_{i+1}, \ t_j \leq t < t_{j+1} \tag{3.92}$$

where $S_i = [(s-s_i)^3, (s-s_i)^2, (s-s_i), 1]$ and $T_j = [(t-t_j)^3, (t-t_j)^2, (t-t_j), 1]$ are cubic polynomials in each of the dimensions; M_{σ_1} and M_{σ_2} are the tension spline matrices in each of the dimensions and have the same structure as M_σ; and $G_{i,j}$ is the grid of 16 control points $P_{i-k,j-l}, 0 \leq k, l \leq 3$.

For a one-dimensional tension cubic spline curve, the effect of increasing the tension σ is to pull the curve closer to the lines joining successive control points. Similarly, for a two-dimensional tension cubic spline surface, the effect of increasing the tensions σ_1 and σ_2 is to pull the surface closer to the planes defined by adjacent surface control points.

Vemuri and Aggarwal [1986] have used tension bicubic splines to segment a range surface. Given a range image of the form $z = F(x, y)$, a representation of the form $x = f(s,t)$, $y = g(s,t)$, $z = h(s,t)$, where s and t are surface parameters and f, g, and h are tensor products of one-dimensional bicubic splines, is sought. As the first step, the parametric grid of control points (s_i, t_j), $1 \leq i \leq m$, $1 \leq j \leq n$ is obtained such that for each $i \in \{1, \ldots, m\}$ and $j \in \{1, \ldots, n\}$ there exist s_i and t_j such that

$$(x(s_i, t_j), y(s_i, t_j), z(s_i, t_j)) = (x_{ij}, y_{ij}, z_{ij})$$

where x, y, and z are twice differential functions of s and t. Also, it is required that $s_1 = t_1 = 0$ and $s_m = t_n = 1$. The quantity $s_{i+1} - s_i$ is made equal to the average normalized distance between $(x_{i,j+1}, y_{i,j+1}, z_{i,j+1})$ and $(x_{i,j}, y_{i,j}, z_{i,j})$, where the average is taken over $j = 1, \ldots, n$. Similarly, $t_{j+1} - t_j$ is made equal to the average normalized distance between $(x_{i+1,j}, y_{i+1,j}, z_{i+1,j})$ and $(x_{i,j}, y_{i,j}, z_{i,j})$, where the average is taken over $i = 1, \ldots, m$. Thus s_i and t_j are given by

$$s_{i+1} = s_i + \frac{1}{n} \sum_{j=1}^{n} \frac{\| p_{i+1,j} - p_{i,j} \|}{\sum_{l=1}^{m-1} \| p_{l+1,j} - p_{l,j} \|} \tag{3.93}$$

$$t_{j+1} = t_j + \frac{1}{m} \sum_{i=1}^{m} \frac{\| p_{i,j+1} - p_{i,j} \|}{\sum_{l=1}^{n-1} \| p_{i,l+1} - p_{i,l} \|} \tag{3.94}$$

where $p_{i,j} = (x_{i,j}, y_{i,j}, z_{i,j})$, and $\| p_{i+1,j} - p_{i,j} \|$ is the Euclidean distance. The above parameterization satisfies the condition that $s_1 = t_1 = 0$ and $s_m = t_n = 1$.

The surface approximation problem is now reduced to three standard surface fitting problems of the form

$$\begin{aligned} x(s_i, t_j) &= x_{i,j} \quad 1 \leq i \leq m, \ 1 \leq j \leq n \\ y(s_i, t_j) &= y_{i,j} \quad 1 \leq i \leq m, \ 1 \leq j \leq n \\ z(s_i, t_j) &= z_{i,j} \quad 1 \leq i \leq m, \ 1 \leq j \leq n \end{aligned} \tag{3.95}$$

Each of the surface fitting problems can be solved using the formulation by Cline [1981]:

> Given a grid defined by two strictly increasing abscissa sets $\{s_i : 1 \le i \le m\}$ and $\{t_j : 1 \le j \le n\}$, an ordinate set $\{z_{i,j} : 1 \le i \le m, 1 \le j \le n\}$, positive weights $\{\delta s_i : 1 \le i \le m\}$ and $\{\delta t_j : 1 \le j \le n\}$, a non-negative tolerance S, and a non-negative tension factor σ, determine a function F which minimizes the expression
>
> $$\int_{s_1}^{s_m} \int_{t_1}^{t_m} g_{sstt}^2(s,t)\,ds\,dt + \sigma^2 \sum_{i=1}^{m-1}\sum_{j=1}^{n-1} \int_{s_i}^{s_{i+1}} \int_{t_j}^{t_{j+1}} Q_{i,j}^2(s,t)\,ds\,dt \tag{3.96}$$
>
> over all functions $g \in C^2\,[s_1, s_m] \times [t_1, t_n]$ such that
>
> $$\sum_{i=1}^{m}\sum_{j=1}^{n} \left[\frac{g(s_i,t_j) - z_{i,j}}{\delta s_i \delta t_j} \right]^2 \le S \tag{3.97}$$
>
> where
>
> $$Q_{i,j} = g_{st}(s,t) - \frac{g(s_{i+1},t_{j+1}) - g(s_{i+1},t_j) - g(s_i,t_{j+1}) + g(s_i,t_j)}{(s_{i+1}-s_i)(t_{j+1}-t_j)}.$$
>
> $$g_{st}(s,t) = \frac{\partial^2 g(s,t)}{\partial s \partial t}$$
>
> $$g_{sstt}(s,t) = \frac{\partial^4 g(s,t)}{\partial s^2 \partial t^2} \tag{3.98}$$

Cline has shown that the solution to this problem is a tensor product of splines under tension, that is, the solution F is a one-dimensional spline under tension when restricted to any value of s or t. The fitted surface can be therefore expressed as

$$x(s,t) = \sum_{i=1}^{m}\sum_{j=1}^{n} \alpha_{ij} \Phi_i(s) \Psi_j(t)$$

$$y(s,t) = \sum_{i=1}^{m}\sum_{j=1}^{n} \beta_{ij} \Upsilon_i(s) \Theta_j(t)$$

$$z(s,t) = \sum_{i=1}^{m}\sum_{j=1}^{n} \gamma_{ij} \Lambda_i(s) \Omega_j(t) \tag{3.99}$$

where the functions Φ, Ψ, Υ, Θ, Λ, and Ω are one-dimensional tension splines and α's, β's, and γ's are coefficients of the tensor products. Cline has also shown how these equations can be solved efficiently.

The values of the coefficients of the tensor products can be used to compute surface derivatives and surface curvature values. Vemuri and Aggarwal group surface range pixels into one of five classes based on the surface curvatures computed from these coefficients.

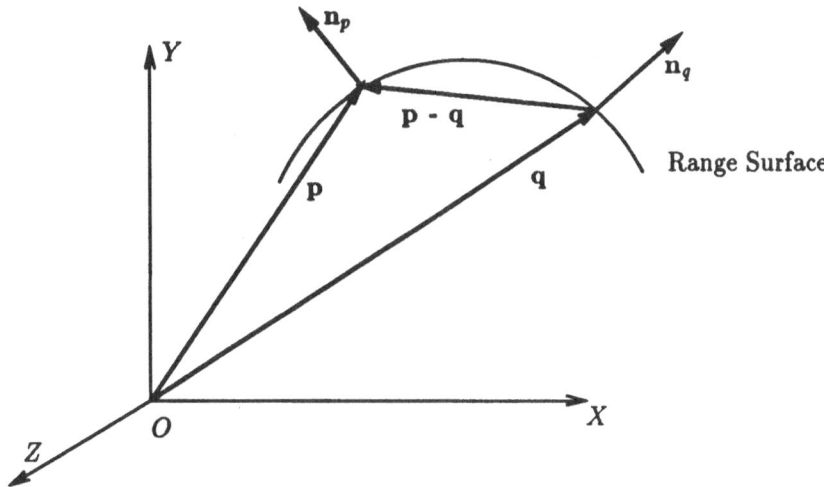

Figure 3.9: Numerical computation of the curvature at p.

1. *Elliptic*, for which the Gaussian curvature $K > 0$.

2. *Parabolic*, for which the Gaussian curvature $K = 0$.

3. *Hyperbolic*, for which the Gaussian curvature $K < 0$.

4. *Umbilic*, for which the Gaussian curvature $K = $ constant.

5. *Planar Umbilic*, for which $\kappa_1 = \kappa_2 = 0$.

Edge pixels are identified as those where the curvature κ_1 or κ_2 exceeds a threshold. Region-growing techniques are then used to cluster pixels belonging to homogeneous classes into surface regions.

Numerical Techniques for Surface Segmentation

Numerical techniques, as opposed to analytical techniques, use range values directly in estimating the surface curvature. Hoffman and Jain [1987] use surface normals in a pixel neighborhood to estimate the surface curvature at a pixel. To estimate the surface normal at a pixel, a least-squares plane fitting is carried out in an $N \times N$ neighborhood centered around a pixel of interest. The equation of the fitted plane is used to compute the surface normal n_p at the pixel location p. Curvature is estimated at each surface point as follows (Figure 3.9): For each range pixel q in an $N \times N$ window centered at p, an estimate of the surface curvature at p is given by

$$\kappa(p,q) \quad = \quad \frac{\|\, \mathbf{n}_p - \mathbf{n}_q \,\|}{\|\, \mathbf{p} - \mathbf{q} \,\|} \quad \text{if } \|\, \mathbf{p} - \mathbf{q} \,\| \le \|\, (\mathbf{n}_p + \mathbf{p}) - (\mathbf{n}_q + \mathbf{q}) \,\|$$

$$= \quad -\frac{\|\, \mathbf{n}_p - \mathbf{n}_q \,\|}{\|\, \mathbf{p} - \mathbf{q} \,\|}, \quad \text{otherwise} \qquad (3.100)$$

The above equation gives a discrete approximation to the one-dimensional curvature along a hypothesized curve from p to q. This expression generally results in an overestimation of surface curvature, since the length of the chord is used instead of the length of the curve between p and q. If we let N_p denote the $N \times N$ window centered around pixel p, then the value of $\kappa(p,q)$ is used to define six curvature measures:

Average curvature at p:

$$\kappa_{avg}(p) = \frac{1}{|N_p|} \sum_{q \in N_p} \kappa(p,q)$$

Minimum curvature at p:

$$\kappa_{min}(p) = min(|\kappa(p,q_i)|) \; \forall q_i \in N_p$$

Maximum curvature at p:

$$\kappa_{max}(p) = max(|\kappa(p,q_i)|) \; \forall q_i \in N_p$$

Mean curvature at p:

$$H(p) = \frac{1}{2}(\kappa_{min}(p) + \kappa_{max}(p))$$

Gaussian curvature at p:

$$K(p) = \kappa_{min}(p) \cdot \kappa_{max}(p)$$

Curvature ratio at p:

$$\kappa_r(p) = \frac{\kappa_{min}(p)}{\kappa_{max}(p)}$$

Hoffman and Jain describe a three-stage segmentation technique that uses surface curvature values computed in the above manner to detect convex, concave, and planar regions of a range image. The first stage segments the range image into surface patches by a clustering algorithm in six-dimensional space, defined by the surface points (i.e., x, y and z values) and the surface normals, that minimizes the squared-error. The second stage classifies the surface patches as either planar, concave, or convex based on a non-parametric statistical test for trend, curvature values, and eigenvalue analysis. In the final stage, the boundaries between the adjacent surface patches are classified as crease or noncrease edges, and this information is used to merge compatible patches to produce reasonable faces of objects in the image. Experimental results have been shown on a variety of real and synthetic range images.

3.4.3 Hybrid Segmentation Techniques

The edge- and region-based segmentation approaches treat the problem of de-tecting surface discontinuities and homogeneous surface regions as distinct from each other. In fact, the problems of detecting edges and detecting smooth sur-face regions are complementary. The knowledge of edge pixels can help to guide region growing techniques, whereas the magnitude of surface fitting error can help infer the presence or absence of edge pixels. Thus hybrid segmentation techniques that exploit the synergy between the problems of detecting edges and detecting smooth surfaces can be expected to perform better than either edge-based or region-based techniques by themselves.

Yokoya and Levine [1989] have described a segmentation approach that com-bines edge- and surface-based segmentation techniques. In their approach, the local curvature values (mean and Gaussian curvatures) at a pixel are computed based on a selective local biquadratic surface fit. A region-based segmentation based on the HK sign map is carried out. The range image is divided into homogeneous surface primitives based on the values of the mean and Gaussian curvatures such that a region does not contain discontinuities in depth or surface orientation. Two additional initial edge-based segmentations are also computed from the partial derivatives and the depth maps, i.e., the jump- and roof-edge maps. The three image maps are then combined to produce a final segmentation.

Jain and Nadabar [1990] describe a Markov random field (MRF) model-based segmentation technique that integrates both region- and edge-based segmenta-tion. The problem of edge detection is treated as a site-labeling problem using the MRF model. MRF models are useful for representing contextual information in the site-labeling problem. A site-labeling problem typically involves classifi-cation of each site (a pixel, edge segment, or region) into a small number of classes based on the observation vector at each site. It is assumed that the class of labels corresponds to true segments or regions in the images. The objective of the site-labeling problem, therefore, can be looked upon as that of recovering the true image from a noisy observed image. Contextual information is used to incorporate *a priori* assumptions or constraints about the scene such as:

1. Neighboring pixels are likely to belong to the same region.

2. Close parallel edges are unlikely.

3. Isolated edge pixels are unlikely.

4. Surface regions are smooth.

Let $\mathbf{X} = \{X_1, X_2, \ldots, X_M\}$ be the M-tuple random vector representing the *true* labels where each X_i takes a value from a set of labels $\{1, \ldots, C\}$. Let $\mathbf{Y} = \{Y_1, Y_2, \ldots, Y_M\}$ represent the observations at the M sites. If the observations are assumed to be statistically independent, then the density of $\mathbf{Y}$ given the true labeling is

$$f_{\mathbf{Y}}(\mathbf{y}|\mathbf{X} = \mathbf{x}) = \prod_{i=1}^{M} f_{Y_i}(y_i|x_i) \qquad (3.101)$$

where each $f_{Y_i}(y_i|x_i)$ is the conditional density function of the observation Y_i, given the true label x_i at the site i. Contextual information is incorporated through an MRF model of the statistical dependence among the labels on neighboring sites in $\mathbf{X}$, which is equivalent to the Gibbs process. The *a priori* probability density function for $\mathbf{X}$ is a Gibbs random field given by

$$P(\mathbf{X} = \mathbf{x}) = \frac{e^{-U(\mathbf{x})}}{Z} \qquad (3.102)$$

where Z is the partition function that is the sum of the numerator over all possible labeling, and $U(\mathbf{x})$ is the energy function given by

$$U(\mathbf{x}) = \sum_{c \in C} V_c(\mathbf{x}) \qquad (3.103)$$

where C is the set of all cliques with respect to the neighborhood system, and $V_c(\mathbf{x})$ are the potential functions. The functions $V_c(\mathbf{x})$ encode the *a priori* knowledge about the spatial dependence of the labels at neighboring sites and can be used to enforce constraints such as smoothness and continuity. The *a posteriori* probability density function of the site labels $\mathbf{X}$, given the observations $\mathbf{Y} = \mathbf{y}$, also has the form of a Gibbs random field

$$P(\mathbf{X} = \mathbf{x}|\mathbf{Y} = \mathbf{y}) = \frac{e^{-U(\mathbf{x}|\mathbf{y})}}{Z_{\mathbf{y}}} \qquad (3.104)$$

where $Z_{\mathbf{y}}$ is a normalizing constant and the corresponding energy function is

$$U(\mathbf{x}|\mathbf{y}) = \sum_{i=1}^{M} -\ln[f_{Y_i}(y_i|x_i)] + \sum_{c \in C} V_c(\mathbf{x}) \qquad (3.105)$$

The site-labeling problem can be treated as one of estimating the labels $\mathbf{x}$ in the true image, given an observation vector $\mathbf{y}$ such that the *a posteriori* probability density function $P(\mathbf{X} = \mathbf{x}|\mathbf{Y} = \mathbf{y})$ is maximized. The value of $\mathbf{x}$ that achieves this is referred to as the *maximum a posteriori* (MAP) estimate. Since $P(\mathbf{X} = \mathbf{x}|\mathbf{Y})$ is a multivariate function of M variables, where $M = N \times N$ for an image of size $N \times N$, determining the MAP estimate is computationally expensive. Geman and Geman [1984] have used simulated annealing to determine the MAP estimate for image restoration. Alternative schemes that approximate the MAP estimate have also been used by some researchers. Marroquin et al. [1987] have suggested minimization of the expected value of an error functional. Besag [1974] has proposed a deterministic iterative algorithm called iterative conditional modes (ICM), in which the labeling of a site is iteratively updated so as to maximize local conditional probabilities. Chou et al. [1987] and Jain and Nadabar [1990] have used the highest-confidence-first (HCF) algorithm, which is similar to the ICM algorithm except for the order in which the sites are visited. The HCF algorithm assigns to each site a confidence value proportional to the maximum amount of energy reduction that would result if the present label were

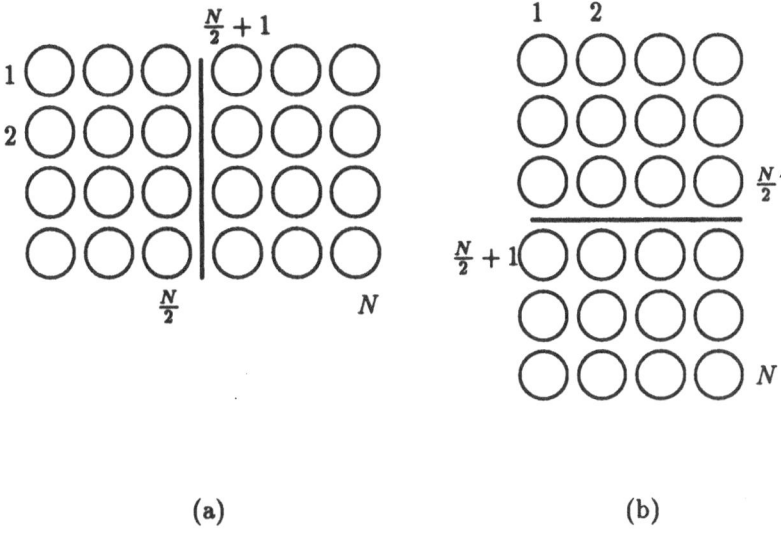

$$(a) \qquad\qquad\qquad\qquad (b)$$

Figure 3.10: Pixel numbering schemes for (a) vertical edge sites and (b) horizontal edge sites used by Jain and Nadabar.

changed to some other. Sites are visited and their confidence values updated in descending order of their confidence values.

Jain and Nadabar [1990] also treat the problem of edge detection as a site-labeling problem. The pixels surrounding horizontal and vertical edge sites are numbered as shown in Figure 3.10a,b. The set of site labels is limited to $C = \{e, \neg e\}$, where e denotes the presence of an edge and $\neg e$ its absence. Whereas the MRF model requires that the observation vector $\mathbf{Y}$, the conditional distribution $f_{Y_i}(y_i|x_i)$, and the clique potential functions $V_c(\mathbf{x})$ be completely specified, in the case of binary labels, only the likelihood ratio $L = f_{Y_i}(y_i|e)/f_{Y_i}(y_i|\neg e)$ and the clique potential functions $V_c(\mathbf{x})$ need be specified. Two statistics are formulated for edge strength at an edge site—one for jump edges and the other for crease edges. Likewise, two likelihood ratios, L_j and L_c, are defined for jump and crease edges, respectively. For each edge site, the greater of the two is chosen. Clique potential functions are defined in the neighborhood of each edge site. Clique potentials are chosen based on the spatial structure or on the constraints that a clique symbolizes. If the spatial structure of a clique does not agree with *a priori* constraints of continuity and smoothness, then that labeling is discouraged by assigning a high potential value to the associated clique (Figure 3.11).

The edge detection algorithm then proceeds as follows:

1. The jump likelihood ratio L_j and the crease likelihood ratio L_c for each edge site are computed.

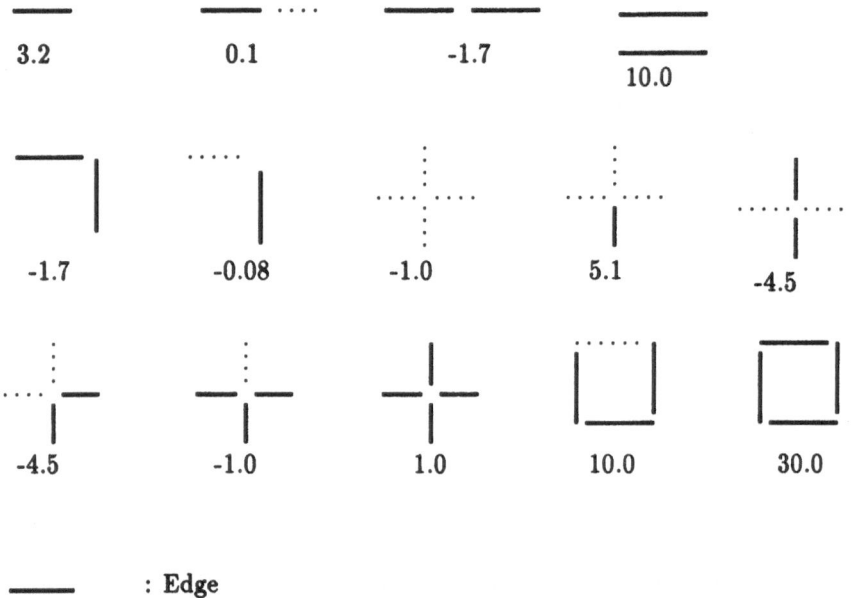

Figure 3.11: Cliques and their potential functions used by Jain and Nadabar.

2. The edge likelihood ratio L_e is computed as $= max(L_j, L_c)$.

3. The HCF algorithm is used to obtain the desired edge labeling.

MRF-based edge-labeling is integrated with a region-based segmentation technique such as the one described in the work of Hoffman and Jain [1987]. Region-based segmentation is carried out independently of edge-labeling. It is assumed that region-based segmentation results in an over-segmented image. The boundary between any two regions in the region-based segmented image is considered. The ratio of the number of pixels on the boundary (within localization accuracy) marked as edge sites by MRF labeling to the total number of pixels on the boundary is computed. If the ratio is below a predefined threshold, the regions are merged. Experimental results on real range data are shown to give results that are better than those obtained by either segmentation technique in isolation.

Bhandarkar and Siebert [1992] have proposed a segmentation technique in which the synergy between the processes of detecting surface discontinuities and surface regions is exploited by using the *geometrical* properties of the detected surface regions. In particular, they demonstrate how their technique can be used to accurately segment scenes containing polyhedral objects. The parameters of the local planar fit at each range pixel is estimated by fitting a planar surface in a local window centered around the pixel. Homogeneous planar regions are extracted using a combination of clustering in parameter space and region growing. The clusters are then subjected to a smoothing operation that eliminates isolated clusters and small clusters surrounded by larger ones. Contours of the resulting clusters are then extracted using a scanning operation (Figure 3.12). Contour pixels are classified as jump or crease edge pixels using a gradient operator, since the response of crease edge pixels to the gradient operator is often negligible compared to that for jump edge pixels. Two clusters are deemed spatially contiguous if their contour pixels are adjacent and have been classified as crease edge pixels. For all spatially adjacent cluster pairs that correspond to non-parallel planes, the direction of the boundary of intersection can be predicted using the parameters of the corresponding planes, i.e., it is the cross product of the normal vectors of the two planes. The boundary of intersection is then projected onto the image plane using an *a priori* model of projection. If the projected boundary does not agree with the actual boundary in the image within a prespecified tolerance, then the image is deemed oversegmented. This forms a cue for merging the corresponding clusters, thereby correcting the initial segmentation. Thus the geometric parameters of the detected surface regions are used to hypothesize the presence of a surface discontinuity in the form of a crease edge boundary and also to accurately compute its parametric form. The presence of the surface discontinuity in the image is used to confirm the hypothesis, whereas its absence is used as a cue to correct the initial region-based segmentation.

The equations of the detected planar facets can then be used to compute accurately the values of the vertex coordinates. For vertices of crease edge boundaries that can be treated as the intersection of three or more contiguous

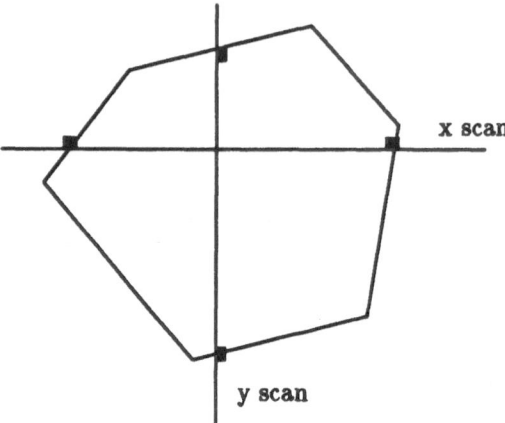

Figure 3.12: Vertical and horizontal scanning of the clustered image to extract contours of clusters.

non-parallel planar facets, the coordinates of the corresponding vertex are accurately determined by solving the system of equations for the intersecting planes. The coordinates of the other vertex are determined using the value of the previous vertex and the equation of the intersection edge. Jump edge boundaries are detected using a two-dimensional Hough transform in the image plane where (ρ, θ) are the parameters for a line. A boundary-tracing procedure determines an initial estimate for the vertices of the jump edge boundary. These initial values are then refined with a constraint propagation procedure that uses the vertices of the crease edges, the equations of the planes and the equations of the intersection boundaries as constraints. Whenever the vertices of a jump edge boundary are refined, two constraints are imposed; (1) the refined vertices are constrained to be collinear with the direction vector of the boundary, and (2) the vertices are constrained to satisfy the equation(s) of the plane(s) the edge belongs to. The overall guiding principle is to compute the new values for the vertices as intersections of two boundaries with known analytic forms whenever possible. The parameters of surface region in a range image can be computed more reliably than those of a boundary using a local edge operator. Since the process of computation of surface parameters involves an averaging or smoothing process over several pixel values, it is expected to be more robust to noise than a local edge operator. Using surface parameters as an aid in computing the parameters of surface boundaries is therefore expected to yield better results than would be possible with an edge-based segmentation scheme alone. The segmentation scheme has been tested on range images containing single and multiple polyhedral objects. Although the segmentation technique is limited to polyhedral objects, it can be extended to include objects with parametric curved surfaces of quadratic order such as conical, cylindrical, and spherical surfaces leading to parametric curves of discontinuity that are conic sections such as circles, ellipses, and parabolas.

3.5 Summary

In spite of the several range image segmentation techniques cited in the research literature, the initial segmentation of a range image remains a very difficult problem. Most segmentation algorithms are application-driven, and there are no standard yardsticks by which their performance can be measured. This is due partly to the difficulty in coming up with good analytical models for range image acquisition on which a universal optimality criterion for the segmentation algorithms can be based. For example, there is no universal choice for the noise process that corrupts a range image during image acquisition. It is widely accepted that range image noise is typically non-Gaussian and non-stationary and consists of random measurement noise, quantization noise, systematic sensor noise, and some amount of *outlier* noise due to specular reflections, multiple reflections, and other factors. Yet, most segmentation algorithms are based on the simplifying assumptions of noise processes that are modeled as additive, Gaussian, and stationary noise. Therefore, most segmentation algorithms, to a degree, tend to be *ad hoc* and their performance assessment is largely subjective. In order to advance the state of the art, more realistic analytical models for range image acquisition, and also standardized segmentation error metrics, need to be formulated.

Chapter 4

Representation

The role of the initial segmentation is to partition a range image into smooth surface regions and to trace the contours of surface discontinuity. After segmenting the image into smooth surface regions and surface discontinuity contours, the next step is to find an appropriate *representation* for the segmented image. The representation should be such that it aids higher level cognitive visual functions. A representation at this level is termed a *feature-level* representation and the process of arriving at such a representation is referred to as *feature extraction*. In order to recognize objects in the scene, it is essential for the computer vision system to have a pre-stored representation of the object(s) it expects to encounter in the scene. The internal representation of an object in the memory of the vision system is referred to as an *object model*, and the process of formulating and implementing an object model is referred to as *representation modeling*. For the purpose of recognition, there should be a one-to-one correspondence between the feature-level representation and the object model representation. In this chapter the term *representation* will be used to denote both the feature level representation and the object model representation. Since objects encountered in range images are primarily three-dimensional with smooth C^2 surfaces, geometric representation schemes for three-dimensional objects are of particular interest.

4.1 Formal Properties of Geometric Representations

Geometric modeling of three-dimensional objects has been a topic of considerable interest in the areas of computer graphics, visualization, and computer-aided design and manufacturing (CAD/CAM). The primary focus in these areas has been on the use of three-dimensional geometric models for the purpose of display and, therefore, the emphasis was on representation schemes that would enable fast and efficient rendering of three-dimensional objects using graphics display algorithms such as ray-tracing and z-buffer. In computer vision, on the other hand, we are interested in representation schemes that are *discriminatory*, i.e., that enable one to recognize and differentiate one object from another. Besl [1988b], Besl and Jain [1985], Requicha [1980], Requicha and Voelcker [1982, 1983], and Brown [1981] provide excellent surveys of three-dimensional geometric modeling.

As proposed by Requicha [1980], a *representation scheme* can be considered to be a relation $\mathcal{M}$ from a set of physical solid objects $\mathcal{O}$ to a set of representations of solid objects $\mathcal{S}$. A representation $m_i \in \mathcal{M}$ is an ordered pair (o_i, s_i) where $o_i \in \mathcal{O}$ is an object drawn from the set of objects and $s_i \in \mathcal{S}$ is a representation drawn from the set of syntactically correct representations. $\mathcal{S}$ can be treated as a language generated by a grammar using a finite alphabet. If $\mathcal{D} \subset \mathcal{O}$ and $\mathcal{R} \subset \mathcal{S}$ are the domain and range of $\mathcal{M}$, then all elements $o \in (\mathcal{O} - \mathcal{D})$ are not representable by $\mathcal{M}$, and elements $s \in (\mathcal{S} - \mathcal{R})$ are syntactically correct representations, but with no corresponding physical object. Such objects are called *invalid* or *nonsense* objects.

Representation schemes can be evaluated based on the following criteria:

1. *Size of $\mathcal{D}$*. The size of the domain $\mathcal{D}$ of any representation scheme $\mathcal{M}$ is indicative of its modeling power. If $\mathcal{D}_1$ is the domain of $\mathcal{M}_1$, and $\mathcal{D}_2$ is that of $\mathcal{M}_2$, and if $\mathcal{D}_1 \subset \mathcal{D}_2$, then the representation scheme $\mathcal{M}_2$ is deemed more powerful than $\mathcal{M}_1$. For example, a representation scheme that can model C^2 or quadric surfaces is more powerful than one that can model only polyhedra, because the class of polyhedral objects is a proper subset of the class of C^2 or quadric surfaces.

2. *Size of $\mathcal{R}$*. If $\mathcal{R} = \mathcal{S}$, then the representation scheme does not permit invalid objects. While such objects may not be intentionally created, it is necessary for the representation to identify such objects as errors in cases where the process of modeling is automated.

3. *Unambiguity of $\mathcal{M}$*. A representation s in $\mathcal{M}$ is said to be *unambiguous* iff

$$(o_1, s) \in \mathcal{M} \wedge (o_2, s) \in \mathcal{M} \Rightarrow o_1 = o_2 \qquad (4.1)$$

A representation scheme $\mathcal{M}$ is deemed unambiguous if every representation $s \in \mathcal{R}$ is unambiguous. If a representation scheme is not unambiguous, then it is possible for more than one object to share the same representation. In such cases it is not always possible to reconstruct the original object from its representation. In areas such as graphics and CAD/CAM where the reconstruction of the object is important for the purpose of display, the representation scheme needs to be unambiguous.

4. *Uniqueness of $\mathcal{M}$*. A representation scheme is deemed *unique* if

$$(o, s_1) \in \mathcal{M} \wedge (o, s_2) \in \mathcal{M} \Rightarrow s_1 = s_2 \; \forall o \in \mathcal{D}, \; \forall s_1, s_2 \in \mathcal{R} \qquad (4.2)$$

If a representation scheme is not unique, then it is possible for a single object to have more than one representation. This results in some redundancy in the representation scheme.

Ideally, we would expect the representation scheme to be rich and powerful so that it is able to model a large class of objects, unambiguous and unique (and hence irredundant). Such a modeling scheme would necessarily be a *bijection* or a one-to-one and onto relation. Most representation schemes fail to satisfy one or more of these criteria. This is one reason why there are several representation schemes used in the areas of computer vision, graphics, and CAD/CAM.

Each representation scheme entails a particular feature extraction process. The choice of features for the representation of the segmented images and the object models is largely application-dependent. There has been no representation scheme to date that could be considered universal in any sense. The choice of representation could be broadly classified as either surface-based or volumetric, and both surface and volumetric representations could be either local or global. Local surface descriptions are typically based on local curvature properties of the surface. Global surface representations, on the other hand, describe the surface in terms of a few global parameters. Representations could also be classified as generic or distinctive. Generic representations cover a broad range of objects under the domain of interest, while distinctive representations make specific assumptions about objects in question.

The following sections present a review of the various representation schemes commonly encountered in computer vision research. For each representation scheme, the corresponding feature extraction process is described. Strengths and limitations of the various representation schemes are also described.

4.2 Wire-Frame Representation

A wire-frame object representation is a graph in which the vertices are three-dimensional points on the object surface (typically junction points), and the graph edges correspond to physical edges between the vertices. The representation does not contain surface information since the *solid* portion between the edges in the wire frame is not defined. The wire-frame representation is therefore not unambiguous. Since the wire frame representation contains only surface discontinuity features (i.e., vertices and edges) the feature extraction process is limited to extracting surface discontinuity contours and corner pixels from a range image. Thus, the feature extraction process cannot use surface information in the range image. Since one of the advantages of using range images is having the surface information explicitly available, it is clear that the wire-frame representation scheme does not take full advantage of range image data. For this reason, the wire-frame representation has not proved popular for range image understanding, although it has been used for polyhedral object recognition from conventional intensity images using such discontinuity features as edge segments and corners [Lowe 1987]. Figure 4.1 shows a wireframe representation of a video terminal. It is apparent that only in the case of polyhedral objects can wire-frame representations be deemed adequate. For an object that consists of nonplanar surfaces, piecewise approximation of the nonplanar surfaces by planar surfaces must be done before arriving at an approximate wireframe representation.

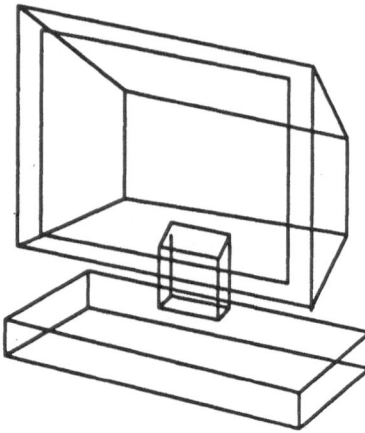

Figure 4.1: An example of the wireframe representation: a video terminal.

4.3   Constructive Solid Geometry (CSG) Representation

In constructive solid geometry (CSG)-based modeling [Foley et al. 1990] [Hoffman 1989], primitive shapes from a finite set are combined using regularized Boolean operations to produce the desired solid (Figure 4.2). The primitive shapes are typically right circular cylinders, right circular cones, spheres, and boxes. A CSG model is stored as a tree where the root node of the tree represents the object and the leaf nodes represent the primitive solids. The other non-leaf nodes of the CSG tree represent regularized Boolean operations such as intersection (I), union (U) and difference (D). The CSG tree, however, contains only a qualitative description of the object, because the final shape of the object depends on the exact relative orientations and positions of the primitive shapes with respect to each other. Thus several objects could be defined by the same CSG tree. CSG has proved to be a convenient modeling technique for CAD/CAM and computer graphics. CSG representations coupled with ray-tracing techniques have been shown to be effective in rendering displays of complex three-dimensional objects. However, the use of CSG representations in computer vision has been limited [Lin and Chen 1988]. This is primarily due to the fact that the CSG representation does not incorporate sufficient *discriminatory* information that is essential for recognition purposes.

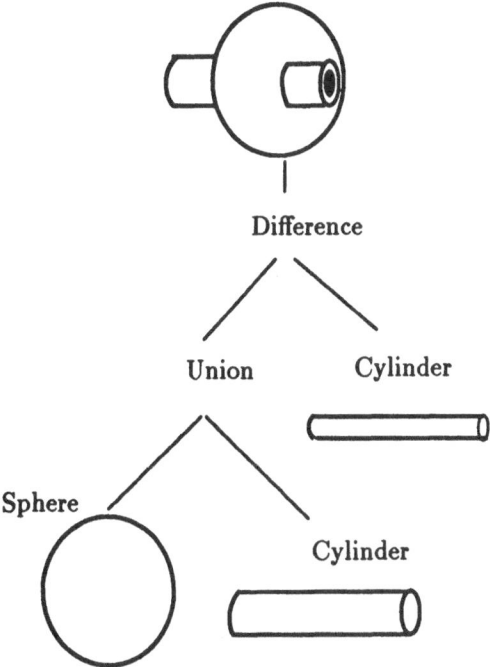

Figure 4.2: An example of the CSG representation of a three-dimensional object.

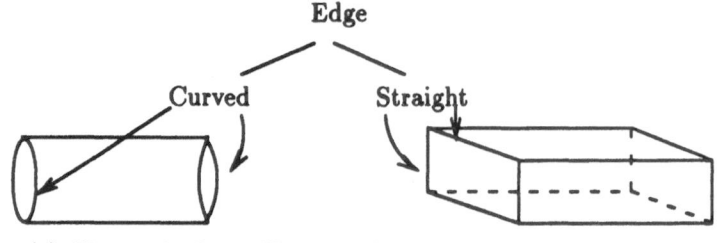

(a) Change in Geon Shape with Variation in Edge Type

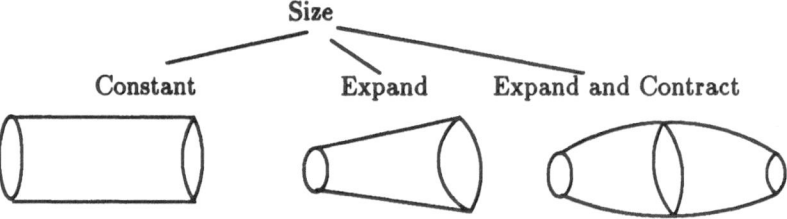

(b) Change in Geon Shape with Variation in Size

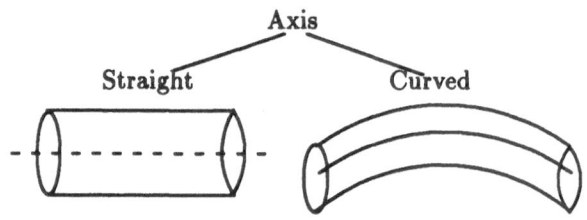

(c) Change in Geon Shape with Variation in Axis

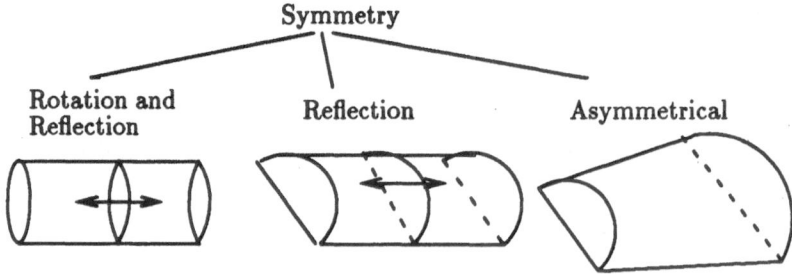

(d) Change in Geon Shape with Variation in Symmetry

Figure 4.3: Different shape of geons resulting from varying the values of qualitative features.

4.4 Qualitative Representation using Geons

Most solid representations used in CAD/CAM or vision systems are quantitative in that they use metrical information. Primitive surfaces or volumes used in representation are described in terms of numerical parameters. Yet, human vision does not rely on such accurate metrical information when recognizing objects in a scene, as it is capable of recognizing objects purely from qualitative descriptions. Biederman [1985, 1987] proposes a qualitative representation in terms of volumetric primitives called *geons* (geometric icons) and argues that, for most visual recognition tasks, the objects to be recognized can be distinguished simply by examining some qualitative features of the segmented primitives. Representations that capture only qualitative features have a considerable advantage in terms of processing requirements.

Biederman presents a catalog of 36 geons with each geon having a unique set of four qualitative features:

1. *Edge*. Straight or curved.

2. *Symmetry*. Rotational/reflective, reflective, asymmetric.

3. *Size variation*. Constant, expanding, expanding/contracting.

4. *Axis*. Straight or curved.

Figures 4.3 (a)–(d) illustrate how variations in the four qualitative features can bring about variations in geon shapes. Biederman shows that most three-dimensional objects of interest can be modeled as piecewise combinations of geon primitives, and he proposes an edge-based procedure for segmenting an image into its geon components. It can be shown that the most likely places where geons may be joined are regions in the image characterized by concavity and nonaccidental alignment of edge features. Psychological experiments have shown that humans are capable of segmenting a given scene into its component geons, even in the face of imperfect or missing edge data, as long as a certain number of nonaccidental alignments in the form of collinear edge segments, co-incident edge segments (corners), and parallel edge segments are preserved. By showing that over 154 million qualitatively different objects can be constructed using three geons and their various inter-geon relationships such as relative sizes, arrangements, and affixments, Biederman argues that geons can be the basis of a versatile and powerful representation scheme for the description of three-dimensional objects. Bergevin and Levine [1989] have designed a model building system that uses two-dimensional line drawings to form geon models.

Although the geon representation scheme is intuitively appealing, it can serve only as a first step in the process of visual recognition, or in cases where only a qualitative scene interpretation is sought. There have been very few vision systems that use geon-based representation schemes. The lack of a powerful mechanism to express inter-geon relations, and the fact that geon-based representation schemes are purely qualitative and incapable of differentiating between qualitatively similar but metrically different objects, have restricted its use in industrial machine vision.

4.5   Aspect Graph Representation

An *aspect graph* representation is a multiple-view representation that describes
a three-dimensional object in terms of its possible two-dimensional projections
or views [Koenderink and Van Doorn 1979]. If a three-dimensional object is
thought of as consisting of a finite number of surface features such as continuous
surface patches and surface discontinuities, then all the possible views, which are
theoretically infinite in number, can be grouped into a finite number of distinct
view classes called *aspects* or *characteristic views*. An aspect is characterized
in terms of the *qualitative topology* of the view it represents. In the context of
range images, each view is 2 1/2-dimensional since depth information is explicitly available for each visible surface in the view. The topology of a view in
such cases can be defined in terms of non-metric properties of surface features
and the relationships between surface features. For example, if the surface features chosen are smooth visible surface patches, then the topology of a view can
be described as a graph wherein each node represents a smooth surface patch
and the arc between nodes indicates that the corresponding surface patches are
adjacent.

Two views are said to belong to a single *aspect* if they are topologically
identical and connected by a continuous path of viewpoints along which the aspect does not change. Thus a set of distinct aspects defines a partition on the
infinite set of views of an object. Since each view, defined in spherical coordinates, represents a point on the surface of a view-sphere, the aspect graph can
be alternatively looked upon as a partition of the surface of a view sphere into
nonoverlapping regions where each region denotes the corresponding aspect. It
must be noted that the definition of an aspect is largely dependent on topological cues used to describe a particular view. Cues based on visible edges, visible
vertices (junctions), and visible surface patches are typically used in most applications. For a particular aspect, suitable features can be computed for the
purpose of recognition. Syntactic, statistical, and graph-theoretic approaches
are typically used for recognition using aspect graph representations.

There are two ways in which aspect graphs can be used:

1. Each aspect is stored as a distinct object in the object model database, in
   which case the representation is ordinarily referred to as a *multiple-view*
   representation.

2. All the aspects can be combined into a single structure called an *aspect
   graph* (Figure 4.4). Each node of the aspect graph refers to a single aspect.
   Two nodes in the aspect graph are connected by an arc if there exists
   a continuous path of viewpoints along which there is a change from one
   aspect to the other. A change of aspect is referred to as a *visual event*.

A considerable amount of research effort in recent years has been devoted
to the development of algorithms for constructing aspect graphs of polyhedral
and non-polyhedral objects. Chakravarty and Freeman [1982] have shown that
imposing certain external constraints on physical objects can drastically reduce

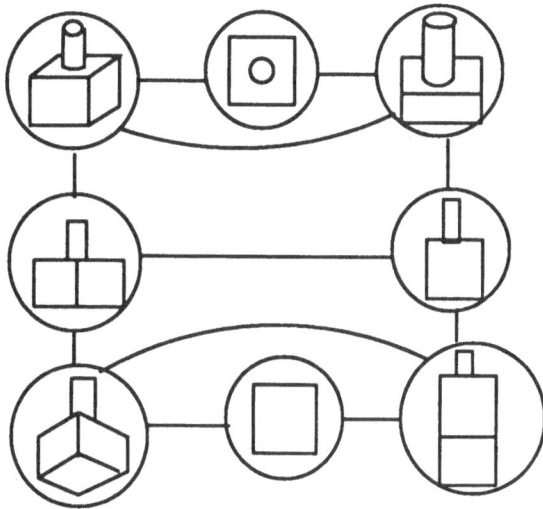

Figure 4.4: An examples of aspect graph representing a simple 3-D object.

the number of aspects that need to be considered. In particular, postulating that the object can appear in the scene only in a certain number of physically stable positions can help to eliminate a large number of aspects and thereby reduce the processing time. Korn and Dyer [1987], Plantinga and Dyer [1986, 1990], Rieger [1987], Gigus and Malik [1990], Eggert and Bowyer [1989], Kriegman and Ponce [1990], and Sripadisvarakul and Jain [1989] have all proposed algorithms for computing aspect graphs of polyhedral and non-polyhedral objects. In spite of extensive research on the aspect graph representation, some basic drawbacks of this scheme still need to be addressed:

1. Most algorithms for aspect graph computation suffer from large space and time complexity. For example, the algorithm by Gigus and Malik [1990] takes $O(n^8)$ time and $O(n^8)$ storage to compute the aspect graph of a non-convex polyhedron of n sides from an orthographic projection. This problem is exacerbated in cases where the object contains curved surfaces.

2. The number of characteristic views becomes very large as the objects become more complex.

Some have taken a more practical approach to computing multiple-view representations [Ikeuchi and Kanade 1988], [Chen and Kak 1989] , [Korn and Dyer 1987], [Jain and Hoffman 1988]. Instead of computing the exact partitioning of the view-sphere into non-overlapping regions, the view-sphere is sampled at a finite number of points that are uniformly distributed over the surface of the sphere. This is tantamount to quantizing or tessellating the surface of the view-

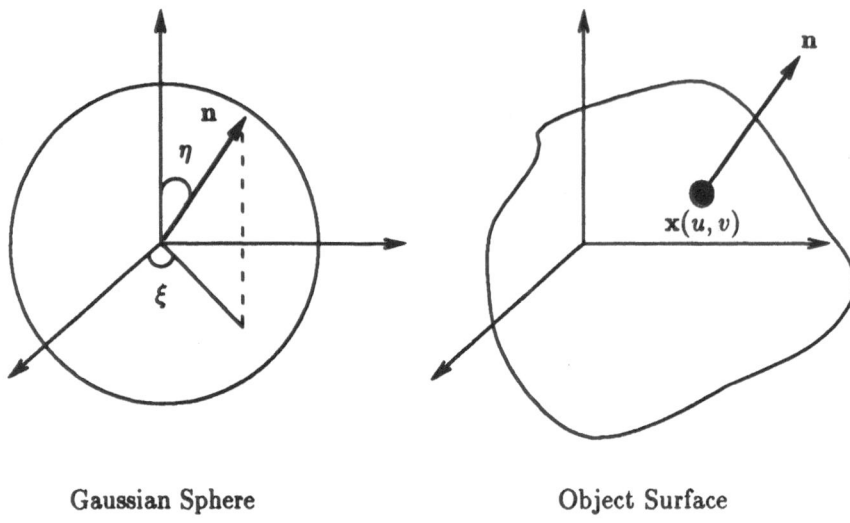

Gaussian Sphere   Object Surface

Figure 4.5: Mapping the surface normal at **x** on the Gaussian sphere.

sphere into uniform regions with the sample points as the region centroids. Views of an object are taken from each sample point. Views that share adjacent regions on the tessellated view-sphere and have identical topographic descriptions are merged into a single aspect. This process results in the labeling of the regions on the tessellated view-sphere as belonging to a particular aspect. Features used for recognition, as also ones extracted from the range image, depend largely on topographic cues used to describe aspects in an aspect graph. If the cues used are based on visibility of edges and vertices, then the corresponding features must be extracted from the image. Cues based on surface features—smooth surface patches and surface discontinuities are commonly used in dealing with range images. Visibility of surface regions and visibility of some important surface discontinuities can be used to classify scene data as instances of aspects of an object.

4.6   EGI Representation

The extended Gaussian image (EGI) is an orientation histogram of points on the surface of a three-dimensional object. For a given point on the surface of a three-dimensional object, we can associate a point on the Gaussian (unit) sphere such that the two points have the same surface normal (Figure 4.5). This mapping is referred to as a Gaussian image and can be seen to map information associated with points on the surface to points on the Gaussian sphere. In the case of a convex object with positive Gaussian curvature everywhere, no two points have the same surface normal and the mapping is invertible. However, the Gaussian image cannot be used to distinguish between objects that have the same shape but are scaled to different sizes. The extended Gaussian image associates the inverse of the Gaussian curvature at each point on the surface of the object with the corresponding point on the Gaussian sphere. If points on the object surface are denoted by $\mathbf{x}(u, v)$ and points on the Gaussian sphere by $\mathbf{g}(\xi, \eta)$, where ξ and η refer to the polar and azimuthal angles in spherical coordinates, then the EGI is defined as

$$\mathbf{g}(\xi, \eta) = \frac{1}{K(u, v)} \qquad (4.3)$$

where $K(u, v)$ is the Gaussian curvature at the point $\mathbf{x}(u, v)$ on the object surface and (ξ, η) is a point on the Gaussian sphere that has the same surface normal as the point $\mathbf{x}(u, v)$. It can be shown that this mapping is unique up to translation for convex objects. In the case of polyhedral objects, the Gaussian curvature is uniformly zero for all points on a planar surface. The EGI $\mathbf{g}(\xi, \eta)$ in this case is an impulse (delta-Dirac function) weighted by the area of the planar surface.

The EGI has some interesting properties:

1. The EGI of an object rotates with the rotation of the object.

2. The center of mass of the EGI of a smoothly curved object is always at the origin.

3. The integration of the EGI of an object over the surface of the Gaussian sphere equals the total surface area of the object, that is

$$\int \int_G \mathbf{g}(\xi, \eta) d\xi d\eta = \int \int_G \frac{1}{K(u, v)} d\xi d\eta = \int \int_S du dv = S \qquad (4.4)$$

Since a range image is a discretized representation of the object surface(s), the EGI of an object is determined from its *needle map*, which denotes the unit surface normal at each range pixel. The needle map of a range image can be obtained by computing the surface normal at each range pixel by fitting a planar surface in a local neighborhood of the range pixel. The EGI of the object is then approximated by impulses contributed by the individual range pixels, where the magnitude of each impulse is the surface area for the corresponding pixel. If the area of a range pixel is A_p, then the surface area covered by the pixel is $S_p = A_p / \cos \theta$, where θ is the angle between the surface normal $\mathbf{n}_p$ at the pixel and the direction of the projection of the pixel on the image plane (Figure 4.6). Although the EGI for a smooth surface is a continuous function, it is convenient to deal with the discretized version of the EGI, which is obtained by tessellating the surface of the Gaussian sphere into a finite number of partitions or cells. The discretized EGI is referred to as an *orientation histogram*. The orientation histogram is computed by using the magnitude or weight of the impulse contributed by each range pixel to increment the appropriate cell in the orientation histogram.

There are several possible ways of tessellating the surface of a Gaussian sphere into a finite number of cells. It is desirable that the cells in the tessellation be

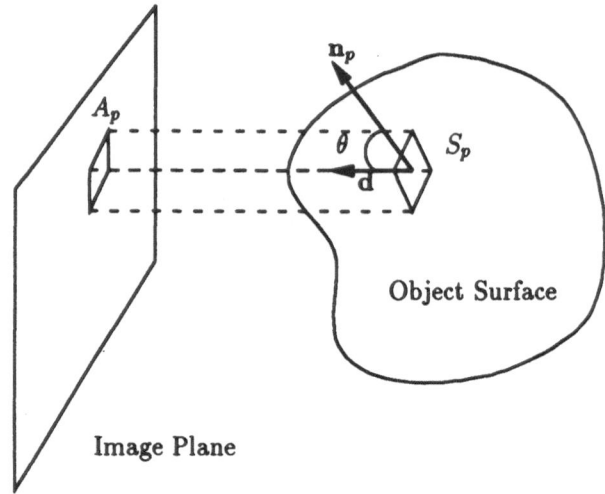

Figure 4.6: Projection of a surface patch on the image plane.

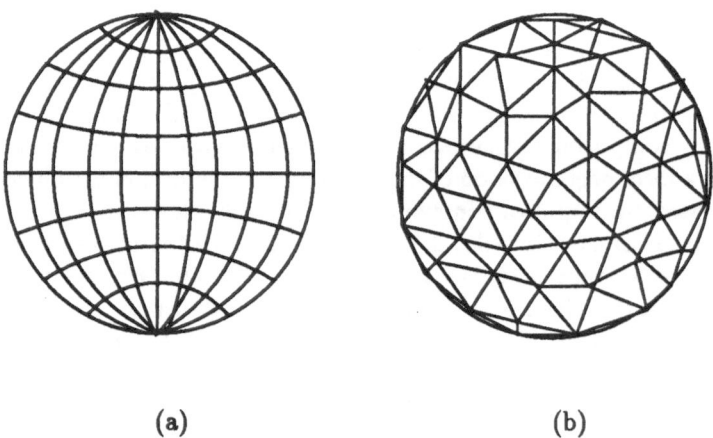

(a)   (b)

Figure 4.7: (a) Tessellation of the Gaussian sphere along latitude and longitude. (b) Geodesic tessellation of the Gaussian sphere.

uniform in shape and area and have compact regular shapes so that the resulting tessellation is fine enough to provide good angular resolution. It is also desirable to have the tessellation allow cells to be brought into alignment for most rotations. The tessellation based on latitude and longitude (Figure 4.7(a)), though simple and intuitive, suffers from the drawback that the resulting cells are not regular. It is possible to obtain a regular tessellation by projecting regular polyhedra (Platonic solids) onto the Gaussian sphere by aligning their centers. However, there are only five regular polyhedra — tetrahedron (four faces), hexahedron (six faces), octahedron (eight faces), dodecahedron (twelve faces) and the icosahedron (twenty faces) — and even the icosahedron with twenty faces provides too coarse a resolution. The geodesic tessellation (Figure 4.7(b)), which divides each triangular face of the icosahedron or each pentangular face of the dodecahedron into an equal number of triangular facets, is a commonly used tessellation since it allows an arbitrarily fine resolution.

The discrete EGI or the orientation histogram can be computed very easily from the needle map. The feature extraction process involved in computing the orientation histogram is fairly straightforward, since it entails estimating the surface normal at each pixel independently. This process can be carried out very efficiently with suitable parallel hardware. The discrete EGI of the visible surfaces in a range image can then be matched with the discrete EGI representation of an object model. In general, the discrete EGI representation of an object model would have to be rotated and matched with the discrete EGI of the visible surfaces in the range image. Efficient algorithms can be designed to rotate the discrete EGI by appropriately shifting the contents of the cells in the orientation histogram. A goodness measure for a match can be defined by determining the sum of squared differences between the cells in the discrete EGI of the object model and those of the visible surfaces in the range image. An appropriate match can be used to obtain both identity and orientation of a three-dimensional object. Horn [1984] presents the basic mathematical issues underlying the EGI representation. Horn and Ikeuchi [1984], Ikeuchi [1981], Brou [1983], and Little [1985] discuss how the EGI representation, computed from the needle map generated by a photometric stereo imaging process, can be used by a robot for bin-picking tasks. One of the principal drawbacks of the EGI representation is that it is unique only for *convex* three-dimensional objects.

4.7 Representation Using Generalized Cylinders

The use of generalized cylinders for representation of three-dimensional objects was first proposed by Binford [1971]. Generalized cylinders can be effectively used to model a large number of natural and man-made shapes, as brought out by the work of Marr and Nishihara [1978], Agin and Binford [1976], and Nevatia and Binford [1977].

A generalized cylinder (GC) (Figure 4.8) is characterized by the following parameters:

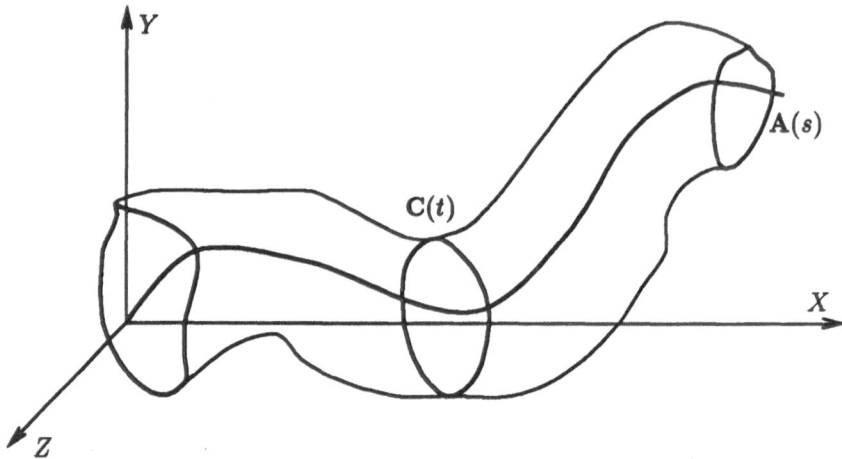

Figure 4.8: A generalized cylinder.

1. *Axis.* The axis of a generalized cylinder is a space curve and is described in parametric form $\mathbf{A}(s) = (x(s), y(s), z(s))$.

2. *Plane of cross section.* At each point on the axis at some fixed angle α to the tangent $\mathbf{A}_s(s)$ to the axis, a *plane of cross section* is defined.

3. *Cross section.* On each plane of cross section a planar curve is defined that constitutes the *cross section* of the generalized cylinder.

4. *Sweeping rule.* This specifies the transformation of the cross section as the plane of cross section is swept along the axis. The sweeping rule is either a continuous function that implies that the cross section varies smoothly along the axis of the generalized cylinder, or a piecewise continuous function that implies that the generalized cylinder under consideration could be treated as a volumetric union of generalized cylinders with smoothly varying cross sections.

Shafer [1985] has presented a general taxonomy for generalized cylinders. Most frequently encountered shapes could be obtained from the general form of the generalized cylinder by imposing additional constraints on the axis, the cross section, the plane of cross section, or the sweeping rule. The first subclass is formed by restricting the axis of the generalized cylinder.

1. *Straight GC.* A straight generalized cylinder (SGC) has a line segment in space as its axis.

2. *Curved GC.* A curved generalized cylinder (CGC) has a space curve as its axis.

3. *Toroidal GC*. A toroidal generalized cylinder (TGC) has a closed curve in space as its axis.

The second subclass is formed by restricting the plane of cross section with respect to the axis of the generalized cylinder:

1. *Right GC*. A right generalized cylinder has cross-sectional planes perpendicular to the tangent to the axis. In the case of a right straight generalized cylinder, the cross section is perpendicular to the axis itself .

2. *Oblique GC*. An oblique generalized cylinder has cross-sectional planes that are not perpendicular to the tangent to the axis.

The third subclass is created by restricting the shape of the cross section:

1. *Circular GC*. A circular generalized cylinder has cross sections that are all circles.

2. *Polygonal GC*. A polygonal generalized cylinder has cross sections that are polygons.

3. *Open GC*. An open generalized cylinder has cross sections that are open curves on the cross-sectional plane. An OGC forms a piece of warped sheet in space.

The fourth subclass is formed by restricting the sweeping rule:

1. *Homogeneous GC's*. A homogeneous generalized cylinder has a transformation rule that allows only uniform scaling of the cross section as it is swept along the axis, i.e., all cross sections have the same shape and are allowed to vary only in size. In the case of a homogeneous circular generalized cylinder, the axis passes through the centers of the circular cross sections.

2. *Linear GC*. A linear generalized cylinder is a special case of the homogeneous generalized cylinder in which the size of the cross section is proportional to the distance from a given point on the axis referred to as the *apex* of the generalized cylinder.

3. *Uniform GC*. A uniform generalized cylinder is a special case of the linear generalized cylinder in which the cross sections are identical in size and shape.

4. *Bilinear GC*. A bilinear generalized cylinder has a cross section that varies along the axis but is scaled differently along two mutually orthogonal directions on the plane of cross section. The bilinear generalized cylinder is a non-homogeneous or a heterogeneous generalized cylinder.

Although modeling with generalized cylinders is a powerful representation mechanism, the number of parameters needed to uniquely specify a general GC can be very large. Consequently, most of the research on GC representation has

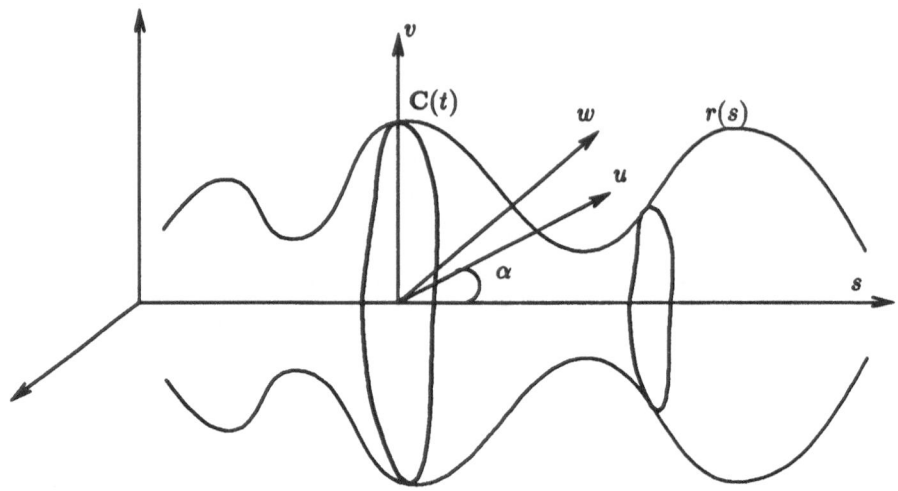

Figure 4.9: An example of a straight homogeneous generalized cylinder.

focused on the subclass of straight homogeneous generalized cylinders (SHGC's).
A SHGC surface (Figure 4.9) is described by two parameters s and t where s
measures the distance along the axis and t measures the distance along the cross
section. A SHGC surface is characterized by the four-tuple $(\mathbf{A}(s), \mathbf{C}(t), r(s), \alpha)$
where:

1. $\mathbf{A}(s) = (x(s), y(s), z(s))$ $s \in [0, 1]$ is the line segment that describes the
   axis.

2. α is the angle of inclination of the cross section plane with the axis. If
   the cross section plane is described by the uv plane, then the u axis is so
   chosen that the angle between the u-axis and the GC-axis is α.

3. Given a cross section plane uv at a given axis point $\mathbf{A}(s)$, the cross section
   is defined by the set of points $r(s)\mathbf{C}(t)$ where the *shape function* $\mathbf{C}(t) =$
   $(u(t), v(t))$ describes the cross section shape and the *radius function* $r(s)$
   describes the cross section size. The SHGC surface is then described as a
   collection of all the points $r(s)\mathbf{C}(t)$ $s \in [0, 1]$, $t \in [0, 1]$.

Any SHGC surface can be described in terms of a *uvs* frame of reference where
the angle between the u and the s axis is α. Alternatively, we can construct an
orthogonal *wvs* frame of reference such that w is orthogonal to v and s and the
angle between u and w is $\pi/2 - \alpha$. Thus any point (u, v, s) in the uvs coordinate
frame can be expressed as $(u \sin \alpha, v, s + u \cos \alpha)$ in the wvs coordinate frame.
Only for a Right SHGC are the two coordinate frames identical. Any point

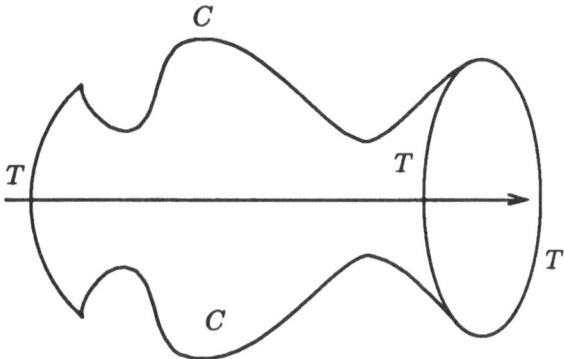

C: Contour Generator

T: Terminator Boundary

Figure 4.10: Contour generators and occluding boundaries for a straight homo-geneous generalized cylinder.

$\mathbf{x}(s,t)$ on the surface of the SHGC can be expressed as

$$\mathbf{x}(s,t) = (u(t)r(s), v(t)r(s), s)_{uvs} \qquad (4.5)$$

in the *uvs* coordinate frame, or as

$$\mathbf{x}(s,t) = (u(t)r(s)\sin\alpha, v(t)r(s), s + u(t)r(s)\cos\alpha)_{wvs} \qquad (4.6)$$

in the *wvs* coordinate frame.

SHGC's have been successfully used in computer vision. Brooks [1981] de-signed a vision system **ACRONYM** for the interpretation of three-dimensional objects in intensity images based on the generalized cylinder representation. Nevatia and Binford [1977] have shown how the generalized cylinder model can be used to model human-like forms. Shafer [1985] has analyzed the occluding contours (silhouettes) of generalized cylinders in an image and the conditions under which the surface of the generalized cylinder can be reconstructed from the occluding contours. Rao and Nevatia [1988] have presented algorithms for extracting parameters of linear straight homogeneous generalized cylinders from sparse range data. Ponce et al. [1989] and Ponce [1990] have analyzed some fun-damental mathematical properties of straight homogeneous generalized cylinders and determined the conditions under which a surface admits unique and multiple descriptions under a generalized cylinder representation.

The feature extraction process for the generalized cylinder representation (Figure 4.10) typically involves:

1. Determining *occluding boundaries* or *contour generators* that are typically jump edges where a visible surface is to one side of the boundary.

2. Determining *terminator boundaries* that define the volumetric extent of the generalized cylinder.

Once occluding and terminator boundaries have been determined, the axis curve, the cross section shape, and the sweeping rule for LSHGC's can be deduced from the range data [Rao and Nevatia 1988].

4.8   Superquadric Representation

Superquadrics are a family of parametric shapes that were discovered by the Danish designer Peit Hein as an extension of basic quadric surfaces and solids. Since then, superquadric surfaces have been used in CAD/CAM, computer graphics and, more recently, computer vision. Superquadric surfaces have been used as primitives for shape representation. Superquadric surfaces have the advantage that a wide variety of shapes can be described in terms of a few parameters. Moreover, superquadric surfaces can be deformed in a systematic manner that enables us to derive secondary shapes from a single canonical shape. Superquadrics can be shown to be able to model most important classes of generalized cylinders. Barr [1981, 1984] has presented the basic mathematical properties of superquadrics and demonstrated their simplicity and versatility in modeling complex shapes for computer graphics. Pentland [1986, 1990], Bajcsy and Solina [1987], Solina and Bajcsy [1990], Boult and Gross [1987, 1988], and Gupta et al. [1989] have demonstrated how superquadrics could be used as an effective representation mechanism in a vision system.

A two-dimensional quadric curve can be expressed in parametric form as follows:

$$\mathbf{x}(\eta) = (x(\eta), y(\eta)) = (a_1 \cos(\eta + \phi_0), a_2 \sin(\eta + \theta_0)) \qquad (4.7)$$

where $0 \leq \eta < 2\pi$ and ϕ_0 and θ_0 are constants. A two-dimensional superquadric curve is a generalization of the two-dimensional quadric curve and is given by

$$\mathbf{x}(\eta, \epsilon) = (x(\eta, \epsilon), y(\eta, \epsilon)) = (a_1 \cos^\epsilon(\eta + \phi_0), a_2 \sin^\epsilon(\eta + \theta_0)) \qquad (4.8)$$

where ϵ is referred to as a *shape parameter*. For example, a superellipse is given by the parametric equation

$$\mathbf{x}(\eta, \epsilon) = (x(\eta, \epsilon), y(\eta, \epsilon)) = (a_1 \cos^\epsilon(\eta), a_2 \sin^\epsilon(\eta)) \qquad (4.9)$$

or by the implicit form

$$\left(\frac{x}{a_1}\right)^{\frac{2}{\epsilon}} + \left(\frac{y}{a_2}\right)^{\frac{2}{\epsilon}} = 1 \qquad (4.10)$$

For $\epsilon = 1$ the superellipse is a regular ellipse (Figure 4.11). As ϵ is varied from 1 to 0, the superellipse becomes progressively squarish. As ϵ is varied from 1 to 2, the ellipse is transformed into a diamond-shaped bevel. As ϵ assumes values

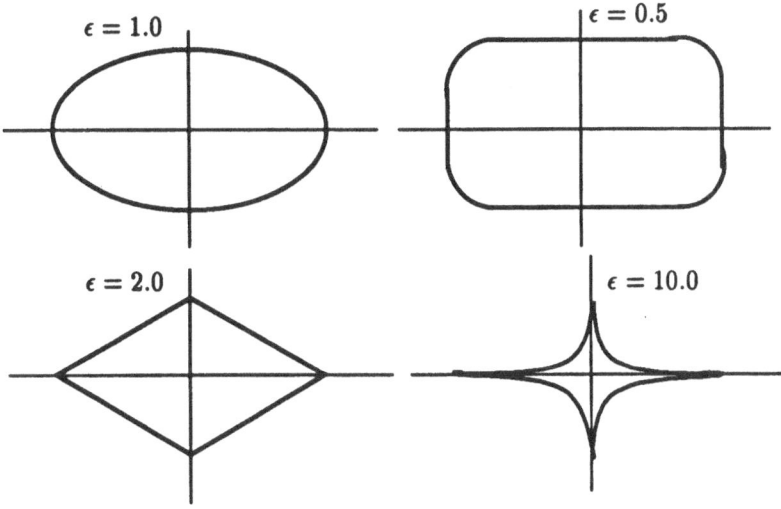

Figure 4.11: Effect of changing ϵ on the shape of a superellipse.

greater than 2, the shape becomes pinched, and, finally, the shape becomes a
cross when ϵ approaches ∞.

The *spherical product* of two two-dimensional curves, $\mathbf{x}(\omega) = (x_1(\omega), x_2(\omega))$,
$\omega_0 \leq \omega \leq \omega_1$ and $\mathbf{y}(\eta) = (y_1(\eta), y_2(\eta))$, $\eta_0 \leq \eta \leq \eta_1$ denoted by $\mathbf{x}(\omega) \otimes \mathbf{y}(\eta)$ is
a surface defined by the equation

$$\mathbf{x}(\omega) \otimes \mathbf{y}(\eta) = \mathbf{S}(\omega, \eta) = (x_1(\omega)y_1(\eta), x_1(\omega)y_2(\eta), x_2(\omega)) \qquad (4.11)$$

A superquadric surface is the spherical product of two two-dimensional superquadric curves and is given by

$$\mathbf{S}(\omega, \eta) = (a_1 \cos^{\epsilon_1}(\omega) \cos^{\epsilon_2}(\eta), a_2 \cos^{\epsilon_1}(\omega) \sin^{\epsilon_2}(\eta), a_3 \sin^{\epsilon_1}(\omega)) \qquad (4.12)$$

$$\text{where } \frac{-\pi}{2} \leq \omega \leq \frac{\pi}{2}, \ -\pi \leq \eta \leq \pi$$

or by the implicit form

$$\left(\left(\frac{x}{a_1} \right)^{\frac{2}{\epsilon_2}} + \left(\frac{y}{a_2} \right)^{\frac{2}{\epsilon_2}} \right)^{\frac{\epsilon_2}{\epsilon_1}} + \left(\frac{z}{a_3} \right)^{\frac{2}{\epsilon_1}} = 1 \qquad (4.13)$$

The parameters a_1, a_2, and a_3 determine the size of the superquadric in the x,
y and z directions, respectively, in the object-centered coordinate frame of reference. The parameters ϵ_1 and ϵ_2 represent the shape parameters in the latitudinal
(xz) and longitudinal (xy) directions respectively. Varying the parameters allows us to model a variety of shapes such as spheres, cones, cylinders, ellipsoids,

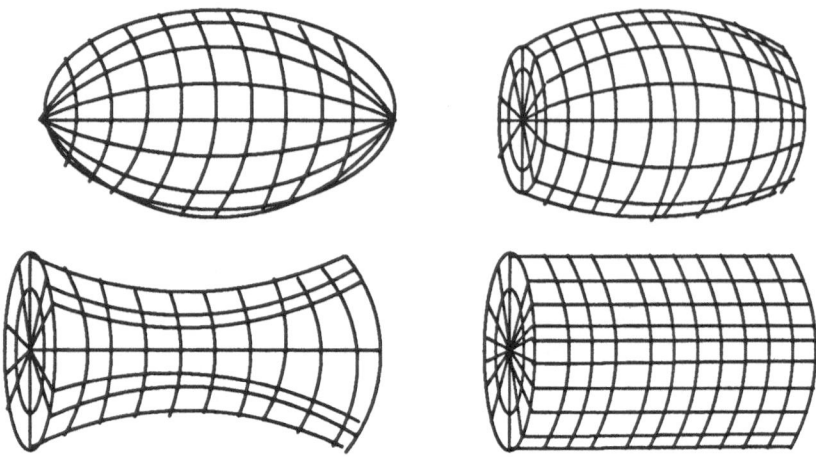

Figure 4.12: Effect of changing ϵ_1 and ϵ_2 on the shape of a superellipsoid

and rectangular parallelepipeds. Figure 4.12 shows how the shape parameters affect the shape of a superellipsoid. Superquadrics define a closed volume with a well defined inside-out function:

$$f(x, y, z) = \left(\left(\frac{x}{a_1} \right)^{\frac{2}{\epsilon_2}} + \left(\frac{y}{a_2} \right)^{\frac{2}{\epsilon_2}} \right)^{\frac{\epsilon_2}{\epsilon_1}} + \left(\frac{z}{a_3} \right)^{\frac{2}{\epsilon_1}} \quad (4.14)$$

where

$$f(x, y, z) \begin{cases} = 1 & \text{if } (x, y, z) \text{ is on the superquadric surface boundary} \\ < 1 & \text{if } (x, y, z) \text{ is inside the superquadric surface boundary} \\ > 1 & \text{if } (x, y, z) \text{ is outside the superquadric surface boundary} \end{cases} \quad (4.15)$$

The representational power of superquadrics can be further enhanced by incorporating deformation parameters to the basic superquadric model. *Tapering* and *bending* are used to derive secondary shapes from a basic superquadric.

Tapering. If a tapering function f is applied along the z axis, then the points on the surface of a basic superquadric $\mathbf{S}(x, y, z)$ are transformed into points on the surface of a tapered superquadric $\mathbf{S}'(x', y', z')$, where the transformation is given by

$$\begin{aligned} x' &= f_x(z)x \\ y' &= f_y(z)y \\ z' &= z \end{aligned} \quad (4.16)$$

For *linear* tapering

$$f_x(z) = \frac{K_x}{a_3}z + 1, \quad -1 \le K_x \le 1$$

$$f_y(z) = \frac{K_y}{a_3}z + 1, \quad -1 \le K_y \le 1 \qquad (4.17)$$

where K_x, K_y represent the tapering in the xy plane relative to the z axis.

Bending. A bending plane is defined by the coordinate axis z and the vector r in the xy plane, whose direction is defined by the angle α. The bending deformation is performed by projecting the x and y components of all points onto the bending plane, performing the bending deformation in that plane, and back-projecting the points to the original plane. The projection of a point (x, y) on the bending plane is

$$r = \cos(\alpha - \beta)\sqrt{x^2 + y^2} \qquad (4.18)$$

where

$$\beta = \tan^{-1}\left(\frac{y}{x}\right) \qquad (4.19)$$

The bending transforms r into

$$r' = \frac{1}{k} - \left(\frac{1}{k} - r\right)\cos\gamma \qquad (4.20)$$

where γ is the bending angle computed from the curvature parameter k

$$\gamma = \frac{z}{k} \qquad (4.21)$$

By projecting r' back to the original plane, the bending deformation of the superquadric $S(x, y, z)$ to the deformed superquadric $S'(x', y', z')$ is given by the transformation:

$$x' = x + (r' - r)\cos\alpha$$
$$y' = y + (r' - r)\sin\alpha$$
$$z' = (\frac{1}{k} - r)\sin\gamma \qquad (4.22)$$

The bending function is therefore specified by the parameters k and α.

A deformed superquadric in a general position with rotation and translation is given by

$$S' = Translation(Rotation(Bending(Tapering(S))))$$

The inside-out function of a deformed superquadric in a general position can be expressed as

$$f'(x, y, z) = f(x, y, z, a_1, a_2, a_3, \epsilon_1, \epsilon_2, p_x, p_y, p_z, \phi, \theta, \psi, K_x, K_y, k, \alpha) \qquad (4.23)$$

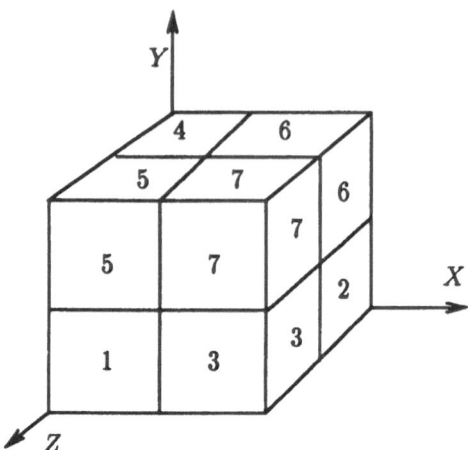

Figure 4.13: Labeling of suboctants in a parent octant.

where $(a_1, a_2, a_3, \epsilon_1, \epsilon_2)$ are the shape parameters, (p_x, p_y, p_z) specify the translation parameters along each of the coordinate axes, (ϕ, θ, ψ) are the *Euler* angles that specify the rotation about each of the coordinate axes, (K_x, K_y) are the tapering deformation parameters, and (k, α) are the bending deformation parameters. Thus, only 15 parameters are needed to model a wide variety of three-dimensional shapes. The segmentation needed for a superquadric representation is minimal. Knowing the values for depth at a sufficient number of pixel locations is all that is needed for single object scenes. For multiple object scenes, it would first be necessary to segment the range image into surface patches belonging to a single object before considering the depth values at those pixel locations. In certain cases, the direction of the surface normal along the occluding contour is also needed and can easily be estimated.

4.9 Octree Representation

The *octree* representation is based on a recursive subdivision of 3-D Euclidean space into *cubes* or *octants*. The octree space is modeled as a cubical region consisting of $2^n \times 2^n \times 2^n$ unit cubes, where n is the resolution parameter and 2^n is the length of the octree. For a given three-dimensional object, each cube can be assigned a value of 0 or 1, depending on whether it is inside or outside the volume bound by the object. The octree representation is obtained by recursively subdividing the cubic space into octants. A $2^d \times 2^d \times 2^d$, $1 \le d \le n$, octant is divided into eight $2^{d-1} \times 2^{d-1} \times 2^{d-1}$ smaller octants if not all the eight octants are $0's$ or $1's$. The subdivision process is carried out recursively until each octant contains suboctants of a single value. Each suboctant generated from a parent

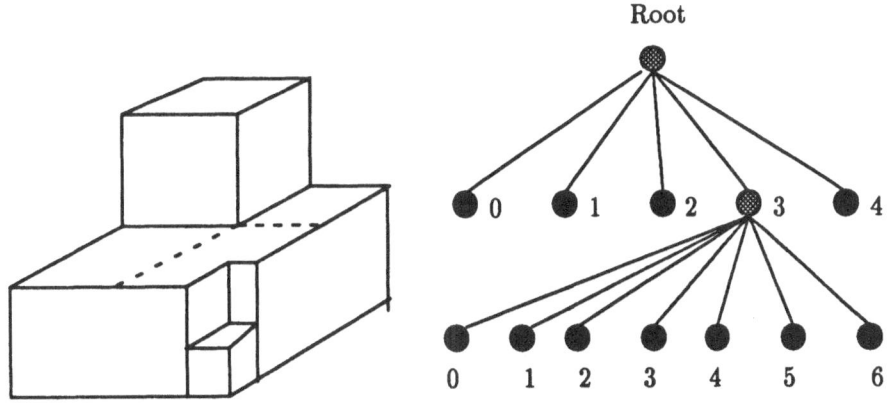

Figure 4.14: A three-dimensional object and its octree representation.

octant is assigned an octal label from 0 to 7 (Figure 4.13). This label reflects the *relative* position of the suboctant to the parent octant from which it is generated.

The result of the recursive subdivision process is represented as a tree of degree 8 whose nodes are either leaves or have eight children. The tree is referred to as an *octree*. Leaf nodes in the tree are marked 0 or 1, whereas internal nodes are marked I. In many cases the leaf nodes marked 0 are not shown. Figure 4.14 shows a three-dimensional object and its octree representation. The length of a $2^d \times 2^d \times 2^d$ octant is defined to be 2^d. The depth of the node in the octree corresponding to this octant is $(n-d)$. To specify the global position of an octant in space, we can set up a coordinate system such that one corner of the octree space is at the origin and three of its edges lie on the positive x, y and z axis, respectively. Thus any octant can be represented by its size and the location of one of its vertices. The vertex chosen for this purpose is the one closest to the origin. This representation scheme can be made more compact by using a *binary address* of the form

$$[X_1 X_2 \cdots X_d; \ Y_1 Y_2 \cdots Y_d; \ Z_1 Z_2 \cdots Z_d] \qquad (4.24)$$

for the vertex of the octant of size $(n-d)$. The depth d does not have to be explicitly stated, since it is embedded in the length of the binary address.

If $(P_{d,x}, P_{d,y}, P_{d,z})$ is the position of a suboctant within its parent octant, where $P_{d,x}, P_{d,y}, P_{d,z}$ are three binary digits, and d is the depth of the suboctant, then the octal label of the suboctant is

$$P_d = P_{d,z} 2^2 + P_{d,y} 2^1 + P_{d,x} \qquad (4.25)$$

Any node in the octree can be specified by a path P originating from the root of the tree and terminating on that node. The path P can be represented as a sequence of octal labels of the nodes that lie on P:

$$P = P_1 P_2 \cdots P_d \qquad (4.26)$$

If the octal label P_i has the binary form $(P_{i,x}, P_{i,y}, P_{i,z})$, then the binary address of the node is

$$[P_{1,x} P_{2,x} \cdots P_{d,x}; P_{1,y} P_{2,y} \cdots P_{d,y}; P_{1,z} P_{2,z} \cdots P_{d,z}] \qquad (4.27)$$

Alternatively, given the binary address of an octant, we can compute the sequence of octal labels along the path from the root node to the corresponding node in the octree. To check if a particular point is within the volume bound by a 3-D object, we must convert the coordinates of the point to the corresponding octal code and check if the corresponding node in the octree is marked 1 or 0.

An excellent survey of algorithms for the construction and manipulation of octrees can be found in Chen and Huang [1988]. There are several algorithms based on ray-tracing and z-buffer techniques for the rendering of octree representations of three-dimensional objects [Jacklins and Tanimoto 1980] [Meagher 1982a]. Algorithms for rotation, translation, clipping, and scaling of octree representations of three-dimensional objects are also fairly common [Meagher 1982b] [Gargantini 1982] [Yamaguchi et al. 1984] [Samet 1990]. In the area of CAD/CAM the research is focused on the conversion of other representations such as CSG representation [Lee and Requicha 1982], boundary representation [Tamminen et al. 1984], and cylinder representation [Requicha 1980] to the equivalent octree representation, and vice versa. In the area of computer vision there are several algorithms for generating octree descriptions from two-dimensional projections [Chien and Aggarwal 1985] [Veenstra and Ahuja 1986], silhouette images [Martin and Aggarwal 1983], 3-D arrays [Samet 1980], and quadtrees of volume sections [Yau 1984]. There also exist algorithms for generating octrees from range images. There are several alternative ways of generating an octree description from the range image(s) of an object. One class of techniques generates the 3-D arrays from the range image and then computes the octree representation. Another class of techniques segments the range data into primitive surface patches and converts the surface description to an octree representation. The corresponding surface patches in multiple views of an object are identified, and the octree is progressively refined by taking the intersection of the bounding volumes of the corresponding surface patches in each view.

Chien and Aggarwal [1985] and Chien et al. [1988] have described how the inertia matrices of a three-dimensional object can be computed from an octree representation. Computation of an inertia matrix requires that the second-order moments of the three-dimensional object be computed, which can be done directly from the octree representation. The directions along the eigenvectors of the inertia matrix denote the principal viewing directions of the object. The two-dimensional projections of the object along the principal viewing directions–termed as *principal projections*–are invariant to rigid body motion in Euclidean space. The principal views of an object model can be stored in memory. Multiple views of an object from range images can be used to generate the octree and the principal projections. The principal projections of the object in the scene can then be matched with those of the object models. If a match of sufficiently high degree is found, then the identity of the object in the scene can be determined. Alternatively, the three-dimensional moment invariants of the object can be computed from its octree representation and matched with those of the object models as proposed by Sadjadi and Hall [1980].

4.10 Summary

There exist several representation schemes in computer vision. Each representation scheme entails a certain feature extraction process. For the purpose of matching, it is essential that the features extracted from the object model be identical to those extracted from the image. In this sense, the representation and feature extraction are inseparable. Volumetric representations like the octree require global features such as moment invariants. Comparison of global features enables rapid recognition in situations where there is little or no occlusion. Presence of partial occlusion, commonly encountered in multiple-object scenes, renders the use of global features ineffective. The aspect graph representation allows the use of local features in the form of smooth surface patches and significant surface discontinuities. However, recognition procedures that use local features tend to be slow unless suitable parallel hardware is used. In general, representations used in graphics and CAD/CAM, such as CSG, are more suited for rendering or display algorithms and often do not incorporate the discriminatory information needed for recognition purposes. There have been recent attempts to automate the process of conversion of representations generated by CAD/CAM packages into relational graph theoretic descriptions suitable for visual recognition [Flynn and Jain 1991a]. The choice of representation granularity (i.e., local vs. global features) is crucial to the process of recognition. In practice, the choice of representation has been largely application dependent, resulting in a wide variety of representation schemes encountered in the literature.

Chapter 5

Recognition and Localization Techniques

Having obtained a feature-level description of the scene, the next step is matching these features with those computed from the internal representation of the object models. The purpose of the matching process is two-fold—first, to label the features in the scene as an instance of an object model and, second, to determine the position and orientation of the object in the scene with respect to a reference coordinate frame. The process of labeling scene features as having arisen from a particular object model is referred to as *recognition*, whereas determining the position and orientation of an object in the scene is referred to as *localization*. In fact, most matching techniques treat recognition and localization as two inseparable issues of the same overall problem, to the extent that the term *recognition* is often used to denote both *recognition* and *localization*.

5.1 Recognition and Localization Techniques— An Overview

The process of recognition and localization can be treated as a *consistent labeling* or a *constraint satisfaction* problem. There are two broad paradigms for constraint satisfaction used in computer vision that differ in the manner in which they deal with the twin issues of recognition and localization—*recognition-followed-by-localization* and *recognition-via-localization*. In the recognition-followed-by-localization paradigm, a relational or graph-theoretic description of the scene is matched against a similar description of the object model(s). In the recognition phase, the components of the scene graph are labeled as instances of object model graphs. Recognition is typically based on graph-theoretic techniques such as sub-graph isomorphism or maximal clique detection. After the recognition phase, the localization phase uses either global shape descriptors or object-specific features to compute the location and orientation of the object. The recognition-followed-by-localization approach enables rapid recognition in those situations where the scene graph can be easily labeled—for example, single-object scenes or multiple-object scenes with little or no occlusion. In multiple-object scenes with substantial partial occlusion, however, global shape descriptors or object-specific features get so distorted as to become inapplicable. On the other hand, in the recognition-via-localization paradigm, primitive geometric features that are invariant to viewpoint are extracted from the scene. These features are matched against similar features from the object model representation. Matches are checked for local consistency using simple geometric constraints such as distance and angle measurements. A set of locally consistent matches is then determined using a constraint propagation procedure that propagates the local constraints. A global solution to the recognition problem is then determined from the set(s) of locally consistent matches. Since the features used in the recognition-via-localization paradigm are primitive, they tend to be generic (i.e., capable of modeling a wide class of solid objects) and also have local support, which ensures robustness to occlusion. The disadvantage is that since local constraints must be propagated, the recognition and localization process tends to be slow, especially when implemented on a conventional uniprocessor architecture.

In either paradigm, recognition-via-localization or recognition-followed-by-localization, a scene interpretation can be looked upon as a solution to a constraint satisfaction problem. The problem of arriving at a consistent scene interpretation could therefore be viewed as a constraint-directed search through the space of possible scene interpretations. Three-dimensional object recognition systems can be classified according to the search strategy used:

1. *Model-driven search.* Used when the identity of the object is known *a priori.* Issues regarding what object model features to use and the order in which they are to be matched with corresponding features in the scene are governed largely by the nature of the representation of the object model. Consequently, the recognition and localization process can be tailored to a specific object model, making it fast and efficient. A model-driven search is an effective strategy when the recognition is *goal-driven,* i.e., the goal of a vision system is recognizing certain specific objects in a scene. A model-driven search is commonly used for bin-picking tasks.

2. *Data-driven search.* Used when few assumptions can be made about the nature of the scene. The constraints used in the search are generic in that they make only general assumptions about the physical and geometrical properties of the scene and the imaging process. The fact that the assumptions made in a data-driven search are not too restrictive makes it better suited for general three-dimensional scene interpretation. A data-driven search proceeds in a strictly bottom-up manner through the various phases of three-dimensional scene interpretation, i.e., image preprocessing, segmentation, feature extraction, and recognition. Data-driven search strategy, although having wider applicability, is slow and inefficient for a problem with a specific purpose, since the generic constraints tend to be

weak in their ability to prune the search space.

3. *Interpretive search strategy.* An interpretive control strategy uses the object model interpretively, that is, the knowledge extracted from the model is transformed into an execution strategy at run time. The system relies on a generic constraint propagation mechanism such as numerical optimization, constraint satisfaction by symbolic reasoning, or a tree search by hypothesize-and-test. An interpretive system sacrifices speed for generality and flexibility.

4. *Precompiled search strategy.* Relevant control knowledge is embedded in the object model and compiled into a recognition strategy *off line*. As a result, little computation is needed during the process of recognition. The advantage of precompilation is that recognition is fast, but at the cost of loss of generality.

5. *Centralized search strategy.* The search process is controlled by a single control *module* or *agent* that decides upon how the most promising portion of the search tree should be explored. It chooses the nodes in the search tree that need to be expanded and the order in which the expansion should be scheduled. A centralized search strategy is most naturally implemented on a conventional uniprocessor architecture. Most existing three-dimensional vision systems employ a centralized search strategy.

6. *Distributed search strategy.* The search is carried out *collectively* or *cooperatively* by a group of *autonomous* agents. The agents may communicate with each other to share data or partial results. Significant advantages of a distributed search strategy are increased fault tolerance and its inherent parallelism. Distributed search strategies can be implemented on SIMD and MIMD multiprocessor architectures. However, crucial design issues such as the nature of interaction between agents, means of communication between agents, stability of the system, and convergence to a solution need to be addressed.

Some of the most commonly used recognition and localization techniques for three-dimensional object recognition from range images are reviewed below and analyzed for their advantages and shortcomings.

5.2 Interpretation Tree Search

The *interpretation tree* (IT) search has been one of the most popular and widely used constraint propagation techniques for object recognition and localization within the recognition-via-localization paradigm. Given a set of scene features $S = \{s_i, \ 1 \leq i \leq N\}$ and a set of model features $\mathcal{M} = \{m_j, \ 1 \leq j \leq M\}$, a match of a scene feature s_i with a model feature m_j is represented by a node (s_i, m_j) in the interpretation tree (Figure 5.1). The branching factor of the tree is M where the children of the node (s_i, m_j) are the nodes

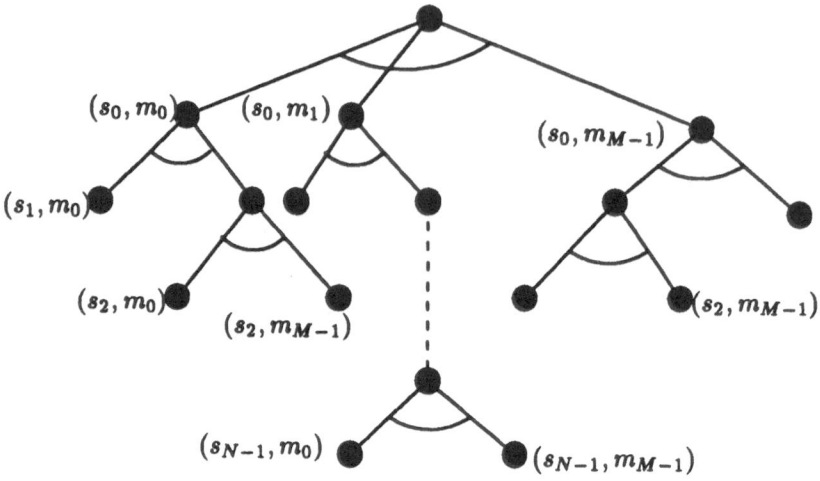

Figure 5.1: An interpretation tree search.

$(s_{i+1}, m_1), (s_{i+1}, m_2), ..., (s_{i+1}, m_M)$. The root node being at level 0, the interpretation tree has N levels and M^N leaf nodes. A *locally* consistent set of pairings, $\mathcal{I} = \{(s_i, m_j); 1 \leq i \leq M, 1 \leq j \leq N\}$, is called a *locally valid scene interpretation* and is represented by a path in the interpretation tree from the root node to one of the leaf nodes. A locally valid scene interpretation has to be checked for *global* consistency before it can be accepted as a *globally valid scene interpretation*.

To determine the local consistency of scene feature-model feature pairings, unary and binary constraints on local feature measurements are used. The scene feature-model feature pairings generated during the course of interpretation tree search are subjected to these local constraints. Higher order constraints (i.e., ternary, quaternary, and so on) are possible, but in practice, unary and binary constraints have been found to be adequate for most problems. Local constraints can be used to selectively prune the interpretation tree so that the entire interpretation tree does not have to be explored in order to arrive at a *locally valid scene interpretation*.

A unary constraint is of the form $match(s_i, m_j)$, which is *true* if the scene feature s_i can be matched to the model feature m_j, and *false* otherwise. Nodes that are found to satisfy all possible unary constraints are retained for further expansion, whereas those found to be inconsistent with any of the unary constraints are pruned. Typical unary constraints are attributes based on the three-dimensional shape of the scene and model features. It is desirable that the attributes be viewpoint-independent and robust to occlusion so that unary constraints based on *equality* of feature attributes can be derived. For example, qualitative curvature attributes (spherical, cylindrical, etc.) are viewpoint-independent and can be used to formulate a unary constraint requiring the scene feature s_i to have the same qualitative curvature attribute as model feature m_j if they are to be matched. Viewpoint-dependent features or features that are not robust to occlusion, on the other hand, are typically metric and can be used in deriving unary constraints based on *inequality*. For example, in the case of linear features, the unary constraint based on length, the inequality $length(s_i) \leq length(m_j)$, is justified since the scene feature s_i could be occluded. Unary constraints based on equality are more effective than ones based on inequality in terms of their ability to prune the interpretation tree. Checking for the validity of a unary constraint is also referred to as checking for *node consistency*.

A binary constraint is of the form $match((s_i, m_j), (s_k, m_l))$, which is *true* if the scene feature-model feature pairs (s_i, m_j) and (s_k, m_l) satisfy the binary constraint, and *false* otherwise. A node (s_i, m_j) in the interpretation tree has to be checked for all possible binary constraints with the nodes (s_k, m_l); $1 \leq k \leq i - 1$, that is, all nodes along the path from the root node to the node under consideration. Binary constraints arise from relational attributes. If the scene features s_i and s_k are related via a relational attribute R, i.e., $(s_i, s_k) \in R$, then the model features m_j and m_l need also be similarly related, i.e., $(m_l, m_j) \in R$ in order to satisfy the binary constraint $match((s_i, m_j), (s_k, m_l))$. As in the case of unary constraints, it is desirable that the relational attributes underlying the binary constraints be viewpoint-independent and robust to occlusion. Checking for the validity of a binary constraint is also referred to as checking for *arc consistency*.

Recognition and localization via interpretation tree search consists of the following three subproblems:

1. Selecting an appropriate object model from a library of object models.

2. Arriving at a locally valid interpretation through searching the interpretation tree.

3. Computing the rigid-body transformation that would place the object model in registration with the scene features.

The size of the search space for selecting an appropriate object model is dependent on the number of object models K in the object model library. For a data-directed search of the interpretation tree with M model features and N scene features, the size of the search space of scene interpretations is M^N, whereas for a model-directed search it is N^M. The size of the search space for estimating the rigid-body transform $\mathbf{T}$ is given by

$$\mathcal{R}^{\mathbf{T}} = \mathcal{R}^3 \times [0, 2\pi] \times [0, 2\pi] \times [0, 2\pi] \qquad (5.1)$$

where $\mathcal{R}^3$ is the three-dimensional Euclidean space of all possible translations, and $[0, 2\pi]$ is the space of all possible angular orientations for each of the *Euler* angles of rotation ϕ, ψ and θ about the x, y, and z axis, respectively. The size of the overall search space is therefore $K \times M^N \times \mathcal{R}^{\mathbf{T}}$ or $K \times N^M \times \mathcal{R}^{\mathbf{T}}$ which, in either case, is of exponential complexity.

Grimson and Lozano-Perez [1984, 1987] have proposed a constrained search of an interpretation tree in order to arrive at a locally valid interpretation using a simple *generate-and-test* control strategy. In particular, Grimson [1986] has shown how the use of simple unary and binary constraints can reduce the complexity of the search from exponential to $O(M^2)$ in the case of single-object scenes when the scene features are in the form of sparse depth and surface orientation measurements, typical of tactile range sensors. To account for multiple object scenes, Grimson [1990] assigns a null feature ϕ to each object model. Matching a scene feature to the null feature ϕ of an object model is tantamount to saying that the particular scene feature cannot be considered as having arisen from an instance of the object model under consideration. The match of a scene feature to the null feature of an object model is not checked for the unary and binary constraints. In the case of multiple-object scenes with occlusion and clutter, the complexity of interpretation tree search using simple unary and binary constraints was found to be of $O(M^N)$, which is of an exponential order. When a locally valid interpretation is determined via interpretation tree search, the global transformation **T** that would place the object model in registration with the object in the scene is determined. The locally valid interpretation is deemed to be globally consistent if all the transformed model features are in registration with the corresponding scene features within the bounds of error for the computation of the transform.

Chen and Kak [1989] in their vision system 3D-POLY, Flynn and Jain [1991b] in their vision system BONSAI, and Faugeras and Herbert [1986] in their experiments in 3-D object recognition from range data, have modified the constrained search so as to allow for premature verification of a partial scene interpretation before a leaf node in the interpretation tree is encountered. Chen and Kak define a hypothesis generating feature (HGF) set containing certain locally connected scene and model features. A match between the features of a scene HGF set with those of a model HGF set allows us to compute the rigid-body transformation that would place the object model in registration with the objects in the scene. Searching an interpretation tree is carried out in two phases: (1) a hypothesis generation phase in which the HGF set and the corresponding pose hypothesis is generated, and (2) a hypothesis verification phase in which the pose hypothesis is verified. If the hypothesis is generated via an exhaustive enumeration process, the complexity of the hypothesis generation phase is $O(M^h)$ where h is the size of the HGF set, which is equal to 3 in most cases. If hypothesis verification is done via an exhaustive enumeration of all possible matches of M model features with N scene features, then the complexity of the hypothesis verification phase is $O(NM)$. Thus a brute force approach would result in an $O(NM^{h+1})$ overall complexity for the interpretation tree search process. However, Chen and Kak have shown how the use of attribute (unary) constraints and relational (binary) constraints can reduce the complexity of the hypothesis generation phase to $O(M)$. Once the rigid-body transformation is computed at the end of the hypothesis generation phase, it can be used to constrain the relative orientations of the scene and model features with respect to the corresponding features in the HGF set. Typical orientation constraints in 3D-POLY are the directions of the

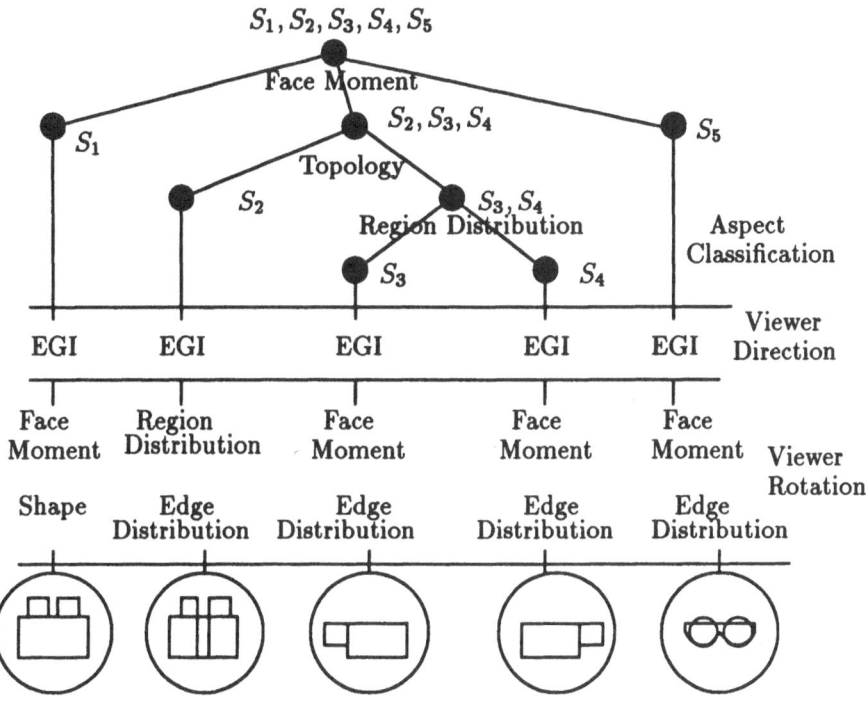

Figure 5.2: Precompiled interpretation tree search.

axes of conical and cylindrical surfaces, direction of the surface normal of planar surfaces, direction of linear features, and direction of the position vector of point features. Orientation constraints can be expressed as points on the surface of the Gaussian sphere which as in 3-D POLY, is referred to as a *feature sphere*. It can be shown that the complexity of hypothesis verification with orientation constraints is $O(N)$. Therefore, the overall complexity of the interpretation tree search is $O(NM)$.

The interpretation tree search techniques by Grimson, Chen and Kak, and Flynn and Jain are examples of an *interpretive* control strategy for object recognition and localization. Constraints derived from the object model are used at run time in conjunction with a generic constraint propagation technique based on a *hypothesize-and-test* paradigm. Interpretive techniques are flexible and have wider applicability, but tend to be slow for a problem with a specific purpose. Ikeuchi [1987], Ikeuchi and Kanade [1988], and Ikeuchi and Hong [1991] have demonstrated how a recognition strategy can be *compiled* off-line into an interpretation tree for object recognition in bin-picking tasks. Each object is modeled as a collection of aspects or characteristic views (Figure 5.2). The process of generating the interpretation tree consists of two phases: (1) decomposing the object model into its constituent aspects, and (2) determining the features needed to compute the orientation of the object model within the aspect. Aspects are defined based on face visibility. For an object with n faces, each aspect is assigned a binary n-tuple label $L = (l_1, l_2, l_3, \ldots l_n)$ where

$$l_i = \left\{ \begin{array}{ll} 1 & \text{if the } i^{th} \text{ face is visible in the aspect} \\ 0 & \text{otherwise} \end{array} \right. \tag{5.2}$$

The aspects of an object can be obtained by analytic means; however, the algorithm for doing so gets very complex for objects with a large number of faces. A more practical alternative is viewpoint sampling. The Gaussian sphere of viewpoints is tessellated into a finite number of cells and each cell is assigned a label based on the above mentioned criterion. Spatially connected cells on the surface of the Gaussian sphere that have the same labels are grouped into the same aspect.

The aspect classification phase of the interpretation tree generation process starts with all possible aspects at the root node. At each level of the interpretation tree a particular feature is used to split the set of aspects into two or more subsets such that one subset of aspects is distinguished from the other(s) by that feature. The aspect classification phase halts when each subset or node of the interpretation tree contains a single aspect. The orientation computation phase records, at each leaf node of the interpretation tree, the features needed to compute the exact orientation of that particular aspect. The features, such as moments of inertia of the visible faces, inter-face relationships, and face-edge relationships, can be used for aspect classification, whereas distinctive features within an aspect, such as the magnitude and direction of moments of inertia of significant faces and the EGI of the aspect, are used to compute the orientation of the particular aspect.

Object recognition proceeds in two phases: first, the aspect of the object is determined using the aspect classification portion of the interpretation tree, and second, the distinctive features within the aspect are used to compute the orientation of the object. Since the interpretation tree can be generated (or compiled) for each object model off-line, the interpretation tree search process is essentially model-driven. However, the precompiled interpretation tree search procedure assumes that the identity of the object in the scene is known *a priori* and the role of the vision system is limited to computing the orientation of the predetermined object (i.e., the vision system is goal-driven). Ikeuchi has used the precompiled interpretation tree search procedure for bin-picking tasks that are largely goal-driven, but the applicability of precompiled interpretation tree search for general purpose 3-D scene interpretation has not yet been fully explored.

5.3   Hough Clustering

The Hough transform or Hough clustering, as originally proposed by Hough [1962], was for the detection of straight line segments in an image. If the equation

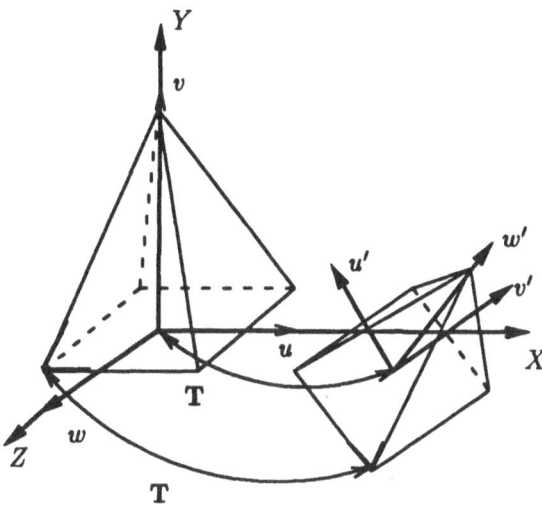

Figure 5.3: Determining the object pose by a rigid-body transform.

of a straight line in the x, y plane is given by

$$x \cos \theta + y \sin \theta = \rho \qquad (5.3)$$

the parameters (ρ, θ) of all the possible lines that pass through a given point (x_0, y_0) in the xy plane form a sinusoidal curve in the (ρ, θ) space. This sinusoidal curve in the (ρ, θ) space is the *Hough image* of the point (x_0, y_0) in the image plane. The Hough transform can thus be looked upon as a mapping from the xy plane to the parameter space or Hough space (ρ, θ). The sinusoidal curves of all the points that lie on a single line in the xy plane intersect in a single point in the (ρ, θ) space. If the (ρ, θ) space is discretized in the form of an array (referred to as the Hough array or Hough accumulator), then each image pixel (x, y) can cast a *vote* for the appropriate locations or bins in the Hough array that correspond to the parameters (ρ, θ) of all the possible lines that pass through the point (x, y). A line segment in the xy plane, characterized by parameters (ρ_0, θ_0), would result in a large number of votes cast by the points on that line segment in the bin corresponding to the parameters (ρ_0, θ_0) in the Hough array. Thus the problem of line detection in the xy plane has been effectively translated to that of detecting maxima or peaks in the Hough array. The Hough transform for line detection has been generalized to detect features with parametric descriptions such as circles and ellipses. As the features become more complex, the number of parameters needed to describe them increases, resulting in a Hough space of higher dimensions. The basic principle of vote accumulation and maxima detection in the Hough space, however, remains the same.

Hough clustering, or the generalized Hough transform for 3-D object recognition and localization, is based on the same principle as the conventional Hough transform for feature detection. Given a set of scene features $S = \{s_i, 1 \leq i \leq N\}$ and a set of model features $M = \{m_j, 1 \leq j \leq M\}$, a match of a scene feature s_i with a model feature m_j, denoted by (s_i, m_j), is used to compute a rigid-body transform $T_{i,j}$ that would place the model feature m_j in registration with the scene feature s_i (Figure 5.3). The scene and model features are so chosen that computation of the rigid-body transform is possible for a successful match. Such features are referred to as *transform generating features* (TGF's). Matches of scene and model features can be constrained by local length and angle measurements that are viewpoint-invariant. In the case of a two-dimensional image with two-dimensional object models, the transform $T_{i,j}$ has three degrees of freedom—two translational degrees of freedom in the xy image plane along each of the x and y coordinate axes, and one rotational degree of freedom about the z axis that is perpendicular to the xy image plane. In the case of a range image with three-dimensional object models, the transform has six degrees of freedom—three translational degrees of freedom t_x, t_y, and t_z along the x, y and z coordinate axes, respectively, and three rotational degrees of freedom characterized by Euler angles of rotation ψ, η and θ about the x, y and z coordinate axes, respectively. The transform can thus be mapped to a point in parameter (Hough) space where each parameter denotes a degree of freedom associated with the transform. Under the constraint of rigidity, a cluster in transform space would indicate the identity and pose of the object. If a discrete version of the transform space in the form of a Hough accumulator composed of a finite number of bins is considered, then each computed transform $T_{i,j}$ can be made to cast its vote in the appropriate bin. The bin containing the maximum number of votes would then indicate the identity and pose of the object.

Stockman [1987] has discussed various aspects of Hough clustering for the recognition and localization of three-dimensional polyhedral objects. Local sets of primitive features such as, (1) pairs of noncollinear straight edge segments, (2) triads of planar patches, no two of which are coplanar, and (3) a pair of two planar patches sharing one edge, can be used as TGF's. TGF's extracted from the scene are matched with those from the object model to compute the rigid-body transform. Umeyama et al. [1988] use pairs of adjacent planar facets as TGF's for polyhedral objects. The angle between the normals to the planar facets and the areas of the planar facets are constraints to be used when matching scene and model features. Rotation is computed by aligning the surface normals in the scene TGF with those in the corresponding model TGF. Translation is computed by aligning the corresponding edges of the matched scene and model facets.

Dhome and Kasvand [1987], in their experiments on polyhedral object recognition using Hough clustering, also use pairs of adjacent planar facets as TGF's. The angle between the normals to the planar facets is used to constrain scene-model feature matches. Rotation is determined in two steps: (1) determining the view axis, and (2) determining the orientation around the view axis. Since the z axis in the scene is deemed to be the view axis, the view axis can be determined by identifying the axis in the model coordinate frame of reference

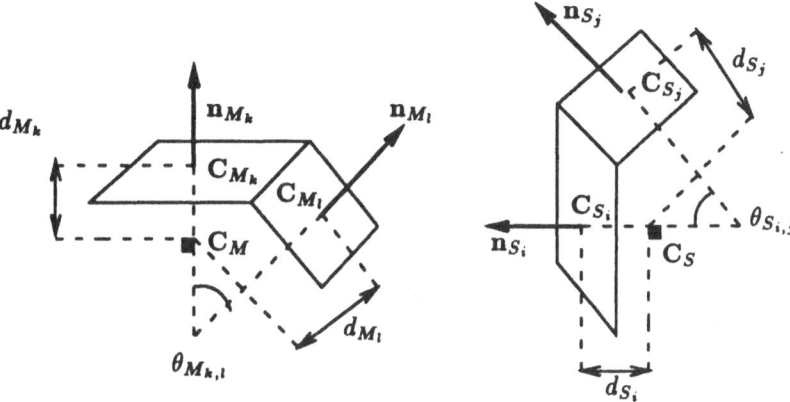

Figure 5.4: Model and scene TGF's for polyhedral objects.

that is equivalent to the z axis in the scene. Similarly, the orientation can be determined by identifying the axis in the model coordinate frame of reference that is equivalent to the x axis in the scene. The scene facet pair (S_i, S_j) is matched with the model facet pair (M_k, M_l) if $\theta_{S_{i,j}} = \theta_{M_{k,l}}$ (Figure 5.4). The view axis $\mathbf{V}_a$ is then determined by requiring that the projections of the model surface normals $\mathbf{n}_{S_i}$ and $\mathbf{n}_{S_j}$ on $\mathbf{V}_a$ be equal to the projections of the scene surface normals $\mathbf{n}_{M_k}$ and $\mathbf{n}_{M_l}$ on the z-axis $\mathbf{V}_z$. This results in the system of equations that can be solved for $\mathbf{V}_a = (V_{ax}, V_{ay}, V_{az})$.

$$
\begin{aligned}
\mathbf{n}_{M_k} \cdot \mathbf{V}_a &= \mathbf{n}_{S_i} \cdot \mathbf{V}_z \\
\mathbf{n}_{M_l} \cdot \mathbf{V}_a &= \mathbf{n}_{S_j} \cdot \mathbf{V}_z \\
(\mathbf{n}_{M_k} \times \mathbf{n}_{M_l}) \cdot \mathbf{V}_a &= (\mathbf{n}_{S_i} \times \mathbf{n}_{S_j}) \cdot \mathbf{V}_z
\end{aligned}
\tag{5.4}
$$

The orientation axis $\mathbf{V}_o$ is similarly determined by solving the following set of linear equations for $\mathbf{V}_o = (V_{ox}, V_{oy}, V_{oz})$

$$
\begin{aligned}
\mathbf{n}_{M_k} \cdot \mathbf{V}_o &= \mathbf{n}_{S_i} \cdot \mathbf{V}_x \\
\mathbf{n}_{M_l} \cdot \mathbf{V}_o &= \mathbf{n}_{S_j} \cdot \mathbf{V}_x \\
(\mathbf{n}_{M_k} \times \mathbf{n}_{M_l}) \cdot \mathbf{V}_o &= (\mathbf{n}_{S_i} \times \mathbf{n}_{S_j}) \cdot \mathbf{V}_x
\end{aligned}
\tag{5.5}
$$

The translation vector is determined by computing the location of the center of the model in the scene. If the centers of the scene surface patches S_i and S_j are C_{S_i} and C_{S_j}, respectively, in the scene coordinate frame of reference, and if the model center is located at distances d_{M_k} and d_{M_l} from the planes M_k and M_l, respectively, in the model coordinate frame of reference, then the location of the model center in the scene is determined as follows:

1. For each matched pair (S_i, S_j) and (M_k, M_l), the equations of the planes parallel to the planes S_i and S_j and located at distances d_{M_k} and d_{M_l} from C_{S_i} and C_{S_j}, respectively, are determined.

2. The above mentioned planes intersect in a line that passes through the model center. The equation of the line of intersection is determined from the equations of the above mentioned planes.

3. The intersection of all such non-parallel lines results in the coordinate values of the model center.

One salient feature of the technique used by Dhome and Kasvand is that the recognition problem has been decomposed into three independent Hough clustering problems, each of which is carried out in a parameter space of reduced dimensionality. This alleviates the problem of having to carry out the Hough clustering process in a high-dimensional parameter space. Object recognition by decomposed Hough clustering can be summarized as:

1. All possible matches of scene and model TGF's are generated.

2. Model view axis is computed for each successful match.

3. Parameters of the model view axis are clustered on the Gaussian sphere and the dominant clusters identified.

4. Model orientations around the view axis for the matches in the dominant clusters in 3 are computed.

5. Parameters of the model orientation axis are clustered on the Gaussian sphere and the dominant clusters identified.

6. Model centers are computed for the matches in the dominant clusters resulting from 5.

7. Model centers are clustered in a three-dimensional Hough space defined by the model center coordinates.

The pose hypothesis generated at the end of the Hough clustering process is verified by explicit depth comparison with the objects in the scene.

Krishnapuram and Casasent [1989] describe a three-dimensional Hough transform that is an extension of the conventional two-dimensional Hough transform for line detection. A series of unit vectors (Figure 5.5)

$$\mathbf{u}_n = \alpha_n \mathbf{i} + \beta_n \mathbf{j} + \gamma_n \mathbf{k} = (\xi_n, \eta_n) \tag{5.6}$$

in three-dimensional space are defined where $\sqrt{\alpha_n^2 + \beta_n^2 + \gamma_n^2} = 1$ and (ξ_n, η_n) are the spherical coordinates of the vector in terms of the polar and azimuthal angles. The points corresponding to the unit vectors $\mathbf{u}_n$ are uniformly distributed on the surface of the Gaussian sphere. The three-dimensional Hough transform for a point $\mathbf{x} = (x, y, z)$ in the range image is defined as

$$\rho_n = \mathbf{x} \cdot \mathbf{u}_n \tag{5.7}$$

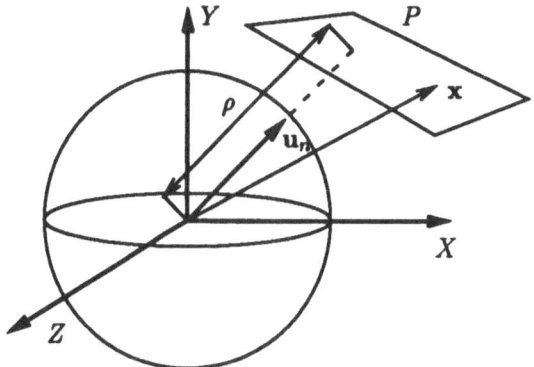

Figure 5.5: The 3-D Hough transform for detecting planes.

and is represented by a point in the (ρ_n, ξ_n, η_n) space. By the nature of this mapping, a plane with surface normal (ξ_0, η_0) and at a distance ρ_0 from the origin, will result in a maxima or peak at the point (ρ_0, ξ_0, η_0) in the Hough space. Krishnapuram and Casasent demonstrate the effect of scaling, rotation, and translation in the scene on the Hough image.

1. *Scaling.* If a point (x, y, z) is uniformly scaled to the point (sx, sy, sz), then the resulting Hough image H_s is related to the original Hough image H by the relation

$$H_s(\rho, \xi, \eta) = H\left(\frac{\rho}{s}, \xi, \eta\right) \tag{5.8}$$

The effect of scaling is thus either to stretch or collapse the 3-D Hough accumulator along the ρ index.

2. *Translation.* If a point (x, y, z) is translated to the point $(x - t_x, y - t_y, z - t_z)$, then the resulting Hough image is given by the relation

$$H_t(\rho, \xi, \eta) = \begin{cases} H(\rho - t \cdot u_n, \xi, \eta) & \text{if } t \cdot u_n < \rho \\ H(-\rho + t \cdot u_n, \xi, \eta) & \text{if } t \cdot u_n > \rho \end{cases} \tag{5.9}$$

Translation results in the shifting of the contents of the Hough accumulator along the ρ index. The extent of the shift is different for different vectors u_n.

3. *Rotation.* If a point $x = (x, y, z)$ is transformed by a rotation to a point $x' = Ax$ where A is the matrix of rotation, then the transformed image is

$$H_r(\rho, \xi, \eta) = H(\rho, \xi', \eta') \tag{5.10}$$

where $(\xi', \eta') = A^T(\xi, \eta)$. Rotation results in a uniform shift of the Hough accumulator along the indices (ξ, η) for all vectors u_n.

For each polyhedral object model the Hough image is computed for several characteristic views. The Hough image of the range image is computed using Eq. (5.7). Krishnapuram and Casasent present an algorithm by which the Hough image of the range image is systematically shifted and matched with the Hough images of the object models. A match of sufficient degree yields both the identity and pose of the object in the range image. The 3-D Hough transform is three-dimensional and, for a given resolution of the Hough accumulator array, requires less memory as compared to the generalized Hough transform, which is six-dimensional. Recognition and localization using a 3-D Hough transform entails extra processing in terms of shifting and matching operation as compared to the relatively simpler operation of maxima detection in the case of the generalized Hough transform. This is an example of the tradeoff between memory requirements and processing requirements that is typical of most computer algorithms. For single-object scenes the processing requirements of the 3-D Hough transform may be acceptable, but for multiple-object scenes it may turn out to be prohibitive.

In spite of its popularity, Hough clustering suffers from certain inherent drawbacks. Errors resulting from sensor inaccuracy and subsequent feature extraction cause a deviation of the computed transform from its true value. This in turn causes peaks in the Hough space to be *smeared* and thus harder to detect. Occlusion and clutter cause formation of spurious peaks in the Hough space arising out of accidental alignment of random features. If peaks in the Hough array are detected using classical feature vector clustering techniques, the resulting algorithms tend to be slow due to their iterative nature and are sensitive to the threshold values chosen for splitting or merging clusters. If a binning approach to peak detection is taken, then the choice of quantization of the Hough accumulator array is both critical and difficult. Too fine a quantization would result in fragmentation of the peaks into several bins and would also increase memory requirements. Too coarse a quantization would result in several peaks being placed in the same bin, resulting in loss of localization accuracy. One way of alleviating these problems is to employ a *coarse-to-fine* strategy for Hough clustering called a *hierarchical* generalized Hough transform. Starting with an initial coarse quantization, the bins containing votes above a certain threshold are selected and quantized at progressively finer resolutions at each successive iteration of the algorithm. Peaks detected at the finest possible resolution are then used to identify and localize the objects in the scene. As an alternative to binning, a hierarchical feature vector clustering technique could be used. One advantage of the generalized Hough transform is its potential for parallelization on fine-grained SIMD architecture. The hierarchical generalized Hough transform has also proven itself amenable to parallelization on the pyramidal architecture.

5.4   Matching of Relational Structures

Matching of relational structures in particular, *attributed relational graphs* (ARG's) has been a popular and well researched technique in structural pattern

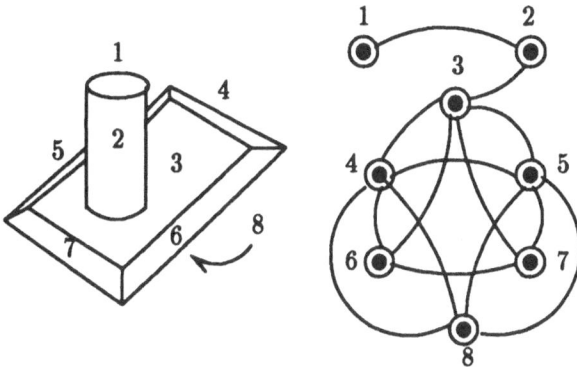

Figure 5.6: The ARG representation of a three-dimensional object.

recognition [Eshara and Fu 1984, 1988]. More recently it has also proved to be a valuable technique for three-dimensional object recognition from range data. In this section some of the basic concepts underlying recognition by matching ARG's are reviewed, along with their application to three-dimensional object recognition from range images.

An *attribute pair* is an ordered pair $a = (a_l, a_v)$ where a_l is an attribute label or attribute name describing the attribute and a_v is the value for that attribute—for example, *(Area, 3.0)*. An *attribute set* is a set of attribute pairs $\{a_1, a_2, \ldots, a_n\}$ where each a_i is an attribute pair. An *attributed vertex* v_i is a vertex with an associated attribute set called a *vertex attribute set*. An *attributed edge* $e_{i,j}$ is an edge between vertices v_i and v_j with an associated attribute set called an *edge attribute set*. An attributed edge is also referred to as an *attributed arc* or an *attributed relation*. If $e_{i,j} = e_{j,i}$ (i.e., possess the same attribute set), then the edge $e_{i,j}$ (or $e_{j,i}$) is said to be *undirected*. An ARG is a graph $G = (V, E)$, where $V = \{v_1, v_2, \ldots, v_n\}$ is a set of attributed vertices and $E = \{e_{i,j}\}$ is a set of attributed edges such that an attributed edge $e_{i,j}$ represents an attributed relation between the attributed vertices v_i and v_j. An ARG is said to be undirected if all of the edges in E are undirected and is possible iff the binary relation signified by the edges in E is symmetric. For most problems in computer vision or pattern recognition the ARG is assumed to be undirected.

If the scene features are organized in the form of an ARG, and so also the features derived from the object model, then the problem of recognition can be suitably paraphrased as matching of the scene ARG with the model ARG. In the context of three-dimensional object recognition from range images, it is typical for the vertices of the ARG to represent surface features, whereas the edges denote relationships between surface features (Figure 5.6). Given two primitive elements (i.e., vertices or edges) P_{si} and P_{mj} from the scene ARG and the model

ARG, respectively, P_{si} and P_{mj} are said to match completely iff

$$|A_{mi}^k - A_{sj}^k| < T_k \text{ for all attribute labels } k \text{ in the attribute set} \qquad (5.11)$$

where A_{si}^k is the value of the attribute with label k in the attribute set of P_{si} in the scene ARG, A_{mj}^k is the value of the corresponding attribute in the attribute list of P_{mj}, and T_k is a predefined threshold. Since it is possible for a feature in the object model not to appear in a scene due to occlusion, the feature in the object model can be deemed to match a *null* feature. So P_{si} and P_{mj} can be defined as being partially matched when

$$
\begin{aligned}
|A_{si}^k - A_{mj}^k| \quad &< \quad T_k \text{ whenever attribute label } k \\
&\qquad \text{is present in the attribute list of } P_{si}, \text{ or} \\
A_{si}^k \quad &= \quad null \qquad\qquad\qquad\qquad\qquad\qquad (5.12)
\end{aligned}
$$

The partial match of P_{si} to P_{mj} is denoted as $P_{si} \to P_{mj}$.

A scene ARG is considered to match a model ARG if the scene ARG has a monomorphism onto the model ARG. In formal terms, a scene ARG $G_s = (V_s, E_s)$ has a monomorphism onto a model ARG $G_m = (V_m, E_m)$ denoted by $G_s \Rightarrow G_m$ if

1. $\forall v_i \in V_s, \exists v_j' \in V_m$ such that $v_i \to v_j'$

2. $\forall e_{ij} \in E_s, \exists e_{kl}' \in E_m$ such that $e_{ij} \to e_{kl}'$ whenever $v_i \to v_k'$ and $v_j \to v_l'$.

The problem of graph monomorphism or subgraph isomorphism (finding a subgraph in G_m that is isomorphic to G_s) is known to be NP-complete, that is, there is no known algorithm that has polynomial complexity in the number of vertices and edges of G_m or G_s. In fact, the worst case complexity of matching two ARG's with m and n vertices (where $m \le n$) by exhaustive exploration of the search space is known to be of the order of $n!/(n-m)!$. Thus most techniques for graph-matching use constraints derived from the scene and model features to control the combinatorial complexity of the search.

Fan et al. [1989] have implemented a three-dimensional object recognition system based on the matching of ARG's. The input range image is segmented into smooth surface patches and surface discontinuities. Surface discontinuities are classified as *jump* edges and *crease* edges. Crease edges are further classified as *concave* or *convex* crease edges. Jump edges where the surface normal is perpendicular to the line of sight are further classified as *limb* edges. The scene features are organized in the form of an ARG where the vertices (or nodes) represent smooth surface patches. Surface feature attributes such as principal surface curvatures values, location of the centroid of the surface patch, orientation of the surface patch as measured from the directions of the principal curvatures, and the visible area of the surface patch are used to construct the vertex attribute set. Two vertices in the ARG are connected by an attributed edge if the corresponding surface patches share a common edge in the image. The edge attribute set is constructed using attributes based on

1. the nature of the edge (in the image) joining the surface patches—whether jump edge, crease edge, or limb;

2. the possibility p of the surface patches being connected: If the edge (in the image) between the surface patches happens to be a convex crease edge, then $p = 1.0$. For a concave crease edge $p = 0.75$. For jump and limb edges p, is assigned a value between 0.3 and 0.5, depending on the extent of the depth discontinuity;

3. the angular difference in orientations of the surface patches;

4. the inter-centroid distance between the surface patches.

Each object model consists of a collection of ARG's, each ARG representing a characteristic view of the object model. A preprocessing module matches the scene ARG with all model ARG's using gross properties of the two ARG's. Properties such as the total number of nodes, the total number of nodes of a certain surface type, and the visible three-dimensional area of the largest surface patch can be used to reject certain model ARG's. The problem of ARG monomorphism or graph-matching is cast as one of depth-first search through the space of possible pairings of vertices of the scene ARG with vertices of the model ARG. This is an approach similar to the one followed in searching an interpretation tree. All possible matches of scene ARG vertices with model ARG vertices based on vertex attribute sets (unary constraints) are generated and ranked, based on a match quality. The best few matched pairs are then retained as possible starting points for the search process. The search proceeds by extending a given set of vertex pairs using both vertex attribute sets (unary constraints) and edge attribute sets (binary constraints) in a manner similar to the interpretation tree search. Once a set contains four pairs, a rigid-body transform is computed and the value of the transform is used to constrain future matches. A heuristic match quality is assigned to the set of vertex pairings after it has been fully extended. If the match quality exceeds a certain predefined threshold, the match is accepted, else another set of vertex pairs is considered for extension. If none of the candidate sets qualify as a match, another model ARG is invoked for matching. A match of a model ARG with the scene ARG is also used to refine the earlier data-driven segmentation. If the number of vertices in the scene ARG that do not correspond to any vertex in the model ARG exceeds a certain threshold, the scene ARG is split between the vertices having low connection possibilities. On the other hand, if the number of vertices in the model ARG that do not correspond to any vertex in the scene ARG exceeds a certain threshold, the set of scene ARG's is scanned to determine whether other ARG's could be merged with the scene ARG under consideration. The candidate ARG's for merging are considered in the order of their spatial proximity to the scene ARG under consideration.

Kim and Kak [1991] have proposed a three-dimensional object recognition system based on bipartite graph matching coupled with discrete relaxation. Surface features derived from the scene and those from the object models are rep-

resented in the form of a scene ARG and model ARG's, respectively. The node
(or vertex) attribute set in this case consists of:

1. *Intrinsic* attributes that do not depend on the location and orientation
   of the surface feature in three-dimensional space. This class includes
   viewpoint-independent attributes such as the qualitative surface type (planar, spherical, etc.), and *viewpoint-dependent* attributes such as surface
   area. The surface area is viewpoint-dependent because it is subject to
   change as a result of occlusion.

2. *Extrinsic* attributes that depend on the location and orientation of the
   surface feature in three-dimensional space. This class includes attributes
   based on surface orientation such as the orientation of the normal of a
   planar surface or the axis of a cylindrical surface. It also includes attributes
   based on surface position such as the location of the centroid of a spherical
   surface patch or the apex of a conical surface patch.

Similarly, the edge or arc attribute set consists of intrinsic attributes such as
the edge type (jump, crease, or limb), the angle between the orientations of the
surfaces associated with the arc vertices, and the inter-centroid distance.

In the approach taken by Kim and Kak, the *global* problem of matching scene
and model ARG's is decomposed into subproblems wherein each subproblem is
concerned with the *local consistency* of a match of a vertex in the scene ARG
with a vertex in the model ARG. A vertex v_i in the scene ARG G_s is said to be
locally consistent with a vertex v_j' in the model ARG G_m if

1. $v_i \rightarrow v_j'$, that is, v_i and v_j' satisfy the same unary constraints and the
   vertex attribute set of v_i is a subset of that of v_j'.

2. for each vertex $v_k \in G_s$ that is adjacent to v_i there exists a vertex $v_l' \in G_m$
   that is adjacent to v_j' such that $v_k \rightarrow v_l'$ and $e_{i,k} \rightarrow e_{j,l}'$, where $e_{i,k}$ is the
   attributed edge between vertices v_i and v_k and $e_{j,l}'$ is the attributed edge
   between vertices v_j' and v_l'.

Proving that v_i and v_j' are locally consistent is equivalent to proving the monomorphism $ET_i \Rightarrow ET_j'$ (Figure 5.7), where ET_i is an elementary tree in G_s with its
root at the vertex v_i and with all the vertices v_k adjacent to v_i as the leaves,
and ET_j' is the corresponding elementary tree in G_m with its root at v_j' and all
the vertices v_l' adjacent to v_j' as leaves.

In order to determine whether the scene ARG G_s is a monomorphism onto
a model ARG G_m, Kim and Kak use a series of filtering steps to reject false
matches. The first filtering step carries out a coarse comparison of the two ARG's
based on gross properties of the two ARG's such as the total number of vertices
and edges, the total number of nodes denoting a certain surface type, or the
total number of nodes of a certain degree. A match that does not qualify, based
on any of the above mentioned properties, is rejected. The second filtering step
determines for each vertex $v_i \in G_s$ the corresponding vertices $v_j' \in G_m$ such that
$v_i \rightarrow v_j'$. The result is a bipartite graph between the vertices of G_s and those of

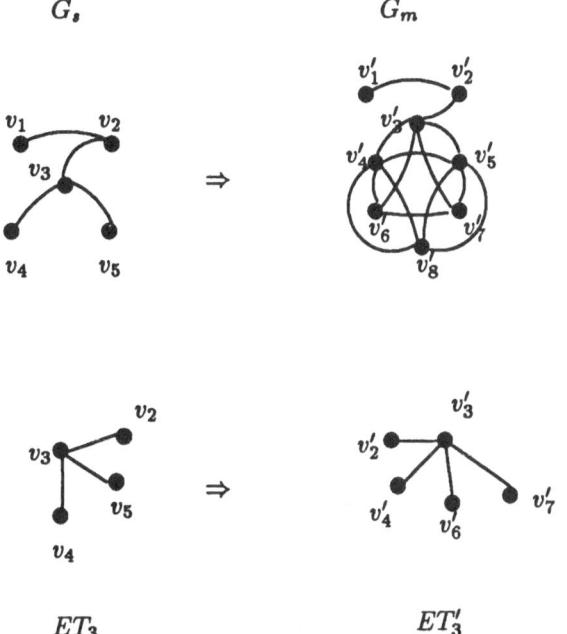

Figure 5.7: The monomorphism problem $G_s \Rightarrow G_m$ is decomposed into elementary monomorphism problems $ET_i \Rightarrow ET_j'$, where ET_i is the elementary tree rooted at v_i.

G_m that can be represented as a vertex compatibility table. If there exists any $v_i \in G_s$ that has no corresponding matching $v_j' \in G_m$, then the match between the two ARG's is rejected. The third filtering step determines whether the bipartite graph based on vertex compatibility has within it a bipartite subgraph representing a one-to-one injective mapping. This is a problem in bipartite graph matching for which algorithms of quadratic complexity are known. If no such bipartite subgraph can be shown to exist, the match is rejected.

The ARG matches that survive the filtering steps are input to a pruning module that checks for *local consistency* among the vertices in the vertex compatibility table based on the edge attributes. Elementary trees are constructed for each vertex in G_s and G_m. The matching of two elementary trees can be done in quadratic time using the bipartite graph matching algorithm. If a vertex in $v_i \in G_s$ is found to be locally inconsistent with a vertex in $v_j' \in G_m$, then the $(i, j)^{th}$ entry in the vertex compatibility table is changed from a *1* to a *0*. The effect of this change is propagated using a discrete relaxation labeling algorithm to the elementary trees that are affected by the change. If at any stage a vertex $v_i \in G_s$ results in being incompatible with all the vertices $v_j' \in G_m$, then the match is rejected. Pruning halts when there are no more changes in the vertex compatibility table. If pruning results in a one-to-one injective mapping, then the pose is computed and the match is verified for a consistent pose. If pruning results in a mapping that is not one-to-one and injective, then subsets of the assignment table are extracted using a generate-and-test with backtracking procedure, as in the case of interpretation tree search, and verified for a consistent pose. The ARG matching technique of Kim and Kak implicitly assumes that either the scene contains a single object or, in the case of multiple-object scenes, the scene has been appropriately segmented so as to delineate the features belonging to a single object. This approach does not take into account segmentation errors, nor does it try to correct them.

Wong et al. [1989] use an attributed *hypergraph* representation of three-dimensional objects in order to reduce the combinatorial complexity. For a three-dimensional object, an *elementary area attributed graph* $G_a = (V_a, E_a)$ is defined for representing a face bound by distinct and well-defined edges. Each vertex in V_a is a set of attributed vertices representing the boundary segments, whereas E_a is the set of attributed edges representing the relations between the boundary segments such as the angle between them. A complex three-dimensional object can be decomposed into primitive blocks wherein each primitive block represents a convex solid bound by the faces of the object. A *primitive block attributed graph* $G_b = (V_b, E_b)$ is defined to represent a primitive block of an object where each attributed vertex in V_b represents a face of the primitive block, and each attributed edge in E_b represents the geometric relation between the faces.

A *hypergraph* is an ordered pair (V, E) where $V = \{v_1, v_2, \ldots, v_m\}$ is a set of attributed vertices and $E = \{e_1, e_2, \ldots, e_n\}$ is a set of hyperedges such that

1. $e_i \neq \phi, 1 \leq i \leq n.$

2. $\bigcup_{i=1}^{n} e_i = V$

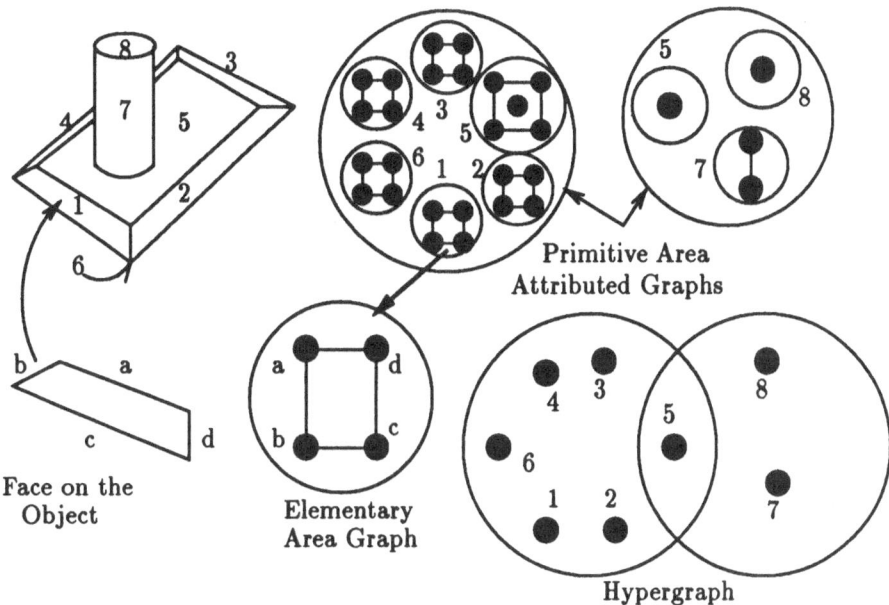

Figure 5.8: Hypergraph representation of a three-dimensional object.

$|V| = m$ is said to be the order of the hypergraph. An *object attributed hypergraph* $H = (V, E)$ consists of a set of attributed vertices V and a set of hyperedges E where each vertex $v_i \in V$ represents an elementary area attributed graph G_{v_i} and each hyperedge $e_j \in E$ is associated with a primitive block attributed graph G_{e_j}. A vertex is said to be common to two hyperedges if the face corresponding to the vertex is common to the primitive blocks corresponding to the hyperedges (Figure 5.8).

Wong et al. extend the concept of ARG monomorphism to the monomorphism of object attributed hypergraphs. A scene-attributed hypergraph $H_s = (V_s, E_s)$ is said to have a monomorphism onto a model-attributed hypergraph $H_m = (V_m, H_m)$, denoted by $H_s \Rightarrow H_m$ if

1. $\forall v_i \in V_s, \exists v_j' \in V_m$ such that $v_i \rightarrow v_j'$, that is, $G_{v_i} \Rightarrow G_{v_j'}$.

2. $\forall e_i \in E_s, \exists e_j' \in E_m$ such that $e_i \rightarrow e_j'$, that is, $G_{e_i} \Rightarrow G_{e_j'}$.

3. if $v_i = e_j \cap e_k$ and $v_p' = e_q' \cap e_r'$, then $e_j \rightarrow e_q'$ and $e_k \rightarrow e_r'$ whenever $v_i \rightarrow v_p'$.

The advantage of using object-attributed hypergraphs over ARG's is that they induce a hierarchical matching that leads to an overall reduction in complexity.

For two ARG's with n and m vertices, the order of complexity of the monomorphism problem is $\binom{n}{m}m!$ If the same problem is translated into a matching of two hypergraphs with p and q vertices such that $\sum_{i=1}^{p} n_i = n$ and $\sum_{j=1}^{q} m_j = m$ where n_i is the number of vertices in the elementary area attributed graph which the ith vertex in the hypergraph represents, then the overall order of complexity of the hypergraph monomorphism problem is $\sum_{i=1}^{p} \sum_{j=1}^{q} \binom{n_i}{m_j}m_j!$ which is much less than $\binom{n}{m}m!$. Wang et al. have described algorithms for generating the hypergraph representation from a series of range images of an object viewed from different directions. They have tested the hypergraph monomorphism algorithm on range images of single-object scenes. The hypergraph monomorphism algorithm, however, implicitly assumes that the scene has been correctly segmented and does not attempt to correct errors in the initial segmentation.

Relational structures, such as ARG's, are intuitively appealing since they capture the most structural properties and their geometrical inter-relationships of objects. However, the fact that ARG representation is so well suited for most vision tasks does not make the recognition and localization problem any easier, since most ARG matching algorithms are known to be NP-complete problems. This is particularly true when dealing with multiple-object scenes with partial occlusion. It can be shown that, in the worst case, all the various approaches to ARG matching require algorithms with exponential order of complexity, just as would techniques like interpretation tree search. However, since ARG represents unary and binary constraints explicitly, these constraints can be brought directly to bear during the matching process, thereby improving the average order of complexity.

5.5   Geometric Hashing

Geometric hashing is another procedure widely used for recognition and localization of objects in multiple-object scenes in the presence of occlusion. The central idea behind the geometric hashing paradigm is the creation of a redundant representation of each object model in terms of all possible transformation invariant coordinate frames. This redundant representation is stored in a hash table that is indexed during the recognition process by using minimal transformation invariant features derived from scene data. One advantage of the geometric hashing paradigm is that the process of creating the hash table, though computationally intensive, is carried out *off line*. Moreover, the hash table can be incrementally generated for each object model without having to recompute it from scratch every time a new object model is added to the object model library. The size of the hash table is dependent solely on the size of the object-model library and not on the complexity of the scene. If indexing into the hash table is done efficiently, the recognition process can be seen to have a fairly low order of complexity. Also, the process of indexing into the hash table can be parallelized in a straightforward manner that makes geometric hashing very attractive.

The primary step in geometric hashing is to determine a set of transformed (translated, rotated, scaled, etc.) model features that match a subset of the scene features. Features in the object model are represented in terms of a set of *basis* features. For example, for a three-dimensional object, four non-coplanar points $\{v_0, v_1, v_2, v_3\}$ on the object surface can adequately represent any other surface point v_s and can thus be considered to be a set of basis features for representing the three-dimensional object. Any surface point v_s can be expressed as a linear combination of the basis set $\{v_0, v_1, v_2, v_3\}$, i.e., $v_s = \alpha(v_1 - v_0) + \beta(v_2 - v_0) + \gamma(v_3 - v_0) + v_0$. Alternatively, we could use the basis set $\{v_0, t_1, t_2\}$ where v_0 is a point feature and t_1 and t_2 non-collinear direction vectors that signify either the orientation of an edge feature or the normal to a planar surface. Any surface point v_s can then be represented as $v_s = \alpha t_1 + \beta t_2 + \gamma(t_1 \times t_2) + v_0$ where $\times$ denotes the vector cross product. The coordinates (α, β, γ) can be shown to be invariant to rigid-body motion in 3-D Euclidean space. The elements of the basis set are typically features of geometrical significance such as surface normals of the planar facets, edges, corners (junction vertices), or points of high curvature and are referred to as *interest* features.

For a given object model having m point interest features, we can construct $\binom{m}{4} = O(m^4)$ different basis sets. Alternatively, with m point interest features and $m_1 = O(m)$ directional interest features, we can construct $m\binom{m_1}{2} = O(mm_1^2) = O(m^3)$ different basis sets. The following preprocessing steps are followed in generating the hash table:

1. For a particular object model, the interest features are selected.

2. All possible basis sets are generated from the interest features. In general, we would have $O(m^3) - O(m^4)$ possible basis sets.

3. Each interest feature is expressed in terms of all possible basis sets. For a given basis set, the coordinates (α, β, γ) of an interest feature are used as an address or index to a hash table. The corresponding location in the hash table contains the pair (*model_id, basis_id*) where *model_id* refers to a particular object model and *basis_id* to a particular basis set.

The complexity of the hash table generation process is $O(m^4) - O(m^5)$ per object model, since each of the m interest features is expressed in terms of the $O(m^3) - O(m^4)$ possible basis sets. The major advantage of this redundant representation is that it is possible to recognize objects in the scene even in the face of partial occlusion.

During the recognition phase, the following steps are carried out:

1. The interest features are extracted from the scene.

2. A basis set is chosen from the scene interest features. For n scene interest features there are $O(n^3) - O(n^4)$ possible choices for a basis set. A particular basis set could be chosen at random, or if the scene interest features are assigned degrees of importance, then a choice of a basis set could be selectively made.

3. The coordinates of each scene interest feature are computed with respect to the basis set selected in 2.

4. For each set of coordinates, the corresponding entry in the hash table is obtained. For each (*model_id, basis_id*) pair that resides at that particular location in the hash table, a vote is accrued.

5. A (*model_id, basis_id*) pair that scores a high number of votes is conjectured to be one corresponding to the basis set selected from the scene interest features. The coordinate transform between the model basis set referred to by *basis_id* and the basis set selected from the scene interest features is then considered to be the appropriate rigid-body transform between the object model and the object in the scene.

6. If all the model-image feature pairings that voted for a particular (*model_id, basis_id*) pair are noted, then a rigid-body transformation that yields the least-squared match between the corresponding feature pairs can be determined. This transformation could be expected to be more accurate than the one computed in 5.

7. The object model is projected onto the scene using the rigid-body transformation computed in 6, and the transformation is verified. In the event that the verification fails, the process loops back to 2 for another basis set to be chosen from the scene interest features.

With suitable parallelization, the voting can be done simultaneously for all possible object models and basis sets defined for an object model. The voting process is linear in the number of interest features in the scene and is hence dependent on the scene complexity.

Although the principle of vote accumulation is common to both the generalized Hough transform and geometric hashing, there are certain important differences. The generalized Hough transform determines a rigid-body transformation that would place the model interest features in registration with the scene interest features. For this purpose, the transformation is determined by voting for its parameters in parameter space. In the case of geometric hashing, on the other hand, voting is done for the model basis sets that are known *a priori*. The accumulator array used by the generalized Hough transform as a discretized representation of the parameter space has its equivalent–in the case of geometric hashing–not in the hash table, but in the discrete accumulator of votes used by different basis sets. Geometric hashing processes model and scene data independently of each other, which is not the case with the generalized Hough transform. In the case of geometric hashing, voting is done for one image basis set at a time, whereas the generalized Hough transform can be looked upon as comparing all image basis sets with all the basis sets of the object model. The equivalent of the hash table used in geometric hashing does not exist for the generalized Hough transform. Serial implementation of the generalized Hough transform with N object models, n interest features per object model, and m scene interest features has a worst case complexity of $O(Nm^3n^3) - O(Nm^4n^4)$. For geometric hashing, on the other hand, the recognition phase has a worst case complexity of $O(n^4) - O(n^5)$, the worst case being when all possible basis sets of the image features must be tried.

Geometric hashing has been studied by several researchers. Wolfson [1990], Lamdan and Wolfson [1988], and Grimson and Huttenlocher [1990b] have studied the effect of errors due to noise and occlusion on the performance of geometric hashing. In particular, Grimson and Huttenlocher have noted that geometric hashing works well for single-object scenes or for exact data without measurement errors. However, in the presence of noise or clutter due to occlusion, the probability of false positive recognition becomes significant, leading to a degradation in performance. As in the case of the Hough transform or the interpretation tree search, geometric hashing must be coupled with good segmentation techniques for grouping significant features so that the ratio of spurious data to real data is significantly reduced. However, the fact that geometric hashing can be parallelized on a fine-grained SIMD architecture in a natural manner, as brought out by the work of Bourdon and Medioni [1989], makes it attractive for recognition tasks in well constrained environments.

5.6 Iterative Model Fitting

Iterative model fitting is a recognition technique that can be used in situations where the underlying representation is given in a parametric form. The parameters characterizing the representation scheme need to satisfy the following conditions:

1. The parameters need to be robust to changes in viewpoint.

2. The parameters need to capture the *global* properties of shape and yet allow for shape deformations.

3. The parameters need to have local support so that they are robust to occlusion and can be recovered from a sparse set of image data.

4. The parameters should enable a description of a wide class of objects.

5. The parameters should result in a unique description that makes recognition unambiguous.

As noted in the previous chapter, the superquadric representation satisfies all the above conditions, which makes it an ideal candidate for three-dimensional object recognition via iterative model fitting. A deformed superquadric in a general position has an *inside-out* function of the form

$$f'(x, y, z) = f(x, y, z, a_1, a_2, a_3, \epsilon_1, \epsilon_2, p_x, p_y, p_z, \phi, \theta, \psi, K_x, K_y, k, \alpha) \quad (5.13)$$

where $(a_1, a_2, a_3, \epsilon_1, \epsilon_2)$ are the shape parameters, (p_x, p_y, p_z) the translation parameters along each of the coordinate axes, (ϕ, θ, ψ) the *Euler* angles that specify the rotation about each of the coordinate axes, (K_x, K_y) the tapering deformation parameters, and (k, α) the bending deformation parameters. The process of recognizing a superquadric in a general position is tantamount to recovering the 15 parameters $(a_1, a_2, a_3, \epsilon_1, \epsilon_2, p_x, p_y, p_z, \phi, \theta, \psi, K_x, K_y, k, \alpha)$ from

the range image. The 15 shape, position, orientation, and deformation parameters can be represented by the parameter vector $\mathbf{a} = [a_1, a_2, \ldots, a_{15}]$. Since,
$f'(x_s, y_s, z_s) = 1$ for a point (x_s, y_s, z_s) on the surface of the superquadric, one
way of recovering the parameters $[a_1, a_2, \ldots, a_{15}]$ is by sampling the range z_i at
a number of pixel locations (x_i, y_i) and fitting a superquadric model to the set
of 3-D points $\{(x_i, y_i, z_i) : 1 \le i \le N\}$ where $N \gg 15$. The parameters of the
best superquadric fit are those minimizing the sum of the squared deviations F

$$F = \sum_{i=1}^{N} [f'(x_i, y_i, z_i) - 1]^2 \qquad (5.14)$$

Since $N \gg 15$ in most practical cases, the resulting system of non-linear equations is *overconstrained* and can be solved using an iterative non-linear least
squares minimization technique such as the Levenberg-Marquardt or the Gauss-
Newton technique. The partial derivatives $\partial F / \partial a_i$ needed for the minimization
procedure can be computed analytically.

Solina and Bajcsy [1990], Boult and Gross [1987], and Pentland [1990] have
discussed issues regarding the convergence of the non-linear least squares minimization technique for superquadratic model fitting, and the accuracy and sta-
bility of the solution vector $\mathbf{a} = [a_1, a_2, \ldots, a_{15}]$ to perturbations in the viewpoint
and sensor noise. It has been noted that the addition of Poisson noise to the
residual prevents the minimization technique from being trapped in a local minimum. It has also been noted that estimates for the parameter vector tend to be
inaccurate when the number of data points is small or if the system is given only
a partial view of the object. Estimates are found to improve substantially when
multiple views of the object are used. Solina and Bajcsy have noted that in certain cases wherein the object in the scene was substantially occluded, the objective function based on the inside-out function, i.e., $F = \sum_{i=1}^{N} [1 - f'(x_i, y_i, z_i)]^2$,
was unable to come up with a unique solution for the parameter vector. In such
cases the objective function needs to be modified in order that the superquadric
fit with the smallest volume be selected. The objective function,

$$F' = \sum_{i=1}^{N} a_1 a_2 a_3 [1 - f'(x_i, y_i, z_i)]^2 \qquad (5.15)$$

has been found to be a suitable since $[1 - f'(x_i, y_i, z_i)]^2$ is zero for all points
(x_i, y_i, z_i) on the surface, and the factor $a_1 a_2 a_3$ ensures that the minimum corresponds to the superquadric with the least volume.

As noted by Bajcsy and Solina, in cases where the occluding contour(s) of
the object is available, the constraint imposed by the surface normal along the
occluding contour could be incorporated into the objective function. From the
parametric equation of the superquadric surface,

$$\mathbf{S}(\omega, \eta) = \begin{bmatrix} a_1 C_\omega^{\epsilon_1} C_\eta^{\epsilon_2} \\ a_2 C_\omega^{\epsilon_1} S_\eta^{\epsilon_2} \\ a_3 S_\omega^{\epsilon_1} \end{bmatrix} \qquad (5.16)$$

where $C_\omega = \cos\omega$, $S_\omega = \sin\omega$, $C_\eta = \cos\eta$, $S_\eta = \sin\eta$, $-\frac{\pi}{2} \le \omega \le \frac{\pi}{2}$ and $-\pi \le \eta \le \pi$, the equation of the surface normal $\mathbf{n}(\omega, \eta)$ can be derived as

$$\mathbf{n}(\omega, \eta) = \frac{\partial \mathbf{S}(\omega, \eta)}{\partial \omega} \times \frac{\partial \mathbf{S}(\omega, \eta)}{\partial \eta} = \begin{bmatrix} \frac{1}{a_1} C_\omega^{2-\epsilon_1} C_\eta^{2-\epsilon_2} \\ \frac{1}{a_2} C_\omega^{2-\epsilon_1} S_\eta^{2-\epsilon_2} \\ \frac{1}{a_3} S_\omega^{2-\epsilon_1} \end{bmatrix} \tag{5.17}$$

From Eq. (5.17) the components (n_x, n_y, n_z) of the surface normals should satisfy the implicit equation

$$N(n_x, n_y, n_z) = \left[\left[(n_x a_1)^{\frac{2}{2-\epsilon_2}} + (n_y a_2)^{\frac{2}{2-\epsilon_2}} \right]^{\frac{2-\epsilon_2}{2-\epsilon_1}} + (n_z a_3)^{\frac{2}{2-\epsilon_1}} \right]^{2-\epsilon_1} = 1$$

$$\tag{5.18}$$

If the viewing axis is along the z axis of the world coordinate system, then for all points on the occluding contour $n_z = 0$. Since the direction of the surface normal is invariant to translation, the implicit equation obeyed by the components of the surface normals along the occluding contour of a superquadric in a general position subject to deformation is given by

$$N'(n_x, n_y, n_z) = N'(n_x, n_y) = N(n_x, n_y, a_1, a_2, a_3, \epsilon_1, \epsilon_2, \phi, \theta, \psi, K_x, K_y, k, \alpha) \tag{5.19}$$

Since $N(n_x, n_y, a_1, a_2, a_3, \epsilon_1, \epsilon_2, \phi, \theta, \psi, K_x, K_y, k, \alpha) = 1$ for points along the occluding contour, the objective function can be modified to incorporate the constraint imposed by the surface normal

$$F'' = \sum_{i=1}^{N} a_1 a_2 a_3 [1 - f'(x_i, y_i, z_i)]^2 + \sum_{i=1}^{M} [1 - N'(n_{x_i}, n_{y_i})]^2 \tag{5.20}$$

where N is the number of points where the range is sampled and M is the number of points where the estimates of the surface normal along the occluding contour are available. Solina and Bajcsy [1990] have noted that the incorporation of the surface normal constraint achieves faster convergence of the model fitting algorithm.

Object recognition via iterative model fitting is an attractive paradigm since it reduces the problem of object recognition and localization to that of estimating the parameters of the model. Moreover, the iterative non-linear optimization techniques used for parameter estimation can be easily parallelized on a fine-grained SIMD mesh architecture or a systolic array. However, this technique implicitly assumes that the scene has been correctly segmented into surface patches so that the model fitting algorithm could assume that the data points belong to a single surface patch with a unique superquadric description. If the scene is incorrectly segmented, we could expect errors in the parameter estimates, or even failure of the model fitting algorithm to converge to a unique solution, which are problems far from trivial.

5.7 Indexing and Qualitative Features

As is evident from discussions in previous sections, the constraint satisfaction process involved with the recognition of three-dimensional objects from multiple-object scenes in the presence of occlusion and clutter exhibits an order of complexity that is exponential in the number of scene and model features. One way of controlling the combinatorial complexity of the search space of possible interpretations is to limit the search to a small number of object models. The process of focusing the search on a small subset of object models is referred to as *indexing* into the object model database.

The process of indexing can best be visualized as a set of mappings from the domain of scene features to a range of index values, referred to as the *index space*, and also from the domain of model features to the index space. Given a set of N scene features, we could form a group of G (where $G \ll N$) scene features to constitute an *index*. The index value could be generated by a suitable parameterization of the group and could be represented as a point in index space. If the model database contains K object models such that the ith model has M_i features, then, similarly, by forming groups of model features, we could generate a set of index values for each group of features for each object model. The set of index values generated by the object models could then be used to generate an index table that contains for each index value i a list of ordered pairs (j, k), where j and k denote the jth feature group in the kth object model that gave rise to that particular index value. The index table could be generated *off line*. During recognition a group of scene features can be used to compute an index. The corresponding (j, k) entries in the index table corresponding to the computed index would indicate all possible feature groups for all possible object models that could have given rise to the group of scene features as observed. This enables the recognition process to limit its match to the set of object models compatible with the computed index value.

In order that the indexing be effective, it is essential that the number of entries in the index table consistent with a particular index value be as small as possible. A large number of entries indicates that the ratio of false hypotheses to the correct ones is very high. The number of entries could thus be considered a measure of the discriminating ability of the group containing G scene features. In general, there are $\binom{N}{G}$ possible distinct feature groups of size G in the scene and $\sum_{i=1}^{K} \binom{M_i}{G}$ possible distinct model groups. Since $G \ll N$ and $G \ll M_i$ $1 \le i \le K$, $\binom{N}{G} = O(N^G)$ and $\sum_{i=1}^{K} \binom{M_i}{G} = O(M^G)$ where $M = max(M_i)$. Increasing the value of G has the effect of making the feature group more *structured*, thereby increasing its discriminatory ability. This results in a decreasing number of entries. But increasing the value of G also increases the number of scene feature groups to be considered. Thus the key to successful indexing lies in not having to consider all possible feature groups of size G, but only those likely to have arisen from a single object.

Grimson [1990] has studied the effect of indexing on the performance of interpretation tree search for object recognition. He has shown how indexing,

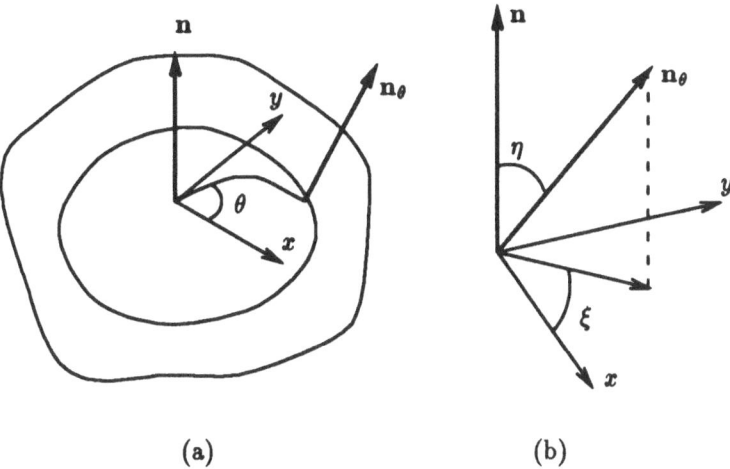

Figure 5.9: Representation of surface patches by splashes: (a) the surface normal **n** at the centroid of a patch, and the surface normal $\mathbf{n}_\theta$ at a point on the circumference of a geodesic circle centered at the centroid; (b) $\mathbf{n}_\theta$ can be expressed in terms of η and ξ.

coupled with the grouping of scene features into subsets likely to have arisen from an instance of a single object model, can reduce the complexity of object recognition in multiple-object scenes with occlusion and clutter from exponential to cubic. On the other hand, with simple indexing that relies on exhaustive grouping of features, the complexity of the search process remains exponential. Clemens and Jacobs [1991] have shown that simple indexing with an exhaustive grouping of features cannot result in any significant speedup. On the other hand, speedup achievable by indexing coupled with proper grouping of features is of the order β^G for a constant $\beta > 1$. Thus the speedup has an order that is exponential in the size of the feature group.

Stein and Medioni [1992] have implemented an indexing scheme that they term *structural indexing*. As feature groups they have used curves of discontinuity that correspond to crease edges and representations of curved surface patches in terms of *splashes*. A curve of discontinuity corresponding to a crease edge is represented by a series of line segments $\{\mathbf{s}_i \ : \ 1 \le i \le L\}$. For each line segment the curvature angle κ_i and the torsion angle τ_i are computed as follows:

$$\kappa_i = \cos^{-1}\left(\frac{\mathbf{s}_{i+1} \cdot \mathbf{s}_i}{|\mathbf{s}_{i+1}||\mathbf{s}_i|}\right) \tag{5.21}$$

$$\tau_i = \cos^{-1}(\mathbf{b}_i \cdot \mathbf{b}_{i+1}) \tag{5.22}$$

where $b_i's$ are the binormal vectors given by the equation

$$b_i = \frac{s_{i+1} \times s_i}{|s_{i+1}||s_i|} \tag{5.23}$$

and where $\cdot$ denotes the vector scalar or dot product and $\times$ denotes the vector cross product. The curve of discontinuity is then encoded as a list $\{(\kappa_i, \tau_i) : 1 \leq i \leq L\}$. A surface patch is described by a Gaussian map or a *splash* of surface normals along the circumference of a geodesic circle of radius ρ centered at the centroid of the surface patch. Let n be the reference surface normal at the centroid of the surface patch and θ be the polar coordinate (relative to a reference) of a surface point along the circumference of the geodesic circle. Then the surface normal n_θ at the surface point can be expressed in terms of the spherical coordinates $(\eta(\theta), \xi(\theta))$ (Figure 5.9). If the geodesic circle is sampled at regular intervals of $\Delta\theta$ along the circumference, then the coordinates of the of n_θ constitute a space curve $(\eta(\theta), \xi(\theta), \theta)$ where $0 \leq \theta < 2\pi$. This space curve can then be decomposed into a series of line segments and encoded in a similar manner as the curves of discontinuity. A surface patch can be represented by splashes for different values of the geodesic radius ρ. The encoded curves of discontinuity and splashes can then be used as an index into an index table. The index table is created off line for a variety of object models. During the recognition phase, the indexing of the encoded curves of discontinuity and splashes of the scene object in the index table is used to generate candidate matches of scene and model features. The candidate matches are clustered and verified using binary and transformational constraints on the splashes. Binary constraints are based on the distance between centroids and the relative orientations of the reference normals of the splash. The transformational constraint requires that in a cluster of candidate matches every triad of scene splash-model splash pairs result in a unique pose. The constraints are imposed using an interpretation tree search similar to the one used by Chen and Kak [1989]. The structural indexing technique has been shown to work fairly reliably in both single-object and multiple-object scenes. Since partial matches of splashes are permitted and splashes are local features, scenes with partially occluded objects can be handled as well. The performance of structural indexing is found to degrade with the presence of noise in the scene data. The performance is also found to deteriorate when objects in the scene have many features in common. This reduces the discriminating ability of the indexing features, producing a great number of candidate hypotheses. The verification stage is then forced to filter true hypotheses from several false ones, causing loss of efficiency.

From the above discussion, it is obvious that indexing can yield significant speedup only when accompanied by an intelligent grouping operation that places features most likely to have arisen from a single object into a single group. The grouping is data-driven and is done using *qualitative* attributes such as parallelism, continuity, co-termination, proximity, and containment that could be assigned to features or groups of features. The features are either edge segments or elementary regions. This grouping, known as Gestalt clustering, is characteristic of most biological vision systems, but has proved very difficult to emulate in computer vision systems. In fact, none of the computer vision systems developed to date are capable of equaling, let alone surpassing, biological vision systems (in particular, the human vision system) in terms of speed and robustness. One reason cited by psychologists and researchers in computer vision is that biological vision systems, for the most part, aim at a *qualitative* interpretation of a scene rather than rely on precise *quantitative* measurements. Quantitative or metric information is sought and processed only under specific circumstances. Qualitative descriptions of the visual environment are therefore receiving greater interest in computer vision. This recent increase in interest is due partly to the difficulties that often arise in the practical application of more quantitative methods. These quantitative approaches tend to be computationally expensive, complex, and brittle, and they require constraints that limit generality. Moreover, inaccuracies in input data often do not justify such precise methods. Alternatively, physical constraints imposed by application domains such as mobile robots and real-time visual perception have prompted the exploration of qualitative mechanisms that require less computation, have better response time, focus on salient and relevant aspects of the environment, and use environmental constraints more effectively.

It has been shown that the grouping of intensity discontinuities based on qualitative Gestalt properties serves as an excellent criteria for the initial segmentation of the image and also as an indexing criterion for recognition of objects in the image. Julez and Bergen [1983] have used Gestalt properties to group primitive patterns called *textons* for texture-based segmentation. Guzman [1968], Clowes [1971], Huffman [1971], Waltz [1975], and Malik [1987] have researched on qualitative description of shape. Their works deal with junction labeling of trihedral solids and curved solids. Horn's shape-from-shading algorithm [Horn 1977] [Ikeuchi and Horn 1981] and Witkin's shape-from-texture algorithm [Witkin 1981] use qualitative information conveyed by junctions and occluding boundaries as boundary conditions. Shape-from-stereo [Barnard and Fischler 1982] uses the presence of intensity discontinuities as a means of limiting the search for correspondence. Malik [1989] uses the shape-from-shading algorithm in conjunction with the junction labeling algorithm to derive quantitative description of shape. Verri and Poggio [1989] have shown how smoothed optical flow and the motion field can be interpreted as vector fields tangent to the flows of planar dynamical systems and how stable qualitative properties of the motion field can be obtained from the optical flow. These stable qualitative properties of the motion field are shown to give useful information about the 3-D velocity field and the 3-D structure of the scene. Weinshall [1990] has shown how qualitative depth information can be obtained from stereo disparities by ordering matched points in a depth-consistent fashion from image coordinates only. Levitt and Lawton [1990] and Kuipers and Byun [1988] present qualitative models of map representation for mobile robots based on landmarks and topological inter-relationships between landmarks. Qualitative models are shown to be more robust than their metrically accurate counterparts, since the latter are prone to multiplicative accumulation of error.

Given the robustness of biological vision systems over computer vision sys-

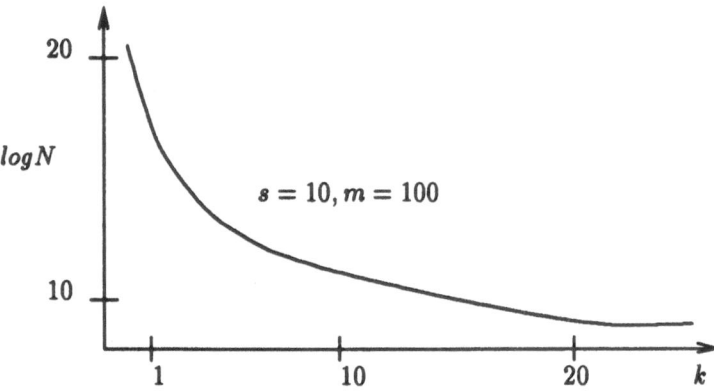

Figure 5.10: The size of the search space vs. the number of feature types k identified by qualitative features.

tems, trying to arrive at an entirely qualitative model for human vision could be worthwhile. That problem lies beyond our present scope; however, we can show that, by using qualitative features as an indexing criterion, the size of the search space can be dramatically reduced. Given a scene interpretation problem with s scene features and m model features, the size of the search space is given by $m!/(m-s)!$ under the assumption that $s < m$ and the *unique interpretation constraint* is satisfied, i.e., a single model feature matches only a single scene feature, and a single scene feature matches only a single model feature.

If scene features and model features can both be classified as belonging to one of k qualitative feature types, and assuming that both the model and the scene features are equally distributed in one of the k classes, the size of the search space can be reduced to $[(m/k)!/((m-s)/k)!]^k$ under the unique interpretation constraint. For a given value of s and m, the size of the search space is shown to decrease exponentially with increasing k (Figure 5.10). Thus, using qualitative features as an indexing criterion leads to an exponential reduction in the search space. However, it must be noted that the effort involved in the process of extracting these features should be minimal; otherwise, the cost of feature extraction can very well offset the advantages of having restricted the search space. The use of qualitative features in object recognition is the main subject of Part II.

If the scene contents and the contents of the object model library are organized along an object-oriented hierarchy, then qualitative features can serve as a useful indexing criteria into such a hierarchy. This has two advantages: (1) The combinatorial complexity of the search space of possible scene interpretations is reduced, and (2) A recognition/localization technique specific to a certain qualitative feature can be used. This ensures that the combinatorial complexity of the search space is not only reduced, but is also more efficiently traversed.

The use of qualitative features in an object-oriented representational hierarchy is further elaborated in the following section.

5.8 Vision Systems as Coupled Systems

As already mentioned, in spite of the several advances made in the area of three-dimensional scene interpretation, existing computer vision systems do not exhibit the speed and robustness of most biological vision systems. This is primarily due to the following shortcomings:

1. *Inadequacy of any single level of representation.* Of the many representation schemes used in existing computer vision systems, no single representation scheme has been able to satisfy the conflicting requirements of global scalability and richness of local support.

2. *Inadequacy of a constraint propagation technique based on matching of features at a single level of representation.* Techniques such as Hough clustering, which are based on propagation of local geometric constraints arising out of matches of local features, are robust to occlusion but are computationally intensive and are prone to false interpretations, whereas matching techniques based on global features are fast but not robust to occlusion.

3. *Inflexible control strategies.* Most existing computer vision systems are pre-committed to a particular control strategy and are incapable of varying the control strategy based on the state of the recognition process.

4. *Need for effective integration of symbolic and numerical processing.* In computer vision problems the role of numerical processing is largely in segmentation, feature extraction, and constraint propagation/constraint satisfaction techniques that operate on numerical data. Symbolic constraint propagation/constraint satisfaction techniques, on the other hand, are used for symbolic reasoning. Both symbolic and numerical processing techniques need to be integrated based on the chosen granularity of representation.

5. *Need for parallelism.* Given the combinatorial complexity of most computer vision tasks, parallelization of segmentation and feature extraction algorithms, and also the parallelization of both symbolic and numeric constraint propagation techniques, is necessary.

Coupled systems [Kowalik 1986] [Kowalik and Kitzmiller 1988], i.e. knowledge-based systems in which the symbolic and numerical processing are closely coupled, are viewed as an important aspects of problem-solving in scientific and engineering problem domains. A coupled-systems approach within an object-oriented framework can be viewed as one way of addressing the above mentioned shortcomings of computer vision systems. The primary issues in coupled systems are:

1. incorporating representation at multiple levels of granularity along part-subpart and class-subclass object hierarchies;

2. making the constraint propagation technique a part of the representation;

3. integration of symbolic and numerical processing;

4. incorporating flexibility into the control structure;

5. exploiting parallelism in both the symbolic and numerical processing within an object-oriented framework.

Since the problem of three-dimensional object recognition is essentially a constraint satisfaction problem, the two most important issues that need to be addressed in formulating a coupled-systems approach for object recognition are: (1) choice of representation, and (2) choice of constraint propagation technique. Recognition techniques developed for single-object scenes rely on a single granularity of representation for image and model features and on a constraint propagation technique tuned to that particular granularity of representation. This has been the case with all the recognition and localization techniques reviewed in the previous sections. In the case of a multiple-object scene with partial occlusion, the combinatorial explosion of the search space renders infeasible the straightforward application of recognition techniques developed for single-object scenes. Recognition techniques developed for single-object scenes exhibit poor performance, both in lack of efficiency because of the combinatorial explosion of the search space, and in lack of robustness because of the generation of several spurious scene interpretations. Clearly, the key to efficient and robust recognition in a multiple-object scene with partial occlusion lies in: (1) intelligent selection of representation for image and model features and constraints that arise from the matching of image and model features, and (2) intelligent selection of a constraint propagation technique tuned to the granularity of the selected representation.

5.8.1   Object-Oriented Representation for Coupled Systems

Object-oriented representation techniques have at their core the primary entity called the *object*[1] [Ramamoorthy and Sheu 1988]. An object is an entity that combines the properties of both procedures and data. An object can perform computations and save the local state. Procedural knowledge is *encapsulated* within an object as *methods* attached to an object. All operations (such as procedure invocation) are achieved by the process of message-passing between objects. Objects can be structured hierarchically along two principal hierarchies. The *class* hierarchy is a semantic hierarchy that classifies objects into classes and subclasses. The *part-subpart* hierarchy is a structural hierarchy that decomposes a complex object into its constituent parts or composes a complex object from its constituent parts.

---

[1]Note that the term *object* is used in two different contexts: physical objects for recognition, and abstract objects used in object-oriented programming.

Object-oriented representation has some inherent advantages. First, the object-oriented representation supports the concept of *data abstraction* at various levels. Data abstraction means that various procedures specific to a particular data-type or *class* can be encapsulated together, thus increasing the modularity of the object model database. Second, an object-oriented representation supports *specialization* and *inheritance*. For instance, a certain class of objects can be made a specialization of another class of objects wherein it inherits the properties of the original class, but also has additional class descriptors of its own. The new class is then a subclass of the original class, and thus hierarchical information is easily modeled in such a representation without unnecessary duplication.

5.8.2   Object-Oriented   Representation   for   3-D Object Recognition

The entities encountered in a three-dimensional vision problem can be naturally represented at multiple levels of representation granularity and are thus ideal candidates for object-oriented representation. In the context of an object-oriented representation scheme for the problem of three-dimensional object recognition from range images, the issues to be addressed are: (1) choice of objects, (2) choice of descriptors for each object, and (3) representation of methods associated with each object.

Choice of Objects

A crucial issue in an object-oriented representation is the choice of object classes. The object classes would typically consist of: (1) primitive objects, (2) composite objects, (3) constraint objects, (4) class objects, and (5) matched objects. Each of these object classes could be described as follows:

1. *Primitive objects.* In the context of three-dimensional object recognition, surface patches and surface boundary segments are natural choices for primitive objects from which all other objects can be derived.

2. *Composite objects.* Composite objects can be created from primitive objects. The process of composition creates a *part-of* hierarchy. Composite objects typically contain a list of component parts and constraints between their component parts.

3. *Constraint objects.* Constraints between objects can be represented explicitly as objects. Each constraint object typically contains slots for the constraint type, the list of object types that qualify for the constraint, and symbolic/numerical representation of the constraint.

4. *Class objects.* Objects can be arranged along a *class-subclass* hierarchy. A typical class object contains slots for object type, constraint(s) on the

object type that provide(s) the class definition, and slots for class specialization and generalization. For surface regions, the classification is typically based on the signs of the mean and Gaussian curvatures. Mean and
Gaussian curvature values are used to classify surfaces into eight qualitative surface types. For surface boundary segments, the classification can
be done based on metrical properties of curvature. Object models can be
classified based on the number and orientation of their subparts and on the
dimension and orientation of the object models and/or dimension of their
subparts, etc. Constraints can be typically classified as either relational
or transformational. Relational constraints constrain the relative geometry of the two objects, whereas transformational constraints compute the
relative coordinate transformation between two objects. Relational constraints are typically based on qualitative properties such as adjacency and
containment. These constraints can be further refined based on the distance between centroids, relative orientations based on curvature values,
length of the common boundary, etc. These classifications need not be
strictly tree-based. A lattice-based hierarchy with multiple inheritance is
also a possibility.

5. *Matched objects.* Matches generated from the scene description and pre-
   stored objects can be represented as objects. Matched objects typically
   contain slots for describing the objects matched and for constraints imposed by the matching process. Constraints imposed by the matching
   process serve two purposes: refining classification of objects by propagation of constraints through the *class-subclass* hierarchy and determining or
   refining the pose of the object with respect to the viewer.

Choice of Descriptors for Objects

The descriptors for objects are used to form the indexing criteria by which the
objects can be accessed. These descriptors are qualitative at coarse levels of
description. For surface regions the signs of the mean and Gaussian curvatures
serve as qualitative indexing criteria, whereas, for boundary segments, qualitative attributes such as *crease, jump, straight*, and *curved* can serve as qualitative
indexing criteria. These qualitative descriptors can be further refined to more
quantitative or metrical descriptions based on curvature properties.

Representation of Methods Associated with Each Object

In object-oriented approaches the numerical procedures (or methods) are *encapsulated* along with the symbolic description of the objects they act upon, thus
clearly outlining their inter-dependence. In the context of three-dimensional object recognition, the important classes of procedures that need to be represented
are: (1) low-level algorithms such as segmentation and feature extraction, and
(2) control procedures such as constraint propagation and precompiled recognition strategies. Typical methods that could be associated with each object
are:

1. *Segmentation algorithms associated with a certain object type.* Most image segmentation algorithms are fine-tuned for a certain object type. For example, the detection of jump or step edges needs a different set of operations than does the detection of roof or crease edges. Segmentation algorithms can also be refined based on the object type. Segmentation algorithms for general surfaces incorporate weak criteria based on qualitative properties for clustering, such as continuity, adjacency, and containment. Segmentation algorithms for specific surfaces can incorporate clustering criteria based on very specific assumptions about the surface type. For example, clustering of surfaces based on assumption of cylindrical surfaces would typically incorporate the assumption of zero Gaussian curvature.

2. *Algorithms for feature extraction associated with a certain object type.* Feature extraction algorithms are also tuned for a certain granularity of representation of the associated object type. A point-wise surface normal and surface curvature representation is the most general representation of the object type *surface*. Feature extraction algorithms for the extraction of point-wise surface curvatures and surface normals are encapsulated in the object-type *surface*. For cylindrical surfaces a representation based on the length and the direction of the axis and radius of curvature is more appropriate. Likewise, feature extraction algorithms for the extraction of the magnitude and direction of the axis could be made a part of the object *cylindrical-surface*.

3. *Algorithms for constraint propagation and constraint satisfaction suited for a certain granularity of representation of an object type.* Constraint propagation and constraint satisfaction techniques for matching are well suited for a certain granularity of representation. Hough clustering techniques are well suited for fine-grained representation, whereas graph-theoretic techniques based on subgraph isomorphism and maximal clique detection are better suited for symbolic representations. These constraint propagation and constraint satisfaction algorithms are made a part of the representation of the appropriate object.

4. *Precompiled recognition strategies.* The problem of precompiling recognition strategies for object recognition in a bin-picking scenario has been addressed in a previous section. The bin-picking scenario is a simple case, since we are generally interested in the topmost object in a pile of objects, and the identity of the object is often known *a priori*. In a general object recognition scenario precompiled recognition strategies would have to be triggered when there is sufficient evidence available for the presence of a certain object. The precompiled recognition strategies, along with the triggering criteria, can be made a part of the representation of the object model.

One principal advantage of an object-oriented coupled system for object recognition is that the recognition strategy can be fine-tuned to the appropriate representation class and granularity. Generic constraint propagation techniques are encapsulated within generic representations, whereas constraint propagation techniques specific to specialized representations are encapsulated therein. This allows the integration of both symbolic and numerical constraint propagation techniques within a common representation framework. The overall control strategy can then be seen as a search through the various levels of representational hierarchy. By appropriate indexing into the appropriate level in the object hierarchy, the appropriate recognition/localization technique can be invoked.

5.8.3   Embedding Parallelism in an Object-Oriented Coupled System

It is possible to embed parallelism into an object-oriented coupled system. In any parallel environment there are two levels of parallelism—functional parallelism and data parallelism. In functional parallelism or pipelining, a data set is processed by several processing functions in a series. Parallelism is achieved by executing the functions at the same time on different data sets. Data parallelism is achieved by partitioning the data set into subsets and processing them simultaneously by multiple processing elements. Most parallel processing systems employ one or a combination of both levels of parallelism.

Numerical methods, in the form of segmentation and feature extraction algorithms, operate on pixel-level data and are easily parallelized on a SIMD mesh, pyramid or systolic architecture. Parallelization of segmentation and feature extraction algorithms has been studied extensively, and there exist systematic methodologies for mapping algorithms onto architectures. In contrast, parallelization of constraint satisfaction problems that arise from matching scene features with features extracted from the object models in the model database is an area that has not been as well explored. Constraint satisfaction problems are either numerical or symbolic, depending on the granularity of representation of the scene and model features. Hough clustering and geometric hashing are typical examples of numerical constraint satisfaction techniques, whereas graph-theoretic constraint satisfaction techniques are essentially symbolic in nature. Parallelization of constraint satisfaction techniques is typically a three-step process that involves:

1. Deriving a suitable representation for the constraint satisfaction problem. This representation can be loosely termed as a *problem graph* wherein the nodes denote the tasks/subtasks to be solved and the arcs between nodes denote a communication link for inter-task or inter-subtask communication.

2. Mapping the problem graph onto the topology of the underlying architecture. The underlying architecture is represented as a *system graph* wherein each node in the graph represents a processing element, and an arc between nodes a communication channel for inter-processor communication.

3. An optimization criterion for the matching of a problem graph with a system graph. For a given set of architectures and for a certain object

representation, the mapping procedure (or method) can also be embedded within the object representation.

As can be seen from the discussion in this section, an object-oriented coupled-systems approach to computer vision problems is very promising in that it offers an integrated framework in which to address some of the major shortcomings of existing computer vision systems. Given the fact that considerable research has been devoted in recent years to low- and intermediate-level computer vision problems, there is a need to address problems regarding high-level vision such as control strategies and systems integration. Object-oriented coupled systems can offer an integrated framework in which problems regarding high-level vision can be studied. Qualitative features play an important role in an object-oriented coupled-systems approach. Qualitative features constitute the descriptors by which objects are initially indexed in a representational hierarchy. This indexing provides a criterion for activating the methods—whether segmentation algorithms or constraint propagation techniques—associated with that particular object. Qualitative features could be further refined, as and when needed, based on metrical properties allowing more specialized objects to be indexed and more specialized methods to be invoked allowing a coarse-to-fine-tuning of the selected representation and control strategy. This not only reduces the combinatorial complexity of the search space, but allows specific portions of the search space to be explored by specialized and more efficient techniques. This enables control strategies that are robust, flexible, and adaptable.

5.9 Summary

In this chapter we have reviewed some commonly used recognition and localization techniques for three-dimensional object recognition. The choice of representational granularity and the constraint propagation technique are the two critical issues that need to be addressed when designing a three-dimensional object recognition system. The choice of representation granularity greatly affects the choice of the constraint propagation technique, and vice versa. Most existing constraint propagation techniques for recognition and localization are fine-tuned for a certain representation granularity. Techniques such as the generalized Hough transform and geometric hashing are well suited for fine-grained, largely numerical representations, whereas graph-theoretic techniques are well suited for coarse-grained symbolic representations. Given that the scene contents can be represented at multiple-levels of representation granularity, from the pixel level to the symbolic level that describes objects and object classes, there is no single level that can reconcile the often conflicting demands of locality of support and the need to capture the global aspects of three-dimensional shape. Consequently, most existing three-dimensional object recognition systems that restrict themselves to a single level of representation granularity and a constraint propagation technique suited to that single representation level suffer from several shortcomings. One major shortcoming is the combinatorial explosion of search space of possible scene interpretation hypotheses and the subsequent degradation of performance when faced with multiple-object scenes with partial occlusion. It will be shown in Section III that the use of qualitative features can effectively control the combinatorial complexity of the search space and can also provide a criterion for using powerful specialized techniques to explore certain subspaces of the search space whenever possible. An object-oriented coupled-systems approach with qualitative features as the initial indexing criteria has great potential for addressing most of the shortcomings of existing vision systems and thereby providing a framework for vision systems that are robust, flexible and adaptable.

Part II

Three-Dimensional Object Recognition Using Qualitative Features

Chapter 6

Polyhedral Object Recognition

We consider in this chapter the problem of recognition and localization of polyhedral objects from range images. Of particular interest are scenes that contain multiple polyhedral objects with objects partially occluding each other. As we have pointed out in the previous chapter, global shape descriptors are ineffective in the face of occlusion and clutter. Recognition-via-localization using only local shape descriptors in conjunction with a proper constraint propagation technique proves to be effective for solving this particular problem. We consider both the interpretation tree (IT) search and the generalized Hough transform in this chapter. In particular, we show that the use of *qualitative* features can achieve a significant reduction in the combinatorial complexity of the search space of scene interpretations, resulting in fewer spurious scene interpretation hypotheses being generated and greater robustness and efficiency for the recognition and localization process.

First, we discuss the segmentation of scenes containing polyhedral objects, and then the feature extraction process that constructs a description of the scene in terms of planar surface patches and edges. Next, we discuss the interpretation tree search and generalized Hough transform that process the feature-level description to arrive at the identity and location of objects in the scene. We discuss the use of *qualitative* features in controlling the combinatorial complexity of the search space of scene interpretations in cases of both, interpretation tree search and the generalized Hough transform. We present experimental results on real and synthetic range images showing the advantages of using *qualitative features* in each case.

6.1 Preprocessing and Segmentation

Figure 6.1 shows the flow chart for the segmentation algorithm we used in conjunction with the recognition techniques for polyhedral objects described in this

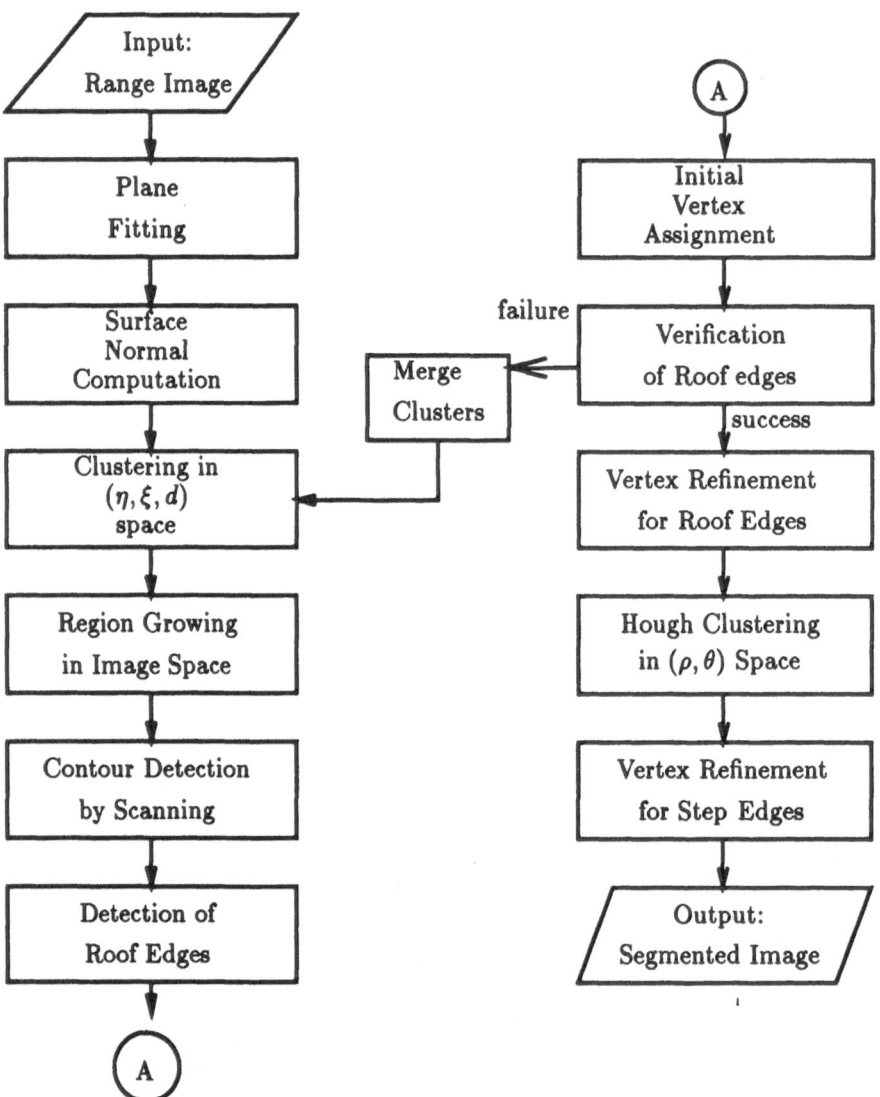

Figure 6.1: The flowchart of the segmentation process used for polyhedral object recognition.

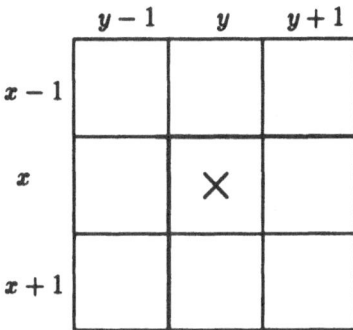

Figure 6.2: Results of plane fitting are averaged over four quadrants to improve accuracy.

chapter. The algorithm is different from conventional edge-based or region-based segmentation schemes. The algorithm exploits the synergy between the processes of detecting surface discontinuities and surface regions by using the *geometrical* properties of the detected surface regions. Homogeneous surface regions are extracted using a combination of clustering in parameter space and region-growing. It is known that the parameter estimation of surface regions in a range image is more reliable than edge detection using a local operator. Since the process of computing surface parameters involves averaging over several pixel values, it is more robust to noise than a local edge operator. In the following segmentation scheme, therefore, the geometric parameters of the surface regions are used to hypothesize the presence of surface discontinuities and accurately compute their parametric form. The hypothesis verification process incorporates the projection geometry as an *a priori* constraint to verify the hypothesized surface discontinuities.

The major components of the segmentation scheme are: (1) plane fitting to the pixel data, (2) clustering in the parameter domain, (3) region-growing, (4) contour detection and classification, (5) roof edge detection and initial vertex assignments, (6) verification using projection resulting in the possible merging of clusters, (7) refinement of vertex values, (8) step edge detection using the two-dimensional Hough transform, and (9) refinement of vertex values producing the final segmented image.

6.1.1 Plane Fitting to Pixel Data

Rosenfeld and Kak [1982] discuss a plane-fitting technique for fitting a plane $z = kx + ly + m$ to four pixel values $f(x,y)$, $f(x+1,y)$, $f(x,y+1)$, and $f(x+1,y+1)$ such that the quadratic error is minimized. The values of k,

l, and m for such a minimum quadratic error fit are given by:

$$k = \frac{1}{2}[(f(x+1,y)+f(x+1,y+1))-(f(x,y)+f(x,y+1))]$$

$$l = \frac{1}{2}[(f(x,y+1)+f(x+1,y+1))-(f(x,y)+f(x+1,y))]$$

$$m = \frac{1}{4}[3f(x,y)+f(x+1,y)+f(x,y+1)-f(x+1,y+1)]$$
$$-xk-yl \tag{6.1}$$

If the plane is written as $ax+by+cz+d=0$, the parameters a, b, c and d are related to the parameters k, l, and m by $a=k$, $b=l$, $c=-1$, and $d=m$ where (a,b,c) is the normal vector to the plane and d is the distance of the plane from the origin. The parameters are normalized such that $|(a,b,c)|=1$. The results of plane-fitting can be improved by averaging the values of a, b, c, and d over four 2×2 quadrants that include $f(x,y)$ (Figure 6.2).

6.1.2   Clustering in Parameter Space

The best fitting plane can be represented by another set of parameters (η,ξ,d) where $a = \sin\eta \cos\xi$, $b = \sin\eta \sin\xi$, $c = \cos\eta$, $0 \le \eta \le \pi$, and $0 \le \xi < 2\pi$. Planar facets in the image are identified by grouping pixels with similar values for (η,ξ,d), i.e., by clustering in the parameter space (η,ξ,d). An iterative clustering algorithm with a fixed number of cluster centers minimizing the squared error is used [Jain and Dubes 1988]. The algorithm consists of the following steps:

1. Select an initial partition with K initial cluster centers.

2. Compute new cluster centers as the centroids of the clusters.

3. Generate a new partition by assigning each point to its closest cluster center.

4. Repeat steps 2 and 3 a fixed number of times.

5. Adjust clusters by merging or removing some clusters.

The number of seed points, K, for the initial partition needs to be chosen beforehand. The K seed points for the initial partition can be selected randomly from the image data. However, better results can be expected if the seed points are spread over the range in parameter space where the cluster centers are expected to lie. In this case, the maximum and minimum values for d are computed from the image data, whereas the maximum and minimum values for η and ξ are known a priori. The number of seed points, K, (and therefore the maximum number of clusters) is chosen such that it is always larger than the maximum number of visible planes in the scene. This prevents the planes from being improperly merged due to unavailability of the requisite number of cluster centers. The assignment of each point to a cluster center requires the definition of a distance measure. Many useful distance measures are possible [Tou and Gonzalez

1974]. In our work, a weighted square-distance measure was found adequate. If (η, ξ, d) is a point in the parameter space and (η_0, ξ_0, d_0) is a cluster center, then the distance between the two in the parameter space is defined as

$$D = (d - d_0)^2 + W_1(d_{max} - d_{min})(\eta - \eta_0)^2 + W_2(d_{max} - d_{min})(\xi - \xi_0)^2 \quad (6.2)$$

where W_1 and W_2 are weights to account for the scaling problem, and d_{max} and d_{min} are the maximum and minimum values for d in the image, respectively. There is no general solution to the scaling problem, i.e., the problem of selecting weights in the distance measure so as to obtain the best result at the end of the clustering process has no general solution. The weights in our work are so chosen that all the variables are of the same order of magnitude.

The required number of iterations can be made to depend on a certain halting criterion. However, endless oscillations could occur if the criterion is not met. Since the algorithm converges fast, it is easier to limit the number of iterations to a fixed small number, typically 5 or 6. The number of clusters at the end of the iteration process is usually larger than the number of planar facets in the image. (We chose a large enough K to ensure this.) Some cluster centers may not contain any points at all and can be eliminated immediately. Some planes may be improperly divided into two clusters. Typically, such clusters are spatially adjacent and are merged if they meet the merging criterion. Again, several useful merging criteria can be conceived. The one used here uses a different threshold for each cluster parameter. If (η_1, ξ_1, d_1) is the center of the first cluster and (η_2, ξ_2, d_2) the center of the second cluster, then the merging criterion is given by :

$$
\begin{aligned}
|d_2 - d_1| &< D_0 \\
|\eta_2 - \eta_1| &< H_0 \\
|\xi_1 - \xi_2| &< R_0 \ or \ 2\pi - |\xi_1 - \xi_2| < R_0
\end{aligned}
\quad (6.3)
$$

where D_0, H_0 and R_0 are appropriately chosen constants. Small clusters are considered unlikely to represent actual planes. Rather, they are considered to represent noise or edge points between planes. Such clusters are normally caused by the averaging process during the computation of surface normals. Characteristically, these small clusters cannot be merged with neighboring clusters since the distance in parameter space between the cluster centers is too large. As these clusters are not of direct use, they are *dissolved* by merging each pixel of such a cluster with the cluster of a neighboring pixel, assuming that the neighboring pixel belongs to a different cluster. If no such neighboring pixel exists, the pixel is arbitrarily assigned to any other cluster. The smoothing process described next can remove such pixels.

6.1.3 Post Processing of Clustering Results

The range sensor used to acquire the range images in this chapter was an active triangulation-based sensor using vertical stripe light for scene illumination. Pixels within the field of view of the camera that are not illuminated by the stripe light source are called *shadow* pixels. Since the range cannot be computed at these shadow pixel locations, these pixels are marked as *invalid* pixels. With this in view, the quality of the range image, segmented thus far, is adversely affected by three factors:

1. There could be invalid pixels surrounded by valid pixels.

2. There could be pixels from one cluster that actually belong to different surfaces.

3. There could be a ragged line between clusters as a result of the preceding dissolving process.

These problems can be solved by smoothing the clusters in the image domain with masks of size $N \times N$ (typically 7×7). The mask is applied to every pixel p in the image. The number of valid points and the number of points belonging to each cluster within the mask centered around pixel p are counted. The pixel p is assigned to the cluster with the largest number of points in the mask if there is a sufficiently high number of valid points within the mask. Ties are broken arbitrarily. When an invalid pixel p is made valid using the smoothing technique, a new value is assigned to the pixel p by averaging the values of other valid pixels in the mask belonging to the same cluster to which the pixel p has been assigned. The smoothing process can be repeated, but more than two iterations are rarely required. The smoothing process is computationally expensive. The computational effort is directly proportional to the number of iterations and the size of the mask. At the end of the smoothing process there could exist clusters containing pixels belonging to distinct non-contiguous planar facets that coincidentally have the same parameters. These clusters are split into spatially connected components using a region-growing algorithm.

During the process of smoothing and region-growing, the cluster centers are recomputed, taking into consideration all reassignments of pixels to clusters. The cluster centers represent the average (η, ξ, d) values of all points belonging to that cluster. The averaging process is known to suppress noise (especially Gaussian noise), thereby enabling us to recover the parameters of the plane(s) with high accuracy.

6.1.4   Contour Extraction and Classification

The pixels constituting the contour lines of each plane can be extracted by using a simple scan line algorithm. The segmented image is scanned by rows, and those pixels at which the cluster labels change are marked as pixels on the contour lines (Figure 6.3). The scan is repeated vertically, i.e., for each column in the image. New contour line pixels are added during the vertical scan if they are different from the ones already extracted by the horizontal scan. Necessarily, the contour lines are only one pixel thick and closed. The contour lines of convex as well as concave objects can be correctly identified. This contour extraction algorithm does not need a sophisticated edge detection operator or thresholding or thinning procedure since it is applied after the previously mentioned smoothing process.

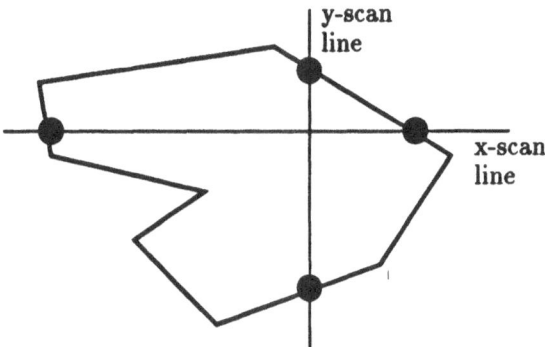

Figure 6.3: Horizontal and vertical scans detect pixels on contour lines.

Contour pixels can be classified as step (jump) or roof (crease) edge pixels by using a simple gradient edge operator along the X and Y directions, centered on the contour pixel. The response of a step edge pixel to a gradient operator is typically much greater than that of a roof edge pixel. The thresholded gradient values enables us to distinguish step edge pixels from roof edge pixels. Roof edge pixels can be further classified as *concave* or *convex* by using a Laplacian operator centered around the pixel. The sign of the result of Laplacian operator is used to classify the edge pixel as either *convex* or *concave*. It is to be noted, however, that the edge operator is not used to *compute* the edge parameters such as length, direction vector, etc., but only for *classification*. Edge parameters are computed far more accurately using the parameters of the planar facets already extracted. Moreover, the edge pixels thus labeled are also verified for conformity with the parameters of the planar facets.

6.1.5 Computation of Edge Parameters

Given the contour pixels, the computation of edge parameters (i.e., end points, length, and direction vector) proceeds in two parts. The roof edge parameters are computed first since they can be computed with a high degree of accuracy. Then the parameters for the step edges are determined using a Hough clustering algorithm coupled with a constraint propagation algorithm that propagates the values of the parameters of the roof edges and those of the planar facets.

Computation of Roof Edge Parameters

For all pairs of non-parallel planes, the direction vector of the line of intersection of each pair is predicted from the parameters of the planes, i.e., it is the cross product of the normal vectors of the two planes; however, the predicted line might not be found in the given image since we are dealing with finite planar

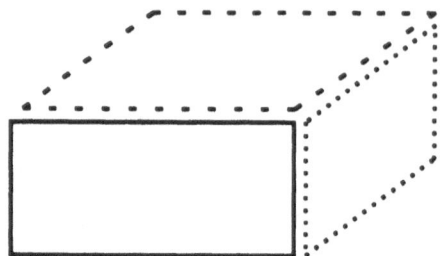

Figure 6.4: A contour line between spatially contiguous surface patches is a roof edge.

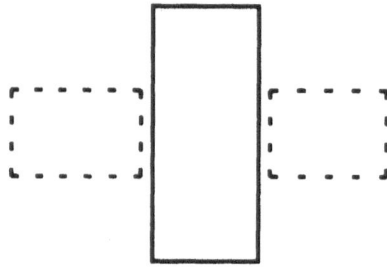

Figure 6.5: A contour line between two spatially non-contiguous patches is a step edge.

facets. Therefore, only spatially contiguous non-parallel planes are considered. Two clusters are considered spatially contiguous if their contour pixels are next to each other and have been labeled as roof edge pixels (Figure 6.4). It is possible, however, for two clusters to have adjacent contour pixels but have the corresponding contour pixels labeled as step edge pixels (Figure 6.5). Such clusters are not considered to be spatially contiguous.

To check whether the predicted line of intersection really exists in the image, the line is projected on the xy plane using the *a prior* constraints derived from the knowledge of the projection geometry (orthographic, perspective, affine, etc.). In this chapter the projection is assumed to be orthographic, but the approach is general enough to incorporate other types of projection geometry as well. If the projected line has a slope of less than 45°, then a pixel (x, y) on the projected line is checked for edge pixels from spatially contiguous clusters at locations (x, y) and $(x, y + 1)$ or locations (x, y) and $(x, y - 1)$. If the projected line has a slope of greater than 45°, then a pixel (x, y) on the projected line is checked for edge pixels from spatially contiguous clusters at locations (x, y)

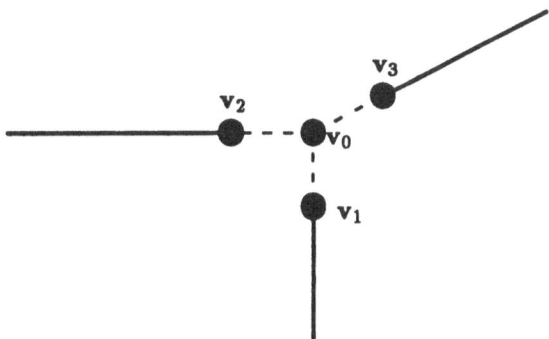

Figure 6.6: Refinement of a vertex formed by roof edges: v_0 replaces v_1, v_2, and v_3.

and $(x-1, y)$ or locations (x, y) and $(x+1, y)$. The hypothesis verification thus assumes a localization accuracy tolerance of ± 1 pixel. It is possible, however, to incorporate any other prespecified tolerance. If the projected line does not satisfy the above conditions, then the image is assumed to be *oversegmented*. This forms a cue for merging the corresponding clusters, as shown in the flow chart (Figure 6.1). If the projected line does satisfy the conditions mentioned above, then the x and y coordinates of the extremal points on the projected line are retained during the process of checking the neighborhood of the pixels that lie on the projected line. The corresponding z coordinates are determined from the equations of the planar facet. These (x, y, z) values are preliminary values for the end points of the edges and the vertices of the object.

Vertex Refinement for Roof Edges

The initial values of the vertices computed above are not always accurate. To refine the values, the following approach is taken:

1. Three nonparallel planes define a point of intersection if their corresponding clusters, considered pairwise, are spatially contiguous. If the equations of the planes are $a_i x + b_i y + c_i z + d_i = 0$ where $1 \le i \le 3$, then the point of intersection can be computed by solving the three plane equations for x, y, and z. Since each pair of the above planes has a common roof edge, the value of the computed vertex replaces the value of one of the endpoints of each of the roof edges (Figure 6.6).

2. By the end of Step 1 most roof edges would have one vertex accurately determined. The other vertex would have a less accurate value, as determined by the neighborhood checking procedure described previously. If one vertex (x_1, y_1, z_1) and the direction vector of the edge (d_x, d_y, d_z) are

accurately known, then the value of the less accurate vertex can be refined by constraining it to lie on the line defined by the first vertex and the direction vector. If the second vertex has an initial value (x_2, y_2, z_2), then we compute the parameter ν to be the average of $(x_2 - x_1)/d_x$ and $(y_2 - y_1)/d_y$. The refined value of the second vertex is then computed as $(x_1 + \nu d_x, y_1 + \nu d_y, z_1 + \nu d_z)$.

Computation of Step Edge Parameters

A two-dimensional Hough clustering procedure is applied to the contour pixels labeled as step edges. The two-dimensional projection on the xy plane of a three-dimensional edge is a two-dimensional line represented by the equation $r = x \cos \theta + y \sin \theta$, where r is the distance of the line from the origin and θ is the angle between the normal to the line and the X axis. The direction vector of the two-dimensional line is $\mathbf{p} = (\sin \theta, -\cos \theta, 0)$. An iterative Hough clustering technique based on histogramming in the (r, θ) accumulator array is used. Whenever a peak in the accumulator array is detected, the corresponding contour pixels are traced using a line tracing algorithm. The response of these pixels for subsequent iterations of the algorithm is selectively suppressed. The accumulator array is reset at the beginning of every iteration and when the peak value in the array falls below a threshold the process is terminated. For pixels that correspond to a peak detected above, the line tracing algorithm computes the extremal pixels, which are retained as end points of the edge. Since the edge lies in three-dimensional space, whereas the line is a two-dimensional projection, the z-coordinates of the extremal points are computed by constraining the points to lie on the corresponding plane. If the equation of the plane is $ax+by+cz+d = 0$, then the z coordinate of a point (x, y) on the two-dimensional orthographic projection of the edge is given by $z = -(ax + by + d)/c$. Since the normal to the plane is $\mathbf{n} = (n_x, n_y, n_z) = (a, b, c)$, the direction vector of the edge $\mathbf{d} = (d_x, d_y, d_z)$ is determined by the set of equations

$$
\begin{aligned}
d_x &= \sin \theta \\
d_y &= -\cos \theta \\
\mathbf{d} \cdot \mathbf{n} &= 0
\end{aligned}
\tag{6.4}
$$

The coordinates for the endpoints as computed above serve as initial estimates for the corresponding vertices.

Vertex Refinement for Step Edges

In order to refine the coordinate values of a vertex for a step edge, a proximity function is defined between the given vertex and a previously computed (and refined) vertex. The proximity function decides whether the two vertices are close enough to be deemed identical. If (x_1, y_1, z_1) and (x_2, y_2, z_2) are the vertices under consideration, then they are deemed identical if $|x_2 - x_1| < D_x$, $|y_2 - y_1| < D_y$, and $|z_2 - z_1| < D_z$, where D_x, D_y, and D_y are appropriately chosen thresholds.

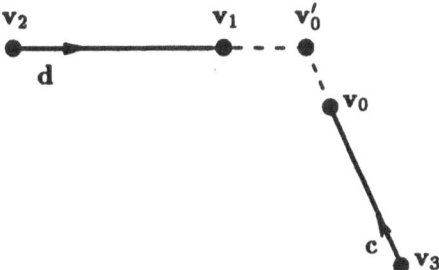

Figure 6.7: Refinement of a vertex formed by step edges: $v_0{}'$ replaces v_0 and v_1.

The vertices of a step edge are refined under the two constraints:

1. The refined vertices should be collinear with the direction vector d of the edge.

2. The vertices must satisfy the equation(s) of the plane(s) to which the edge belongs.

We consider three cases for vertex refinement of step edges. The basic underlying principle in each of these cases is to compute the new vertices as the points of intersection of two lines whenever possible. If we let $v_1 = (x_1, y_1, z_1)$ and $v_2 = (x_2, y_2, z_2)$ be the vertices derived from step edges, and $d = (d_x, d_y, d_z)$ the direction vector of the edge as determined in Eq. (6.4), then the three different cases to be considered are:

1. Neither vertex is close to any previously computed and refined vertex. In this case, $\nu = (x_2 - x_1)/d_x$ and the refined vertices of the edge are $v_1 = (x_1, y_1, z_1)$ and $v_2 = (x_1 + \nu d_x, y_1 + \nu d_y, z_1 + \nu d_z)$.

2. One of the vertices is proximate to a previously computed and refined vertex $v_0 = (x_0, y_0, z_0)$. Let v_1 be proximate to v_0 and let v_2 not be proximate to any previously computed and refined vertex. In this case the following two subcases have to be dealt with:

    (a) The degree of vertex v_0 is 1, i.e., there is only one edge incident on vertex v_0. Let $v_3 = (x_3, y_3, z_3)$ be the other vertex of that edge. A new vertex $v_0{}'$ is computed that is the intersection of the edge (v_3, v_0) and the edge (v_1, v_2) (Figure 6.7). Let $c = (c_x, c_y, c_z)$ be the direction vector in the direction of edge (v_3, v_0). The coordinates of $v_0{}' = (x_0{}', y_0{}', z_0{}')$ are determined as follows:

$$
\begin{aligned}
x_0{}' &= x_2 + \mu_1 d_x \\
&= x_3 + \mu_2 c_x
\end{aligned}
$$

and

$$y_0' = y_2 + \mu_1 d_y$$
$$= y_3 + \mu_2 c_y$$

therefore,

$$x_2 + \mu_1 d_x = x_3 + \mu_2 c_x \qquad (6.5)$$
$$y_2 + \mu_1 d_y = y_3 + \mu_2 c_y \qquad (6.6)$$

Solving Eqs. (6.5) and (6.6) for μ_1 and μ_2 yields the values x_0' and y_0'. The value of z_0' is determined from the equation of the corresponding plane. Thus the vertex v_0' replaces the vertices v_0 and v_1 in the corresponding edges.

(b) The degree of vertex v_0 is greater than 1. In this case v_0 is already computed as the intersection of edges and v_0 replaces v_1 in the edge (v_1, v_2). If $d = (d_x, d_y, d_z)$ is the direction vector of (v_1, v_2), then the coordinates of v_2 are updated to $(x_0 + \nu d_x, y_0 + \nu d_x, z_0 + \nu d_z)$, where $\nu = (x_2 - x_1)/d_x$.

3. Both vertices v_1 and v_2 are proximate to previously computed and refined vertices v_3 and v_4, respectively. In this case there are three subcases to be considered:

(a) v_3 and v_4 are both of degree 1. In this subcase both the vertices v_3 and v_4 are modified as described in 2(a). An edge joining the modified vertices is created. The edge (v_1, v_2) is deleted.

(b) One of the vertices, say v_3, is of degree greater than 1 and the other, v_4, is of degree 1. In this case v_3 is left unchanged and v_4 is modified as discussed in 2(a). An edge joining v_3 and the modified value of v_4 is created. The edge (v_1, v_2) is deleted.

(c) Both v_3 and v_4 are of degree greater than 1. In this case both v_3 and v_4 are left unchanged. A new edge (v_3, v_4) is created. The edge (v_1, v_2) is deleted.

In the approach outlined above, a modified vertex v_0' might be significantly away from v_0 if the two edges intersecting at v_0' form an acute angle, say, less than 20°. In such cases it is preferable to keep v_0 rather than modify it. For most objects in the object model database in this chapter, however, the assumption that two edges of a facet incident on a common vertex do not form an acute angle less than 20° is a reasonable one.

The final output of the segmentation step is a high-level description of the polyhedral object(s) in the scene in terms of their facets, edges, and vertices (junctions), along with their underlying parameters—for a facet it is the equation of the plane containing the facet, for an edge it is the endpoints, the direction vector and its length, and for a vertex it is the coordinate values along the X, Y, and Z axes. The segmentation scheme works well on both, single- and multiple-object scenes. The clustering in the (η, ξ, d) parameter space for detecting planar facets can be done reliably in both single- and multiple-object scenes. It is possible for facets belonging to different objects to be put into the same cluster, but this happens only if the facets are adjacent in the scene and also proximate in the parameter space. However, this phenomenon is rarely observed. A range image of poor quality can cause a breakup of a facet into different clusters, but most clusters of such nature are eventually merged by the cluster merging process. The application of masks to smooth the clusters blurs the contour lines only insignificantly. The blurs are usually noticeable only near corner regions (vertices) of the objects. Since the positions of the vertices are determined by computing the intersections of the corresponding edges and planes, the blurring does not affect the accuracy of the vertex parameters. The equation of a planar facet can be determined accurately even if the planar facet is partially occluded. One problem, however, that is encountered when carrying out Hough clustering for detection of 2-D line segments in the image is that line segments corresponding to a single peak in the Hough space need not always be contiguous. The line-tracing algorithm must be designed to take care of this contingency. The thresholds D_x, D_y, and D_z in the proximity function also have to be carefully chosen. If the thresholds D_x, D_y, and D_z chosen are too small, spurious vertices and edges can be included in the final segmented description, whereas, if they are too large, distinct edges can be coalesced into a single edge.

6.2 Feature Extraction

Having segmented the input range image into planar surface patches that are expected to correspond to the planar facets of the objects, and into surface discontinuities that are expected to correspond to the edges of the objects, the next logical step is to extract appropriate features from the segmented image. As explained earlier, the choice of representational granularity for the features (i.e., whether to choose local or global features) greatly affects the choice of the constraint propagation technique used for recognition and localization. Since the scenes considered contain multiple objects with cases of partial occlusion, the use of global features is ruled out. Thus, only local features are used in the recognition process, and the constraint propagation technique should be capable of propagating constraints arising from the matches of local scene and model features in order to come up with a global scene interpretation. In this chapter both the generalized Hough transform and the interpretation tree search are presented as examples of constraint propagation techniques that satisfy this requirement. There is a wide variety of local features that could be used for matching and pose computation for polyhedral objects. They are (Figure 6.8):

1. Two non-parallel edges (which may be coplanar).

2. One edge and one face normal that are neither parallel nor perpendicular to each other.

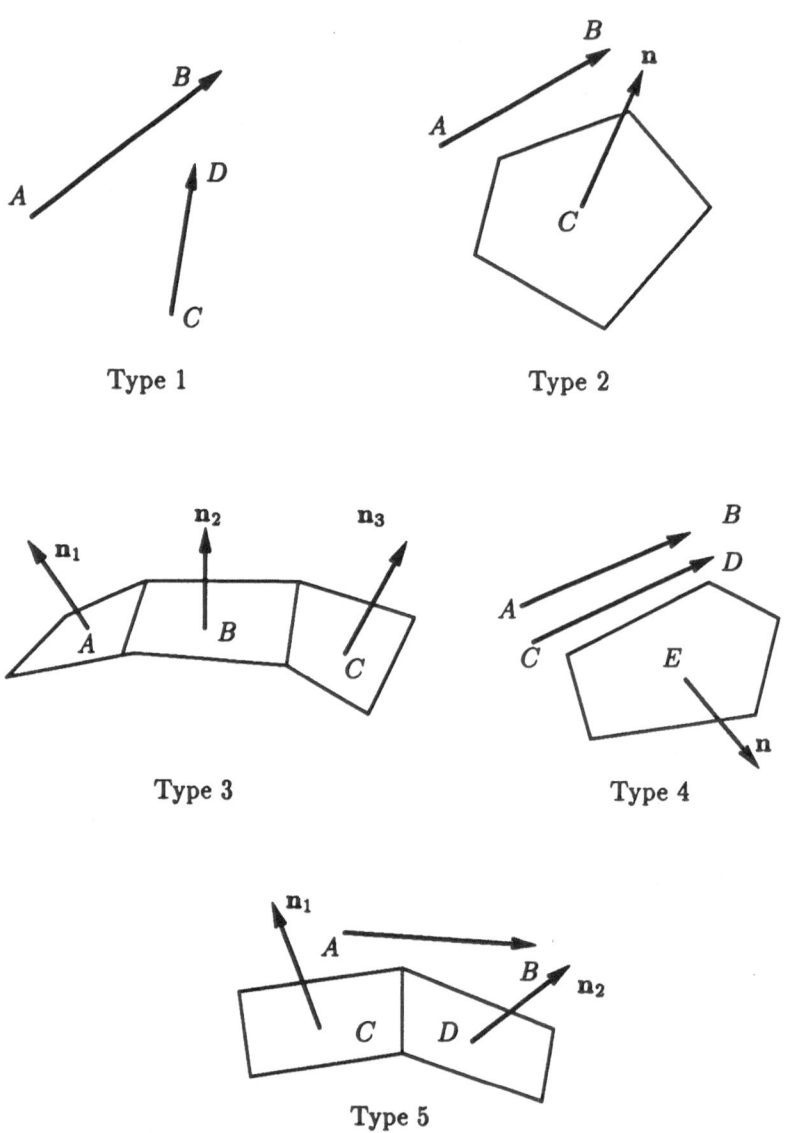

Figure 6.8: Five feature types used in polyhedral object recognition.

3. Three face normals, no two of which are parallel.

4. Two parallel edges and one face normal that is not perpendicular to either parallel edge.

5. Two face normals and one edge which is not perpendicular to either face normal.

These features could also be used as a hypothesis generating feature (HGF) set for interpretation tree search [Chen and Kak 1989].

As mentioned previously, the use of qualitative features is an effective way of controlling the combinatorial complexity of the search space of possible scene interpretations. In the present context, the term *qualitative features* is used to signify scene and model features with *qualitative attributes* assigned to them. These qualitative attributes can then be used to group features into feature classes that are subject to constraints specific to these feature classes. This results in a reduction in the combinatorial complexity of the search space. The qualitative features should be relatively easy to compute and should not entail elaborate segmentation of the image. In many ways the problem of three-dimensional object recognition can be looked upon as a trade-off between the complexity of representation and the computational complexity of the constraint propagation technique. The more complex or higher-level the representation is, the more computationally intensive the segmentation and feature extraction processes should be to arrive at the representation. A higher-level representation often reduces the computational complexity of the constraint propagation process that is used for recognition and localization. On the other hand, a lower-level representation requires less computational effort on the part of segmentation and feature extraction processes, but involves a computationally more complex constraint propagation process. By requiring that qualitative features do not entail an elaborate segmentation or feature extraction process, we can ensure that the benefit of reducing the combinatorial complexity of the search space is not offset by the demands of segmentation or feature extraction processes. As will be shown in this chapter, a simple and easily computable qualitative attribute based on *occlusion* can greatly reduce the combinatorial complexity of the search space.

A boundary segment $\mathbf{A} = (\mathbf{v}_1, \mathbf{v}_2)$ is considered to be *occluded* if it ends at a T junction with a *jump* boundary segment $\mathbf{B} = (\mathbf{v}_3, \mathbf{v}_4)$. $\mathbf{A}$ defines a T junction with $\mathbf{B}$ if the following conditions are satisfied (Figure 6.9):

1. Consider the projections $\mathbf{A}' = (\mathbf{v}_1', \mathbf{v}_2')$ and $\mathbf{B}' = (\mathbf{v}_3', \mathbf{v}_4')$ of $\mathbf{A}$ and $\mathbf{B}$ on the xy plane, respectively. The point of intersection $\mathbf{v}'$ of the two-dimensional lines defined by $(\mathbf{v}_1', \mathbf{v}_2')$ and $(\mathbf{v}_3', \mathbf{v}_4')$ should lie between $(\mathbf{v}_3', \mathbf{v}_4')$. That is to say, $(\mathbf{v}' - \mathbf{v}_3') = \alpha(\mathbf{v}_4' - \mathbf{v}_3')$ where $\alpha < 1$.

2. The point of intersection $\mathbf{v}'$ should be equal to or proximate to (within a threshold) either $\mathbf{v}_1'$ or $\mathbf{v}_2'$.

A simple algorithm classifying boundary segments as either *occluded* or *not occluded* can be designed. The algorithm considers each jump boundary segment

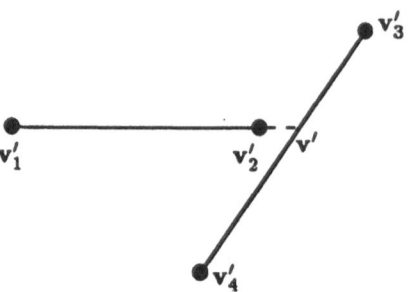

Figure 6.9: **A T** junction defined by two edge segments.

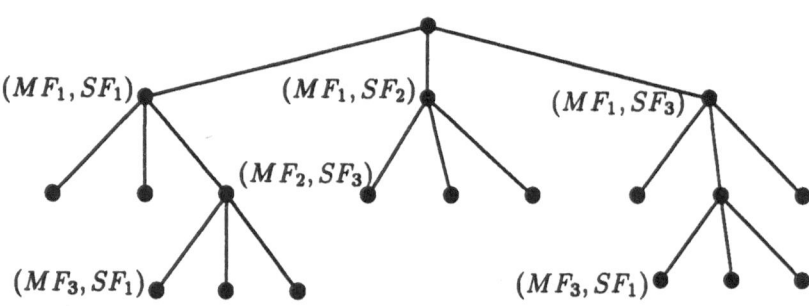

Figure 6.10: An example of interpretation tree search.

and determines which of the remaining boundary segments forms a **T** junction with the jump edge under consideration using the conditions cited above. This algorithm can be seen to have a worst case quadratic complexity in the number of edges of the object. For the generalized Hough transform, dihedral junctions, i.e., junctions with one vertex and two incident edges, are used as the transformation generating feature (TGF), whereas for interpretation tree search, three non-coplanar facets are used as the hypothesis generating feature set. In each case, the use of qualitative features can be seen to greatly reduce the combinatorial complexity of the search space of possible scene interpretations.

6.3 Interpretation Tree Search

In this chapter, the hypothesis generation feature set needed in the interpretation tree search consists of three non-coplanar pairwise adjacent facets. The primary motive behind this choice was that planar facets could be extracted with a high degree of accuracy during the segmentation process. At each node in the interpretation tree, a planar facet from the model is matched with a planar facet from the scene (Figure 6.10). The height of the interpretation tree is three, and a scene interpretation hypothesis consists of three matched pairs of facets $\{(MF_i, SF_j) \mid 1 \le i, j \le 3\}$ where MF_i, $1 \le i \le 3$ are the model facets from some model in the database, and SF_j, $1 \le j \le 3$ are the scene facets from the segmented range image.

The search through the interpretation tree follows the depth-first *hypothesize-and-test* paradigm. Backtracking occurs whenever no consistent hypothesis can be found or when a hypothesis cannot be verified. The tree search is data-driven because the sequence of matches is controlled by the order of the scene features SF_i. For each model in the database a different tree is searched. Since the number of paths in the interpretation tree increases exponentially with the number of features in the scene and in the model, pruning of the interpretation tree is essential.

The following geometric constraints are used to identify inconsistent hypotheses thus enabling us to prune the interpretation tree at an early stage:

1. *Area constraint.* A model facet is matched with a scene facet only if the area of the model facet is larger than or equal to that of the scene facet. A scene facet is considered to be occluded if at least one of its bounding boundary segments has been classified as occluded; otherwise, a scene facet is considered to be unoccluded. For a match of an unoccluded scene facet SF_i to a model facet MF_j, the area constraint can be specified as:

$$|area(SF_i) - area(MF_j)| < \epsilon \qquad (6.7)$$

where ϵ is a tolerance bound. For a match of an occluded scene facet SF_i to a model facet MF_j, the area constraint can be specified as:

$$area(SF_i) \le area(MF_j) \qquad (6.8)$$

The use of the qualitative attribute based on occlusion allows us to select a more rigorous area constraint based on equality (within tolerance bounds) for unoccluded scene facets, whereas for occluded scene facets we can only formulate an area constraint based on inequality. In the absence of this qualitative attribute we would be restricted to the use of the weaker constraint based on inequality for all matches.

2. *Neighborhood constraint.* Only scene facets that are pairwise adjacent are used in a scene interpretation hypothesis. We can assume that the position and orientation of an object in the scene constitutes a *generic* viewpoint. Therefore, the object to be recognized exposes at least three contiguous facets to the viewer. This is a reasonable assumption in scenes with moderate occlusion.

3. *Angle constraint.* If scene facet SF_i is matched with model facet MF_k, and scene facet SF_j is matched with model facet MF_l, then α_s, which is the

angle between SF_i and SF_j, and α_m, which is the angle between MF_k and MF_l, should be equal. Since the computation of the scene facet normals is subject to noise, in practice we impose the constraint that $|\alpha_m - \alpha_s| \leq \alpha_T$, where α_T is an appropriately defined threshold.

4. *Unique interpretation constraint.* In any single interpretation hypothesis we require that a single model facet be matched to a single scene facet, and vice versa.

Scene facets are ordered by decreasing area to maximally exploit the area constraint. Owing to occlusion, the area of a scene facet can be significantly smaller than the area of the model facet to which it is being matched. However, in the area constraint based on equality of the areas of the unoccluded scene facets and model facets, allowance is made for the fact that a scene facet could have an area slightly larger than that of the model facet to which it is being matched, since there could be misclassification of some pixels or errors in range sensing. Once a scene interpretation hypothesis has been generated, the transformation matrix $\mathbf{T}$ can be computed using the three matched pairs of scene facets and model facets. Details of the computation of $\mathbf{T}$ are given in the following section.

6.3.1   Pose Determination

Given three model facets MF_i, $1 \leq i \leq 3$ with equations $A_i x + B_i y + C_i z + D_i = 0$, and three scene facets SF_j, $1 \leq j \leq 3$ with equations $a_j x + b_j y + c_j z + d_j = 0$, we can determine a transformation matrix $\mathbf{T}$ that will place the object model in registration with the object in the scene. In order to compute $\mathbf{T}$ it is convenient to use homogeneous coordinates that allow us to treat rotational and translational transformations in a unified manner [Paul 1981] [Korn and Korn 1972]. Each point (x, y, z) in 3-D space is represented by a four-dimensional column vector $[x, y, z, 1]^T$ in homogeneous coordinates. A position vector $\mathbf{p}$ can be transformed into another vector $\mathbf{p}'$ by premultiplying it by a 4×4 matrix $\mathbf{M}$, i.e., $\mathbf{p}' = \mathbf{M} \cdot \mathbf{p}$.

The matrix $\mathbf{T}$ that describes a global transformation consists of two rotations and one translation. Therefore, $\mathbf{T}$ can be expressed as the product of two rotational transformations, $\mathbf{R}_1$ and $\mathbf{R}_2$, and a translational transformation, $\mathbf{R}_3$.

$$\mathbf{T} = \mathbf{R}_3 \cdot \mathbf{R}_2 \cdot \mathbf{R}_1 \qquad (6.9)$$

The computation of $\mathbf{R}_1$, $\mathbf{R}_2$ and $\mathbf{R}_3$ is described below.

Determination of $\mathbf{R}_1$

Consider a scene interpretation hypothesis

$$S = \{(MF_i, SF_l), (MF_j, SF_m), (MF_k, SF_n)\} \qquad (6.10)$$

The matrix $\mathbf{R}_1$ defines a rotation that aligns the unit normal to the model facet MF_i, denoted by $\mathbf{N}_i = (A_i, B_i, C_i)$ with the unit normal to the scene facet SF_l

denoted by $\mathbf{n}_l = (a_l, b_l, c_l)$. If $\mathbf{N}_i = \pm\mathbf{n}_l$, then the two normals are already aligned and $\mathbf{R}_1 = \pm\mathbf{I}$, where $\mathbf{I}$ is the identity transformation. If $\mathbf{N}_i \neq \pm\mathbf{n}_l$, then consider the vector,

$$\mathbf{d} = \frac{\mathbf{N}_i \times \mathbf{n}_l}{|\mathbf{N}_i \times \mathbf{n}_l|} \tag{6.11}$$

where $\times$ denotes the vector cross product. Clearly, $\mathbf{d}$ is normalized so that $|\mathbf{d}| = 1$. $\mathbf{L} = \mu\mathbf{d}$ (where μ is a scalar parameter) is a line through the origin that is perpendicular to both $\mathbf{N}_i$ and $\mathbf{n}_l$. Let $\theta = \cos^{-1}(\mathbf{N}_i \cdot \mathbf{n}_l)$. Since θ is the angle between $\mathbf{N}_i$ and $\mathbf{n}_l$, a rotation about $\mathbf{L}$ by θ aligns $\mathbf{N}_i$ with $\mathbf{n}_l$.

The rotation about a general line $\mathbf{L} = \mu\mathbf{d}$ through the origin can be decomposed into five independent rotations, each of which is an elementary rotation about one of the coordinate axes. We proceed by aligning $\mathbf{d}$ with the z axis, performing the rotation about the z axis and then undoing the alignment. This involves the following steps.

1. Rotation about the y axis such that $\mathbf{d} = (d_x, d_y, d_z)$ lies in the plane $x = 0$. The transformation $\mathbf{P}_1$ that defines a rotation about the y axis by an angle α is given by

$$\mathbf{P}_1 = \begin{bmatrix} \cos\alpha & 0 & -\sin\alpha & 0 \\ 0 & 1 & 0 & 0 \\ \sin\alpha & 0 & \cos\alpha & 0 \\ 0 & 0 & 0 & 1 \end{bmatrix} \tag{6.12}$$

where $\cos\alpha = d_z/\nu$, $\sin\alpha = d_x/\nu$, and $\nu^2 = d_x^2 + d_z^2$.

2. Rotation about the x axis such that $\mathbf{d}$ lies along the z axis. A matrix $\mathbf{Q}_1$ that defines a rotation about the x axis by angle β is given by

$$\mathbf{Q}_1 = \begin{bmatrix} 1 & 0 & 0 & 0 \\ 0 & \cos\beta & -\sin\beta & 0 \\ 0 & \sin\beta & \cos\beta & 0 \\ 0 & 0 & 0 & 1 \end{bmatrix} \tag{6.13}$$

where $\cos\beta = \nu$, $\sin\beta = d_y$, and $\nu^2 = d_x^2 + d_z^2$.

3. Rotation about the z axis, i.e., the main rotation. The matrix $\mathbf{R}_1'$ that defines a rotation about the z axis by an angle γ is given by

$$\mathbf{R}_1' = \begin{bmatrix} \cos\gamma & -\sin\gamma & 0 & 0 \\ \sin\gamma & \cos\gamma & 0 & 0 \\ 0 & 0 & 1 & 0 \\ 0 & 0 & 0 & 1 \end{bmatrix} \tag{6.14}$$

where $\gamma = \theta = \mathbf{N}_i \cdot \mathbf{n}_l$.

4. Undoing the rotation about the x axis, which involves multiplication by $\mathbf{Q}_1^{-1}$.

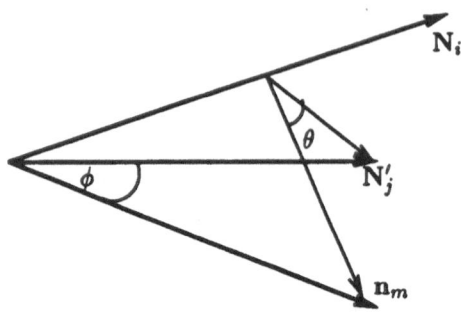

Figure 6.11: Computation of the angle of rotation to align $N_j{}'$ with $\mathbf{n}_m$.

5. Undoing the rotation about the y axis, which involves multiplication by $\mathbf{P}_1{}^{-1}$.

   The rotation matrix $\mathbf{R}_1$, which describes the overall rotation about $\mathbf{L}$, is the product of the matrices

$$\mathbf{R}_1 = \mathbf{P}_1^{-1} \cdot \mathbf{Q}_1^{-1} \cdot \mathbf{R}_1' \cdot \mathbf{Q}_1 \cdot \mathbf{P}_1 \tag{6.15}$$

Determination of $\mathbf{R}_2$

Let $\mathbf{N}_j = (A_j, B_j, C_j)$ be the unit normal to the model facet MF_j and $\mathbf{n}_m = (a_m, b_m, c_m)$ the unit normal to the scene facet SF_m. Let $\mathbf{N}_j'$ be the unit normal produced by the multiplication of $\mathbf{N}_j$ by $\mathbf{R}_1$, i.e., $\mathbf{N}_j' = \mathbf{N}_j \cdot \mathbf{R}_1$. Let $\mathbf{d} = \mathbf{N}_i$ and $\cos\phi = \mathbf{N}_j' \cdot \mathbf{n}_m$. Then $\mathbf{N}_j'$ can be aligned with $\mathbf{n}_m$ by rotating $\mathbf{N}_j'$ by an angle θ about $\mathbf{d}$ given by

$$
\begin{aligned}
\cos\theta &= 1 - \frac{[1 - \cos\phi]}{[1 - (\mathbf{d} \cdot \mathbf{N}_j')(\mathbf{d} \cdot \mathbf{n}_m)]} \\
&= 1 - \frac{[1 - \cos\phi]}{[1 - (\mathbf{N}_i \cdot \mathbf{N}_j')(\mathbf{N}_i \cdot \mathbf{n}_m)]}
\end{aligned} \tag{6.16}
$$

as shown in Figure 6.11. Steps 1 through 5 given previously can be repeated to compute $\mathbf{R}_2$, as follows

$$\mathbf{R}_2 = \mathbf{P}_2^{-1} \cdot \mathbf{Q}_2^{-1} \cdot \mathbf{R}_2' \cdot \mathbf{Q}_2 \cdot \mathbf{P}_2 \tag{6.17}$$

where

$$\mathbf{R}_2' = \begin{bmatrix} \cos\theta & -\sin\theta & 0 & 0 \\ \sin\theta & \cos\theta & 0 & 0 \\ 0 & 0 & 1 & 0 \\ 0 & 0 & 0 & 1 \end{bmatrix} \tag{6.18}$$

and $\mathbf{P}_2$ and $\mathbf{Q}_2$ are defined in the same manner as previously.

Determination of R_3

The scene facets (SF_i, SF_j, SF_n) and the model facets (MF_l, MF_m, MF_n) are pairwise adjacent and non-coplanar, and each defines a point of intersection $\mathbf{v}_s = (v_{s_x}, v_{s_y}, v_{s_z})$ and $\mathbf{V}_m = (V_{m_x}, V_{m_y}, V_{m_z})$, respectively. The overall transformation has to transform $\mathbf{V}_m$ into $\mathbf{v}_s$, i.e., $\mathbf{T} \cdot \mathbf{V}_m = \mathbf{v}_s$. Let $\mathbf{V}_m''$ be the vertex obtained from $\mathbf{V}_m$ by multiplying it by $\mathbf{R}_2 \cdot \mathbf{R}_1$. The translation matrix $\mathbf{R}_3$ translates the model facets rotated by $\mathbf{R}_2 \cdot \mathbf{R}_1$, into the appropriate scene facets.

$$\mathbf{R}_3 = \begin{bmatrix} 1 & 0 & 0 & t_x \\ 0 & 1 & 0 & t_y \\ 0 & 0 & 1 & t_z \\ 0 & 0 & 0 & 1 \end{bmatrix} \tag{6.19}$$

where

$$\begin{aligned} t_x &= v_{s_x} - V_{m_x}'' \\ t_y &= v_{s_y} - V_{m_y}'' \\ t_z &= v_{s_z} - V_{m_z}'' \end{aligned} \tag{6.20}$$

6.3.2 Scene Interpretation Hypothesis Verification

The verification process uses the computed transformation matrix $\mathbf{T}$ to project an object model onto the scene and verifies the existence of an object in the scene at the given position with the given orientation. The verification process is a combination of junction matching and constraint propagation.

Junction Matching

Given a scene interpretation hypothesis

$$S = \{(MF_i, SF_l), (MF_j, SF_m), (MF_k, SF_n)\} \tag{6.21}$$

let $\mathbf{T}$ be the corresponding pose as computed in the previous section. Let M_j be the model from which the three model facets MF_i, MF_j and MF_k are chosen. Let m be the number of vertices of M_j, $\mathbf{V}_i$, $1 \le i \le m$ the vertices of M_j, and $\mathbf{V}_i' = \mathbf{T} \cdot \mathbf{V}_i$ the vertices of M_j after transformation $\mathbf{T}$. Let s be the number of scene vertices denoted by $\mathbf{v}_i$, $1 \le i \le s$. For the selected pose hypothesis denoted by $\mathbf{T}$, the model M_j is projected on the scene. A three-dimensional window is defined around the projection, which serves as a crude filter. If the number of unlabeled scene vertices is fewer than a predefined threshold, the hypothesis is rejected. For the hypotheses that pass the crude filter test, a more detailed comparison based on junction matching is carried out. A model vertex $\mathbf{V}_i'$ and a scene vertex $\mathbf{v}_j$ within the window are matched based on the following constraints.

  1. *Proximity constraint.* The distance between the vertices should be less than a predefined threshold d_{max}, i.e., $|\mathbf{V}_i' - \mathbf{v}_j| \le d_{max}$. For a match that

satisfies the proximity constraint we define a match quality

$$M_p = K_1(d_{max} - |\mathbf{V}'_i - \mathbf{v}_j|) \tag{6.22}$$

where K_1 is a constant.

2. *Object consistency constraint.* The scene vertex $\mathbf{v}_j$ should belong to the same object as the scene facets SF_l, SF_m, and SF_n. Two facets are defined to belong to the same object if they share a common roof edge. Beginning with SF_l, SF_m, and SF_n, and using the above definition, all the facets that belong to the same object as do the facets SF_l, SF_m and SF_n, are recursively determined. Since the segmentation process determines which planar facets $\mathbf{v}_j$ belongs to, we can decide whether $\mathbf{v}_j$ belongs to the same objects as do the scene facets SF_l, SF_m, and SF_n.

3. *Degree constraint.* The degree (number of incident edges) of $\mathbf{v}_j$ should not exceed the degree of $\mathbf{V}'_i$.

4. *Orientation constraint.* The angles between the corresponding edges of $\mathbf{V}'_i$ and $\mathbf{v}_j$ should be less than a predefined threshold. For each edge of $\mathbf{V}'_i$ and the corresponding edge of $\mathbf{v}_j$ such that the angular separation ϕ between the edges is $\leq \phi_{max}$, we define a match quality

$$M_\phi = K_2(\phi_{max} - \phi) \tag{6.23}$$

where K_2 is a constant.

5. *Length constraint.* The length of a scene edge incident on $\mathbf{v}_j$ should be less than or equal to the length of the corresponding model edge incident on $\mathbf{V}'_i$. For *unoccluded* scene boundary segments the length constraint can be written as

$$|L_m - l_s| \leq \epsilon_l \tag{6.24}$$

where ϵ_l is a predefined threshold, L_m is the length of the model edge, and l_s is the length of the scene edge. For *occluded* scene boundary segments the length constraint can be written as

$$l_s \leq L_m \tag{6.25}$$

For edges which satisfy the length constraint we define a match quality

$$M_L = K_3(L_m - |L_m - l_s|) \tag{6.26}$$

where K_3 is a constant.

Again, the qualitative attribute based on occlusion ensures that unoccluded scene edges are subjected to a more rigorous verification test than occluded ones. With the proper choice of threshold ϵ_l the match quality for unoccluded scene edge segments can be made higher than for occluded scene edge segments.

The total match quality of the match $(\mathbf{V}'_i, \mathbf{v}_j)$ is the sum of the individual match quality measures.

For the projected model, a match matrix Γ is defined wherein the element $\Gamma_{i,j}$ denotes the match quality between the transformed model vertex $\mathbf{V}'_i$ and scene vertex $\mathbf{v}_j$. Rejected matches are assigned a match quality of zero. The matrix Γ need not be square. In cases of partially occluded objects the number of scene vertices within the window would be less than that of the projected model vertices. The problem, therefore, is to determine an optimal set of pairings $(\mathbf{V}'_i, \mathbf{v}_j)$ such that the total match quality is maximized. The pairings should be unique, i.e., no scene vertex $\mathbf{v}_j$ should be matched to more than one transformed model vertex $\mathbf{V}'_i$, and no model vertex $\mathbf{V}'_i$ should be matched to more than one scene vertex $\mathbf{v}_j$. This is clearly an *optimal assignment problem*, which is also referred to as the *Hungarian marriage problem* in the literature. The algorithm by Munkres [1957] can be used for the solution of this problem.

Constraint Propagation

The solution of the optimal assignment problem consists of a set of assignments of model vertices to scene vertices $L \subset \{(\mathbf{V}_i, \mathbf{v}_j) | 1 \leq i \leq m, 1 \leq j \leq s\}$. In order for the scene interpretation hypothesis to be considered verified, the elements in L should satisfy binary and higher-order constraints. In practice it is adequate to check for satisfaction of binary constraints using a simple constraint propagation procedure.

A pair of model vertex-scene vertex assignments $(\mathbf{V}_i, \mathbf{v}_k)$ and $(\mathbf{V}_j, \mathbf{v}_l)$, determined by the optimal assignment problem, are deemed consistent if they satisfy the following binary constraints:

1. *Distance constraint.* The distance $d_{i,j}$ between the vertices $\mathbf{V}_i$ and $\mathbf{V}_j$ should equal distance $d_{k,l}$ between the vertices $\mathbf{v}_k$ and $\mathbf{v}_l$. In practice, we require that $| d_{i,j} - d_{k,l} | \leq D_{max}$, where D_{max} is an appropriately chosen threshold.

2. *Edge constraint.* If there exists an edge between the vertices $\mathbf{v}_k$ and $\mathbf{v}_l$ in the scene, then there should also exist an edge between vertices $\mathbf{V}_i$ and $\mathbf{V}_j$ in the model. The reverse implication is not always true, since it is possible for an edge in the object model to be occluded in the scene.

The set of model vertex-scene vertex assignments L is deemed consistent if every pair $(\mathbf{V}_i, \mathbf{v}_k)$ and $(\mathbf{V}_j, \mathbf{v}_l)$ in L satisfies the binary constraints mentioned above. A simple constraint propagation procedure, outlined below, can be used to check if a set of model vertex-scene vertex assignments is consistent.

1. Consider a list L_1 of model vertex-scene vertex assignments resulting from having solved the optimal assignment problem previously mentioned. Let L_2 be a list of model vertex-scene vertex assignments wherein every pair of model vertex-scene vertex assignments satisfies the binary constraints. Initially, L_2 is an empty list.

2. Remove the first element from list L_1 and place it in list L_2.

3. Carry out the following steps until either L_1 is empty or an inconsistent pair of model vertex-scene vertex assignments is encountered.

   (a) Remove an element x from list L_1.

   (b) Check to see if the element x and every existing element y in list L_2 satisfy the binary constraints.

   (c) If element x and every existing element y in list L_2 satisfy the binary constraints, add x to list L_2, else flag an inconsistency.

If constraint propagation procedure does not encounter an inconsistency, the corresponding scene interpretation hypothesis is deemed to be verified. Once a scene interpretation hypothesis is deemed verified, the corresponding scene features (vertices, edges, and planar facets) are removed from future consideration. The process is halted when all object models are exhausted or when no more scene features are to be accounted for.

The Effect of Errors in the Initial Segmentation

In spite of the rather elaborate segmentation process used in this chapter, the initial segmentation is rarely perfect. Noise and sensor inaccuracy very often lead to misclassification of pixels, which causes oversegmentation of the range image, i.e., a single planar facet in the object model is divided into two or more regions. Oversegmentation poses two problems for the interpretation tree search. First, it results in an increase in the number of scene features under consideration, causing in turn an exponential increase in the number of possible scene interpretation hypotheses. Second, it results in the reduction in the efficacy of the area constraint used for pruning the interpretation tree. However, it should be noted that oversegmentation does not cause the interpretation tree search process to miss any scene interpretation hypothesis—it will simply cause the interpretation tree search process to report a greater number of scene interpretation hypotheses than would have been the case had the image not been oversegmented.

Oversegmentation, however, can result in the failure of a scene interpretation hypothesis during the verification stage. In fact, a scene interpretation hypothesis is rejected on the basis of the edge constraint during the constraint propagation process. This is because in an oversegmented image there exist spurious edges between adjacent fragments of a single planar facet that obviously do not exist in the object model. We can keep track of scene interpretation hypotheses that are not deemed verified due to failure to satisfy the edge constraint alone (with all other constraints satisfied). If no other object model in the model database matches the corresponding scene features, the corresponding fragments are merged and the separating edge deleted as shown in the flowchart (Figure 6.2), and the matching and localization processes are reinitiated.

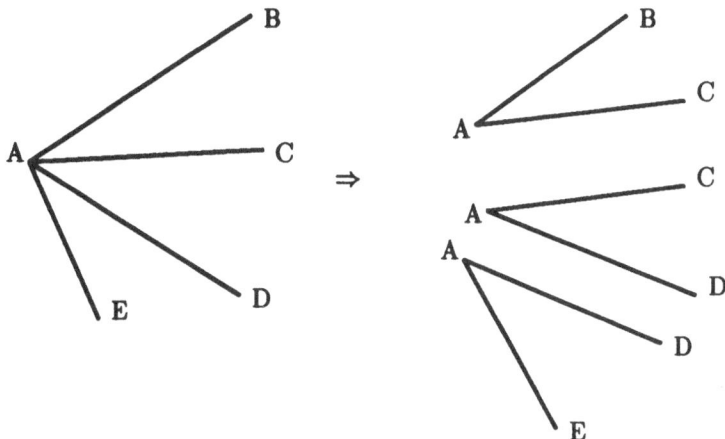

Figure 6.12: Decomposition of a junction into dihedral junctions.

6.4 Generalized Hough Transform

For the generalized Hough transform or Hough clustering, *dihedral* junctions are used as the transformation generating features or TGF's. A dihedral junction consists of a single vertex with two incident edges. These features can be easily extracted from the segmented image. Since the segmented image contains the coordinates of each scene vertex and the coordinates of the end points of each scene edge segment, we can determine the scene edges incident on each scene vertex. Each scene vertex has a degree that is the number of edges incident on the junction vertex. Scene vertices of degree greater than 2 are decomposed into dihedral junctions. The decomposition process ensures that the dihedral junctions satisfy the following properties:

1. The edges of the dihedral junction are *adjacent* in the original scene junction. Two edges in the scene junction are said to be adjacent if one edge can be rotated about the junction vertex and aligned with the second edge without crossing any other edge belonging to the same junction. Edges *AB* and *AC* are adjacent, whereas *AB* and *AD* are not (Figure 6.12).

2. The edges of the dihedral junction should enclose a visible face of the object. Two adjacent edges of a scene junction of degree greater than 2 are deemed to enclose a visible face if they are not both step edges. Only step edges of a scene junction of degree 2 can be said to enclose a visible face. If *AB* and *AE* are step edges, then the dihedral junction consisting of edges *AB* and *AE* cannot be deemed to enclose a visible face of the object (Figure 6.12).

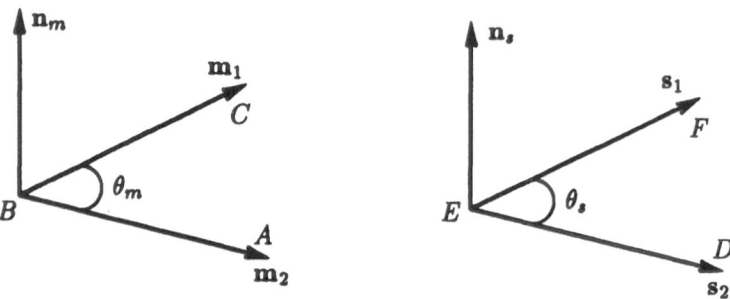

Figure 6.13: Matching a model dihedral junction with a scene dihedral junction.

The edges of a dihedral junction are so ordered that the vector cross product of the unit vector in the direction of the first edge with the unit vector in the direction of the second edge is in the direction of the outward surface normal. Face visibility is used as a constraint in the matching process described next.

6.4.1   Feature Matching

The dihedral junctions extracted from the range image are matched against the dihedral junctions in the object model. Figure 6.13 shows a candidate scene junction to be matched with a candidate model junction. Each match between a candidate scene and model junction was subjected to a series of tests in which the *qualitative* feature attributes were used to determine a weight for each match.

Angle Constraint

The scene and model dihedral junctions are subjected to the angle constraint based on the value of the included angle between the edges that form the junction.

$$M_\theta = \begin{cases} \left(1 - \frac{|\theta_m - \theta_s|}{\epsilon_\theta}\right)^\alpha & \text{if } \theta_m - \epsilon_\theta \le \theta_s \le \theta_m + \epsilon_\theta \text{ and } \alpha \ge 1 \\ 0 & \text{otherwise} \end{cases} \tag{6.27}$$

where ϵ_θ is the maximum allowed deviation in angle, and θ_m and θ_s the angles enclosed by the scene and model junctions, respectively (Figure 6.13). The value of M_θ is deemed to be the weight of the match based on the angle constraint.

Length Constraint

The scene and model dihedral junctions are subjected to the length constraint based on the lengths of the corresponding edges. The weight of the match, M_l, is computed as follows: If the scene edge is unoccluded, then

$$
M_l = \begin{cases} \left[1 - \frac{|L_m - l_s|}{L_m}\right]^{\alpha} = (1 - |1 - \beta|)^{\alpha} \\ \quad \text{if } L_m - \epsilon_p \leq l_s \leq L_m + \epsilon_p \,, \text{ where } \alpha \geq 1 \\ 0 \text{ otherwise} \end{cases} \tag{6.28}
$$

or else, if the scene edge is occluded, then

$$
M_l = \begin{cases} (1 - |1 - \beta|)^{\alpha} = \beta^{\alpha} & \text{if } l_s \leq L_m, \text{ where } \alpha \geq 1 \\ 0 & \text{otherwise} \end{cases} \tag{6.29}
$$

where L_m is the length of the model edge, l_s that of the scene edge and, $\beta = l_s/L_m$ a measure of the extent of occlusion. The overall weight for the match of a model dihedral junction with a scene dihedral junction is considered to be the product of the weights M_θ and M_l, which corresponds to the joint satisfaction of each of the corresponding constraints.

6.4.2   Computation of the Transform

For a successful match between a scene feature and a model feature, the resulting pose is computed in terms of a homogeneous coordinate transformation. The coordinates (x, y, z) refer to the model coordinate system and (u, v, w) to the scene coordinate system. The operations $\times$ and $\cdot$ denote the vector cross product and the vector scalar product, respectively.

Let $\mathbf{m}_1$ be the unit vector in the direction $\mathbf{BA}$ and $\mathbf{m}_2$ the unit vector in the direction $\mathbf{BC}$ (Figure 6.13). Similarly, let $\mathbf{s}_1$ be the unit vector in the direction $\mathbf{ED}$ and $\mathbf{s}_2$ the unit vector in the direction $\mathbf{EF}$. The homogeneous coordinates of B in the model coordinate system are given by the column vector $[x_0, y_0, z_0, 1]^T$, and the homogeneous coordinates of E in the scene coordinate system are given by the column vector $[u_0, v_0, w_0, 1]^T$. The goal, therefore, is to find a transformation $\mathbf{T}$ such that

$$
\mathbf{T}[x_0, y_0, z_0, 1]^T = [u_0, v_0, w_0, 1]^T \tag{6.30}
$$

There is an inherent ambiguity in the matching of the junctions in the sense that whether $\mathbf{m}_1$ should match $\mathbf{s}_1$ and $\mathbf{m}_2$ should match $\mathbf{s}_2$ or vice versa (Figure 6.13). The directions of the outward normals $\mathbf{n}_s$ and $\mathbf{n}_m$ to the faces bound by the corresponding scene and model junctions can be used to resolve the ambiguity. Since $\mathbf{n}_s = \mathbf{m}_1 \times \mathbf{m}_2$ and $\mathbf{n}_m = \mathbf{s}_1 \times \mathbf{s}_2$, $\mathbf{m}_1$ should match $\mathbf{s}_1$, and $\mathbf{m}_2$ should match $\mathbf{s}_2$ (Figure 6.13).

The transformation $\mathbf{T}$ is determined in a stepwise manner as below:

1. Points B and E are translated to their respective origins. Let TRANS$(-B)$ and TRANS$(-E)$ denote the respective homogeneous transformations. This ensures that both junctions have their vertices translated to the origin.

2. The vectors m_1 and m_2 are rotated about k by an angle θ so as to be aligned with s_1 and s_2, respectively; k is determined by the requirement that it be perpendicular to both $m_1 - s_1$ and $m_2 - s_2$ or, equivalently, that the projections of m_1 and s_1 along k be equal and the projections of m_2 and s_2 along k be equal, i.e.,

$$k \cdot m_1 = k \cdot s_1 \Rightarrow k \cdot (m_1 - s_1) = 0 \tag{6.31}$$

$$k \cdot m_2 = k \cdot s_2 \Rightarrow k \cdot (m_2 - s_2) = 0 \tag{6.32}$$

Thus

$$k = \frac{(m_1 - s_1) \times (m_2 - s_2)}{|(m_1 - s_1) \times (m_2 - s_2)|} \tag{6.33}$$

The angle of rotation θ is determined by (Figure 6.11)

$$\cos\theta = \frac{[m_1 - (m_1 \cdot k)k] \cdot [s_1 - (s_1 \cdot k)k]}{[1 - (m_1 \cdot k)(s_1 \cdot k)]} \tag{6.34}$$

$$= 1 - \frac{[1 - (m_1 \cdot s_1)]}{[1 - (k \cdot m_1)(k \cdot s_1)]} \tag{6.35}$$

3. The final transformation can be thus written as:

$$ROT(k,\theta)\,TRANS(-B)[x_0, y_0, z_0, 1]^T = TRANS(-E)[u_0, v_0, w_0, 1]^T \tag{6.36}$$

From Eq. (6.30) and Eq. (6.36)

$$T = TRANS^{-1}(-E)\,ROT(k,\theta)\,TRANS(-B) \tag{6.37}$$

The transformation T from the model coordinate system to the scene coordinate system could thus be written as [Paul 1981] [Korn and Korn 1972]:

$$T = ROT(k,\theta)\,TRANS(t_x, t_y, t_z) \tag{6.38}$$

$$T = \begin{bmatrix} r_{11} & r_{12} & r_{13} & 0 \\ r_{21} & r_{22} & r_{23} & 0 \\ r_{31} & r_{32} & r_{33} & 0 \\ 0 & 0 & 0 & 1 \end{bmatrix} \begin{bmatrix} 1 & 0 & 0 & t_x \\ 0 & 1 & 0 & t_y \\ 0 & 0 & 1 & t_z \\ 0 & 0 & 0 & 1 \end{bmatrix} \tag{6.39}$$

where

$$\begin{aligned} r_{11} &= k_x^2(1 - \cos\theta) + \cos\theta \\ r_{12} &= k_x k_y(1 - \cos\theta) - k_z \sin\theta \\ r_{13} &= k_x k_z(1 - \cos\theta) + k_y \sin\theta \\ r_{21} &= k_x k_y(1 - \cos\theta) + k_z \sin\theta \end{aligned}$$

$$
\begin{aligned}
r_{22} &= k_y^2(1 - \cos\theta) + \cos\theta \\
r_{23} &= k_y k_z(1 - \cos\theta) - k_x \sin\theta \\
r_{31} &= k_x k_z(1 - \cos\theta) - k_y \sin\theta \\
r_{32} &= k_y k_z(1 - \cos\theta) + k_x \sin\theta \\
r_{33} &= k_z^2(1 - \cos\theta) + \cos\theta
\end{aligned}
\tag{6.40}
$$

and

$$
\begin{aligned}
t_x &= u_0 - r_{11}x_0 - r_{12}y_0 - r_{13}z_0 \\
t_y &= v_0 - r_{21}x_0 - r_{22}y_0 - r_{23}z_0 \\
t_z &= w_0 - r_{31}x_0 - r_{32}y_0 - r_{33}z_0
\end{aligned}
\tag{6.41}
$$

The axis of rotation **k** could be alternatively expressed by the pair (ξ, η), where

$$
\begin{aligned}
k_x &= \cos\xi \, \sin\eta \\
k_y &= \sin\xi \, \sin\eta \\
k_z &= \cos\eta
\end{aligned}
\tag{6.42}
$$

where $-\pi < \eta < \pi$ and $0 < \xi < 2\pi$.

The transformation **T** is thus uniquely specified by the 6-tuple $(t_x, t_y, t_z, \xi, \eta, \theta)$.

6.4.3 Pose Clustering

The dihedral junctions of each object model are matched against the scene dihedral junctions, and the value of the computed transform is used to increment the appropriate bin in the six-dimensional accumulator, which is a discrete representation of the six-dimensional Hough space corresponding to the transformation parameters $(t_x, t_y, t_z, \xi, \eta, \theta)$. The corresponding bin could either be incremented by 1 for each successful match of a scene dihedral junction to a model dihedral junction or by the match quality assigned to the match. The maxima in the bins of the Hough accumulator are taken to represent peaks in the Hough space that correspond to a globally consistent pose of the object. Thus each maximum in the Hough accumulator can be treated as a pose hypothesis. The maxima are considered in the order of their magnitude and verified against the scene dihedral junctions.

6.4.4 Veriification of the Pose Hypothesis

The pose hypothesis is used to project the object model onto the image. A dihedral junction-based comparison technique is used to compare dihedral junctions in the scene with those in the projected model. The comparison process is similar to the junction matching process used for hypothesis verification in the

case of interpretation tree search and is therefore not discussed in great detail in
this section. The constraints used to compare a scene dihedral junction with a
dihedral junction in the projected model are based on the angle and the lengths
of the edges. A match quality is assigned to the comparison using Eqs. (6.27),
(6.28), and (6.29). A match matrix is defined wherein the $(i, j)^{th}$ element in
the matrix represents the quality of the match between the ith model dihedral
feature junction with the jth scene dihedral feature junction. Just as in the case
of hypothesis verification for interpretation tree search, the problem of determining a maximally compatible set of matches from the match matrix is cast as an
optimal assignment or Hungarian marriage problem and solved likewise. If the
overall match quality, as determined by solving the Hungarian marriage problem, is above a certain threshold defined in terms of the fraction of the model
features that are matched to the scene features, then the pose hypothesis is accepted, else rejected. For an accepted pose hypothesis, the corresponding scene
features are labeled as being an instance of the object model under consideration
and are removed from any further processing. The pose hypotheses generated
by each object model are considered and subjected to the verification process.
The recognition and localization process halts when either all pose hypotheses
for all object models have been exhausted or there are no more scene features
to be considered.

6.5   Experimental Results

Both interpretation tree search and the generalized Hough transform were experimentally verified on a database of real range images that contained one or
two objects out of a set of five different polyhedral objects. In Figures 6.14 and
6.15 two range images are shown. The corresponding images resulting from the
segmentation process are shown in Figures 6.16 and 6.17. The output of the
segmentation process is a data structure that contains the high-level description
of each scene, i.e., the parameters for the facets, edges, and vertices. An instance
of this data structure is created for each range image.

   The efficiency of interpretation tree search and the generalized Hough transform can be measured in terms of the number of hypotheses tested before a
hypothesis is successfully verified, and also in terms of the total number of scene
hypotheses generated. Experiments were conducted both with and without the
use of qualitative features. In the case of interpretation tree search, the absence of the qualitative attribute based on *occlusion* meant that the stronger
constraint based on the equality of areas for unoccluded scene facets had to be
replaced by the weaker constraint based on inequality of areas for *all* scene facets.
This implies that a larger number of scene hypotheses had to be generated and
tested before one hypothesis could be verified. The use of the qualitative attribute based on occlusion allows the scene facets to be ordered such that the
unoccluded scene facets are matched before the occluded ones. Within each
category, i.e., unoccluded and occluded, the scene facets can be arranged in decreasing order of size (area) so that larger prominent facets are matched before

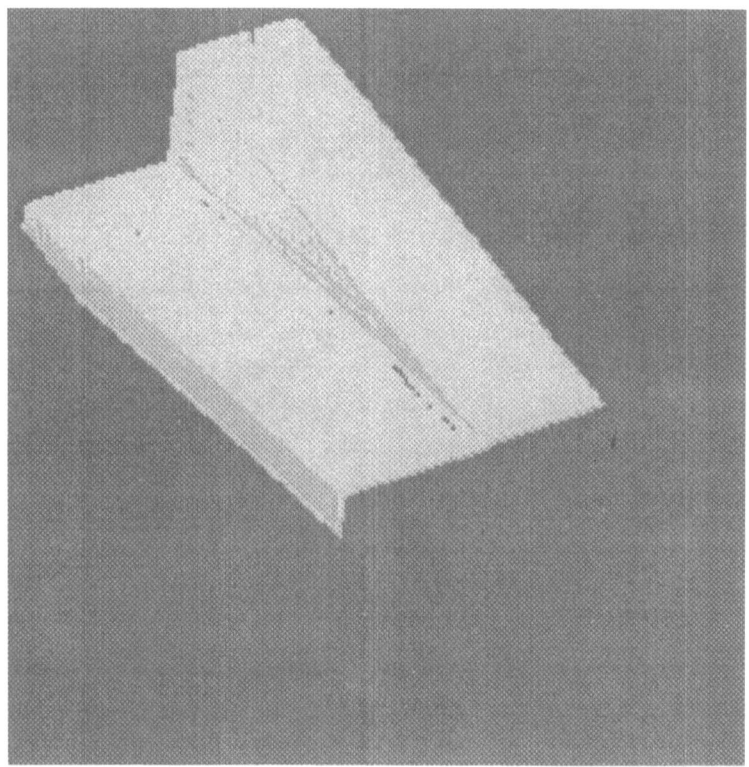

Figure 6.14: Scene I containing a single polyhedral object.

Figure 6.15: Scene II containing multiple polyhedral objects.

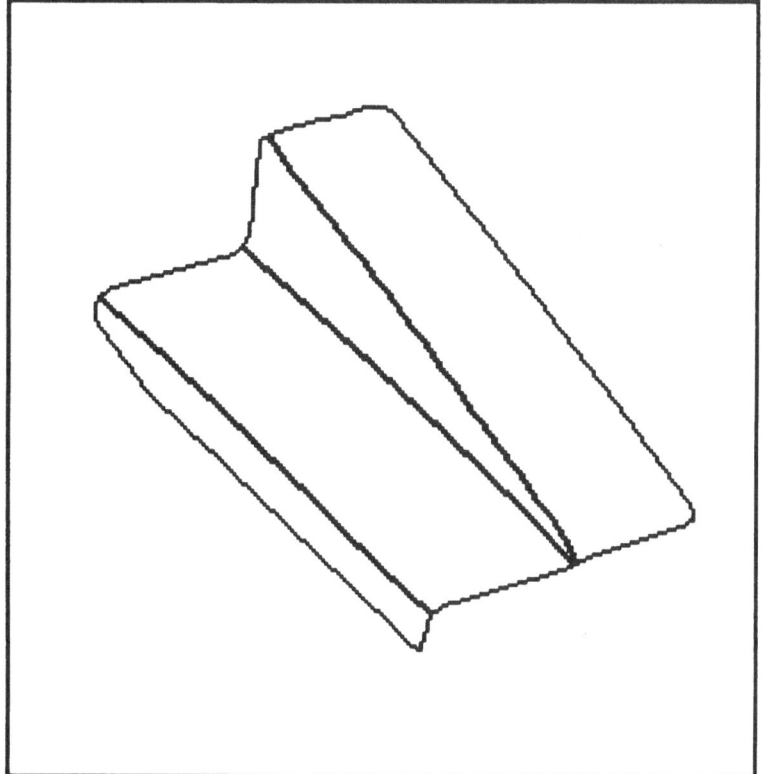

Figure 6.16: Segmented image of Scene I.

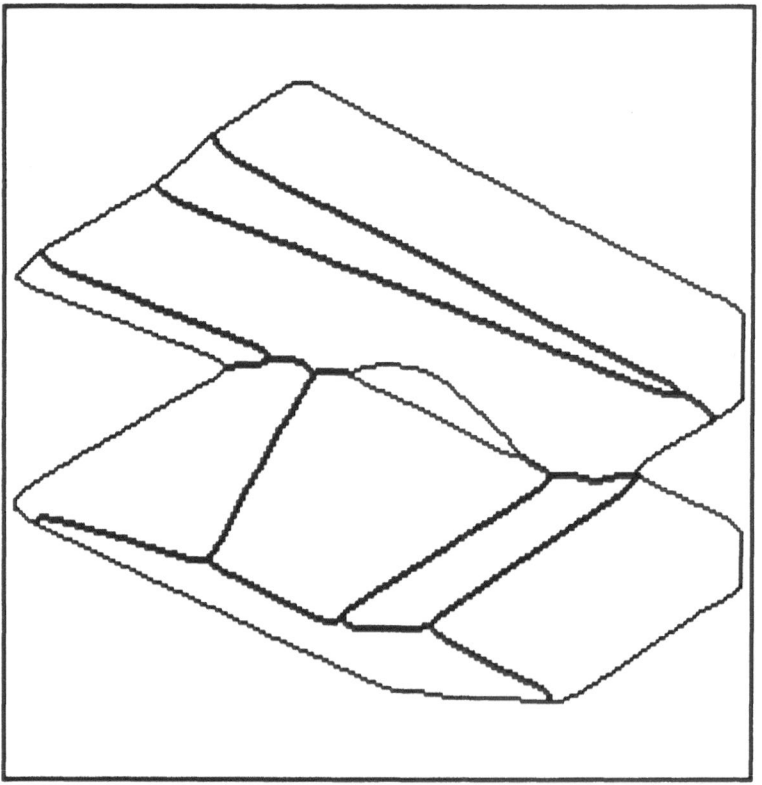

Figure 6.17: Segmented image of Scene II.

Table 6.1: Performance of the interpretation tree search with and without qualitative features.

Scene No.	With Qualitative Feat.		Without Q. F.	
	H1	H2	H1	H2
1	8	1	11	2
2	13	3	21	7

H1: Total number of hypotheses generated
H2: Total number of hypotheses tested during verification

smaller ones. In the case where the qualitative attribute is not used, scene facets can only be ordered in decreasing order of size (area). In Table 6.1 the total number of scene hypotheses and the total number of hypotheses tested before a hypothesis was successfully verified are tabulated for the two scenes in Figures 6.14 and 6.15 both with and without the use of qualitative features using the interpretation tree search approach.

In the case of Hough clustering, the qualitative attribute based on occlusion of the scene edges was used to assign a match quality to the match of a scene feature with a model feature. The matching function was designed to ensure that the matches based on unoccluded scene features has a higher match quality assigned to them, as compared to ones based on occluded scene features. The use of the qualitative attribute based on occlusion also allows matches of unoccluded scene edges to be subject to a more rigorous constraint based on length equality, in the absence of which all scene edges are subject to the weaker constraint based on inequality. The absence of qualitative features has two consequences: (1) The number of false matches of scene features to model features increases, and (2) The Hough clustering process is unable to distinguish between matches containing unoccluded scene features and those containing occluded scene features. Since the use of qualitative features lends a higher match quality to features containing unoccluded scene features, it increases the likelihood of significant peaks or maxima in the Hough accumulator array containing *true* matches, rather than those that could have arisen due to random matches. Also, since the pose hypotheses are verified in descending order of magnitude of the corresponding maxima in the Hough array, the use of qualitative features ensures that pose hypotheses with a greater number of matches containing unoccluded scene features are verified before the others. This is reasonable and intuitive because the object containing the maximum number of unoccluded scene features is likely to be the topmost object in a pile of objects in a bin and therefore should be expected to be recognized first. The performances of Hough clustering with qualitative features and the Hough clustering without the use of qualitative features are

Table 6.2: Performance of the generalized Hough transform with and without using qualitative features.

Scene No.	With Qualitative Feat.		Withoout Q. F.	
	H1	H2	H1	H2
1	13	4	23	9
2	27	6	41	14

H1: Total number of hypotheses generated
H2: Total number of hypotheses tested during verification

compared in Table 6.2 for the two scenes in Figures 6.14 and 6.15. In the case of straightforward Hough clustering, the bin was used to accumulate simple votes rather than accumulate the match quality, since the match quality was assigned based on qualitative features. This means that for each successful match of a scene and model feature, the straightforward Hough clustering incremented the appropriate bin by 1, as opposed to the Hough clustering with qualitative features that incremented the appropriate bin by the match quality. Table 6.2 summarizes the comparison of the two Hough clustering schemes based on the total number of scene hypotheses generated and the total number of hypotheses tested before a hypothesis is successfully verified for the two scenes in Figures 6.14 and 6.15.

As can be seen from the experimental results, both interpretation tree search and Hough clustering performed better with the use of qualitative features. In Chapter 8 a formal study of the impact of the use of qualitative features on the generalized Hough transform will be presented and a fuzzy-probabilistic model for the generalized Hough transform will be introduced. The fuzzy-probabilistic model would provide analytical justification for the use of qualitative features in the generalized Hough transform in particular, and recognition and localization techniques in general.

6.6   Summary

In this chapter, two techniques for the recognition and localization of polyhedral objects were examined: interpretation tree search and the generalized Hough transform. These techniques were tested on real range images containing single and multiple polyhedral objects with clutter and partial occlusion. A qualitative attribute based on occlusion was assigned to edges and facets in the scene. Scene features were classified as occluded or unoccluded based on this qualitative attribute and were termed as qualitative features. The use of qualitative features enabled us to use stronger constraints when matching unoccluded scene features to model features. On the other hand, in the absence of qualitative features, weaker constraints used for occluded scene features had to be used for all scene features. This was reflected in the performance of interpretation tree search and the generalized Hough transform when used to recognize and localize objects in real range images. The number of scene hypotheses generated and the number of scene hypotheses that had to be tested before the true hypothesis could be verified are much fewer for both the interpretation tree search and the generalized Hough transform with the use of qualitative features than without the use of qualitative features. These experimental results prompted the formulation of a fuzzy-probabilistic model, presented in Chapter 8, for the generalized Hough transform that provides the analytical justification for the use of qualitative features in the generalized Hough Transform in particular, and for recognition and localization techniques in general.

Chapter 7

Recognition of Curved Objects

In this chapter we consider the problem of recognition and localization of objects with curved surfaces. Although polyhedral objects are encountered more frequently than curved objects in an industrial environment, objects with curved surfaces are more prevalent in natural scenes. One simple way of dealing with curved objects is to approximate them by polyhedral objects—an approach commonly used in earlier vision systems. However, such an approach has certain fundamental shortcomings in that the resulting description is not rich enough to capture the *intrinsic* properties of curved surfaces, is not stable to changes in viewpoint, and suffers from approximation errors. In this chapter, invariant surface curvatures, viz. the mean and Gaussian and principal curvatures, are used to come up with a description of curved surfaces that is invariant to viewpoint. As in the case of polyhedral objects, multiple-object scenes with clutter and partial occlusion are considered. This precludes the use of global shape descriptors, which means that only local shape descriptors based on the invariant surface curvatures can be used. The generalized Hough transform, on account of its ease of parallelization, is chosen as the constraint propagation technique.

The generalized Hough transform is, in a sense, a brute-force enumeration of the search space of scene interpretations, since all possible pairings of scene and model features are considered in order to determine a globally consistent pose. When using the generalized Hough transform in a multiple-object scene with partial occlusion, two major problems need to be addressed: first, the combinatorial explosion of the search space of scene interpretations and, second, the difficulty of accurate localization in the presence of spurious interpretations. We will show in this chapter that the use of qualitative features can ensure effective pruning of the search space of scene hypotheses, as well as an efficient exploration of the search space. Two significant advantages of using qualitative features are:

1. Qualitative features provide an effective means of reducing the combinato-

rial complexity of the search space of possible scene interpretations. In the context of the generalized Hough transform, this means that we are able to suppress spurious peaks in the Hough space. The generation of spurious peaks is a problem that is endemic to the generalized Hough transform. Since the technique relies on the accumulation of local evidence to come up with a global pose hypothesis, spurious accumulation of local evidence can result from false matches of scene features to model features. In single-object scenes the spurious peaks corresponding to false hypotheses tend to be insignificant in comparison to the true peak that corresponds to the globally consistent pose. However, in multiple-object scenes with partial occlusion the spurious accumulation of evidence from false matches for each object could be reinforced, thereby causing spurious hypotheses to be greater or comparable in magnitude to the true pose hypothesis. Qualitative features are useful in restricting the number of false matches and thereby suppressing false peaks in the Hough space.

2. Qualitative features provide effective criteria for the selection of an appropriate parameter space in which the global pose is to be determined. The parameter space can be made specific to a certain qualitative surface type and can thereby incorporate certain characteristics typical of that surface type, such as the axis of symmetry for a conical or cylindrical surface.

In this chapter we describe a generalized Hough transform technique that uses a dense point-wise curvature description of curved surfaces. The curved surfaces considered are spherical, cylindrical, and conical surfaces. Although these surface types constitute a small subset of all possible curved surfaces, studying them is important since a large majority of man-made industrial objects are composed of these surfaces. The shortcomings of the generalized Hough transform technique that uses such a dense point-wise curvature description are then described. Classification of the surfaces into qualitative surface classes based on the signs of the mean curvature and Gaussian curvature is shown to provide a means of describing a surface in a parameter space specific to the qualitative surface type, a method that alleviates the shortcomings of the generalized Hough transform technique, which uses a dense point-wise curvature description. A generalized Hough transform technique using dihedral feature junctions as the transformation generating features (TGF's) is shown to provide a means for recognizing complex curved objects composed of piecewise composition of spherical, cylindrical conical, and planar objects. Dihedral feature junctions are shown to be robust to occlusion and to provide a viewpoint-independent representation scheme. These techniques are then tested on range images containing curved surfaces.

7.1   Representation of Curved Surfaces

As mentioned in Chapters 3 and 4, the desired characteristics of features chosen for the representation of curved surfaces are:

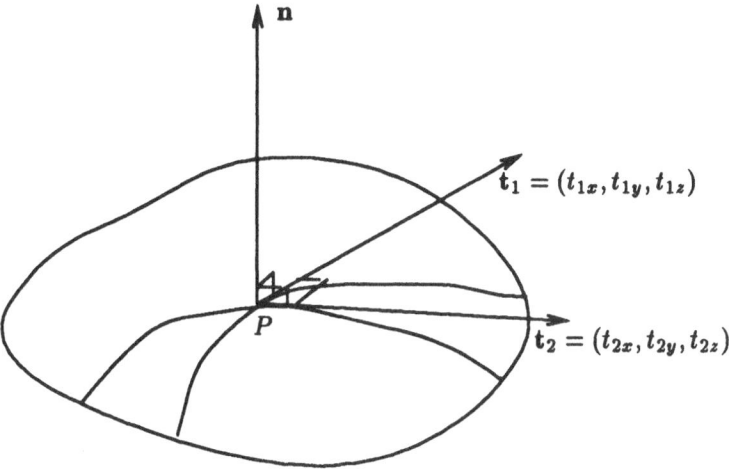

Figure 7.1: An orthogonal coordinate system formed by t_1, t_2, and n.

1. Viewpoint invariance so that they can be used for matching.

2. Richness of local support, which ensures robustness to occlusion.

3. Ease of extraction so that the effort involved in segmentation is minimal.

4. Generality of representation so that a wide range of surface types can be covered.

The representation of surfaces in terms of the mean, Gaussian, and principal curvatures exhibits the above characteristics. As has been mentioned in Chapter 3, it is a well-known result from surface differential geometry that surface curvature properties such as the mean curvature (H), Gaussian curvature (K), the maximum principal curvature (κ_1), and the minimum principal curvature (κ_2) are invariant to rigid-body motion (i.e., rotations and translations) in 3-D Euclidean space. Moreover, the unit vectors in the directions of the principal curvatures κ_1 and κ_2, denoted by t_1 and t_2, respectively and the unit normal n form an orthogonal coordinate system at every non-umbilic and non-planar point on the surface (Figure 7.1). Any two of H, K, κ_1, and κ_2 are adequate to characterize the surface locally. The invariance of these surface curvature properties forms the underlying basis of several surface segmentation and feature extraction techniques as discussed in Chapter 3.

7.1.1 Extraction of Surface Curvature Features from Range Images

Since digital range images are typically noisy, direct determination of surface curvatures and surface normals from raw range data is very unreliable. A more reliable technique for surface curvature extraction is to approximate the digital range surface by an analytic surface within a local window using a least-squares surface-fitting technique or a functional optimization technique. The equation of the fitted analytic surface is used to compute the values of surface curvatures and surface normals. Typical surface-fitting techniques include least-square surface-fitting using bivariate polynomial approximations [Besl and Jain 1988], parametric surface approximation techniques such as B-splines [Naik and Jain 1988], tensor products of splines under tension [Vemuri and Aggarwal 1987], and tensor product of discrete Chebychev polynomials [Haralick 1984].

In this chapter we consider the approximation of a digital range surface by using discrete bi-orthogonal Chebychev polynomials [Haralick 1984]. Discrete bi-orthogonal Chebychev polynomials are used as basis functions in a local $N \times N$ (where N is odd) window centered about the point of interest. The orthogonality of the basis functions enables efficient computation of the coefficients of the functional approximation. The first four orthogonal polynomials are:

$$\phi_0 = 1$$
$$\phi_1 = u$$
$$\phi_2 = u^2 - \frac{\mu_2}{\mu_0}$$
$$\phi_3 = u^3 - (\frac{\mu_4}{\mu_2})u$$
$$where \ \mu_k = \sum_{u=-M}^{i=+M} u^k$$
$$and \ M = \frac{(N-1)}{2} \tag{7.1}$$

A discrete biorthogonal basis is created from the $\phi_i's$:

$$\phi_{i,j}(u,v) = \phi_i(u)\phi_j(v) \tag{7.2}$$

The surface function estimate that minimizes the sum of squared surface-fitting error within the window is given by

$$\hat{f}(u,v) = \sum_{i,j=0}^{3} a_{i,j}\phi_i(u)\phi_j(v) \tag{7.3}$$

where the coefficients of the functional approximation are given by

$$a_{i,j} = \sum_{(u,v)=(-M,-M)}^{(u,v)=(+M,+M)} f(u,v)b_i(u)b_j(v) \tag{7.4}$$

and $b_i(u)$ is the normalized version of the polynomial $\phi_i(u)$.

The estimates of the first- and second-order derivatives of the surface are given by:

$$f_u = a_{10} - \frac{\mu_2}{\mu_0}a_{12} - \frac{\mu_4}{\mu_2}a_{30} + \frac{\mu_4}{\mu_0}a_{32}$$

$$f_v = a_{01} - \frac{\mu_2}{\mu_0}a_{21} - \frac{\mu_4}{\mu_2}a_{03} + \frac{\mu_4}{\mu_0}a_{23}$$

$$f_{uu} = 2a_{20} - 2\frac{\mu_2}{\mu_0}a_{22}$$

$$f_{vv} = 2a_{02} - 2\frac{\mu_2}{\mu_0}a_{22}$$

$$f_{uv} = a_{11} - \frac{\mu_4}{\mu_2}a_{31} - \frac{\mu_4}{\mu_2}a_{13} + \frac{\mu_4^2}{\mu_0}a_{33} \tag{7.5}$$

Estimates of the partial derivatives are used to compute the coefficients of the first- and second-fundamental forms of the surface [Faux and Pratt 1979]. $\mathbf{G} = \begin{bmatrix} g_{11} & g_{12} \\ g_{21} & g_{22} \end{bmatrix}$ is the *First fundamental form* of the surface, where

$$g_{11} = 1 + f_u^2$$

$$g_{22} = 1 + f_v^2$$

$$g_{12} = g_{21} = f_u f_v \tag{7.6}$$

$\mathbf{B} = \begin{bmatrix} b_{11} & b_{12} \\ b_{21} & b_{22} \end{bmatrix}$ is the *Second fundamental form* of the surface, where

$$b_{11} = \frac{f_{uu}}{\sqrt{1 + f_u^2 + f_v^2}}$$

$$b_{12} = b_{21} = \frac{f_{uv}}{\sqrt{1 + f_u^2 + f_v^2}}$$

$$b_{22} = \frac{f_{vv}}{\sqrt{1 + f_u^2 + f_v^2}} \tag{7.7}$$

The principal curvatures are the roots of the quadratic equation [Faux and Pratt 1979]

$$|\mathbf{G}|\kappa_n^2 - (g_{11}b_{22} + b_{11}g_{22} - 2g_{12}b_{12})\kappa_n + |\mathbf{B}| = 0 \quad n = 1, 2 \tag{7.8}$$

The directions of the principal curvatures are given by $\mathbf{t}_n = (1, \lambda_n, f_u + \lambda_n f_v)$ where

$$\lambda_n = \frac{b_{11} - \kappa_n g_{11}}{b_{12} - \kappa_n g_{12}} = \frac{b_{21} - \kappa_n g_{21}}{b_{22} - \kappa_n g_{22}} \tag{7.9}$$

The mean curvature H and the Gaussian curvature K are given by:

$$H = \frac{\kappa_1 + \kappa_2}{2} \tag{7.10}$$

$$K = \kappa_1 \kappa_2 \tag{7.11}$$

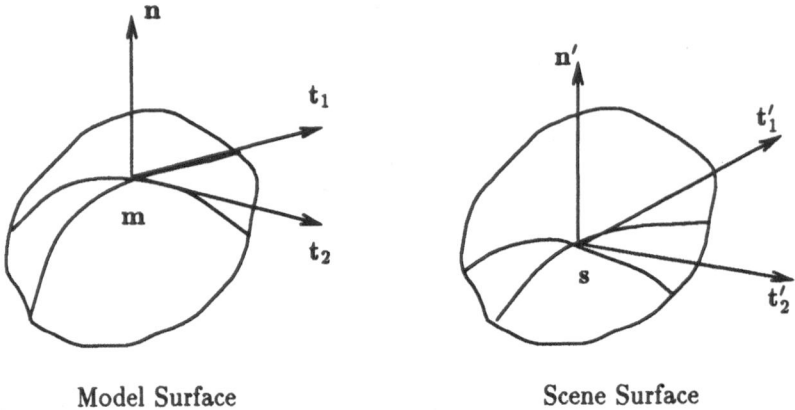

Figure 7.2: Matching a model point **m** and a scene surface point **s**.

7.2 Recognition Using a Point-Wise Curvature Description

Since the direction of the principal curvatures and the direction of the surface normal constitute a local orthogonal coordinate system at a non-planar or non-spherical surface point, they can be used as the TGF for a generalized Hough transform scheme that is based on the matching of points on a model surface with corresponding points on the scene surface. The values of the mean curvature and Gaussian curvature can be used to constrain the matches of such points, that is, a scene surface point is matched to a model surface point only if the values of the mean curvature and Gaussian curvature at the two points are the same. The directions of the principal curvatures and the surface normals at these points can then be used to compute the geometric transformation that would place the point on the model surface in registration with the corresponding point on the scene surface. In this section, the steps followed in computing the geometric transform are outlined.

With reference to Figure 7.2, given two points (expressed as position vectors) $\mathbf{m} = [x_0, y_0, z_0, 1]$ and $\mathbf{s} = [u_0, v_0, w_0, 1]$ (in homogeneous coordinates) on the model surface and the scene surface, respectively, we are interested in: (1) knowing if **m** and **s** are actually one and the same, differing in their positions in 3-D space on account of a rigid-body motion (three translations and three rotations about the coordinate axes) of the model surface, and if so, (2) computing the rigid-body motion or pose, which would place the model point **m** in registration with the corresponding point **s** in the scene. Two points **m** and **s** are matched *iff* the values of H and K or, alternatively, the values of κ_1 and κ_2 at the two points are the same. If the two points **m** and **s** represent a match, then the pose is determined by computing the transformation T that would place m in registration with s. In order to determine T such that

$$T[x_0, y_0, z_0, 1]^T = [u_0, v_0, w_0, 1]^T \qquad (7.12)$$

we use the fact that the directions of the principal curvatures and the surface normals form an orthogonal coordinate system at every non-umbilical and non-planar point.   If (n, t_1, t_2) is an orthogonal coordinate system associated with m, and (n', t_1', t_2') is the one associated with s (Figure 7.2), then the transformation T is determined as follows:

Let C_1 denote the coordinate system at point m, C_2 the coordinate system at point s, and W the world coordinate system. Let T_1 be the coordinate frame transformation from C_1 to W, and T_2 the coordinate frame transformation from C_2 to W. Then

$$T_1[0, 0, 0, 1]^T = [x_0, y_0, z_0, 1]^T \qquad (7.13)$$

where

$$T_1 = \begin{bmatrix} \kappa_{1x} & \kappa_{2x} & n_x & x_0 \\ \kappa_{1y} & \kappa_{2y} & n_y & y_0 \\ \kappa_{1z} & \kappa_{2z} & n_z & z_0 \\ 0 & 0 & 0 & 1 \end{bmatrix} \qquad (7.14)$$

and

$$T_2[0, 0, 0, 1]^T = [u_0, v_0, w_0, 1]^T \qquad (7.15)$$

where

$$T_2 = \begin{bmatrix} \kappa'_{1x} & \kappa'_{2x} & n'_x & u_0 \\ \kappa'_{1y} & \kappa'_{2y} & n'_y & v_0 \\ \kappa'_{1z} & \kappa'_{2z} & n'_z & w_0 \\ 0 & 0 & 0 & 1 \end{bmatrix} \qquad (7.16)$$

From Eqs. (7.13) and (7.15)

$$T_1^{-1}[x_0, y_0, z_0, 1]^T = T_2^{-1}[u_0, v_0, w_0, 1]^T = [0, 0, 0, 1]^T \qquad (7.17)$$

from which

$$T_2 T_1^{-1}[x_0, y_0, z_0, 1]^T = [u_0, v_0, w_0, 1]^T \qquad (7.18)$$

hence from Eqs. (7.12) and (7.18)

$$T = T_2 T_1^{-1} \qquad (7.19)$$

The transformation T can be decomposed into a translation vector $t = [t_x, t_y, t_z]$ and an equivalent axis of rotation whose direction is given by the unit vector $k = [k_x, k_y, k_z]$ and an angular rotation of magnitude θ about k (details of the derivation are given in [Paul 1981]). The axis of rotation k could be alternatively expressed by the pair (ξ, η) where

$$\begin{aligned} k_x &= \cos\xi \sin\eta \\ k_y &= \sin\xi \sin\eta \\ k_z &= \cos\eta \end{aligned} \qquad (7.20)$$

Figure 7.3: Scene I containing multiple objects made up of simple curved surfaces.

where $-\pi < \eta < \pi$ and $0 < \xi < 2\pi$.

The transformation $\mathbf{T}$ is thus uniquely specified by the 6-tuple $(t_x, t_y, t_z, \xi, \eta, \theta)$, which can be represented as a point in six-dimensional Hough space. Clustering of such points in Hough space can be used to recognize and localize the surface in the scene. Thus a straightforward generalized Hough transform can be formulated for the recognition of curved surfaces based on a point-wise curvature description. However, an obvious limitation of this technique is that it cannot be used to match locally planar or spherical surface points, since at such points the values of the principal curvatures are equal and uniform (and, in the case of planar surfaces, uniformly zero) in all directions. Thus two mutually orthogonal principal directions cannot be defined at such surface points.

Figure 7.4: Scene II containing multiple objects made up of simple curved surfaces.

7.2.1   Object Recognition Using Point-Wise Surface Matching

A series of experiments were carried out using the straightforward generalized Hough transform based on the point-wise surface matching scheme. Two scenes consisting of simple curved objects were considered (Figures 7.3 and 7.4). The objective of these experiments was to evaluate the performance of the generalized Hough transform based on a point-wise curvature representation where the recognition and pose determination were achieved by maxima detection in the parameter space of rigid-body motion parameters. The scenes contained multiple 3-D objects consisting of cylindrical, conical, and spherical surfaces. Surfaces were allowed to occlude one another. The performance of the generalized Hough transform was evaluated based on the following criteria:

1. The number of false interpretations generated.

2. Limitations of the technique in terms of its ability to identify and localize certain surface types.

3. Accuracy of localization.

The steps used in recognition by straightforward generalized Hough transform are:

1. *Surface feature extraction.* Using the analytic surface-fitting technique described in Section 7.1.1 the values of the mean, Gaussian, and principal curvatures, the directions of the principal curvatures, and the surface normal were computed for each pixel in the range image.

2. *Surface matching and pose determination.* As discussed in Section 7.2, each pixel in the range image was matched against potential surface points on the model surface. Since the model surfaces (cones, cylinders, and spheres) in this experiment were generated analytically, the relevant surface features were computed as needed from the appropriate analytic expression. Each valid match was mapped to a point in the six-dimensional Hough space.

3. *Maxima detection in Hough space.* A conventional binning approach to maxima detection in Hough space was found to be impractical, since the memory requirements for a Hough accumulator array with a reasonable degree of resolution were found to be prohibitive. Instead, the K-means clustering algorithm [Tou and Gonzalez 1974] was used. The maxima in the Hough array were approximated by the values of the cluster centers. The algorithm was run for different values of K (number of clusters).

The experimental results were analyzed in terms of the following parameters:

1. *The magnitude of the largest peak in the Hough space.* M_{peak} gives a measure of the quality of the most significant hypothesis. M_{peak} is expressed as a percentage of the total number of points in the Hough space.

2. *The magnitude of the peak closest to the actual solution.* M_{min} gives a measure of the quality of the best hypothesis. The best hypothesis is the one closest to the theoretically computed solution based on Euclidean distance in the six-dimensional parameter space. M_{min} is expressed as a percentage of the total number of points in the Hough space.

3. *The distance measure d_{peak}.* d_{peak} is the Euclidean distance in parameter space of the most significant hypothesis from the theoretically computed solution.

4. *The distance measure d_{min}.* d_{min} is the Euclidean distance in parameter space of the best hypothesis from the theoretically computed solution.

5. *Relative significance of the best hypothesis.* $R = (M_{min}/M_{peak}) \times 100$ is a measure of the relative magnitude of the best hypothesis with respect to the most significant hypothesis.

The values of d_{peak} and d_{min} are measures of the localization accuracy, whereas the values of M_{peak}, M_{min}, and R are measures of the number of spurious hypotheses in the Hough space. The ideal behavior desired from the straightforward Hough clustering algorithm would be as follows:

1. With increasing values of K, the true maxima in the Hough space should be emphasized, whereas the spurious maxima should be suppressed. M_{peak}, M_{min}, d_{peak}, and d_{min} should approach constant values.

2. The most significant hypothesis should also be the best hypothesis. This means that $M_{peak} = M_{min}$ and $R = M_{min}/M_{peak} \times 100 = 100.0\%$.

3. The values of d_{peak} and d_{min} should tend to zero with increasing K. Both the most significant hypothesis and the best hypothesis should approach the theoretical value.

Figures 7.5 (a) and (b) show the experimental results for recognition and localization of the conical surface in the scene described by Figure 7.3. M_{min}, M_{peak}, R, d_{min}, and d_{max} are plotted as functions of K. Similar graphs were obtained for the conical surface in the scene in Figure 7.4 and for the cylindrical surface in the scenes in Figures 7.3 and 7.4. The experimental results showed that although M_{peak}, M_{min}, d_{peak} and d_{min} approach more or less constant values with increasing values of K, there were significant deviations from the ideally desired values. M_{min} tended towards a value that was a minor fraction of M_{peak}. This is a measure of the number of spurious hypotheses in the Hough space. The values of d_{peak} and d_{min} should approach zero with increasing K, but they tended to finite non-zero values, which indicate limited accuracy of localization. These experiments brought out the limitations of the use of the straightforward generalized Hough transform technique:

1. Limitations intrinsic to the fundamental nature of the straightforward Hough clustering algorithm.

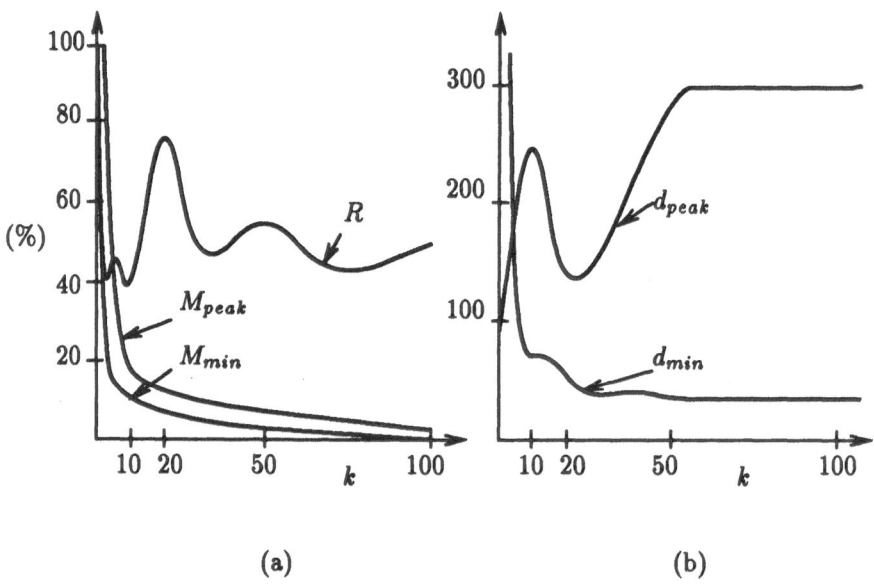

(a)   (b)

Figure 7.5: Experimental results for the recognition and localization of the conical surface in Figure 7.3.

2. Limitations arising out of the application of the Hough clustering algorithm to a multiple-object scene with partial occlusion.

The fundamental limitations of the Hough clustering algorithm in this case are:

1. *Inability to detect planar and umbilic (spherical) surfaces.* For planar surfaces the surface curvature is identically zero in all directions. For umbilic surfaces the surface curvature has an identical non-zero value in all directions. Thus at planar or umbilic surface points it is not possible to compute two unique directions for the maximum and minimum principal curvatures.

2. *Inability to take into account axes of symmetry of the modeled objects.* For objects with an axis of symmetry, rotations about the axis of symmetry are not distinguishable. For a given 3-D object model with axis of symmetry in the Z direction and with the observed axis direction $[a_x, a_y, a_z]$ in the scene, we are interested in the rotation matrix $\mathbf{R}$ such that:

$$\mathbf{R}[0, 0, 1]^T = [a_x, a_y, a_z]^T \qquad (7.21)$$

The above equation does not uniquely specify the rotation matrix $\mathbf{R}$. If the rotation matrix $\mathbf{R}$ is specified by the triple (ξ, η, θ), then the possible rotations can be shown to span a subspace Ω of the six-dimensional parameter space $(t_x, t_y, t_z, \xi, \eta, \theta)$ denoted by Π. The subspace Ω is given by the equations:

$$\begin{aligned}
\cos \xi \cos \eta \sin \eta (1 - \cos \theta) + \sin \xi \sin \eta \sin \theta &= a_x \\
\sin \xi \cos \eta \sin \eta (1 - \cos \theta) - \cos \xi \sin \eta \sin \theta &= a_y \\
\cos^2 \eta (1 - \cos \theta) + \cos \theta &= a_z \qquad (7.22)
\end{aligned}$$

In order to take into account the indistinguishability of the rotations in Ω, the clustering should be done in a subspace Ψ, where $\Pi = \Omega \oplus \Psi$, where $\oplus$ denotes the direct sum of the two vector spaces. The straightforward Hough clustering technique has no such provision.

Limitations of straightforward Hough clustering when applied to multiple-object scenes with partial occlusion are:

1. *Increased number of false hypotheses generated.* As can be observed from Figure 7.5 (a), M_{min} and M_{peak} approach more or less constant values. This value is a small fraction of the total number of hypotheses in the Hough space (values ranging from 0.7% to 1.5%). The presence of spurious peaks in the Hough space is brought out by the value of M_{peak}. The value of M_{min} is a fraction of the value of M_{peak} (values ranging from 12% to 52%).

2. *Accuracy of the localization process.* The value of d_{min} is a measure of the accuracy of the localization process. The value of d_{min} approaches

Table 7.1: Eight qualitative surface types distinguished by the signs of mean and Gaussian curvatures.

H K	$-$	0	$+$
$-$	Saddle Ridge Type = 4	Minimal Surface Type = 6	Saddle Valley Type = 8
0	Ridge Surface Type = 3	Planar Surface Type = 2	Valley Surface Type = 7
$+$	Peak Surface Type = 1	None	Pit Surface Type = 5

a constant value with increasing K (Figure 7.5(b)). Ideally, d_{min} should approach zero. The finite value of d_{min} represents the inherent inaccuracies in feature extraction, matching, and peak detection.

3. *Extensive memory and computational requirements.* A binning approach to peak detection is extensive in terms of memory requirement. To represent a six-dimensional Hough space as an accumulator array with sufficient degree of resolution, the memory requirement would be prohibitive. Clustering algorithms, on the other hand, take a long time to converge to a solution.

The overall conclusion is that straightforward Hough clustering is fairly ineffective in object recognition and localization in complex 3-D scenes with partial occlusion. None of the three objects in either scene was reliably identified and localized. On the other hand, as described in the following sections, the generalized Hough transform coupled with qualitative features is more effective in the recognition of 3-D objects in a multiple-object scene with partial occlusion. The use of qualitative features in conjunction with the generalized Hough transform enables us to alleviate some of the shortcomings mentioned above.

7.3   Recognition Using Qualitative Features

The signs of the mean curvature and the Gaussian curvature are used to define eight qualitative surface types [Besl and Jain 1986]. These surface types are tabulated in Table 7.1. The surface types of interest are cylindrical, conical,

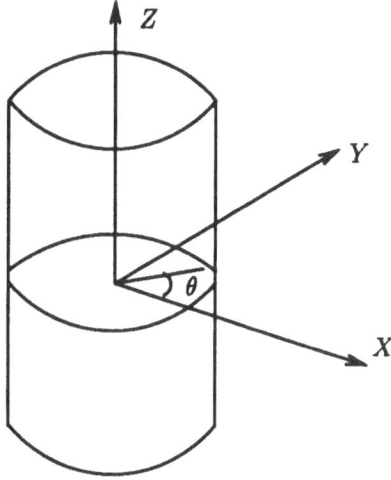

Figure 7.6: A cylindrical surface.

and ellipsoidal surfaces. Cylindrical and conical surfaces are characterized by zero Gaussian curvature and non-zero mean curvature (types 3 and 7), whereas ellipsoidal surfaces are characterized by positive Gaussian curvature (types 1 and 5). The ellipsoidal surfaces of special interest are spherical surfaces, for which $H^2 = K$. The qualitative surface descriptions enable the use of localization techniques specific to that particular surface type.

7.3.1 Cylindrical and Conical Surfaces

Cylindrical surfaces (Figure 7.6) are represented by the parametric equation $\mathbf{x}(\theta, z) = (x(\theta),\ y(\theta),\ z)$ [Faux and Pratt 1979]. The equation for the surface normals is given by

$$\mathbf{n}(\theta, z) = \frac{\mathbf{x}_\theta \otimes \mathbf{x}_z}{|\mathbf{x}_\theta \otimes \mathbf{x}_z|} \tag{7.23}$$

where $\otimes$ denotes the vector cross product. For right circular cylindrical surfaces $x(\theta) = r\cos\theta$ and $y(\theta) = r\sin\theta$. Hence $\mathbf{n}(\theta, z) = (\cos\theta, \sin\theta, 0)$. Mapping the surface normals (needle map) onto the Gaussian sphere yields a great circle with the orientation of the plane of the great circle in the direction of the axis of the cylindrical surface.

Conical surfaces are represented by $\mathbf{x}(\theta, z) = (r(z)\cos\theta,\ r(z)\sin\theta,\ z)$ [Nagata and Jha 1988]. For right circular conical surfaces (Figure 7.7), $r(z) = R(1 - z/H)$, hence the equation for the surface normals is given by

$$\mathbf{n}(\theta, z) = \frac{\mathbf{x}_\theta \otimes \mathbf{x}_z}{|\mathbf{x}_\theta \otimes \mathbf{x}_z|} = \frac{(\cos\theta, \sin\theta, \frac{R}{H})}{\sqrt{1 + (\frac{R}{H})^2}} \tag{7.24}$$

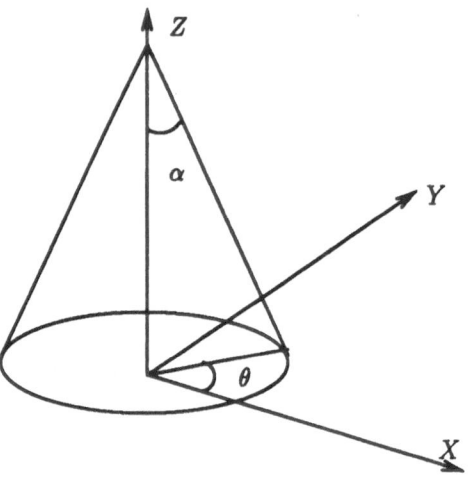

Figure 7.7: A conical surface

The needle map maps onto a small circle with the orientation of the plane of the small circle the same as the axis of the conical surface. The distance of the small circle from the origin is given by $d = R/\sqrt{R^2 + H^2} = \sin \alpha$. Thus detecting the orientation of the axis of a cone or a cylinder is reduced to estimating the orientation of the plane of the great or small circle on the Gaussian sphere on which the needle map of the surface is mapped.

As shown in Figure 7.8, the equation of a plane on the Gaussian sphere is given by

$$d = n_{xi} \cos \xi \sin \eta + n_{yi} \sin \xi \sin \eta + n_{zi} \cos \eta \qquad (7.25)$$

where $\mathbf{n}_i = (n_{xi}, n_{yi}, n_{zi})$ is the input needle map. The plane on the Gaussian sphere is uniquely characterized by the triple (d, ξ, η). A Hough clustering technique is the most obvious way of estimating the parameters (d, ξ, η) from the input needle map. The parameter d distinguishes cylindrical surfaces from conical surfaces, since $d = 0$ for cylindrical surfaces, whereas for conical surfaces d is nonzero. The parameters ξ and η give the orientation of the axis of the conical or cylindrical surface on the Gaussian sphere.

7.3.2 The Recognition Process Using Qualitative Features

Recognition and localization using qualitative features proceed in the following steps:

1. *Feature extraction.* The analytic surface-fitting technique described in the previous section is used to compute the mean, Gaussian, and principal

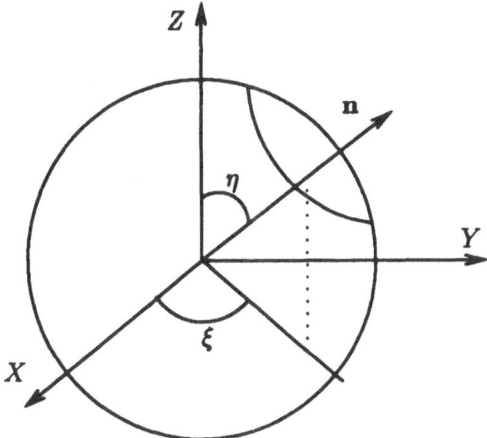

Figure 7.8: Mapping of surface normals on the Gaussian sphere.

curvature values, the directions of the principal curvatures, and the surface normal at each pixel in the range image.

2. *Detection of surface discontinuities.* Two types of surface discontinuities are detected: (a) step edges, which indicate discontinuity in depth, and (b) roof edges, which indicate continuity in depth but discontinuity in surface normal. Since depth discontinuities denote a high value for the surface gradient, the square root of the determinant of the first fundamental form matrix is used as a criterion for the detection of step edges:

$$\sqrt{|G|} = \sqrt{g_{11}g_{22} - g_{12}^2} = \sqrt{1 + f_u^2 + f_v^2} \qquad (7.26)$$

The range image pixels where $\sqrt{|G|}$ exceeds a predefined threshold are selected as step edge points. Roof edges are detected by computing the maximum angular difference between adjacent surface normals, giving the roof edge magnitude M_{roof} at a particular pixel location in the image.

$$M_{roof}(x,y) = max[\cos^{-1}[\mathbf{n}(x,y) \cdot \mathbf{n}(x+k, y+l)], -1 \le k, l \le +1] \quad (7.27)$$

The range image pixels where M_{roof} exceeds a predefined threshold are selected as roof edge pixels.

3. *Pixel classification.* Based on the signs of the mean curvature and the Gaussian curvature (HK signs), the range pixels are classified as belonging to one of the eight qualitative surface types described in Table 7.1.

4. *Pixel grouping.* Pixels are grouped spatially into surface patches homogeneous in the HK signs using a region-growing algorithm. Knowledge

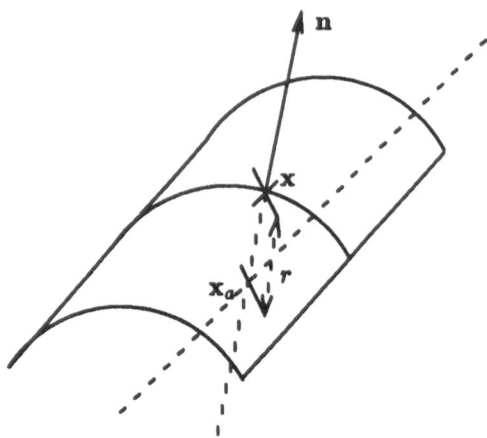

Figure 7.9: Determining the axis point of a cylindrical surface where x_a is the axis point estimated from x.

of the location of the step and roof edges is used to prevent accidental region-growing over the surface discontinuities.

5. *Identification and localization of surface patches.* Surface patches are localized in 3-D space using localization techniques specific to the qualitative surface types. The surface types of interest are conical, cylindrical, and spherical, and the localization techniques specific to these surface types are presented in the following subsections.

7.3.3   Localization of a Cylindrical Surface

A cylindrical surface can be localized by the orientation of its axis, the value of its radius, and the location of its centroid. The location of the centroid of the cylinder is not robust in cases of severe occlusion, but is fairly robust in most cases of partial occlusion. The orientation of the axis is estimated, as mentioned in the previous section. The radius of the cylinder is obtained by averaging the maximum principal curvature κ_1 over the cylindrical surface. The centroid is obtained by finding the mean of the axis points. For each point x on the cylindrical surface (Figure 7.9), the corresponding axis point is given by

$$x_a(x) = x - n(x)(\frac{1}{\kappa_1(x)}) \qquad (7.28)$$

The centroid and radius are given by the equations

$$x_0 = \frac{1}{N}\sum x_a(x) \qquad (7.29)$$

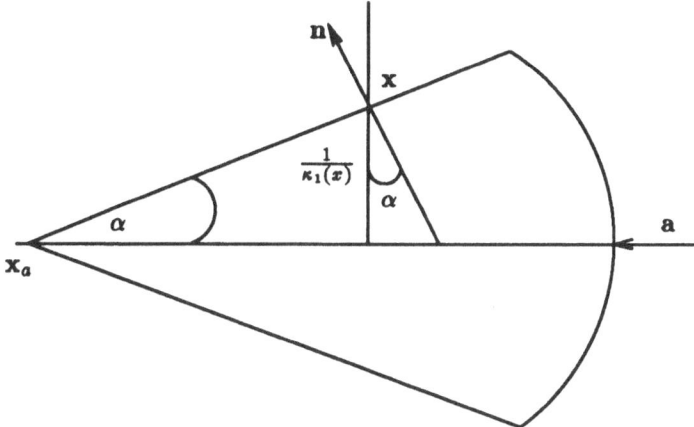

Figure 7.10: Determining the apex of the conical surface where x_a is the apex point estimated from x.

$$R = \frac{1}{N} \sum \frac{1}{\kappa_1(\mathbf{x})} \qquad (7.30)$$

7.3.4 Localization of a Conical Surface

A conical surface can be localized by the orientation of its axis, the value of α (Figure 7.10), and the location of the apex of the cone. The location of the apex of the cone with respect to a single point $\mathbf{x}$ on the conical surface is given by

$$\mathbf{x}_a(\mathbf{x}) = \mathbf{x} - \mathbf{n}(\mathbf{x})(\frac{1}{\kappa_1(\mathbf{x})\cos\alpha}) + \mathbf{a}(\frac{2}{\kappa_1(\mathbf{x})\sin 2\alpha}) \qquad (7.31)$$

where $\mathbf{n}(\mathbf{x})$ is the unit surface normal at point $\mathbf{x}$ on the conical surface, $\kappa_1(\mathbf{x})$ is the maximum principal curvature at $\mathbf{x}$, and $\mathbf{a}$ is the unit vector in the direction of the axis of the conical surface. The points $\mathbf{x}_a$ computed for each surface point on the conical surface form a cluster in 3-D space. The actual value of the apex is taken to be the average of the $\mathbf{x}_a$ values

$$\hat{\mathbf{x}}_a = \frac{1}{N} \sum \mathbf{x}_a(\mathbf{x}) \qquad (7.32)$$

The apex of the conical surface is computed independently at each surface point on the conical surface and is hence robust, even to severe occlusion.

7.3.5 Localization of a Spherical Surface

The needle map of a spherical surface is uniformly distributed on the Gaussian sphere. Consequently, the process of histogramming on the Gaussian sphere

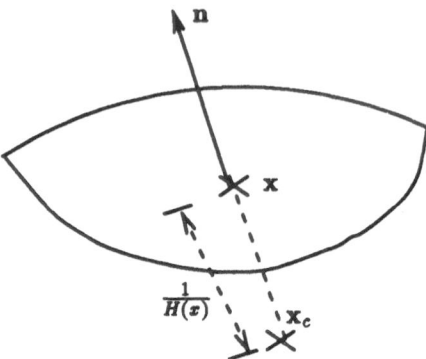

Figure 7.11: Determining the center of a spherical surface where x_c is the center estimated from x.

does not yield the parameters of the spherical surface. A simple technique of determining the parameters of a sphere is by using the equation of the spherical surface

$$(x - a)^2 + (y - b)^2 + (z - c)^2 = r^2 \qquad (7.33)$$

Since a spherical surface can be localized by the location of its center and the value of its radius, histogramming and maxima detection in the (a, b, c, r) parameter space localizes the sphere.

Alternatively, the spherical surface can be localized by clustering in the image domain instead of in the parameter domain. The location of the center of the sphere (Figure 7.11), with respect to a point x on the spherical surface, is given by

$$x_c(x) = x - n(x)\frac{1}{H(x)} \qquad (7.34)$$

The points x_c computed for each point on the spherical surface form a cluster in 3-D space. The center of this cluster is taken to be the center of the spherical surface. Since the center of the spherical surface is computed independently at each surface point on the spherical surface, it is robust even to severe occlusion:

$$\hat{x}_c = \frac{1}{N}\sum x_c \qquad (7.35)$$

7.3.6 An Experimental Comparison

Recognition and localization using qualitative features was tested on range images (Figures 7.3 and 7.4). Results of the experiments are summarized in Tables 7.2, 7.3, 7.4 and 7.5. From these results, we can summarize the advantages of using qualitative features in the recognition and localization process:

Table 7.2: Results of recognition and localization of a cylindrical surface using qualitative features.

Scene No.		Centroid	Axis	Radius
1	Theoretical Computation	60.00 60.00 600.00	0.853 -0.146 0.500	25.00
	Experimental Result	61.98 60.70 600.10	0.790 -0.168 0.590	23.70
2	Theoretical Computation	60.00 60.00 300.00	0.625 -0.217 0.750	25.00
	Experimental Result	61.98 60.70 600.60	0.604 -0.220 0.766	24.55

Table 7.3: Results of recognition and localization of a conical surface using qualitative features.

Scene No.		Apex	Axis	α (deg)
1	Theoretical Computation	16.70 42.50 278.40	-0.866 -0.250 -0.433	21.80
	Experimental Result	15.35 43.00 278.17	0.864 0.248 -0.438	21.72
2	Theoretical Computation	60.00 60.00 300.00	-0.707 0.500 -0.500	21.80
	Experimental Result	69.60 60.33 278.79	-0.727 0.528 -0.438	16.70

Table 7.4: Results of recognition and localization of a spherical surface using qualitative features.

Scene No.		Centroid	Radius
1	Theoretical Computation	75.00 100.00 900.00	25.00
	Experimental Result	75.01 100.07 900.23	25.11
2	Theoretical Computation	75.00 75.00 900.00	25.00
	Experimental Result	could not be localized due to excessive occlusion	

Table 7.5: Comparison of localization accuracy.

Surface Type	Scene No.	d_{peak}	d_{min}	d_{qual}
Cylindrical	1	128.39	13.57	6.79
	2	142.93	15.64	21.25
Conical	1	318.37	36.09	0.381
	2	89.11	43.74	22.19

1. A representation that is more specific to the surface type in question can be used for recognition. This is in contrast to the more generic representation of the surface in terms of point-wise surface curvature and surface normal values. Making the representation specific to the surface type enables the detection and localization of spherical surfaces, which was not possible using the generic representation of the surface.

2. The choice of localization parameters can be made specific to the representation of that particular surface type, which is in contrast to the more generic localization parameters based on three-dimensional rigid-body motion. This allows us to take into account the axes of symmetry of the modeled objects. For both conical and cylindrical surfaces, a parameter space that takes into account the axis of symmetry of these surface types is used in the Hough clustering process. This enables us to overcome the indistinguishability of the rotations about the axis of symmetry. All this is made possible by the classification of the surfaces based on qualitative surface types.

3. Use of qualitative features leads to better localization accuracy. In Table 7.5, a quantitative comparison of the localization accuracy of the straightforward Hough clustering algorithm vs. the use of qualitative features is made. The parameters of interest were d_{peak} and d_{min}, which characterize the localization accuracy of the straightforward Hough clustering algorithm, and d_{qual}, which characterizes the localization accuracy with the help of qualitative features. Since d_{peak} and d_{min} are functions of K, the smallest values of d_{peak} and d_{min} over the range of values of K were considered for comparison. The distance measure d_{qual} is in the parameter space specific to that particular surface type. It measures the parametric distance between the theoretically computed viewpoint and the experimentally computed viewpoint. The parameter space for the cylindrical surface is $(c_x, c_y, c_z, \xi, \eta, r)$, where (c_x, c_y, c_z) is the location of the centroid of the cylinder, (ξ, η) is the orientation of the axis of the cylinder, and r is the radius of the cylinder. The parameter space for the conical surface is $(a_x, a_y, a_z, \xi, \eta, \alpha)$, where (a_x, a_y, a_z) is the location of the apex of the cone, (ξ, η) is the orientation of the axis of the cone, and α is the angle of the cone. The distance measurements are not strictly comparable, since they are in different parameter spaces. However, the numerical figures do give a good indication of the relative localization accuracy.

Since local pixel-level operations such as surface-fitting, region growing, edge detection, and histogramming are used extensively in the process of extracting the localization parameters for the primitive surface types, the feature extraction process is amenable to parallelism. In particular, these algorithms are easily parallelized on an SIMD mesh architecture. Since the Connection Machine can be configured as an n-dimensional mesh, all of these procedures can be easily parallelized on the Connection Machine. (See Chapter 9.)

7.4   Recognition of Complex Curved Objects

As discussed earlier, the process of matching can be viewed as a constraint propagation/constraint satisfaction problem. In fact, the problem of 3-D object recognition most often involves a trade-off between the complexity of representation and the complexity of constraint propagation/constraint satisfaction technique used. A higher-order relational description of the image data would imply a graph-theoretic constraint propagation technique based on subgraph isomorphism or maximal clique detection, whereas a description in terms of primitive geometric features implies a constraint propagation technique based on Hough clustering or searching through an interpretation tree. A more complex representation reduces the time complexity of the constraint propagation/constraint satisfaction process, and vice versa.

In Section 7.2 surfaces were matched by matching each point on the model surface with an appropriate point on the scene surface. The values of the mean curvature and the Gaussian curvature were used to restrict the possible matches and the local coordinate system at each point formed by the directions of the principal curvatures, and the direction of the surface normal was used to compute the transformation that would place the point on the model surface in registration with the point on the scene surface. Hough clustering in the six-dimensional parameter space of rigid-body motion parameters was used to compute the global pose. The segmentation effort in this case was minimal, since all that was involved was the fitting of an analytic surface in a local window centered around a surface point and computing the surface curvature properties from the parameters of the analytic surface. This approach, apart from being memory intensive and time consuming, also caused a number of spurious peaks in the Hough space, especially when dealing with a multiple-object scene with partial occlusion. This made recognition and localization very difficult.

The approach followed in Section 7.3 involved, in addition to computation of the curvature values at every point, classification of surfaces into one of the eight surface types based on the signs of the mean curvature and the Gaussian curvature (HK signs), grouping of surface pixels identical in HK signs into homogeneous regions, and the extraction of recognition and localization features characteristic of that particular surface type. Although this approach involves a greater effort in segmentation, it is far less than the segmentation effort required to come up with a relational description. The fact that most of the segmentation techniques shown in this chapter are based either on pixel-level operations in a local window or on histogramming makes the segmentation easily amenable to parallelism on a SIMD mesh architecture.

The classification of surfaces into qualitative surface types also enables the recognition and localization of complex curved objects that are made up of a piecewise combination of spherical, conical, cylindrical, and planar surfaces. *Dihedral feature junctions* are shown to be well suited for the recognition and localization of such objects. Dihedral feature junctions are shown to be robust to occlusion and offer a viewpoint-independent representation scheme for modeling complex objects. Moreover, dihedral feature junctions can be easily extracted from the localization parameters of the qualitative surface types.

7.5 Dihedral Feature Junctions

The recognition and localization features for conical, cylindrical, and spherical surfaces can be used to form what are termed *dihedral feature junctions*. Dihedral junctions are junctions with a single vertex and two incident edges. The use of dihedral junctions in the recognition and localization of polyhedral solids has already been explored with satisfactory results in the previous chapter. *Dihedral feature junctions* differ from *dihedral junctions* in polyhedra in the sense that dihedral feature junctions do not correspond to physical junctions in the scene, but are junctions formed from the recognition and localization features for the aforementioned surface types. Representation of object models in the form of dihedral feature junctions is viewpoint independent. This offers a considerable advantage in terms of memory requirements over representation techniques that are viewpoint dependent and need to store several characteristic views of the objects [Ikeuchi 1987].

7.5.1 Types of Dihedral Feature Junctions

Two types of dihedral feature junctions are encountered in the recognition and localization of curved objects made up of piecewise combinations of conical, cylindrical, spherical and planar surfaces:

1. **Type I**: *Dihedral feature junction pair*, which is encountered when dealing with pairwise combinations of conical, cylindrical, and planar surfaces. A typical dihedral feature junction pair is shown in Figure 7.12

2. **Type II**: *Dihedral feature junction*, which is encountered when dealing with a spherical surface in combination with a conical, cylindrical, or planar surface. A typical dihedral feature junction is shown in Figure 7.13.

A pair of spherical surfaces does not constitute a valid dihedral feature junction and is not considered for the purpose of matching and pose computation. Both range image data and models are represented in terms of Type I and Type II dihedral feature junctions.

7.5.2 Matching of Dihedral Feature Junctions

The matching procedure for each of the dihedral feature junction types is as discussed below:

1. **Type I**: With reference to Figure 7.14, the two dihedral feature junction pairs are said to match if they satisfy the following unary and binary constraints.

   Unary Constraints:

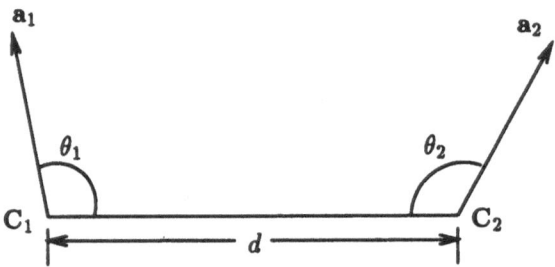

Figure 7.12: A dihedral feature junction pair (Type I).

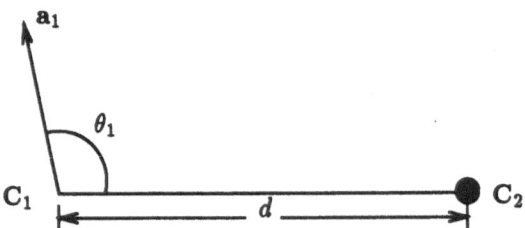

Figure 7.13: A dihedral feature junction (Type II). C_2: center of a spherical surface.

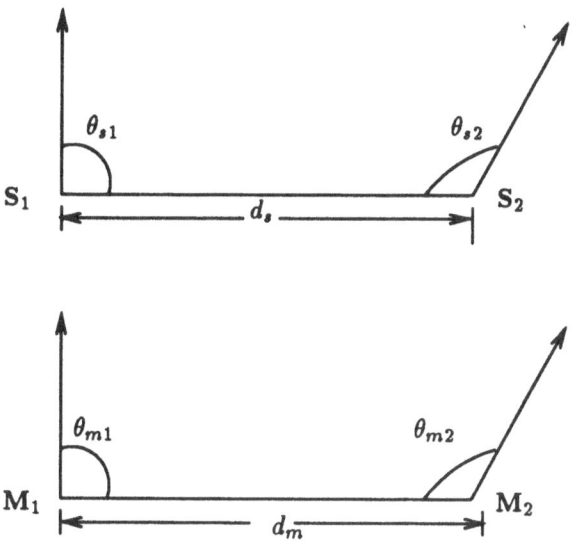

Figure 7.14: Matching two dihedral feature junction pairs (Type I)

(a) Surface type S_1 = Surface type M_1

(b) Surface type S_2 = Surface type M_2

(c) Angle θ_{s1} = Angle θ_{m1}

(d) Angle θ_{s2} = Angle θ_{m2}

(e) If S_1 and M_1 are cylindrical, then radius of S_1 = radius of M_1

(f) If S_1 and M_1 are conical, then angle of S_1 = angle of M_1

(g) If S_2 and M_2 are cylindrical, then radius of S_2 = radius of M_2

(h) If S_2 and M_2 are conical, then angle of S_2 = angle of M_2

Binary constraints:

(a) Distance d_s = Distance d_m

2. **Type 2:** With reference to Figure 7.15, two dihedral feature junctions are said to match if they satisfy the following unary and binary constraints.

Unary constraints:

(a) Surface type S_2 = Surface type M_2 = spherical

(b) Radius of S_2 = Radius of M_2

(c) Surface type S_1 = Surface type M_1

(d) Angle θ_{s1} = Angle θ_{m1}

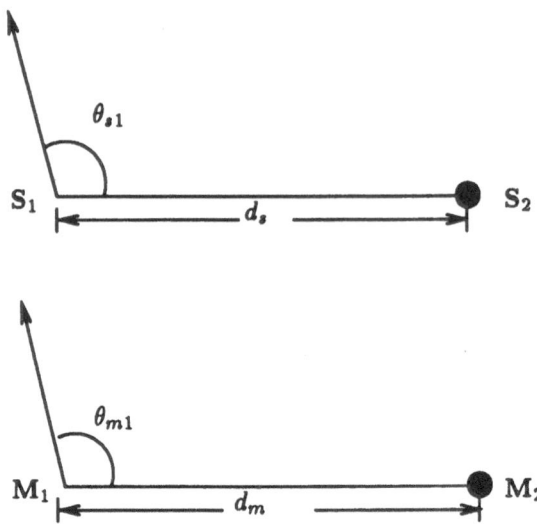

Figure 7.15: Matching two dihedral feature junctions (Type II).

(e) If S_1 and M_1 are cylindrical, then radius of S_1 = radius of M_1

(f) If S_1 and M_1 are conical, then angle of S_1 = angle of M_1

Binary constraints:

(a) Distance d_s = Distance d_m

7.5.3   Pose Determination

We first discuss the technique for pose determination for dihedral feature junction of Type 2. The pose determination technique for the dihedral feature junction of Type 1 is an extension of this.

Pose Determination for Type II Dihedral Feature Junction

Figure 7.16 shows a model dihedral feature junction that is to be matched with a scene dihedral feature junction. Let m_1 be the unit vector in the direction **BA**, and let m_2 be the unit vector in the direction **BC**. Similarly, let s_1 be the unit vector in the direction **ED** and s_2 the unit vector in the direction **EF**. Let the homogeneous coordinates of B in the model coordinate system be $[x_0, y_0, z_0, 1]^T$, and let those of E in the scene coordinate system be $[u_0, v_0, w_0, 1]^T$. The goal is to find a transformation **T** such that

$$\mathbf{T}[x_0, y_0, z_0, 1]^T = [u_0, v_0, w_0, 1]^T \qquad (7.36)$$

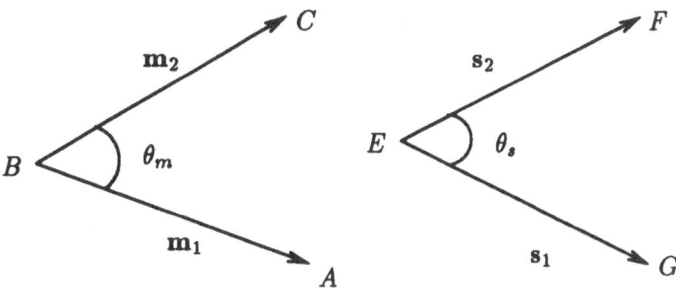

Figure 7.16: Matching a model and scene dihedral feature junction.

T is determined as follows [Korn and Korn 1972]:

1. Points B and E are translated to their respective origins. Let $TRANS(-B)$ and $TRANS(-E)$ denote the respective homogeneous transformations. This ensures that both junctions have their vertices translated to the origin.

2. The vectors $\mathbf{m}_1$ and $\mathbf{m}_2$ are rotated about $\mathbf{k}$ through an angle θ so as to be aligned with $\mathbf{s}_1$ and $\mathbf{s}_2$, respectively; $\mathbf{k}$ is determined by requiring that it be perpendicular to both $\mathbf{m}_1 - \mathbf{s}_1$ and $\mathbf{m}_2 - \mathbf{s}_2$ or, equivalently, that the projections of $\mathbf{m}_1$ and $\mathbf{s}_1$ along $\mathbf{k}$ be equal and the projections of $\mathbf{m}_2$ and $\mathbf{s}_2$ along $\mathbf{k}$ be equal, i.e.,

$$\mathbf{k} \cdot \mathbf{m}_1 = \mathbf{k} \cdot \mathbf{s}_1 \Rightarrow \mathbf{k} \cdot (\mathbf{m}_1 - \mathbf{s}_1) = 0 \tag{7.37}$$

$$\mathbf{k} \cdot \mathbf{m}_2 = \mathbf{k} \cdot \mathbf{s}_2 \Rightarrow \mathbf{k} \cdot (\mathbf{m}_2 - \mathbf{s}_2) = 0 \tag{7.38}$$

Thus

$$\mathbf{k} = \frac{(\mathbf{m}_1 - \mathbf{s}_1) \otimes (\mathbf{m}_2 - \mathbf{s}_2)}{|(\mathbf{m}_1 - \mathbf{s}_1) \otimes (\mathbf{m}_2 - \mathbf{s}_2)|} \tag{7.39}$$

where $\otimes$ denotes the vector cross product. From Figure 7.17

$$\vec{OA} = (\mathbf{m}_1 \cdot \mathbf{k})\,\mathbf{k} = (\mathbf{s}_1 \cdot \mathbf{k})\mathbf{k} \tag{7.40}$$

$$\vec{AC} = \mathbf{m}_1 - (\mathbf{m}_1 \cdot \mathbf{k})\mathbf{k} \tag{7.41}$$

$$\vec{AC} \cdot \mathbf{k} = [\mathbf{m}_1 - (\mathbf{m}_1 \cdot \mathbf{k})\mathbf{k}] \cdot \mathbf{k} = 0 \tag{7.42}$$

Hence OAC is a right angle triangle with OC as the hypotenuse. Also,

$$|\vec{AC}| = |\vec{AB}| = \sqrt{1 - (\mathbf{m}_1 \cdot \mathbf{k})(\mathbf{s}_1 \cdot \mathbf{k})} \tag{7.43}$$

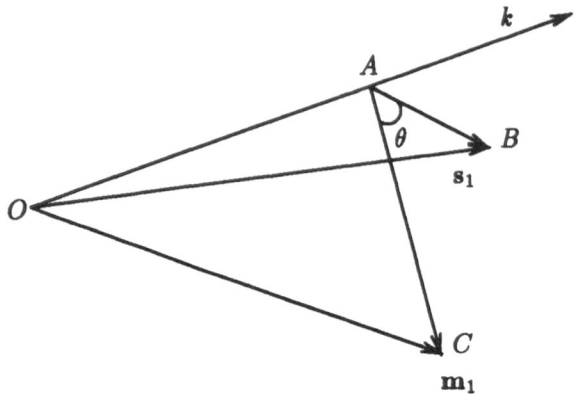

Figure 7.17: Determination of the axis **k** and angle θ for rotation.

(since $\mathbf{m}_1$ is a unit vector). Therefore, θ is determined by

$$\cos\theta = \frac{\vec{AB} \cdot \vec{AC}}{|\vec{AB}|\,|\vec{AC}|} = \frac{[\mathbf{m}_1 - (\mathbf{m}_1 \cdot \mathbf{k})\mathbf{k}] \cdot [\mathbf{s}_1 - (\mathbf{s}_1 \cdot \mathbf{k})\mathbf{k}]}{[1 - (\mathbf{m}_1 \cdot \mathbf{k})(\mathbf{s}_1 \cdot \mathbf{k})]} \qquad (7.44)$$

$$= 1 - \frac{[1 - (\mathbf{m}_1 \cdot \mathbf{s}_1)]}{[1 - (\mathbf{k} \cdot \mathbf{m}_1)(\mathbf{k} \cdot \mathbf{s}_1)]} \qquad (7.45)$$

3. The final transformation can thus be written as:

$$ROT(k,\theta)\,TRANS(-B)[x_0, y_0, z_0, 1]^T = TRANS(-E)[u_0, v_0, w_0, 1]^T \qquad (7.46)$$

From equations (7.36) and (7.46)

$$\mathbf{T} = TRANS^{-1}(-E)\,ROT(k,\theta)\,TRANS(-B) \qquad (7.47)$$

The transformation **T** from the model coordinate system to the scene coordinate system could be written as:

$$\mathbf{T} = ROT(k,\theta)\,TRANS(t_x, t_y, t_z) \qquad (7.48)$$

$$\mathbf{T} =
\begin{bmatrix}
r_{11} & r_{12} & r_{13} & 0 \\
r_{21} & r_{22} & r_{23} & 0 \\
r_{31} & r_{32} & r_{33} & 0 \\
0 & 0 & 0 & 1
\end{bmatrix}
\begin{bmatrix}
1 & 0 & 0 & t_x \\
0 & 1 & 0 & t_y \\
0 & 0 & 1 & t_z \\
0 & 0 & 0 & 1
\end{bmatrix} \qquad (7.49)$$

where

$$r_{11} = k_x^2(1 - \cos\theta) + \cos\theta$$

$$
\begin{aligned}
r_{12} &= k_x k_y(1 - \cos\theta) - k_z \sin\theta \\
r_{13} &= k_x k_z(1 - \cos\theta) + k_y \sin\theta \\
r_{21} &= k_x k_y(1 - \cos\theta) + k_z \sin\theta \\
r_{22} &= k_y^2(1 - \cos\theta) + \cos\theta \\
r_{23} &= k_y k_z(1 - \cos\theta) - k_x \sin\theta \\
r_{31} &= k_x k_z(1 - \cos\theta) - k_y \sin\theta \\
r_{32} &= k_y k_z(1 - \cos\theta) + k_x \sin\theta \\
r_{33} &= k_z^2(1 - \cos\theta) + \cos\theta
\end{aligned}
\tag{7.50}
$$

and

$$
\begin{aligned}
t_x &= u_0 - r_{11}x_0 - r_{12}y_0 - r_{13}z_0 \\
t_y &= v_0 - r_{21}x_0 - r_{22}y_0 - r_{23}z_0 \\
t_z &= w_0 - r_{31}x_0 - r_{32}y_0 - r_{33}z_0
\end{aligned}
\tag{7.51}
$$

The axis of rotation $\mathbf{k}$ could be alternatively expressed by the pair (ξ, η), where

$$
k_x = \cos\xi \, \sin\eta, \; k_y = \sin\xi \, \sin\eta, \; k_z = \cos\eta
\tag{7.52}
$$

where $-\pi < \eta < \pi$ and $0 < \xi < 2\pi$.

The transformation $\mathbf{T}$ is thus uniquely specified by the 6-tuple $(t_x, t_y, t_z, \xi, \eta, \theta)$.

Pose Determination for Type I Dihedral Feature Junction Pair

In order to determine the pose for a dihedral feature junction pair, the pose is computed for each of the constituent dihedral feature junctions as described above. The pose of the dihedral feature junction pair is the average of the poses computed for the individual dihedral feature junctions.

7.5.4   Pose Clustering

The Hough space is represented by a six-dimensional accumulator array. The value of the pose resulting from the matching of a scene dihedral feature junction with a model dihedral feature junction is used to update the appropriate cell in the Hough array. At the end of the matching stage, detecting a peak (or a maximum) in the Hough array yields a globally consistent pose.

7.6   Experimental Results

The matching and localization technique based on dihedral feature junctions, as described in the previous sections, was experimentally verified. The experimental results bring out the advantages of the proposed recognition and localization technique in terms of its ability to handle multiple-object scenes with partial occlusion.

The flow chart of the entire recognition and localization process is shown in Figure 7.18. Three scenes (Figures 7.19, 7.20, and 7.21) were considered. Each scene contained three objects from different viewpoints. The objects partially occlude each other. Table 7.6 shows the experimental results in which both the theoretical and experimentally computed poses are compared.

The experimental findings show that the rotation parameters in the pose computation are quite sensitive to the difference in the angles between the scene and the model dihedral feature junctions. On the other hand, the estimation of translation parameters was found to be far more robust. The experimental findings conformed with a formal sensitivity analysis in Chapter 8. In Scene IV, object 2 is fairly occluded, yet the experimentally computed pose is in close conformity with the theoretical pose. This brings out the robustness of the dihedral feature junctions when used for matching and localization. In Scene V, the experimentally computed pose for object 3 is seen to differ considerably from the theoretical pose. This could be accounted for by the object symmetry. Since the object is symmetrical with respect to a rotation of π about the model z axis, the transform $\mathbf{T}$ is indistinguishable from the transform $\mathbf{T}\mathbf{R}_z(\pi)$ where $\mathbf{R}_z(\pi)$ is the matrix corresponding to the rotation about the model z axis with an angular magnitude of rotation of π . For the theoretical viewpoint of (150.0, 160.0, 1000.0, 347.23, 121.44, 91.74) the corresponding symmetric pose is (150.0, 160.0, 1000.0, 77.236, 138.669, −136.023), which agrees well with the experimentally computed viewpoint of (149.081, 160.763, 997.619, 75.938, 139.219, −132.188). The histogramming technique is not capable of disambiguating symmetric poses.

7.7   Summary

In this chapter we have presented a technique for the recognition and localization of objects with curved surfaces. The input images are range images of 3-D curved objects composed of piecewise combinations of conical, cylindrical, and spherical surfaces. Such objects constitute a significant majority of objects encountered in an industrial environment. Hough clustering is chosen as the constraint propagation technique because of its ease of parallelization. The straightforward generalized Hough transform based on point-wise surface matching leads to a combinatorial explosion of the search space of scene interpretation hypotheses as well as spurious hypotheses in the Hough space. Qualitative surface classification based on the signs of the mean curvature and the Gaussian curvature is shown to enable the formulation of a representation in parameter space that is specific to a qualitative surface type. This reduces the combinatorial complexity of the search space of scene interpretation hypotheses and also reduces the number of spurious hypotheses. Moreover, classification of surfaces into qualitative surface types is used to come up with *dihedral feature junctions* , which are used for matching and pose computation. Dihedral feature junctions are shown to be

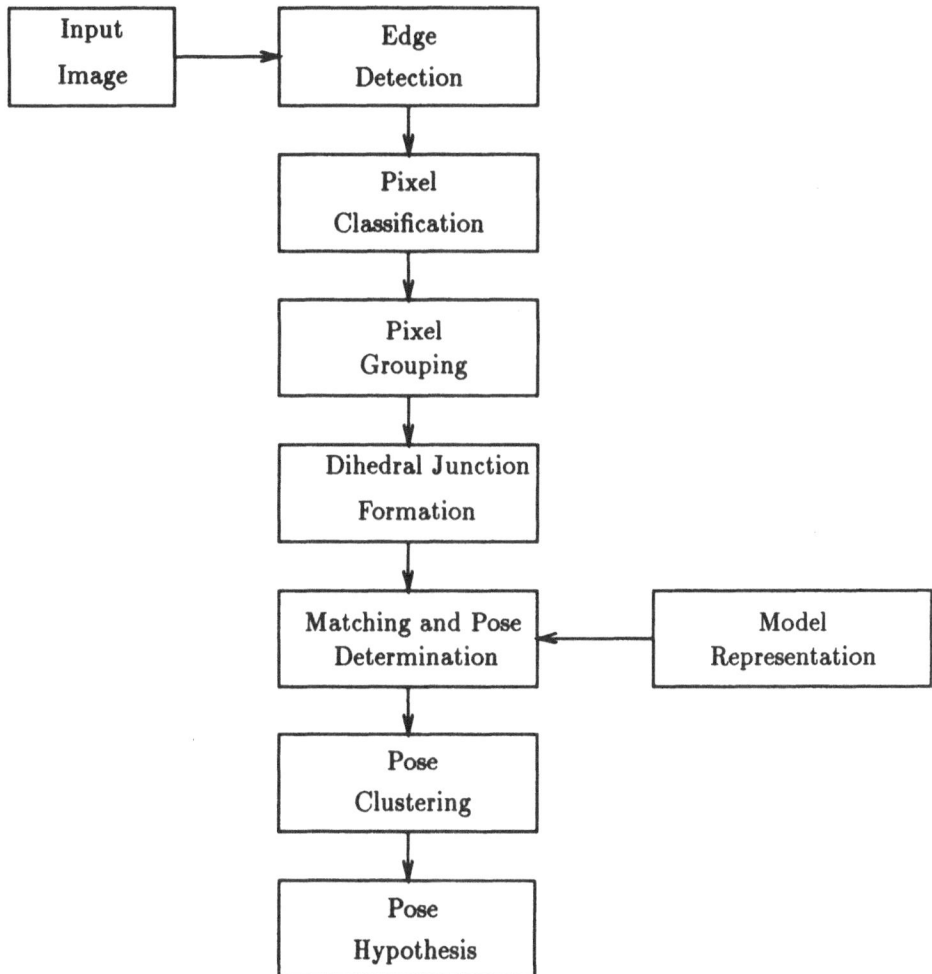

Figure 7.18: The flowchart for the recognition and localization of complex curved objects.

Table 7.6: Experimental results for complex curved objects.

Scene No.		Object 1		Object 2		Object3	
		Th.	Exp.	Th.	Exp.	Th.	Exp.
1	t_x	100.00	95.97	160.00	156.80	200.00	200.31
	t_y	100.00	102.69	160.00	165.33	100.00	99.94
	t_z	1000.00	1000.18	2000.00	1999.08	3000.00	2999.69
	ξ	2.33	2.63	5.26	2.63	327.24	329.06
	η	114.92	116.72	114.60	116.72	133.93	130.78
	θ	-113.48	-109.69	-84.67	-81.56	116.50	126.56
2	t_x	100.00	95.97	160.00	161.43	130.00	129.00
	t_y	100.00	102.69	160.00	159.82	180.00	180.50
	t_z	1000.00	1000.18	3000.00	3011.66	2000.00	1997.38
	ξ	2.33	2.63	5.26	14.06	354.74	357.19
	η	114.92	116.72	114.60	108.28	114.60	116.72
	θ	-113.48	-109.69	-84.67	-70.31	84.67	87.19
3	t_x	180.00	180.97	120.00	121.15	150.00	149.08
	t_y	100.00	98.39	140.00	137.94	160.00	160.76
	t_z	3000.00	2999.70	2000.00	2003.36	1000.00	997.62
	ξ	32.33	30.94	32.26	30.94	347.23	75.94
	η	127.37	127.97	132.77	133.60	121.44	139.22
	θ	-145.22	-143.44	-113.06	-109.69	91.74	-132.19

Th. : Theoretical Viewpoint   Exp. : Experimental Viewpoint

All angles are measured in degrees

Figure 7.19: Scene III containing multiple objects made up of complex curved surfaces.

Figure 7.20: Scene IV containing multiple objects made up of complex curved surfaces.

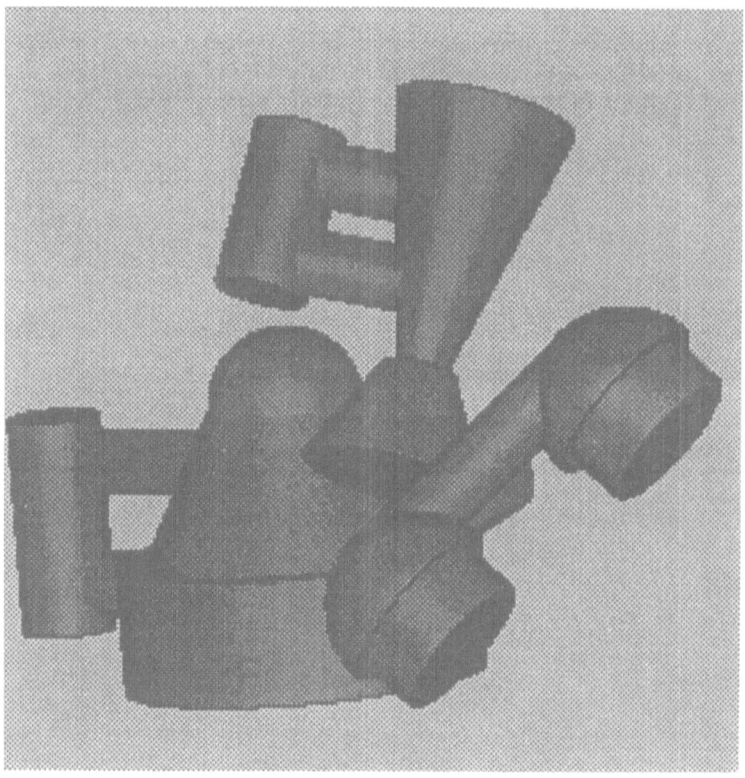

Figure 7.21: Scene V containing multiple objects made up of complex curved surfaces.

robust to occlusion and to offer a viewpoint independent modeling scheme for object models.

The proposed technique could be extended in several directions. Certain features used in the proposed technique, such as centroid of cylindrical surface and centroid of planar surface, are robust in cases of *mild* occlusion, but not *severe* occlusion. Alternative features for making the technique more robust need to be explored. In all the examples shown in this chapter, the corresponding models were generated manually. Techniques for automated model acquisition from images need to be explored. This will be particularly imperative as the objects get more complex, making the task of manually generating the models prohibitive. Although the proposed technique is designed to cover a large number of objects encountered in an industrial scenario, more surface types need to be considered in order to make the technique truly general and powerful.

Part III

Sensitivity Analysis and Parallel Implementation

Chapter 8

Sensitivity Analysis

Owing to errors introduced during the process of segmentation and feature extraction, the matching of scene features with model features may not always be exact. Therefore, a certain amount of tolerance has to be incorporated into the process of matching a scene feature with a model feature. Tolerance in the matching process will cause an error in the computed pose parameters. During the course of experiments based on matching and pose computation using dihedral junctions, the computed pose parameters were found to be sensitive to the difference in the included angles of the model dihedral junction (θ_m) and the scene dihedral junction (θ_s) (Figure 8.1). The rotation parameters were found to be much more sensitive than the translation parameters. The objective of this chapter is to present a formal analysis of the sensitivity of the computed pose to the difference in the included angles of the model and scene dihedral junctions. Based on the sensitivity analysis, a fuzzy-probabilistic model of the generalized Hough transform is proposed. The proposed model provides an analytical explanation of how the use of qualitative features provides greater robustness for

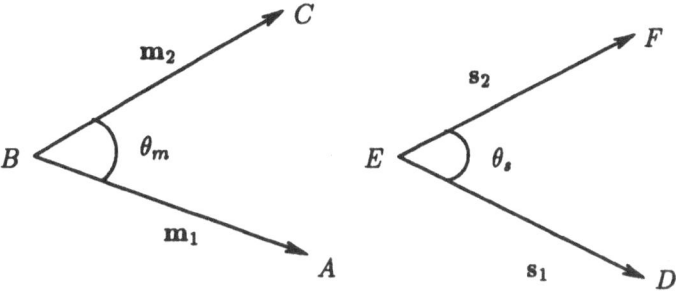

Figure 8.1: Matching model and scene dihedral junctions.

223

the generalized Hough transform. Although the analysis is done for the case of matching dihedral junctions or dihedral feature junctions, the approach taken in the sensitivity analysis is general and can be extended to matching based on other feature types.

8.1   Junction Matching and Pose Determination

This section [1] describes pose determination from dihedral feature junction matching. Figure 8.1 shows a model dihedral junction that is to be matched to a scene dihedral junction.   Let m_1 be the unit vector in the direction $\mathbf{BA}$ and let m_2 be the unit vector in the direction $\mathbf{BC}$. Similarly, let s_1 be the unit vector in the direction $\mathbf{ED}$ and s_2 the unit vector in the direction $\mathbf{EF}$. Let the homogeneous coordinates of B in the model coordinate system be $[x_0, y_0, z_0, 1]^T$, and let those of E in the scene coordinate system be $[u_0, v_0, w_0, 1]^T$. The goal is to find a transformation $\mathbf{T}$ such that

$$\mathbf{T}[x_0, y_0, z_0, 1]^T = [u_0, v_0, w_0, 1]^T \tag{8.1}$$

$\mathbf{T}$ is determined in a stepwise manner as follows:

1. Points B and E are translated to their respective origins. Let $TRANS(-B)$ and $TRANS(-E)$ denote the respective homogeneous transformation. This ensures that both junctions have their vertices translated to the origin.

2. The vectors m_1 and m_2 are rotated about $\mathbf{k}$ through an angle θ so as to be aligned with s_1 and s_2, respectively. $\mathbf{k}$ is determined by requiring that it be perpendicular to both $m_1 - s_1$ and $m_2 - s_2$ or, equivalently, that the projections of m_1 and s_1 along $\mathbf{k}$ be equal and the projections of m_2 and s_2 along $\mathbf{k}$ be equal, i.e.,

$$\mathbf{k} \cdot m_1 = \mathbf{k} \cdot s_1 \Rightarrow \mathbf{k} \cdot (m_1 - s_1) = 0 \tag{8.2}$$

$$\mathbf{k} \cdot m_2 = \mathbf{k} \cdot s_2 \Rightarrow \mathbf{k} \cdot (m_2 - s_2) = 0 \tag{8.3}$$

Thus

$$\mathbf{k} = \frac{(m_1 - s_1) \otimes (m_2 - s_2)}{|(m_1 - s_1) \otimes (m_2 - s_2)|} \tag{8.4}$$

where $\otimes$ denotes the vector cross product. From Figure 8.2,

$$\vec{OA} = (m_1 \cdot \mathbf{k}) \mathbf{k} = (s_1 \cdot \mathbf{k})\mathbf{k} \tag{8.5}$$

$$\vec{AC} = m_1 - (m_1 \cdot \mathbf{k})\mathbf{k} \tag{8.6}$$

---

[1] This section is the same as Section 7.5.3. It is repeated here to make this chapter self-contained.

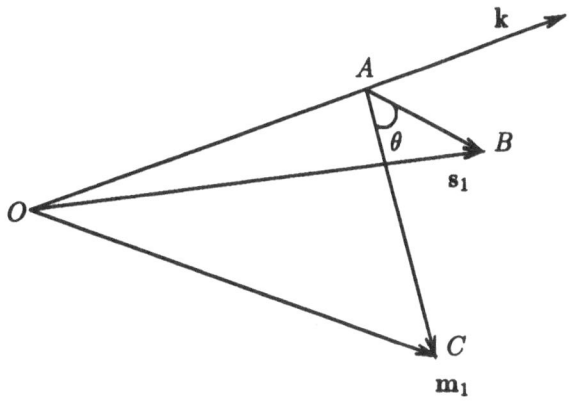

Figure 8.2: Derivation of $\mathbf{k}$ and θ

$$\vec{AC} \cdot \mathbf{k} = [\mathbf{m}_1 - (\mathbf{m}_1 \cdot \mathbf{k})\mathbf{k}] \cdot \mathbf{k} = 0 \qquad (8.7)$$

(since $\mathbf{k}$ is a unit vector as in Eq. (8.4)). Hence OAC is a right angle triangle with OC as the hypotenuse. Also,

$$|\vec{AC}| = |\vec{AB}| = \sqrt{1 - (\mathbf{m}_1 \cdot \mathbf{k})(\mathbf{s}_1 \cdot \mathbf{k})} \qquad (8.8)$$

(since $\mathbf{m}_1$ is a unit vector). Therefore, θ is determined by

$$\cos\theta = \frac{\vec{AB} \cdot \vec{AC}}{|\vec{AB}| \, |\vec{AC}|} = \frac{[\mathbf{m}_1 - (\mathbf{m}_1 \cdot \mathbf{k})\mathbf{k}] \cdot [\mathbf{s}_1 - (\mathbf{s}_1 \cdot \mathbf{k})\mathbf{k}]}{[1 - (\mathbf{m}_1 \cdot \mathbf{k})(\mathbf{s}_1 \cdot \mathbf{k})]} \qquad (8.9)$$

$$= 1 - \frac{[1 - (\mathbf{m}_1 \cdot \mathbf{s}_1)]}{[1 - (\mathbf{k} \cdot \mathbf{m}_1)(\mathbf{k} \cdot \mathbf{s}_1)]} \qquad (8.10)$$

3. The final transformation can thus be written as

$$ROT(\mathbf{k}, \theta)\, TRANS(-B)[x_0, y_0, z_0, 1]^T = TRANS(-E)[u_0, v_0, w_0, 1]^T \qquad (8.11)$$

From Eq. (8.1) and Eq. (8.11)

$$\mathbf{T} = TRANS^{-1}(-E)\, ROT(\mathbf{k}, \theta)\, TRANS(-B) \qquad (8.12)$$

The transformation $\mathbf{T}$ from the model coordinate system to the scene coordinate system could thus be written as:

$$\mathbf{T} = \begin{bmatrix} r_{11} & r_{12} & r_{13} & 0 \\ r_{21} & r_{22} & r_{23} & 0 \\ r_{31} & r_{32} & r_{33} & 0 \\ 0 & 0 & 0 & 1 \end{bmatrix} \begin{bmatrix} 1 & 0 & 0 & t_x \\ 0 & 1 & 0 & t_y \\ 0 & 0 & 1 & t_z \\ 0 & 0 & 0 & 1 \end{bmatrix} \qquad (8.13)$$

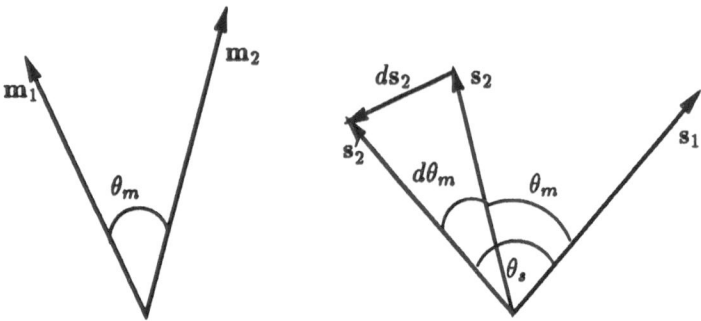

Figure 8.3: Error in matching dihedral junctions.

where

$$
\begin{aligned}
r_{11} &= k_x^2(1 - \cos\theta) + \cos\theta \\
r_{12} &= k_x k_y(1 - \cos\theta) - k_z \sin\theta \\
r_{13} &= k_x k_z(1 - \cos\theta) + k_y \sin\theta \\
r_{21} &= k_x k_y(1 - \cos\theta) + k_z \sin\theta \\
r_{22} &= k_y^2(1 - \cos\theta) + \cos\theta \\
r_{23} &= k_y k_z(1 - \cos\theta) - k_x \sin\theta \\
r_{31} &= k_x k_z(1 - \cos\theta) - k_y \sin\theta \\
r_{32} &= k_y k_z(1 - \cos\theta) + k_x \sin\theta \\
r_{33} &= k_z^2(1 - \cos\theta) + \cos\theta
\end{aligned}
\tag{8.14}
$$

and

$$
\begin{aligned}
t_x &= u_0 - r_{11}x_0 - r_{12}y_0 - r_{13}z_0 \\
t_y &= v_0 - r_{21}x_0 - r_{22}y_0 - r_{23}z_0 \\
t_z &= w_0 - r_{31}x_0 - r_{32}y_0 - r_{33}z_0
\end{aligned}
\tag{8.15}
$$

The axis of rotation $\mathbf{k}$ could be alternatively expressed by the pair (ξ, η) where

$$
k_x = \cos\xi\,\sin\eta,\; k_y = \sin\xi\,\sin\eta,\; k_z = \cos\eta \tag{8.16}
$$

where $-\pi < \eta < \pi$ and $0 < \xi < 2\pi$.
The transformation $\mathbf{T}$ is thus uniquely specified by the 6-tuple $(t_x, t_y, t_z, \xi, \eta, \theta)$.

8.2 Sensitivity Analysis

In this section we formally analyze sensitivity of the pose—rotation parameters (ξ, η, θ) and translation parameters (t_x, t_y, t_z)—to the difference in the included angles of the scene dihedral junction and the model dihedral junction.

As shown in Figure 8.3, two dihedral junctions are said to match if $\theta_s = \theta_m$. To consider the case when they are not exactly equal, let $\theta_s = \theta_m + d\theta_m$, then $s_2' = s_2 + ds_2$ where $|ds_2| = d\theta_m$. Three possible cases that arise in the matching of dihedral junctions need to be explored:

1. **Case 1:**

$$m_1 = s_1 \Rightarrow k = s_1 = m_1 \qquad (8.17)$$

thus

$$dk = 0 \qquad (8.18)$$

$$
\begin{aligned}
m_1 \cdot m_2 &= k \cdot m_2 = \cos \theta_m \\
s_1 \cdot s_2 &= k \cdot s_2 = \cos \theta_m
\end{aligned}
\qquad (8.19)
$$

since

$$\cos \theta = 1 - \frac{[1 - (m_2 \cdot s_2)]}{[1 - (k \cdot m_2)(k \cdot s_2)]} \qquad (8.20)$$

$$d(\cos \theta) = -d \left[\frac{1 - (m_2 \cdot s_2)}{1 - (k \cdot m_2)(k \cdot s_2)} \right]. \qquad (8.21)$$

Using the identities $d(a/b) = (bda - adb)/b^2$ and $d(a \cdot b) = da \cdot b + a \cdot db$

$$d(\cos \theta) = \frac{m_2 \cdot ds_2}{[1 - (m_2 \cdot k)(s_2 \cdot k)]} - \frac{(1 - m_2 \cdot s_2)(m_2 \cdot k)(ds_2 \cdot k)}{[1 - (m_2 \cdot k)(s_2 \cdot k)]^2} \qquad (8.22)$$

$$|d(\cos \theta)| = \left| \frac{m_2 \cdot ds_2}{\sin^2 \theta_m} + \frac{(1 - \cos \theta)d\theta_m}{\tan \theta_m} \right| \qquad (8.23)$$

Since $d(\cos \theta) = -\sin \theta d\theta$

$$|d\theta| = \left| \frac{m_2 \cdot ds_2}{\sin \theta \sin^2 \theta_m} + \frac{(1 - \cos \theta)d\theta_m}{\sin \theta \tan \theta_m} \right| \qquad (8.24)$$

Using Schwartz's inequality we get an upper bound on the value of the error as

$$|d(\cos \theta)| \leq \left| \frac{m_2 \cdot ds_2}{\sin^2 \theta_m} \right| + \left| \frac{(1 - \cos \theta)d\theta_m}{\tan \theta_m} \right| \qquad (8.25)$$

$$|d\theta| \leq \left| \frac{m_2 \cdot ds_2}{\sin \theta \sin^2 \theta_m} \right| + \left| \frac{(1 - \cos \theta)d\theta_m}{\sin \theta \tan \theta_m} \right| \qquad (8.26)$$

Since $|\mathbf{m}_2 \cdot d\mathbf{s}_2| = |\mathbf{m}_2|\,|d\mathbf{s}_2|\cos\beta \le d\theta_m$, where β is the angle between $d\mathbf{s}_2$ and $\mathbf{m}_2$.

$$|d(\cos\theta)| \le \frac{d\theta_m}{\sin^2\theta_m} + |(1-\cos\theta)|\frac{1}{|\tan\theta_m|}d\theta_m \qquad (8.27)$$

$$|d\theta| \le \frac{d\theta_m}{|\sin\theta|\,\sin^2\theta_m} + \left|\frac{(1-\cos\theta)}{\sin\theta}\right|\frac{1}{|\tan\theta_m|}d\theta_m \qquad (8.28)$$

The asymptotic behavior of $|d\theta|$ and $|d(\cos\theta)|$ with respect to θ_m and θ is as follows:

$$\text{As } \theta \to 0;\quad |d\theta| \to \infty,\, |d(\cos\theta)| \to \frac{d\theta_m}{\sin^2\theta_m}$$

$$\text{As } \theta \to \frac{\pi}{2};\quad |d\theta| \to d\theta_m\left(\frac{1}{\sin^2\theta_m} + \frac{1}{|\tan\theta_m|}\right),$$

$$|d(\cos\theta)| \to d\theta_m\left(\frac{1}{\sin^2\theta_m} + \frac{1}{|\tan\theta_m|}\right)$$

$$\text{As } \theta \to \pi;\quad |d\theta| \to \infty,\, |d(\cos\theta)| \to d\theta_m\left(\frac{1}{\sin^2\theta_m} + \frac{2}{|\tan\theta_m|}\right)$$

$$\text{As } \theta_m \to 0;\quad |d\theta| \to \infty,\, |d(\cos\theta_m)| \to \infty$$

$$\text{As } \theta_m \to \frac{\pi}{2};\quad |d\theta| \to \frac{d\theta_m}{|\sin\theta|},\, |d(\cos\theta)| \to d\theta_m$$

$$\text{As } \theta_m \to \pi;\quad |d\theta| \to \infty,\, |d(\cos\theta)| \to \infty$$

For a given value of $d\theta_m$ we have an error surface $\epsilon = \epsilon(\theta, \theta_m)$.

2. **Case 2:**

$$\mathbf{m}_2 = \mathbf{s}_2 \Rightarrow \mathbf{k} = \mathbf{s}_2 = \mathbf{m}_2 \qquad (8.29)$$

thus

$$d\mathbf{k} = d\mathbf{s}_2 \qquad (8.30)$$

$$\mathbf{m}_1 \cdot \mathbf{m}_2 = \mathbf{m}_1 \cdot \mathbf{k} = \cos\theta_m \text{ and } \mathbf{s}_1 \cdot \mathbf{s}_2 = \mathbf{s}_1 \cdot \mathbf{k} = \cos\theta_m \qquad (8.31)$$

since

$$\cos\theta = 1 - \frac{[1 - (\mathbf{m}_1 \cdot \mathbf{s}_1)]}{1 - (\mathbf{k} \cdot \mathbf{m}_1)(\mathbf{k} \cdot \mathbf{s}_1)} \qquad (8.32)$$

$$d(\cos\theta) = -d\left[\frac{1 - (\mathbf{m}_1 \cdot \mathbf{s}_1)}{1 - (\mathbf{k} \cdot \mathbf{m}_1)(\mathbf{k} \cdot \mathbf{s}_1)}\right] \qquad (8.33)$$

Using the results in Eqs. (8.30) and (8.31)

$$|d(\cos\theta)| = |(1-\cos\theta)|\frac{|\cos\theta_m|}{\sin^2\theta_m}|\,\mathbf{m}_1\cdot d\mathbf{s}_2 + \mathbf{s}_1\cdot d\mathbf{s}_2| \qquad (8.34)$$

$$|d\theta| = \left|\frac{(1-\cos\theta)}{\sin\theta}\right|\frac{|\cos\theta_m|}{\sin^2\theta_m}|\mathbf{m}_1\cdot d\mathbf{s}_2 + \mathbf{s}_1\cdot d\mathbf{s}_2| \qquad (8.35)$$

Using Schwartz's inequality

$$|d(\cos\theta)| \leq |(1-\cos\theta)|\frac{|\cos\theta_m|}{\sin^2\theta_m}(|\mathbf{m}_1\cdot d\mathbf{s}_2| + |\mathbf{s}_1\cdot d\mathbf{s}_2|) \qquad (8.36)$$

$$|d\theta| \leq \left|\frac{(1-\cos\theta)}{\sin\theta}\right|\frac{|\cos\theta_m|}{\sin^2\theta_m}(|\mathbf{m}_1\cdot d\mathbf{s}_2| + |\mathbf{s}_1\cdot d\mathbf{s}_2|) \qquad (8.37)$$

Since

$$|\mathbf{m}_1\cdot d\mathbf{s}_2| = |\mathbf{m}_1||d\mathbf{s}_2|\ \cos\gamma \leq d\theta_m$$

where γ is the angle between $\mathbf{m}_1$ and $d\mathbf{s}_2$ and

$$|\mathbf{s}_1\cdot d\mathbf{s}_2| = |\mathbf{s}_1||d\mathbf{s}_2|\ \cos\alpha \leq d\theta_m$$

where α is the angle between $\mathbf{s}_1$ and $d\mathbf{s}_2$

$$|d(\cos\theta)| \leq 2|(1-\cos\theta)|\frac{|\cos\theta_m|}{\sin^2\theta_m}d\theta_m \qquad (8.38)$$

$$|d\theta| \leq \left|\frac{2(1-\cos\theta)}{\sin\theta}\right|\frac{|\cos\theta_m|}{\sin^2\theta_m}d\theta_m \qquad (8.39)$$

The asymptotic behavior of $|d\theta|$ and $|d(\cos\theta)|$ with respect to θ_m and θ is as follows:

$$\text{As } \theta\to 0;\quad |d\theta|\to 0, |d(\cos\theta)|\to 0$$

$$\text{As } \theta\to\frac{\pi}{2};\quad |d\theta|\to\frac{2|\cos\theta_m|}{\sin^2\theta_m}d\theta_m,\ |d(\cos\theta)|\to\frac{2|\cos\theta_m|}{\sin^2\theta_m}d\theta_m$$

$$\text{As } \theta\to\pi;\quad |d\theta|\to\infty, |d(\cos\theta)|\to\frac{4|\cos\theta_m|}{\sin^2\theta_m}d\theta_m$$

$$\text{As } \theta_m\to 0;\quad |d\theta|\to\infty, |d(\cos\theta_m)|\to\infty$$

$$\text{As } \theta_m\to\frac{\pi}{2};\quad |d\theta|\to 0,\ |d(\cos\theta)|\to 0$$

$$\text{As } \theta_m\to\pi;\quad |d\theta|\to\infty, |d(\cos\theta)|\to\infty$$

3. **Case 3:**

$$\mathbf{m}_1 \neq \mathbf{k} \neq \mathbf{s}_1 \text{ and } \mathbf{m}_2 \neq \mathbf{k} \neq \mathbf{s}_2$$

From Eq. (8.4)

$$\mathbf{k} = \frac{(\mathbf{m}_1 - \mathbf{s}_1) \otimes (\mathbf{m}_2 - \mathbf{s}_2)}{|(\mathbf{m}_1 - \mathbf{s}_1) \otimes (\mathbf{m}_2 - \mathbf{s}_2)|} = \frac{(\mathbf{m}_1 - \mathbf{s}_1) \otimes (\mathbf{m}_2 - \mathbf{s}_2)}{M} \tag{8.40}$$

where

$$M \triangleq |(\mathbf{m}_1-\mathbf{s}_1)\otimes(\mathbf{m}_2-\mathbf{s}_2)| = [((\mathbf{m}_1-\mathbf{s}_1)\otimes(\mathbf{m}_2-\mathbf{s}_2))\cdot((\mathbf{m}_1-\mathbf{s}_1)\otimes(\mathbf{m}_2-\mathbf{s}_2))]^{\frac{1}{2}} \tag{8.41}$$

$$d\mathbf{k} = d\left[\frac{(\mathbf{m}_1 - \mathbf{s}_1) \otimes (\mathbf{m}_2 - \mathbf{s}_2)}{|\mathbf{m}_1 - \mathbf{s}_1) \otimes (\mathbf{m}_2 - \mathbf{s}_2)|}\right] \tag{8.42}$$

$$d\mathbf{k} = (M d[(\mathbf{m}_1-\mathbf{s}_1)\otimes(\mathbf{m}_2-\mathbf{s}_2)]-[(\mathbf{m}_1-\mathbf{s}_1)\otimes(\mathbf{m}_2-\mathbf{s}_2)]dM)/M^2 \tag{8.43}$$

On simplification this yields

$$d\mathbf{k} = \frac{1}{M}[d\mathbf{s}_2 \otimes (\mathbf{m}_1 - \mathbf{s}_1)] - \frac{1}{M}\mathbf{k}[\mathbf{k} \cdot [d\mathbf{s}_2 \otimes (\mathbf{m}_1 - \mathbf{s}_1)]] \tag{8.44}$$

Since $\mathbf{k} \cdot \mathbf{k} = 1$,

$$\mathbf{k} \cdot d\mathbf{k} = 0 \tag{8.45}$$

From Eqs. (8.44) and (8.45)

$$d\mathbf{k} = \frac{1}{M}[d\mathbf{s}_2 \otimes (\mathbf{m}_1 - \mathbf{s}_1)] \tag{8.46}$$

$$|d\mathbf{k}| = \frac{1}{M}|d\mathbf{s}_2| \, |\mathbf{m}_1 - \mathbf{s}_1| \sin \beta \tag{8.47}$$

$$|d\mathbf{k}| = \frac{1}{M}d\theta_m|\mathbf{m}_1 - \mathbf{s}_1| \sin \beta \tag{8.48}$$

where β is the angle between $d\mathbf{s}_2$ and $\mathbf{m}_1 - \mathbf{s}_1$

$$|d\mathbf{k}| \leq \frac{1}{M}d\theta_m \tag{8.49}$$

Thus $|d\mathbf{k}|$ is directly proportional to $d\theta_m$ and inversely proportional to M.

(a) **Case 3.1:**

$$\cos\theta = 1 - \frac{[1 - (\mathbf{m}_1 \cdot \mathbf{s}_1)]}{[1 - (\mathbf{k} \cdot \mathbf{m}_1)(\mathbf{k} \cdot \mathbf{s}_1)]} \tag{8.50}$$

Thus,

$$\begin{aligned}
d(\cos\theta) &= -d\left[\frac{1 - (\mathbf{m}_1 \cdot \mathbf{s}_1)}{1 - (\mathbf{k} \cdot \mathbf{m}_1)(\mathbf{k} \cdot \mathbf{s}_1)}\right] \tag{8.51} \\
&= \frac{(1 - \mathbf{m}_1 \cdot \mathbf{s}_1)d[1 - (\mathbf{m}_1 \cdot \mathbf{k})(\mathbf{s}_1 \cdot \mathbf{k})]}{[1 - (\mathbf{m}_1 \cdot \mathbf{k})(\mathbf{s}_1 \cdot \mathbf{k})]^2} \tag{8.52}
\end{aligned}$$

Since $\mathbf{m}_1 \cdot \mathbf{k} = \mathbf{s}_1 \cdot \mathbf{k}$

$$\begin{aligned}
d(\cos\theta) &= \frac{(1 - \mathbf{m}_1 \cdot \mathbf{s}_1)d[1 - (\mathbf{m}_1 \cdot \mathbf{k})^2]}{[1 - (\mathbf{m}_1 \cdot \mathbf{k})^2]^2} \tag{8.53} \\
&= \frac{-2(1 - \mathbf{m}_1 \cdot \mathbf{s}_1)(\mathbf{m}_1 \cdot \mathbf{k})(\mathbf{m}_1 \cdot d\mathbf{k})}{[1 - (\mathbf{m}_1 \cdot \mathbf{k})^2]^2} \tag{8.54}
\end{aligned}$$

From Eq. (8.46)

$$\mathbf{m}_1 \cdot d\mathbf{k} = \frac{\mathbf{m}_1}{M} \cdot [d\mathbf{s}_2 \otimes (\mathbf{m}_1 - \mathbf{s}_1)]. \tag{8.55}$$

Using the trigonometric identity $\mathbf{A} \cdot (\mathbf{B} \otimes \mathbf{C}) = (\mathbf{A} \otimes \mathbf{B}) \cdot \mathbf{C} = (\mathbf{C} \otimes \mathbf{A}) \cdot \mathbf{B}$ and with $\cos\lambda \overset{\Delta}{=} \mathbf{m}_1 \cdot \mathbf{k}$,

$$\mathbf{m}_1 \cdot d\mathbf{k} = \frac{d\mathbf{s}_2}{M} \cdot [(\mathbf{m}_1 - \mathbf{s}_1) \otimes \mathbf{m}_1] \tag{8.56}$$

$$\mathbf{m}_1 \cdot d\mathbf{k} = \frac{d\mathbf{s}_2}{M} \cdot [\mathbf{m}_1 \otimes \mathbf{s}_1] \tag{8.57}$$

$$|\mathbf{m}_1 \cdot d\mathbf{k}| = \frac{|d\mathbf{s}_2|\,|\mathbf{m}_1 \otimes \mathbf{s}_1|\cos\beta}{M} \leq \frac{d\theta_m}{M} \tag{8.58}$$

where β is the angle between $d\mathbf{s}_2$ and $\mathbf{m}_1 \otimes \mathbf{s}_1$

$$|d(\cos\theta)| = 2|(1 - \cos\theta)|\frac{|\cos\lambda|}{\sin^2\lambda}|\mathbf{m}_1 \cdot d\mathbf{k}| \tag{8.59}$$

From Eq. (8.57) and Eq. (8.58)

$$|d(\cos\theta)| \leq \frac{2|(1 - \cos\theta)|\,|\cos\lambda|}{M\,\sin^2\lambda}d\theta_m \tag{8.60}$$

Since $d(\cos\theta) = -\sin\theta\,d\theta$, Eq. (8.58) yields

$$|d\theta| = \left|\frac{2(1 - \cos\theta)}{\sin\theta}\right|\frac{|\cos\lambda|}{\sin^2\lambda}|\mathbf{m}_1 \cdot d\mathbf{k}| \tag{8.61}$$

From Eq. (8.57) and Eq. (8.61) we get

$$|d\theta| \le \left|\frac{2(1-\cos\theta)}{M\sin\theta}\right| \frac{|\cos\lambda|}{\sin^2\lambda} d\theta_m \tag{8.62}$$

The asymptotic behavior of $|d\theta|$ and $|d(\cos\theta)|$ is as follows:

As $\theta \rightarrow 0$; $|d\theta| \rightarrow 0$, $|d(\cos\theta)| \rightarrow 0$

As $\theta \rightarrow \dfrac{\pi}{2}$; $|d\theta| \rightarrow \dfrac{2}{M}\dfrac{|\cos\lambda|}{\sin^2\lambda}d\theta_m$, $|d(\cos\theta)| \rightarrow \dfrac{2}{M}\dfrac{|\cos\lambda|}{\sin^2\lambda}d\theta_m$

As $\theta \rightarrow \pi$; $|d\theta| \rightarrow \infty$, $|d(\cos\theta)| \rightarrow \dfrac{4}{M}\dfrac{|\cos\lambda|}{M\sin^2\lambda}d\theta_m$

As $\lambda \rightarrow 0$; $|d\theta| \rightarrow \infty$, $|d(\cos\theta)| \rightarrow \infty$

As $\lambda \rightarrow \dfrac{\pi}{2}$; $|d\theta| \rightarrow 0$, $|d(\cos\theta)| \rightarrow 0$

As $\lambda \rightarrow \pi$; $|d\theta| \rightarrow \infty$, $|d(\cos\theta)| \rightarrow \infty$

(b) **Case 3.2**

$$\cos\theta = 1 - \frac{[1-(m_2 \cdot s_2)]}{[1-(k \cdot m_2)(k \cdot s_2)]} \tag{8.63}$$

Thus,

$$d(\cos\theta) = -d\left[\frac{1-(m_2 \cdot s_2)}{1-(k \cdot m_2)(k \cdot s_2)}\right] \tag{8.64}$$

Since $m_2 \cdot k = s_2 \cdot k$,

$$
\begin{aligned}
d(\cos\theta) &= -d\left[\frac{1-(m_2 \cdot s_2)}{1-(k \cdot m_2)^2}\right] \\
&= \frac{m_2 \cdot ds_2}{[1-(m_2 \cdot k)^2]} - \frac{(1-m_2 \cdot s_2)2(m_2 \cdot k)(m_2 \cdot dk)}{[1-(m_2 \cdot k)^2]^2}
\end{aligned}
$$

$$\tag{8.65}$$

$$|d(\cos\theta)| = \left|\frac{m_2 \cdot ds_2}{[1-(m_2 \cdot k)^2]} + \frac{(1-m_2 \cdot s_2)(-2)(m_2 \cdot k)(m_2 \cdot dk)}{[1-(m_2 \cdot k)^2]^2}\right| \tag{8.66}$$

Using Schwartz's inequality

$$|d(\cos\theta)| \le \left|\frac{m_2 \cdot ds_2}{[1-(m_2 \cdot k)^2]}\right| + \left|\frac{(1-m_2 \cdot s_2)(-2)(m_2 \cdot k)(m_2 \cdot dk)}{[1-(m_2 \cdot k)^2]^2}\right| \tag{8.67}$$

From Eq. (8.46)

$$\mathbf{m}_2 \cdot d\mathbf{k} = \frac{\mathbf{m}_2}{M} \cdot [d\mathbf{s}_2 \otimes (\mathbf{m}_1 - \mathbf{s}_1)] \tag{8.68}$$

Using the trigonometric identity $\mathbf{A} \cdot (\mathbf{B} \otimes \mathbf{C}) = (\mathbf{A} \otimes \mathbf{B}) \cdot \mathbf{C} = (\mathbf{C} \otimes \mathbf{A}) \cdot \mathbf{B}$ and with $\cos \lambda \triangleq \mathbf{m}_2 \cdot \mathbf{k}$

$$
\begin{aligned}
\mathbf{m}_2 \cdot d\mathbf{k} &= \frac{d\mathbf{s}_2}{M} \cdot [(\mathbf{m}_1 - \mathbf{s}_1) \otimes \mathbf{m}_2] \tag{8.69} \\
&= \frac{|d\mathbf{s}_2|}{M} |[(\mathbf{m}_1 - \mathbf{s}_1) \otimes \mathbf{m}_2]| \cos \beta \tag{8.70} \\
&\leq \frac{|d\mathbf{s}_2|}{M} = \frac{d\theta_m}{M} \tag{8.71} \\
\mathbf{m}_2 \cdot d\mathbf{s}_2 &= |d\mathbf{s}_2| \, |\mathbf{m}_2| \cos \alpha \leq |d\mathbf{s}_2| = d\theta_m \tag{8.72}
\end{aligned}
$$

where α is the angle between $d\mathbf{s}_2$ and $\mathbf{m}_2$ Equations Eqs. (8.67)–(8.72) yield

$$|d(\cos\theta)| \leq \frac{d\theta_m}{\sin^2 \lambda} + \left| \frac{2(1 - \cos\theta)}{M} \right| \frac{|\cos\lambda|}{\sin^2\lambda} d\theta_m \tag{8.73}$$

Using the fact that $|d(\cos\theta)| = |\sin\theta d\theta|$

$$|d\theta| \leq \frac{d\theta_m}{|\sin\theta| \sin^2\lambda} + \left| \frac{2(1-\cos\theta)}{M\sin\theta} \right| \frac{|\cos\lambda|}{\sin^2\lambda} d\theta_m \tag{8.74}$$

The asymptotic behavior of $|d\theta|$ and $d(\cos\theta)|$ is as follows:

$$
\begin{aligned}
\text{As } \lambda &\to 0; \quad |d\theta| \to \infty, |d(\cos\theta)| \to \infty \\
\text{As } \lambda &\to \frac{\pi}{2}; \quad |d\theta| \to \frac{d\theta_m}{|\sin\theta|}, |d(\cos\theta)| \to d\theta_m \\
\text{As } \lambda &\to \pi; \quad |d\theta| \to \infty, |d(\cos\theta)| \to \infty \\
\text{As } \theta &\to 0; \quad |d\theta| \to \infty, |d(\cos\theta)| \to \frac{d\theta_m}{\sin^2\lambda} \\
\text{As } \theta &\to \frac{\pi}{2}; \quad |d\theta| \to \frac{d\theta_m}{\sin^2\lambda} + \frac{2}{M} \frac{|\cos\lambda|}{M\sin^2\lambda} d\theta_m \\
&\qquad |d(\cos\theta)| \to \frac{d\theta_m}{\sin^2\lambda} + \frac{2}{M} \frac{|\cos\lambda|}{\sin^2\lambda} d\theta_m \\
\text{As } \theta &\to \pi; \quad |d\theta| \to \infty, |d(\cos\theta)| \to \frac{d\theta_m}{\sin^2\lambda} + \frac{4}{M} \frac{|\cos\lambda|}{\sin^2\lambda} d\theta_m
\end{aligned}
$$

In all the above three cases it can be seen that the error in $|\theta|$ is higher than the error in $|\cos\theta|$. (Since $|d\theta| = |d\cos\theta|/|\sin\theta|$ and $0 < |\sin\theta| < 1$). Since the axis of rotation $k = [k_x, k_y, k_z] = [\cos\xi \sin\eta, \sin\xi \sin\eta, \cos\eta]$

$$dk_x = -\sin\xi \sin\eta \, d\xi + \cos\xi \cos\eta \, d\eta \tag{8.75}$$

$$dk_y = \cos\xi \sin\eta \, d\xi + \sin\xi \cos\eta \, d\eta \qquad (8.76)$$

$$dk_z = -\sin\eta \, d\eta \qquad (8.77)$$

From Eqs. (8.75)–(8.77)

$$d\xi = \frac{1}{\sin\eta}(\sin\xi \, dk_x - \cos\xi \, dk_y) \qquad (8.78)$$

$$d\eta = \frac{1}{\cos\eta}(\cos\xi \, dk_x + \sin\xi \, dk_y) \qquad (8.79)$$

Thus, as $\eta \to 0$ or π, $d\xi \to \infty$, and as $\eta \to \frac{\pi}{2}$, $d\eta \to \infty$. Assuming that the errors dk_y and dk_z are of the same order as $|d\mathbf{k}|$, the errors in ξ and η are greater than $|d\mathbf{k}|$. From Eq. (8.15), and assuming that there is no error in the model coordinates x_0, y_0 and z_0,

$$
\begin{aligned}
dt_x &= du_0 - dr_{11}x_0 - dr_{12}y_0 - dr_{13}z_0 \\
dt_y &= dv_0 - dr_{21}x_0 - dr_{22}y_0 - dr_{23}z_0 \\
dt_z &= dw_0 - dr_{31}x_0 - dr_{32}y_0 - dr_{33}z_0
\end{aligned}
\qquad (8.80)
$$

From Eq. (8.80) and the expressions for $r_{11}, r_{12}, r_{13}, r_{21}, r_{22}, r_{23}, r_{31}, r_{32}$, and r_{33} in (8.14)

$$(dt_x)_{\max} \approx \max[du_0, d(\cos\theta), d(\sin\theta), dk_x, dk_y, dk_z] \qquad (8.81)$$

$$(dt_y)_{\max} \approx \max[dv_0, d(\cos\theta), d(\sin\theta), dk_x, dk_y, dk_z] \qquad (8.82)$$

$$(dt_z)_{\max} \approx \max[dw_0, d(\cos\theta), d(\sin\theta), dk_x, dk_y, dk_z]. \qquad (8.83)$$

$d(\sin\theta)$ is of the same order of magnitude as $d(\cos\theta)$ if $d(\sin\theta) \le 10.0 \, d(\cos\theta)$ which implies that $5.71 \le \theta \le 174.29$, which is very often the case. From equations Eqs. (8.75)–(8.79) and Eqs. (8.81)–(8.83) it can be seen that the estimates of the rotation parameters ξ, η and θ are more sensitive than the translation parameters t_x, t_y, and t_z (assuming that the error in (u_0, v_0, w_0) is small, which seems reasonable).

The computed pose can be made more robust to the difference in the angle between the model and scene dihedral junctions or dihedral feature junctions simply by introducing redundancy into the parameter space. For example, the axis of rotation $\mathbf{k}$ can be represented by the triple (k_x, k_y, k_z), rather than by the double (ξ, η), since parameters k_x, k_y, and k_z are more robust than the parameters ξ and η. Similarly, the angle of rotation θ can be replaced by the double $(\cos\theta, \sin\theta)$, which uniquely specifies the angle θ in the range $-\pi \le \theta \le \pi$. Since the values of $\sin\theta$ and $\cos\theta$ are less sensitive than the value of θ, replacing θ by the double $(\cos\theta, \sin\theta)$ would ensure greater robustness in the computed pose.

8.3 Qualitative Features

In this section we use the results from the sensitivity analysis to study analytically the effect of qualitative features on the performance of the generalized Hough transform. In doing so, a fuzzy-probabilistic model of the generalized Hough transform is proposed that provides the analytical explanation for the superior performance of the generalized Hough transform when used in conjunction with qualitative features than without. As was mentioned in earlier chapters, both the interpretation tree search and the generalized Hough transform work well in single-object scenes. Multiple-object scenes, however, lead to a combinatorial explosion in the size of the search space of possible scene interpretations and generation of several spurious scene hypotheses. This leads to increased computational complexity for the recognition and localization process, as well as to errors in object identification and localization. The combinatorial complexity of object recognition and localization in single- and multiple-object scenes using the interpretation tree search technique has been investigated by Grimson [1986, 1990]. A set of constraints for sparse sensory data, which are applicable to a wide variety of sensors, are derived and their characteristics examined. Formal bounds on the combinatorial complexity of the interpretation tree search for single- and multiple-object scenes are also derived. It has been shown that a single-object scene results in quadratic complexity, in the number of model and sensory features, for the interpretation tree search process, whereas in the case of multiple-object scenes with partial occlusion the complexity is exponential. The performance of the generalized Hough transform for object recognition in the presence of occlusion and clutter has been studied by Grimson and Huttenlocher [1990a]. Bounds on the set of transformations consistent with each pairing of scene and model features in the presence of noise and occlusion in the image have been presented. The bounds on the likelihood of false peaks in the parameter space as a function of noise, occlusion, and tessellation effects have also been computed. It has been shown how the probability of false peaks can become very high for recognition in complex scenes.

In this chapter the analysis of the generalized Hough transform by Grimson and Huttenlocher is extended in two ways:

1. We show that the use of qualitative features, i.e., scene features with qualitative attributes assigned to them, greatly reduce the combinatorial complexity of a scene interpretation problem by reducing the space of possible scene interpretations.

2. We show that these qualitative attributes enable us to come up with a *weighted* generalized Hough transform where the weights can be interpreted as membership function values for the fuzzy sets defined by these qualitative attributes. The weighted generalized Hough transform is shown to perform better than the straightforward generalized Hough transform for object recognition in multiple-object scenes with partial occlusion.

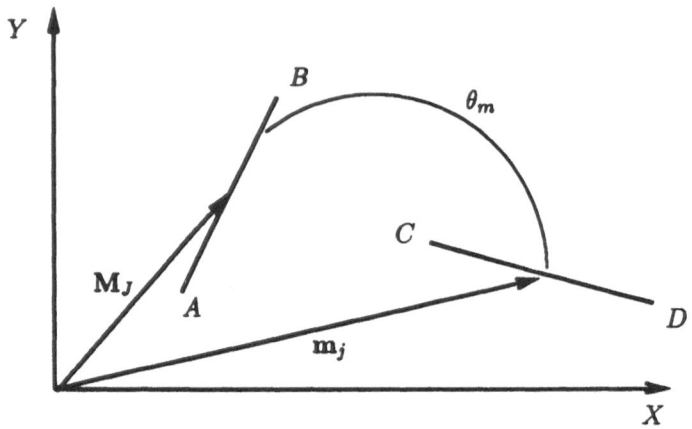

Figure 8.4: Matching a model linear feature to a scene linear feature.

8.4   The Generalized Hough Transform

In this section we present a brief description of the Generalized Hough Transform and a synopsis of the analysis of its performance in the presence of sensor error and occlusion as studied by Grimson and Huttenlocher [1990]. The interested reader could refer to their paper for the details regarding the derivations of the results.

The generalized Hough transform finds possible solutions to the object pose problem by searching for large clusters of evidence in a discrete version of a parameter space. Let $\mathcal{M}$ be the model coordinate frame of reference, $\mathcal{S}$ the scene coordinate frame of reference, $\mathcal{P}$ the n-dimensional parameter space of the geometric transformation that places the model feature in registration with the scene feature to which it is matched, and $\mathcal{H}$ the n-dimensional discrete Hough space (Hough accumulator) resulting from the quantization of each dimension of the n-dimensional parameter space $\mathcal{P}$. $\mathcal{H}$ could be considered as an n-dimensional array of cells or buckets. In order to simplify the analysis, model features and scene features are assumed to be linear segments as in Grimson and Huttenlocher [1990a].

8.4.1   The Generalized Hough Transform in the Absence of Occlusion and Sensor Error

A model feature AB being matched to a scene feature CD is shown Figure 8.4. Let $\mathbf{M}_J$ be the vector to the midpoint of the model edge AB measured in $\mathcal{M}$, $\hat{\mathbf{T}}_J$ the unit tangent to the model edge AB measured in $\mathcal{M}$, L_J the length of the model edge AB, $\mathbf{m}_j$ the vector to the midpoint of the scene edge CD measured in $\mathcal{S}$, $\hat{\mathbf{t}}_j$ the unit tangent to the scene edge CD measured in $\mathcal{S}$, and the l_j length of the scene edge CD. The transformation from $\mathcal{M}$ to $\mathcal{S}$ is represented by

$$\mathbf{v}_s = R_{\theta_m} \mathbf{V}_M + \mathbf{V}_0 \tag{8.84}$$

where $\mathbf{V}_M$ is a vector in $\mathcal{M}$, R_{θ_m} is the rotation matrix corresponding to angle θ_m, $\mathbf{V}_0$ is a translation offset, and $\mathbf{v}_s$ is the resultant vector in $\mathcal{S}$. If $L_J = l_j$, then in the absence of any uncertainty due to sensor error or occlusion

$$\theta_m = \theta_{jJ} = \cos^{-1}(\hat{\mathbf{T}}_J \cdot \hat{\mathbf{t}}_j) \tag{8.85}$$
$$\mathbf{V}_0 = (V_{0x}, V_{0y}) = \mathbf{m}_j - \mathbf{M}_j \tag{8.86}$$

The transform is thus uniquely determined by the 3-tuple $(V_{0x}, V_{0y}, \theta_m)$ and represents a point p in $\mathcal{P}$. In the Hough accumulator $\mathcal{H}$ the point p is represented by incrementing the appropriate bucket in $\mathcal{H}$ by 1. The point p is thus deemed to have cast its vote in the appropriate Hough bucket. A globally consistent pose for a rigid object model can therefore be determined by finding a cluster in $\mathcal{P}$. In $\mathcal{H}$, which is the discretized version of $\mathcal{P}$, it amounts to finding a bucket with the maximum number of votes. In the presence of occlusion and sensor error, the generalized Hough transform suffers from the following problems:

1. The match of a scene feature with a model feature specifies a range of transformations rather than a single transformation. This is referred to as *smearing* of the transform.

2. More than one Hough bucket will be specified due to the smearing of the transform. This is referred to as *fragmentation* of the transform in $\mathcal{P}$ into more than one bucket in $\mathcal{H}$.

3. Due to fragmentation of the computed transform values, spurious maxima (peaks) resulting from random accumulation of votes in $\mathcal{H}$ can be formed.

8.4.2   The Generalized Hough Transform in Presence of Occlusion and Sensor Error

The model edge in Figure 8.4 is specified by the set of points

$$\left\{ \mathbf{M}_J + \alpha \hat{\mathbf{T}}_J \mid \alpha \in \left[\frac{-L_J}{2}, \frac{+L_J}{2} \right] \right\}$$

If the scene edge is occluded, then $l_j \leq L_J$. Occlusion causes the translational component of the transform to be underdetermined. The set of consistent translations is given by

$$\left\{ \mathbf{m}_j - R_{\theta_m} \mathbf{M}_J + \alpha R_{\theta_m} \hat{\mathbf{T}}_J \mid \alpha \in \left[-\frac{L_J - l_j}{2}, \frac{L_J - l_j}{2} \right] \right\}$$

which is a line in parameter space. If the endpoints of the scene edge are known to within a circular region of radius ϵ_p, then the angular uncertainty ϵ_a in the

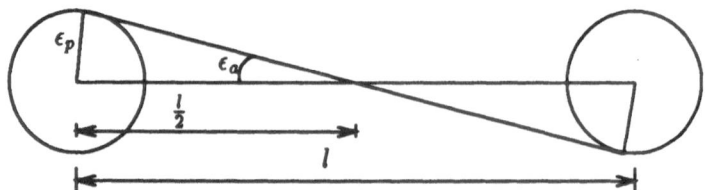

Figure 8.5: The angular uncertainty corresponding to the positional uncertainty of the end points.

orientation of the scene edge is given by

$$\epsilon_a = \tan^{-1}\left(\frac{2\epsilon_p}{\sqrt{l^2 - 4\epsilon_p^2}}\right)$$

as shown in Figure 8.5. The line of consistent translations must therefore be expanded to include any points in the parameter space within ϵ_p of that line. This expansion of a line into a region must be repeated for each value of θ in the range $[\theta_m - \epsilon_a, \theta_m + \epsilon_a]$. This results in a skewed volume in Hough or transform space.

The set of feasible transformations is denoted by the volume

$$V(j, J) = \bigcup_{\theta \in [\theta_m - \epsilon_a, \theta_m + \epsilon_a]} S(\theta, j, J) \tag{8.87}$$

where an individual set of translations $S(\theta, j, J)$ for a given value of θ is denoted by

$$S(\theta, j, J) = \{(\theta, \mathbf{V}_0) \mid \exists \alpha, |\alpha| \leq \frac{L_J - l_j}{2}, |m_j - R_\theta M_J + \alpha \hat{\mathbf{T}}_J - \mathbf{V}_0| \leq \epsilon_p\} \tag{8.88}$$

The volume of the region defined in Eq. (8.87) is given by

$$V(j, J) = 2\epsilon_a[2\epsilon_p(L_J - l_j) + \pi \epsilon_p^2] \tag{8.89}$$

If the dimensions of the Hough buckets are h_θ along the rotational axis and h_t along each of the translational axes, and if $B(\theta, j, J)$ denotes the set of buckets that intersects the slice $S(\theta, j, J)$ at $\theta = \theta_c$, then the entire set of buckets which the volume $V(j, J)$ intersects is given by

$$\bigcup_{\theta \in [\theta_c, \theta_c + h_\theta]} B(\theta, j, J)$$

If the Hough array is decomposed into two arrays—one for the rotation and the other for translation—then the total numbers of buckets in $\mathcal{H}$ that intersect the volume $V(j, J)$ is given by

$$b \geq \left\lceil \frac{2\epsilon_a}{h_\theta} \right\rceil \left\lceil A^*(h_\theta, \epsilon_p^*, M^*, L^*, \beta) \right\rceil \tag{8.90}$$

where

$$\beta = \frac{l_j}{L_J}$$

$$\epsilon_p^* = \frac{\epsilon_p}{h_t}$$

$$l^* = \frac{L}{h_t}$$

$$M^* = \frac{M}{h_t} = \frac{|M|}{h_t}$$

$$\epsilon_a = \tan^{-1}\left(\frac{2\epsilon_p^*}{\sqrt{(l^*)^2 - 4(\epsilon_p^*)^2}} \right)$$

and $A^*(h_\theta, \epsilon_p^*, M^*, L^*, \beta)$ is the area projected on the xy plane by each slice of volume $V(j, J)$ as θ is varied from $\theta_i - h_\theta$ to $\theta_i + h_\theta$. If the accumulator is not decomposed, then

$$b \geq \left\lceil \frac{V(j, J)}{h_\theta h_t^2} \right\rceil \tag{8.91}$$

which is a tighter bound than the one computed in Eq. (8.90). The parameter b is termed the *redundancy* factor of the generalized Hough transform. The redundancy factor is a *quantitative* measure of the fragmentation of the computed transform values into the buckets in $\mathcal{H}$. In order for the generalized Hough transform to be able to localize an object with accuracy, it is necessary to keep the redundancy factor as low as possible.

8.4.3 Probability of Spurious Peaks in the Generalized Hough Transform

The redundancy of the generalized Hough transform is a measure of the fragmentation of the computed transforms in $\mathcal{P}$ among the buckets in $\mathcal{H}$. The other factor that determines the performance of the generalized Hough transform is the likelihood of finding large clusters at random in $\mathcal{P}$. In the Hough accumulator $\mathcal{H}$, this is tantamount to estimating the probability that a Hough bucket will have peaks of size l or more at random. The volumes in transformation space that result from the matching of scene features with model features can be looked upon as independent random events. The tessellation of each volume into the corresponding Hough buckets, however, is not random; but as the number of volumes gets large, compared to the number of buckets defined by each volume, the overall distribution of events into buckets could be considered random. This motivates the use of a *probabilistic occupancy model* for the generalized Hough transform.

Given a distribution of r events into n buckets, let $r_1, r_2, \ldots r_n$ $(r_i \geq 0)$ be the number of events in the corresponding buckets $1, 2, \ldots n$. Obviously, $\sum_{i=1}^{n} r_i = r$. If the events are randomly distributed such that each of the n^r placements are equiprobable with probability n^{-r}, then the probability of a given arrangement with occupancy numbers $r_1, r_2, \ldots r_n$ is given by

$$P(r_1, r_2, \ldots r_n) = \frac{r!}{r_1! r_2! \ldots r_n!} n^{-r} \qquad (8.92)$$

which is the classical Maxwell-Boltzmann statistics [Papoulis 1984]. The probability $P(k)$ that a given cell contains exactly k events is given by the binomial distribution

$$P(k) = \binom{r}{k} \frac{1}{n^k} \left(1 - \frac{1}{n}\right)^{r-k} \qquad (8.93)$$

The probability that a given cell will contain l or more events at random is given by

$$P(k \geq l) = 1 - \sum_{k=0}^{l-1} P(k) \qquad (8.94)$$

The expected number of buckets in a Hough accumulator that will contain peaks of at least size l is given by

$$E(k \geq l) \approx n \cdot P(k \geq l) \qquad (8.95)$$

Computing the value of $P(k)$ for large values of r and k using the binomial distribution can be fairly cumbersome. For large values of n (of the order of 10^4 or greater, which is usually the case), the Poisson approximation to the binomial distribution could be used:

$$P(k) \approx \frac{\lambda^k}{k!} e^{-\lambda} \qquad (8.96)$$

where $\lambda = r/n$, which is the ratio of the number of events (total votes entered in $\mathcal{H}$) to the total number of buckets in $\mathcal{H}$.

If m is the number of model features and s the number of scene features, then the total number of possible matches of scene features to model features, M, is given by $s!/(s-m)!$ if $m < s$, and by $m!/(m-s)!$ if $s < m$. If b is the redundancy of the generalized Hough transform, then $r = Mb$. Thus $\lambda = Mb/n$. For a given value of sensor error ϵ_p and for a given quantization and size of $\mathcal{H}$ (determined by the parameters h_θ, h_t, and n), the parameters b and n are fixed. For different values of m and s we can determine the expected number of buckets in $\mathcal{H}$ that have a value l or larger using Eq. (8.95). Table 8.1 shows the values for the expected number of buckets in $\mathcal{H}$ that have a value greater than $f \cdot m$ where $0 \leq f \leq 1$.

The following problems have been observed in the case of the generalized Hough transform:

Table 8.1: The expected number of Hough buckets that have a value greater than $f \cdot m$ where $0 \leq f \leq 1$, $m = 4$, $s = 8$, $b = 3$ and $n = 10000$.

$l = 0.25m$	$l = 0.5m$	$l = 0.75m$	$l = 1.0m$
3958	914	146	18

1. In the presence of noise and occlusion, the range of transformations consistent with the matching of a scene feature with a model feature can be quite large. As a result, the number of Hough buckets specified by the range of transformations can be quite high. The fraction of the total number of buckets specified by a single scene-model pairing increases with increasing sensor uncertainty, with a reduction in the total number of Hough buckets (i.e., increasing coarseness of $\mathcal{H}$ or, alternatively, decreasing the resolution of $\mathcal{H}$) and with increasing occlusion. The redundancy factor increases when the parameter space is projected onto a subspace.

2. The probabilistic occupancy model shows that the number of buckets having significant spurious peaks due to random accumulation can be quite high. Numerical simulations (such as those shown in Table 8.1) show that the number of scene-model pairings likely to fall into the same bucket at random is often greater than the number of pairings that correspond to a correct solution. This problem is aggravated as the redundancy factor increases. These spurious peaks can cause the vision system to explore large portions of the Hough space in order to verify a correct interpretation.

8.5 The Use of Qualitative Features in the Generalized Hough Transform

The vision system may have to explore large portions of the Hough space in order to verify a correct interpretation due to the redundancy of the generalized Hough transform and the presence of spurious peaks. In order to minimize the effect of the redundancy of the generalized Hough transform and the number of spurious peaks in $\mathcal{H}$, the use of *qualitative* features has been proposed in Part II. Qualitative features are scene features with qualitative attributes assigned to them. The use of qualitative features improves the generalized Hough transform in two ways:

1. The use of qualitative features greatly reduces the combinatorial complexity by drastically pruning the search space of possible scene interpretations. It can be shown that the reduction of the search space greatly reduces the

number of buckets in $\mathcal{H}$ having significant peaks due to random accumulation of votes.

2. Qualitative attributes can be used to come up with a *weighted* generalized Hough transform, where the weights can be interpreted as membership function values for the fuzzy sets defined by these qualitative attributes.

8.5.1 Reduction in the Search Space of Scene Interpretations due to Qualitative Features

Consider an object model consisting of m model features and a scene with s scene features. If $m < s$, then there are s^m possible matches of scene features to model features. If the *unique interpretation constraint* is imposed (i.e., a single scene feature matches a single model feature, and vice versa) then the number of scene interpretations (i.e., possible matches) can be reduced to $s!/(s-m)!$. Furthermore, if each of the s scene features and m model features is classified as belonging to one of k classes based on the qualitative attributes, then the number of scene interpretations is further reduced to

$$\left[\frac{\left(\frac{s}{k}\right)!}{\left(\frac{s-m}{k}\right)!} \right]^k$$

Applying the Poisson approximation to this expression, the probability that a given bucket contains i votes at random is

$$P(i) = \frac{\lambda^i}{i!} e^{-\lambda}$$

where $\lambda = Mb/n$ and M is the number of matches of scene features to model features.

For a given value of i, $P(i)$ is a monotonically decreasing function of λ. For fixed values of b, n, and i, $P(i)$ is a monotonically decreasing function of M. Therefore the expected number of buckets with random votes l or larger is given by

$$E(k \geq l) = n \cdot \left(1 - \sum_{l=0}^{l-1} P(i) \right).$$

which is a monotonically increasing function of M. Since M decreases exponentially with increasing k (number of feature classes), the effect of classifying features based on qualitative attributes is to lower the expected number of Hough buckets with random votes l or larger. Table 8.2 shows the expected number of Hough buckets with random votes l or larger for the cases where $k = 2$ and $k = 4$. Upon comparison with the corresponding quantities in Table 8.1, we can see the improvement in the performance of the generalized Hough transform due to the classification of features based on the qualitative attributes. However, there is one important point to be noted. The amount of preprocessing or segmentation of the image needed in order to come up with the qualitative features should be

Table 8.2: The expected number of Hough buckets that have a value greater than $f \cdot m$ where $0 \leq f \leq 1$, $m = 4$, $s = 8$, $b = 3$ and $n = 10000$.

k	$l = 0.25m$	$l = 0.5m$	$l = 0.75m$	$l = 1.0m$
2	739	28	0	0
4	47	0	0	0

minimal. Otherwise, the benefit from constraining the search space would be offset by the computational cost of preprocessing or segmentation of the image.

8.5.2 Reducing the Effect of Smearing in Parameter Space using Qualitative Features

The straightforward generalized Hough transform computes a range of transform values for a given match of a scene feature to a model feature. The range of transform values is represented by a volume in $\mathcal{H}$, and all the buckets in $\mathcal{H}$ that intersect this volume are incremented. For a given quantization of $\mathcal{H}$ and for given bounds on the sensor accuracy, the primary reason for the redundancy of the generalized Hough transform is the uncertainty in the computed parameters due to occlusion. As will be shown here, computed transform values can be assigned weights based on a *qualitative* estimate of occlusion of scene features. Since the uncertainty in the computed transform is directly proportional to the degree of occlusion of the scene features, these weights can, in effect, be used to selectively emphasize or de-emphasize certain matches of scene features to model features based on the uncertainty in the computed transform. Consider the scene features classified into two categories based on the qualitative attribute of *occlusion*. For *occluded* scene features we can define $1 - \beta$ (where $\beta = l_j/L_I$) to be a measure of the *degree* of occlusion where l_j is the length of scene feature s_j and L_I is the length of model feature M_I with which s_j is matched. The match of a scene feature to a model feature is no longer considered a simple binary relation, but a fuzzy relation [Dubois and Prade 1980] [Kaufmann 1975] [Zadeh 1965] over $\mathcal{M} \times \mathcal{S}$. The membership function of the match (M_I, s_j) is denoted by μ_{Ij}, which can be defined as follows:

1. If s_j is *not occluded*, then for a valid match $L_I - \epsilon_p \leq l_j \leq L_I + \epsilon_p$. For a valid match the membership function is defined as

$$\mu_{Ij} = \begin{cases} \left[1 - \frac{|L_I - l_j|}{L_I}\right]^\alpha = (1 - |1 - \beta|)^\alpha & \text{if } L_I - \epsilon_p \leq l_j \leq L_I + \epsilon_p \\ 0 & \text{otherwise} \end{cases}$$

(8.97)

where $\alpha \geq 1$.

2. If s_j is *occluded*, then for a valid match $l_j \leq L_I$

$$\mu_{Ij} = \begin{cases} (1 - |1 - \beta|)^\alpha = \beta^\alpha & \text{if } l_j \leq L_I \\ 0 & \text{otherwise} \end{cases} \qquad (8.98)$$

where $\alpha \geq 1$.

The straightforward generalized Hough transform increments a bucket in $\mathcal{H}$ by 1 if the volume in parameter space defined by the match (M_I, s_j) intersects the bucket. In the weighted generalized Hough transform the corresponding bucket in $\mathcal{H}$ is incremented by μ_{Ij}. By doing this we achieve the following:

1. Since matches based on unoccluded features are assigned, on an average, a higher weight than those based on occluded features, the weighted generalized Hough transform tends to favor matches with unoccluded features over those with occluded features. Since unoccluded features typically correspond to topmost objects in a pile, the weighted generalized Hough transform can be seen to favor the recognition of such objects, which is as it should be, since these objects are more easily recognizable.

2. The greater the uncertainty in the computed transform value due to occlusion, the smaller the weight assigned to that particular transform value. Thus, the greater the redundancy of a given transform value, the smaller its contribution to the corresponding buckets, and vice versa. This emphasizes the transform values that are computed to a greater degree of accuracy and sharpens the corresponding peaks in the Hough accumulator.

8.5.3   The Probability of Random Peaks in the Weighted Generalized Hough Transform

The occupancy model for the straightforward generalized Hough transform is modified, as shown below, for the weighted generalized Hough transform. Given a distribution of r events into n buckets, let $r_1, r_2 \ldots r_n$ $(r_i \geq 0)$ be the number of events in the corresponding buckets $1, 2, \ldots n$. Since $\sum_{i=1}^{n} r_i = r$ and each of the n^r placements are equiprobable with probability n^{-r}, the probability of a given arrangement with occupancy numbers $r_1, r_2, \ldots r_n$ is given by the Maxwell-Boltzmann statistics, as shown in Eq. (8.92). The probability $P(k)$ that a given cell contains exactly k events is given by the binomial distribution, as shown in Eq. (8.93). For large enough values of n the binomial distribution can be approximated by the Poisson distribution, as shown in Eq. (8.96). In the case of the weighted generalized Hough transform each event is no longer a *discrete event*, but a *fuzzy event* [Zaheh 1968] [Capocelli and DeLuca 1973] [Kandel 1978] [Klir and Folger 1988] with a membership function defined over the real interval [0,1], as shown in Eqs. (8.97) and (8.98). The membership functions described in Eqs. (8.97) and (8.98) are non-decreasing functions and have a maximum value of unity at $\beta = 1$. Since the membership functions are convex and normal, the fuzzy events can be treated as *fuzzy numbers* [Kaufmann and Gupta 1985]. The accumulation of fuzzy events in a bucket in $\mathcal{H}$ corresponds to the summation of the corresponding fuzzy numbers. The probability of k fuzzy events falling into a particular Hough bucket at random is given by

$$P(k) = \int_{-\infty}^{+\infty} \mu_k(x)p_k(x)dx \qquad (8.99)$$

where $\mu_k(x)$ is the membership function of the fuzzy number resulting from the addition of k fuzzy numbers, and $p_k(x)$ is the probability distribution of the accumulated weight in a bucket, given that there are k matches that fall in the bucket [Zadeh 1968]. The problem, therefore, is to determine (approximately, if not exactly) $\mu_k(x)$ and $p_k(x)$.

8.5.4 Determination of $\mu_k(x)$, $p_k(x)$ and $P(k)$

As shown in Eq. (8.98), the fuzzy match relation for matching occluded features has a membership function of the form $\mu_{Ij}(x) = x^\alpha$ where $0 \leq x \leq 1$ and $\alpha \geq 1$. In fact, any normal, non-decreasing, convex function of x would be acceptable. Consider a membership function of the form $\mu_{ij} = x^\alpha$ where $0 \leq x \leq 1$ and α is an integer greater than or equal to 1.

Given n fuzzy numbers $x_1, x_2, \ldots, x_n$ with identical membership functions, $\mu(x) = x^\alpha$, the sum $s_n = \sum_{i=1}^{n} x_i$ can be shown to be a fuzzy number with membership function of the form $\mu_{s_n}(x) = (x/n)^\alpha$, where $0 \leq x \leq n$. It can be shown that $\mu_{s_n}(x)$ is also a normal, non-decreasing, convex function of x [Kaufmann and Gupta 1985]. To determine $p_k(x)$, which is the probability distribution of the accumulated weight in a bucket, given that there are k matches that fall in the bucket, the following approach is taken: If r events are placed at random in n buckets, then the probability of a specific placement is given by the Maxwell-Boltzmann statistics

$$P[N_1 = r_1, N_2 = r_2, \ldots N_n = r_n] = \frac{r!}{r_1!r_2!\cdots r_r}n^{-r}$$

where $\sum_{i=1}^{n} r_i = r$ and N_j denotes the number of events in bucket j. Let us suppose that the weight w of each event is a random variable with a probability density $p_w(x)$. Let $w_1, w_2, \ldots w_k$ be the weights of events $1, 2, \ldots k$, respectively. Then the total weight of k particles is $S_k = \sum_{i=1}^{k} w_i$, $k \geq 1$, where each w_i is an independent and identically distributed random variable. To determine the probability distribution for S_{N_j} for a given value of $N_j = k$, the following relation is used:

$$P[S_{N_j} \leq x | N_j = k] = P[S_k \leq x \mid N_j = k]\, P[N_j = k]$$

$$= P\left[\sum_{i=1}^{k} w_i \leq x \mid N_j = k\right] P[N_j = k] \qquad (8.100)$$

where $P[N_j = k]$, which is a binomial distribution, as shown in equation Eq. (8.93). For large values of n, $P[N_j = k]$ can be approximated using a Poisson distribution shown in Eq. (8.96).

The probability distribution function corresponding to the cumulative distribution function $P[\sum_{i=1}^{k} w_i \leq x | N_j = k]$, which is denoted as p_{S_k}, is given by the relation

$$p_{S_k}(x) = p_{w_1}(w) \otimes p_{w_2}(x) \cdots \otimes p_{w_k}(x) \tag{8.101}$$

where $\otimes$ denotes the convolution operation. Since each w_i is independent and identically distributed, Eq. (8.101) can be written as

$$p_{S_k}(x) = \bigotimes_{i=1}^{k} p_w(x) \tag{8.102}$$

Therefore, the probability distribution function corresponding to the cumulative distribution function $P[S_{N_j} \leq x | N_j = k]$ denoted by $p_{S_{N_j}}(x | N_j = k)$ is given by the equation

$$
\begin{aligned}
p_{S_{N_j}}(x | N_j = k) &= \left[\bigotimes_{i=1}^{k} p_w(x) \right] P[N_j = k] \\
&= p_{S_k}(x) P[N_j = k] \tag{8.103}
\end{aligned}
$$

Since $p_{S_k}(x) = \bigotimes_{i=1}^{k} p_w(x)$, $p_{S_k}(x)$ can be determined for any value of k if $p_w(x)$ is known. Using the central limit theorem, for large values of k

$$\lim_{k \to \infty} \bigotimes_{i=1}^{k} p_w(x) \longrightarrow \mathcal{N}(k\mu, k\sigma^2)$$

where $\mu = E[w]$, $\sigma^2 = var(w)$, and $\mathcal{N}(k\mu, k\sigma^2)$ is a Gaussian random variable with mean $k\mu$ and variance $k\sigma^2$ [Papoulis 1984].

If we assume that $p_w(x)$ is uniformly distributed in the interval [0,1], then $\mu = 1/2$ and $\sigma^2 = 1/12$. Hence

$$p_{S_1}(x) = \begin{cases} 1 & 0 \leq x \leq 1 \\ 0 & \text{elsewhere} \end{cases} \tag{8.104}$$

and

$$p_{S_2}(x) = \begin{cases} x & 0 \leq x \leq 1 \\ 2 - x & 1 \leq x \leq 2 \\ 0 & \text{elsewhere} \end{cases} \tag{8.105}$$

and we can approximate

$$p_{S_k}(x) \approx \mathcal{N}(\frac{k}{2}, \frac{k}{12}), \quad k \geq 3 \tag{8.106}$$

Since $P(N_j = k)$ and $p_{S_k}(x)$ are known for all $k \geq 1$, $p_{S_{N_j}}(x | N_j = k) = p_k(x)$ is known for all $k \geq 1$ using Eq. (8.103). Therefore, the probability $P(k)$ of k

fuzzy events falling into the same Hough bucket at random can be computed for all values of $k \geq 1$ using Eq. (8.99).

$$P(k) = \int_{-\infty}^{+\infty} \mu_k(x)p_k(x)dx$$

$$P(k,\alpha) = \int_{-\infty}^{+\infty} \left(\frac{x}{k}\right)^\alpha ps_k(x)P[N_j = k]dx \qquad (8.107)$$

Using the Poisson approximation for $P[N_j = k]$

$$P(k,\alpha) = \frac{\lambda^k e^{-\lambda}}{k^\alpha k!} \int_{-\infty}^{+\infty} x^\alpha ps_k(x)dx \qquad (8.108)$$

We can compute $P(k,\alpha)$ for different values of k and α. In particular we can show that

$$P(1,\alpha) = \frac{\lambda e^{-\lambda}}{\alpha + 1}$$

$$P(2,\alpha) = \frac{2\lambda^2 e^{-\lambda}}{(\alpha + 1)(\alpha + 2)}[1 - 2^{-(\alpha+1)}]$$

$$P(k,\alpha) \approx \frac{\lambda^k e^{-\lambda}}{k^\alpha k!} M^\alpha\left(\frac{k}{2}, \frac{k}{12}\right) \text{ for } k \geq 3 \qquad (8.109)$$

where $M^\alpha(\mu, \sigma^2)$ is the αth moment of a Gaussian random variable with mean μ and variance σ^2.

The values of $M^\alpha(\mu, \sigma^2)$ for different values of α can be computed using the moment generating function for a Gaussian random variable [Papoulis 1984]. We can show that

$$M^1(\mu, \sigma^2) = \mu$$

$$\text{hence } M^1\left(\frac{k}{2}, \frac{k}{12}\right) = M^1(k) = \frac{k}{2} \qquad (8.110)$$

$$M^2(\mu, \sigma^2) = \mu^2 + \sigma^2$$

$$\text{hence } M^2\left(\frac{k}{2}, \frac{k}{12}\right) = M^2(k) = \frac{1}{12}(3k^2 + k) \qquad (8.111)$$

$$M^3(\mu, \sigma^2) = \mu^3 + 3\sigma^2\mu$$

$$\text{hence } M^3\left(\frac{k}{2}, \frac{k}{12}\right) = M^3(k) = \frac{k^2}{8}(k + 1) \qquad (8.112)$$

$$M^4(\mu, \sigma^2) = \mu^4 + 6\sigma^2\mu^2 + 3\sigma^4$$

$$\text{hence } M^4\left(\frac{k}{2}, \frac{k}{12}\right) = M^4(k) = \frac{k^2}{48}(3k^2 + 6k + 1) \qquad (8.113)$$

Table 8.3: Values of $P(k)$: Probability of k *discrete* random events falling into a bucket for $m = 4$, $s = 8$, $b = 3$ and $n = 10000$.

k	1	2	3	4	5
$P(k)$	0.304	$7.673E(-2)$	$1.829E(-2)$	$1.620E(-3)$	$1.637E(-4)$

$E(x) = 10^x$

$$M^5(\mu, \sigma^2) = \mu^5 + 10\sigma^2\mu^3 + 15\sigma^4\mu$$

$$\text{hence } M^5\left(\frac{k}{2}, \frac{k}{12}\right) = M^5(k) = \frac{k^3}{96}(3k^2 + 10k + 5) \qquad (8.114)$$

In Table 8.3 we tabulate the values of $P(k)$, where $P(k)$ is the probability of k *discrete* random events falling into a bucket in $\mathcal{H}$, using the Poisson probability distribution in Eq. (8.96) for the straightforward generalized Hough transform. In Table 8.4 we tabulate the values of $P(k, \alpha)$, where $P(k, \alpha)$ is the probability of k *fuzzy* random events falling into a bucket in $\mathcal{H}$, using the set of equations in Eq. (8.109) for the *weighted* generalized Hough transform. As can be seen from the corresponding values in Tables 8.3 and 8.4, the weighted generalized Hough transform shows a lower probability of k random events falling into the same bucket in $\mathcal{H}$ as compared to the straightforward generalized Hough transform. The weighted generalized Hough transform thus reduces the probability of large clusters in the parameter space due to the random accumulation of evidence. Furthermore, the parameter α can be used to tune the weighted generalized Hough transform. For a given value of k, $P(k, \alpha)$ can be seen to be a decreasing function of α. Increasing the value of α makes the membership function $\mu(x)$ in Eq. (8.98) more *selective*, favoring matches containing scene features that are less occluded over matches in which scene features are occluded to a greater extent. Since the redundancy of a computed transform value is directly proportional to the extent of occlusion, the parameter α is used to de-emphasize transform values with a higher redundancy and emphasize those with a lower redundancy. We can see that the extent of emphasis/de-emphasis has a direct consequence in lowering the value of $P(k, \alpha)$. The weighted generalized Hough transform can thus control the effect of redundancy or fragmentation of the computed transform values caused by occlusion.

Table 8.4: Values of $P(k, \alpha)$: Probability of k *Fuzzy* random events falling into a bucket for $m = 4$, $s = 8$, $b = 3$ and $n = 10000$.

k $\backslash$ α	1	2	3	4	5
1	0.152	$3.836E(-2)$	$6.445E(-3)$	$8.121E(-4)$	$8.186E(-5)$
2	0.102	$2.238E(-2)$	$3.581E(-3)$	$4.399E(-4)$	$4.366E(-5)$
3	$7.612E(-2)$	$1.439E(-2)$	$2.148E(-3)$	$2.538E(-4)$	$2.456E(-5)$
4	$6.089E(-2)$	$9.911E(-3)$	$1.373E(-3)$	$1.544E(-4)$	$1.446E(-5)$
5	$5.075E(-2)$	$7.193E(-3)$	$9.250E(-4)$	$9.834E(-5)$	$8.868E(-6)$

$E(x) = 10^x$

8.6 Weighted Generalized Hough Transform

We describe here an experiment in which the performance of the straightforward generalized Hough transform is compared with that of the weighted generalized Hough transform. The problem chosen is that of recognition and localization of three-dimensional polyhedral objects from range images. The range images are of scenes containing single objects and multiple objects with partial occlusion. The features used for matching and pose computation are *dihedral junctions*. The various steps, i.e., feature extraction, dihedral junction formation, matching, pose computation, and pose clustering remain the same as in Chapter 6. The only difference is that the results of the sensitivity analysis are used to compute the redundancy of the computed transform and to increment the appropriate bins in the Hough array. The recognition and localization technique proceeds iteratively by recognizing each object in turn, verifying the identity and pose of each object and recomputing the generalized Hough transform until all objects in the scene have been identified and verified.

When the dihedral junctions extracted from the range image are matched against the dihedral junctions in the object model, each match between the candidate scene and model junctions is subjected to a series of tests in which the *qualitative* feature attributes are used to determine the weight for each match, as discussed in Section 8.5.2. The scene and model dihedral junctions are subjected to the angle constraint based on the value of the included angle between the edges that form the junction.

$$M_\theta = \begin{cases} \left(1 - \frac{|\theta_m - \theta_s|}{\epsilon_\theta}\right)^\alpha & \text{if } \theta_m - \epsilon_\theta \le \theta_s \le \theta_m + \epsilon_\theta \text{ and } \alpha \ge 1 \\ 0 & \text{otherwise} \end{cases} \tag{8.115}$$

where ϵ_θ is the maximum allowed deviation in angle, and θ_m and θ_s are the angles enclosed by the scene and model junctions, respectively. The value of M_θ is deemed to be the weight of the match based on the angle constraint. The scene and model dihedral junctions are subjected to the length constraint based on the lengths of the corresponding edges. The weight of the match is M_l, which is the same as the value of μ_{Ij} as computed in Eq. (8.97) or Eq. (8.98), depending on whether the scene edge is unoccluded or occluded, respectively. Match weights M_{l_1} and M_{l_2} are computed for edge of the dihedral junction. The overall weight for the match of a model dihedral junction with a scene dihedral junction is considered to be the product of the weights M_θ, M_{l_1}, and M_{l_2}, which corresponds to the joint satisfaction of each of the corresponding constraints. For a successful match between a scene feature and a model feature, the resulting pose was computed in a manner identical to the one discussed in Chapter 6.

If the uncertainty in the position of the vertices is denoted by the parameter ϵ_p, then the uncertainty in the included angle of the dihedral junction is given by

$$\epsilon_\theta = 2 \tan^{-1}\left(\frac{2\epsilon_p}{\sqrt{l^2 - 4\epsilon_p^2}}\right) \tag{8.116}$$

as shown in Figure 8.6. With reference to Figure 8.6, if $M \triangleq |(\mathbf{m}_1 - \mathbf{s}_1) \times (\mathbf{m}_2 - \mathbf{s}_2)| = [((\mathbf{m}_1 - \mathbf{s}_1) \times (\mathbf{m}_2 - \mathbf{s}_2)) \cdot ((\mathbf{m}_1 - \mathbf{s}_1) \times (\mathbf{m}_2 - \mathbf{s}_2))]^{\frac{1}{2}}$ and $\cos \lambda \triangleq \mathbf{m}_1 \cdot \mathbf{k}$, then from the sensitivity analysis in Section 8.2 we can show the following:

$$\Delta k_x = \Delta k_y = \Delta k_z = \frac{\epsilon_\theta}{M}$$

$$\Delta \theta = \left(\frac{1}{|\sin \theta| \sin^2 \lambda} + \left|\frac{2(1 - \cos \theta)}{M \sin \theta}\right| \frac{|\cos \lambda|}{\sin^2 \lambda}\right) \epsilon_\theta$$

$$\Delta \xi = \frac{1}{\sin \eta}(\sin \xi - \cos \xi)\frac{\epsilon_\theta}{M}$$

$$\Delta \eta = \frac{1}{\cos \eta}(\sin \xi + \cos \xi)\frac{\epsilon_\theta}{M}$$

$$\Delta t_x = \Delta t_y = \Delta t_z = \epsilon_\theta \, max\left(\sin \theta, \cos \theta, \frac{1}{M}\right) \tag{8.117}$$

The volume in parameter space defined by the transform $(t_x, t_y, t_z, \xi, \eta, \theta)$ and denoted by $V(t_x, t_y, t_z, \xi, \eta, \theta)$ is then approximated by $(t_x \pm \Delta t_x, t_y \pm \Delta t_y, t_z \pm \Delta t_z, \xi \pm \Delta \xi, \eta \pm \Delta \eta, \theta \pm \Delta \theta)$. The redundancy of the transform is computed as

$$b \approx \left|\frac{(t_x \pm \Delta t_x, t_y \pm \Delta t_y, t_z \pm \Delta t_z, \xi \pm \Delta \xi, \eta \pm \Delta \eta, \theta \pm \Delta \theta)}{h_{t_x} h_{t_y} h_{t_z} h_\eta h_\xi h_\theta}\right| \tag{8.118}$$

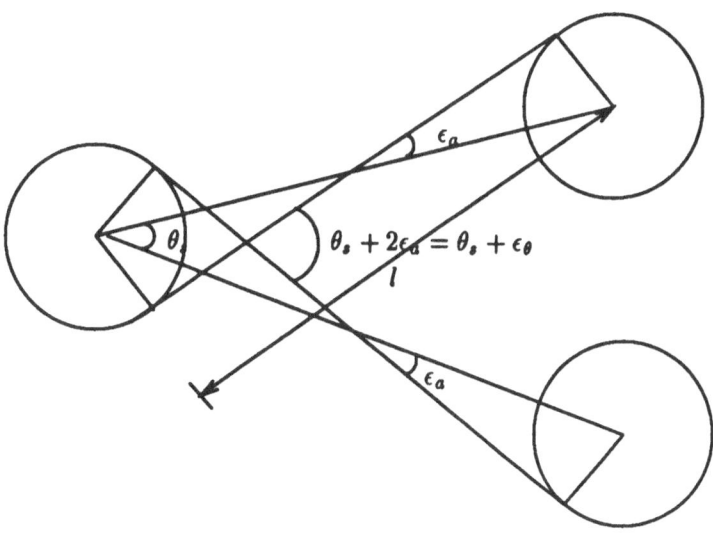

Figure 8.6: Error in included angle due to error in positions of the vertices.

where $h_{t_x}, h_{t_y}, h_{t_z}, h_\eta, h_\xi$ and h_θ are the dimensions of the Hough bucket along the corresponding axis in parameter space. The value of the redundancy obtained by our technique is a more pessimistic estimate than the one that would be obtained by actually computing an analytic expression for the volume $V(t_x, t_y, t_z, \xi, \eta, \theta)$. In the case of the straightforward generalized Hough transform, all the Hough buckets within the volume $(t_x \pm \Delta t_x, t_y \pm \Delta t_y, t_z \pm \Delta t_z, \xi \pm \Delta\xi, \eta \pm \Delta\eta, \theta \pm \Delta\theta)$ are incremented by 1, whereas in the case of the weighted generalized Hough transform, the Hough buckets within the volume are incremented by the weight assigned to the transform.

The pose hypothesis is used to project the object model onto the image. The feature-based comparison technique based on the solution to the optimal assignment problem as discussed in Chapter 6 is used. The recognition algorithm shown in Figure 6.1 was implemented and tested on a set of range images from the range database provided by the Pattern Recognition and Image Processing Laboratory at Michigan State University, East Lansing, Michigan. The performance of the weighted generalized Hough transform was compared with that of the straightforward generalized Hough transform. As a performance criteria, the number of buckets M in the Hough accumulator that had values greater than or equal to the value in the bucket that corresponded to the correct pose hypothesis is used. Obviously, the smaller the value of M, the better the performance of the recognition algorithm. The input scenes are shown in Figures 7–10. The results of our experiments are presented in Table 8.5. In this experiment the sensor (junction vertex) position error ϵ_p was taken to be ≈ 2 pixels, which translated

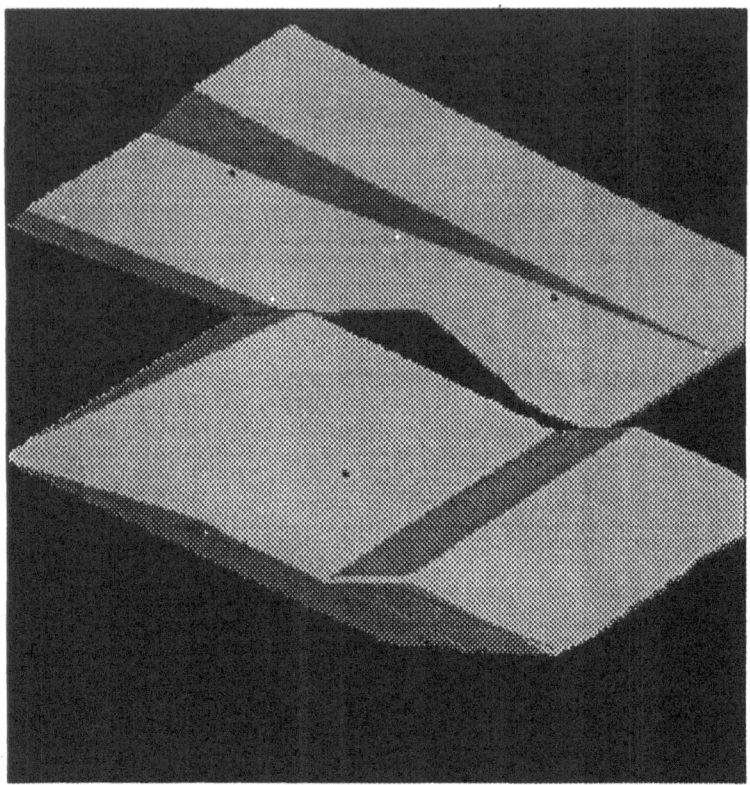

Figure 8.7: Scene I containing polyhedral objects 1 and 2.

to an error in the included angle $\epsilon_\theta \approx 5$ degrees. As can be seen from the experimental results, the weighted generalized Hough transform performs better than the straightforward generalized Hough transform in terms of its ability to reduce the number of spurious peaks that have a magnitude greater than or equal to the peak corresponding to the correct solution.

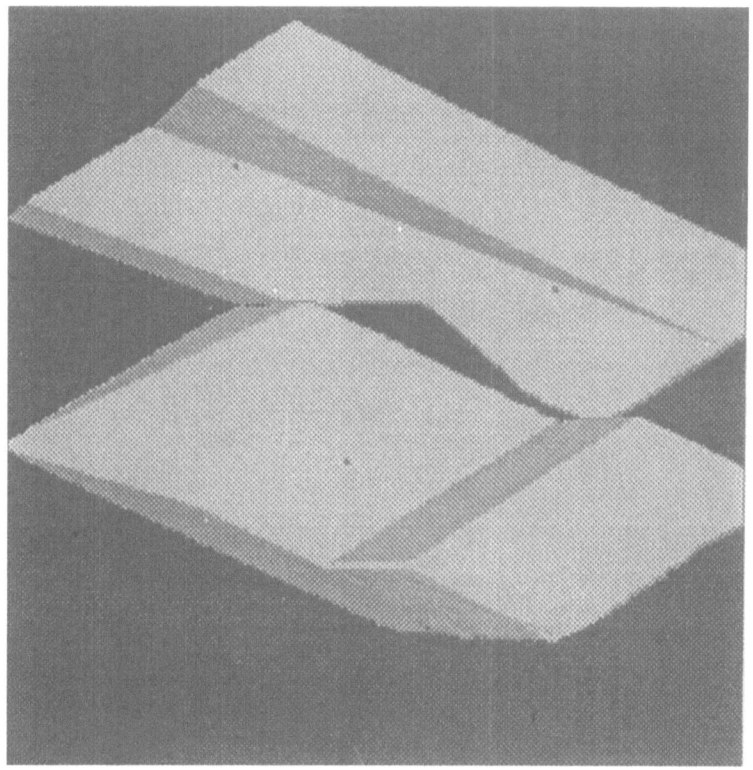

Figure 8.8: Scene II containing polyhedral object 1.

Table 8.5: Performance comparison between the straightforward and weighted generalized Hough transforms.

M	Scene 1		Scene 2	Scene 3	Scene 4
	Object 1	Object 2	Object 1	Object 1	Object 2
WGHT	2	9	5	7	1
GHT	7	24	25	13	23

WGHT: Weighted Generalized Hough Transform
GHT: Straightforward Generalized Hough Transform

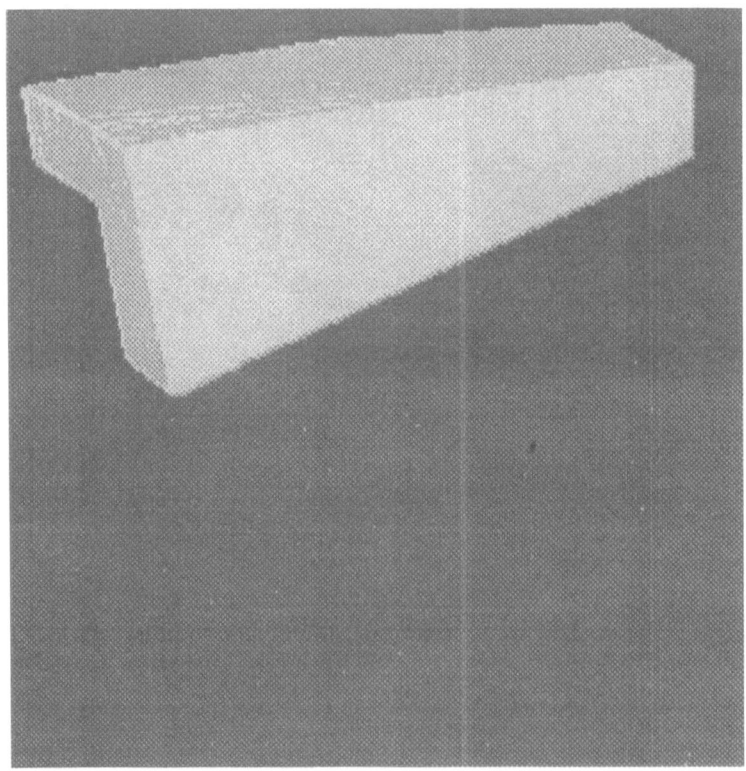

Figure 8.9: Scene III containing polyhedral object 1.

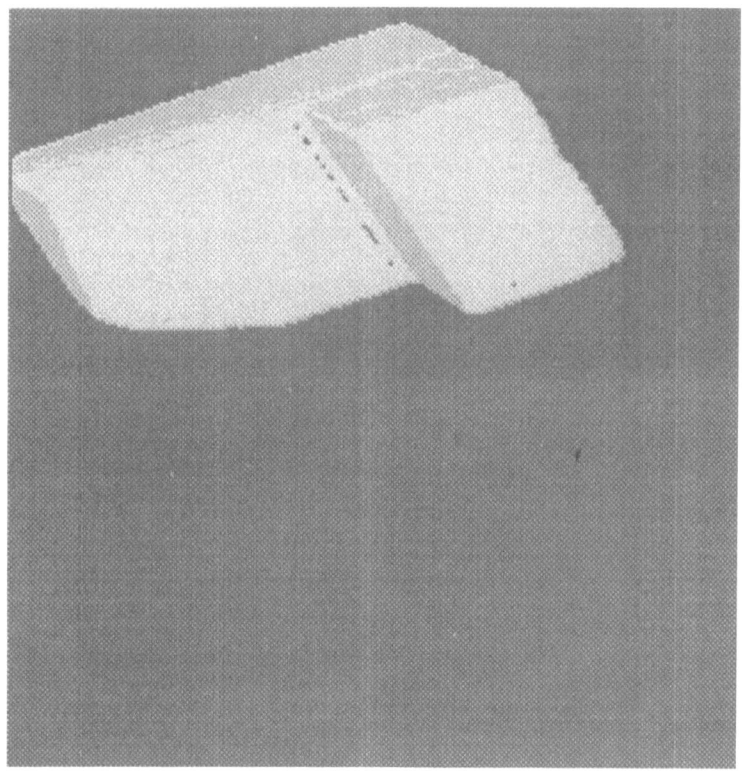

Figure 8.10: Scene IV containing polyhedral object 2.

Chapter 9

Parallel Implementations of Recognition Techniques

Tasks in image processing and computer vision are computationally very intensive. Furthermore, many applications such as robotics, target acquisition, and navigation require real time or near real time processing. Thus, developing efficient algorithms matched to high-performance architectures is a critical area of research in computer vision. In this chapter we describe parallel implementations of the object recognition algorithms described in Part II. The discussion in this chapter is very limited in scope, mainly discussing our work of parallel implementation of algorithms given in Part II using two different parallel architectures, the Connection Machine (CM)[1] and the hypercube. For general discussions of parallel computing in vision, the interested reader could refer to Duff and Levialdi [1981], Duff [1978, 1986], Levialdi [1985], Reeves [1984], Uhr [1984, 1987a, 1978b], Yalamanchili et al. [1985], Cypher and Sanz [1989], Chaudhary and Aggarwal [1990], Crisman and Webb [1991], and Preston and Uhr [1982]. For a general reference for parallel architectures, Almasi and Gottilieb [1989] and Hwang and Briggs [1984] are excellent references.

9.1 Parallel Processing in Computer Vision

Parallel computing in computer vision can be considered from two different aspects—algorithms and architectures.

9.1.1 Parallel Architectures

Parallel computers are usually classified into single instruction stream-multiple data stream (SIMD) and multiple instruction stream-multiple data stream (MIMD) systems [Flynn 1972]. In an SIMD system, all processors are synchronized and engaged in an identical computation at a given moment. The unit of

---

[1] CM is a registered trademark of the Thinking Machines Inc.

computation is very fine-grained in general, and this type of architecture is well suited for implementing data-parallel algorithms that can be found frequently in low-level vision. In an MIMD system all processors are engaged in different computations at the same time. The unit of computation is coarse-grained. MIMD systems find many applications in high-level vision [Preston and Uhr 1982].

Many low-level vision algorithms and image processing algorithms exhibit data-parallelism. For such problems, fine-grained SIMD machines configured as two-dimensional arrays of processors are very useful. The Illiac-IV [Barnes et al. 1968], a mesh-connected SIMD computer developed at the University of Illinois, was a pioneering work of this kind that still provides many useful insights. A 64-processor system was built by the Burroughs Corporation in 1972 that was intended for applications involving matrix computations and solving partial differential equations, thus making it quite useful for vision problems. The Massively Parallel Processor (MPP) [Batcher 1980] by Goodyear Aerospace was developed for satellite image processing for NASA. A 128 × 128 system was built and used for many image processing tasks. A more recent SIMD array computer is the Connection Machine (CM) [Hillis 1985], developed at MIT and built by the Thinking Machines Corporation. A fully configured CM-2 can have up to 64K processors, which can be arranged as a two-dimensional array or as a 16-cube. A detailed description of CM-2 is given in the following section. The Cellular Logic Information Processor 4 (CLIP 4) [Duff 1978], developed at The University College of London, differs from the above computers in that 8 neighboring or 6 neighboring processors in a CLIP computer are connected to each other. The CLIP series is being developed for bit-slice image processing applications. CLIP 4 uses 1-bit processors, while the more recent version, CLIP 7, uses 8-bit processors.

Two MIMD computers developed at Columbia University are based on a tree interconnection. NON-VON [Shaw 1984] is based on binary trees, and a prototype comprised of 63 processors was built. Another tree-connected computer, DADO [Stolfo and Miranker 1986], is based on pure binary trees. A prototype (DADO2) consisting of 1023 processors was built. The primary purpose of these machines is geared toward applications in databases and expert production systems, but they could provide a natural computational structure for certain types of vision algorithms. Another MIMD architecture called a *pyramid computer* combines arrays and tree connections. The HCL Pyramid [Tanimoto et al. 1987], developed at University of Washington, is an example of pyramid computers.

There are many SIMD and MIMD computers based on the hypercube configuration where processors form an n-dimensional hypercube. Cosmic Cube [Seitz 1985] or Caltech Hypercube is an MIMD computer consisting of 64 processors. Commercial hypercube systems include iPSC by Intel (32 and 128 nodes), Floating Point Systems T-series, and NCUBE/ten by N-Cube.

The Butterfly [Crowther et al. 1985], developed by Bolt Beranek and Newman, is an example of an MIMD computer based on reconfigurable networks. It is a shared memory computer based on omega interconnection network. The maximum configuration of the Butterfly can have up to 256 processors. Another parallel computer based on a reconfigurable network is PASM [Siegel 1981], developed at Purdue University. A prototype consisting of 16 processors was built with a maximum configuration that would allow 1024 processors. It has the unique feature of being a partitionable SIMD/MIMD computer, thus being ideal for divide-and-conquer schemes.

A systolic array [Kung 1982] is based on the pipeline concept and is ideal for compute-bound applications. The structure is quite regular, so it is well suited for VLSI implementation. The WARP Computer [Annaratone et al. 1986], developed at Carnegie-Mellon University, consists of ten or more programmable systolic cells connected as a linear array. It has been successfully demonstrated in the Navlab (Navigation Laboratory) environment [Crisman and Webb 1991].

9.1.2   Parallel Algorithms

We are concerned with two aspects of parallel algorithms: mapping vision algorithms developed mainly for sequential computers to chosen parallel architectures so they can be run faster, and developing *new* parallel algorithms specifically for parallel processing.

A large class of vision problems, especially those in low-level vision, falls under the category of data-parallel algorithms. The underlying computation for these algorithms is local in nature: identical computation carried out in small neighborhoods surrounding each pixel of an image, thus exhibiting natural parallelism. Mapping these algorithms onto parallel machines, especially fine-grained SIMD computers, is not difficult. Many steps in object recognition such as convolution (filtering), edge detection, and thinning are included in this category. Other groups of problems that exhibit natural parallelism are those based on *regularlization* and *relaxation*. The computational structures of these algorithms are so regular, involving only immediate neighboring pixels, that they are well suited for VLSI implementation and simulation on many types of parallel computers. Some important algorithms in 3-D object recognition such as stereo, motion, surface reconstruction, and edge-linking belong to this category.

One dilemma in parallel computing concerning computer in vision is that *easy problems are trivial, but difficult problems are extremely difficult*. For many problems in high-level vision, we must try hard to find the best way of parallelization. The information being processed in high-level vision is highly abstract, usually symbolic, and small in quantity. Interaction patterns among symbols are very irregular. MIMD computers are usually preferred for these problems. Since these algorithms are for symbol manipulation involving the use of knowledge, many computers developed for AI applications can also be used [Wah and Li 1985], [Uhr 1987b]. It would often be more beneficial to develop entirely new sets of parallel algorithms, specifically developed with parallelism in mind, instead of trying to "parallelize" existing sequential algorithms. There needs to be a great deal of research in this area. For a good review of parallel algorithms in vision, refer to Cypher and Sanz [1989], Chaudhary and Aggarwal [1990], and Preston and Uhr [1982].

9.2   The Connection Machine

The Connection Machine Model CM-2 is a data-parallel computing system.[2]
Data-parallel computing associates one processor with each data element. This
computing style exploits the natural parallelism inherent in many data-intensive
problems. The CM-2 is an integrated system of hardware and software. The
hardware elements of the system include front-end computers that provide the
development and execution environments for the system software, a parallel
processing unit of 64K processors that execute the data-parallel operations, and
a high performance data parallel I/O system. The system software is based
upon the operating system or environment of the front-end computer. Visible
software extensions are minimal. Users can program using familiar languages
and programming constructs, with all the development tools provided by the
front end. Programs have normal sequential control flow—new synchronization
structures are not needed.

9.2.1   System Organization

The Connection Machine Model CM-2 is a complete computing system that provides both development and execution facilities for data-parallel programs. Its
hardware consists of a parallel processing unit containing thousands of data processors, from one to four front-end computers, and an I/O system that supports
mass storage and graphic display devices (Figure 9.1). The user interacts with
the front-end computer, and all program development and execution takes place
within the front end. The central element in the system is the CM-2 parallel
processing unit, which contains:

- thousands of *data processors*

- an interprocessor communications network

- one or more *sequencers*

- an interface to one or more front-end computers

- zero or more I/O *controllers* and/or *frame buffers*

A parallel processing unit may contain 64K, 32K, or 16K data processors.
Each data processor has 64K bits of bit-addressable local memory and an ALU
that can operate on variable length operands. Each data processor can access its
memory at a rate of at least 5 megabits per second. A fully configured CM-2 thus
has 512 megabytes of memory that can be read or written at about 300 gigabits
per second. When 64K processors are operating in parallel, each performing
a 32-bit integer addition, the CM-2 parallel processing unit operates at about
2500 Mips[3]. In addition to the standard ALU, the CM-2 parallel processing
unit has an optional parallel floating point accelerator that performs at 3500

---

[2]This appendix is adapted from Ramamoorthy [1991].
[3]millions instructions per second

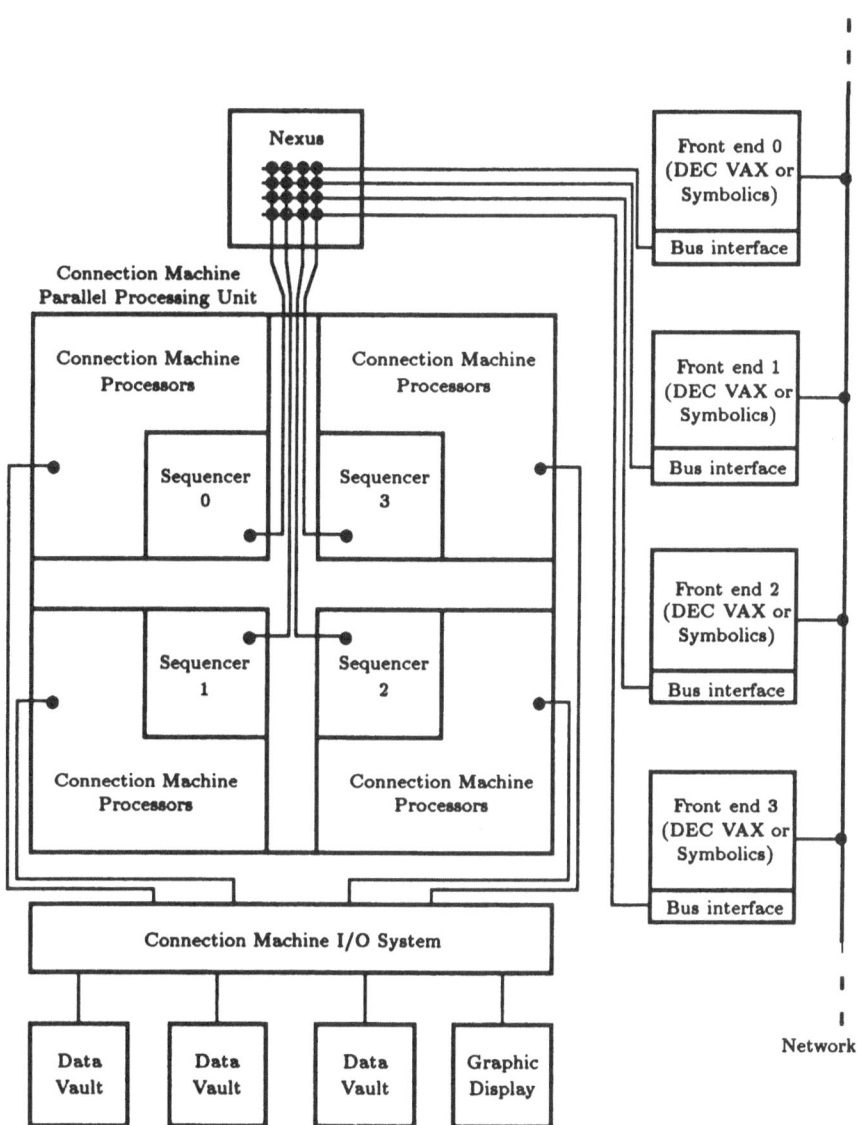

Figure 9.1: Connection Machine system organization.

MFlops[4] (single precision) and 2500 MFlops (double precision). Each physical data processor can also simulate a maximum of 1024 virtual processors, giving a virtual to physical processor ratio of 1024:1. This is done by dividing the local memory of each physical processor among the virtual processors that it simulates.

The CM-2 system provides two forms of communication within the parallel processing unit. The more general mechanism is known as the *router*, which allows any processor to communicate with any other processor. Messages between processors may be of any length. The throughput of the router depends on the message length and on the pattern of accesses; typical values are 80 million to 250 million 32-bit accesses per second. The CM-2 parallel processing unit also has a more structured, somewhat faster communication mechanism called the *NEWS grid*. The CM-2 supports programmable grids with an arbitrary number of dimensions. The NEWS grid allows processors to pass data according to a regular rectangular pattern. The advantage of this mechanism over the router is merely that the overhead of explicitly specifying destination addresses is eliminated; for many applications this is a worthwhile optimization.

The parallel processing unit is designed to operate under the programmed control of a front-end computer, which may be a Symbolics 36xx Lisp machine, a DEC VAX 8000 series computer, a BI bus, or a SUN workstation. The programs execute on the front end; during the course of execution the front end issues instructions to the CM-2 parallel processing unit. The set of instructions sent to the CM-2 is called *Paris*, which includes a variety of instructions such as integer arithmetic, floating point arithmetic, interprocessor communication, vector summation, matrix multiplication, and sorting.

Data processors do not handle Paris instructions directly. Paris instructions from the front end are processed by a *sequencer* in the parallel processing unit. The sequencer breaks down each Paris instruction into a sequence of low-level data processor and memory operations. The sequencer broadcasts these low-level operations to the data processors, which execute them at a rate of several million per second.

To increase the flexibility of program development and execution, the CM-2 can be divided into as many as four sections. Depending on the configuration, each section will have 8K or 16K processors. Each section can be regarded as a complete parallel processing unit by itself, containing its own sequencer, router and NEWS grid. A programmable, bi-directional switch called the *Nexus* allows up to four front-end computers to be attached to a single parallel processing unit.

For every group of 8K processors there is one I/O channel. To each I/O channel may be connected either one high-resolution graphics display framebuffer module or one general I/O controller supporting an I/O bus to which several Data Vault mass storage devices may be connected. The front-end controls I/O transfers in exactly the same manner in which it controls the data processors: by issuing Paris instructions to the sequencer. The sequencer can then send

---

[4] millions of floating point operations per second

low-level commands to the I/O channels and interrogate channel status. Data is transferred directly, and in parallel between the I/O devices and the data processors, without being funneled through the sequencers.

For program development on the front-end computer, the languages available to the user are *Lisp, C* and CM-FORTRAN, which are extensions of Lisp, C, and FORTRAN, respectively, having parallel constructs to handle data-parallel operations efficiently. Users are also permitted to include Paris instructions directly in their programs to quicken execution. Further details can be obtained by referring to the Connection Machine Reference Manuals [Thinking Machines Inc. 1987, 1988].

9.2.2 Performance Specifications

The following specifications assume a fully configured Connection Machine Model CM-2 with 64K data processors and eight I/O channels. Specifications for floating point performance assume the use of a floating point accelerator.

General Specifications

Processors: 65,536
Memory: 512 megabytes
Memory bandwidth: 300 gigabits per second

Input/Output Channels

Number of channels: 8
Capacity per I/O controller: 40 megabytes per second
Total I/O controller transfer rate: 320 megabytes per second
Capacity per framebuffer: 1 gigabit per second

Typical Application Performance (Fixed Point)

General computing: 2500 Mips
Terrain mapping: 1000 Mips
Document search: 6000 Mips

Interprocessor Communication

Regular pattern of 32-bit messages: 250 million per second
Random pattern of 32-bit messages: 80 million per second
Sort 65,536 32-bit keys: 30 milliseconds

Variable Precision Fixed Point

64-bit integer add: 1500 Mips
32-bit integer add: 2500 Mips
16-bit integer add: 3300 Mips

8-bit integer add: 4000 Mips
64-bit move: 2000 Mips
32-bit move: 3000 Mips
16-bit move: 3800 Mips
8-bit move: 4500 Mips

Double Precision Floating Point

4K x 4K matrix multiply benchmark: 2500 MFlops
Dot product: 5000 MFlops

Single Precision Floating Point

Addition: 4000 MFlops
Subtraction: 4000 MFlops   .
Multiplication: 4000 MFlops
Division: 1500 MFlops
4K x 4K matrix multiply benchmark: 3500 MFlops
Dot product: 10,000 MFlops

9.3   Object Recognition on the Connection Machine

Because of its inherent data-parallel nature, the generalized Hough transform technique for the recognition and localization of complex objects with curved surfaces presented in Chapter 7 is very amenable to implementation on the Connection Machine. In this section we present the implementation of the various stages of this technique on the Connection Machine. Two principal features of the Connection Machine that have been exploited are, (1) the availability of *virtual* processors that can be activated or deactivated under software control, and (2) the programmability of communication topology between processors. In our work we have made use of the fact that a K-dimensional Boolean hypercube can be mapped on an N-dimensional wrap-around mesh, and vice versa in $O(1)$ time. The mapping algorithm can be summarized as follows: Given a K-dimensional Boolean hypercube and an N-dimensional wrap-around mesh $D_1 \times D_2 \times ... \times D_N$, where each $D_i = 2^{m_i}$ and $\sum_{i=1}^{N} m_i = K$, let G_{m_i} be the m_i bit gray code representation of each processor along each dimension of the N-dimensional wrap-around mesh. Any processor in the N-dimensional wrap-around mesh can be represented by a sequence of gray codes $< G_{m_i} >$, where each m_i bit gray code value represents the coordinate value of the processor along the ith dimension. It is also known that any processor in the K-dimensional Boolean hypercube can be assigned a unique K-bit gray code value. These K-bit gray code values maintain the adjacency property of the K-dimensional Boolean hypercube in that any two K-bit gray codes which differ in a single bit (i.e., at unit Hamming distance) map onto processors that are adjacent in the K-dimensional Boolean hyper-cube. It can be shown that the concatenation of the gray codes in the sequence $< G_{m_i} >$ of a processor in the N-dimensional wrap-around mesh yields the K-bit gray code of a processor in the K-dimensional Boolean hypercube. This mapping, moreover, preserves the adjacency property, i.e., adjacent processors in the N-dimensional wrap-around mesh map onto adjacent processors in the K-dimensional Boolean hypercube. Similarly, a processor in the K-dimensional Boolean hypercube can be mapped onto an N-dimensional wrap-around mesh by appropriately partitioning the K-bit gray code along each dimension of the mesh. This partitioning yields the gray code sequence $< G_{m_i} >$ for the processor in the mesh. This inverse mapping also preserves the adjacency property, i.e., adjacent processors in the hypercube map onto adjacent processors on the mesh. Since the recognition technique is based on histogramming in N-dimensions, the ability to configure the Connection Machine as an N-dimensional wrap-around mesh is extremely valuable.

Issues regarding implementation on the Connection Machine for various phases of the recognition and localization process are discussed in the following subsections.

9.3.1 Feature Extraction

The process of feature extraction includes surface fitting, curvature computation, step edge detection, roof edge detection, pixel classification, and pixel grouping. All these operations are carried out by configuring the Connection Machine as a two-dimensional grid of the same size as the image. Thus each pixel in the range image is mapped onto a single processor. The surface fitting is carried out in a local $N \times N$ window (where N is odd) centered around each pixel. The computations involve communications in a local pixel neighborhood using the NEWS communication. Curvature computation, roof and step edge detection, and pixel classification are strictly on a single pixel basis and involve no communication between neighboring pixels. Pixel grouping is carried out using an asynchronous region growing algorithm. Each pixel (i, j) is assigned an initial region label $MAX * i + j$ where MAX is the image size. For each non-edge pixel the neighboring pixels are checked for HK signs and their corresponding region labels. If any of the neighboring pixels has the same HK sign and a lower region label, the region label of the center pixel is updated to the value of the lower region label. This process is carried out in parallel for all pixels in the image. The step terminates when no pixel updates its region label.

9.3.2 Localization of Curved Surfaces

The axes of the conical and cylindrical surfaces are determined by histogramming in the (d, ξ, η) space. Each point on the conical or cylindrical surface patch votes for the appropriate buckets in the (d, ξ, η) space, based on the value of the components of the surface normal at that point. This voting process is carried out in parallel for each point on the surface patch. The maxima in the histogram is used to compute the orientation of the axis and so also distinguish between conical and cylindrical surfaces. A parallel averaging process is used to determine the centers and radii of spherical and cylindrical surfaces and the apexes of conical surfaces. Points in each of these regions are represented by a linked list. · The averaging process is essentially a parallel divide-and-conquer technique that computes the average of a pair of elements. The complexity of the algorithm is $O(\log N)$, where N is the length of the list.

9.3.3   Computation of Dihedral Feature Junctions

The surface patches that are identified and localized are allocated to the first row and column of an $M \times M$ grid (where M is the number of surface patches). At each processor (i, j) in the grid the dihedral feature junction corresponding to surface patches i and j is computed. It should be noted that only the upper half or the lower half of the grid along any of the major diagonals is effectively utilized. The mapping, therefore, is not optimal in the sense of processor allocation. Only valid dihedral feature junctions (type I or II) are considered for matching and pose computation.

9.3.4   Matching and Pose Computation

The valid dihedral feature junctions are allocated to the first row and column of an $L \times L$ grid (where L is the number of valid dihedral feature junctions). At each processor (i, j) in the grid the dihedral feature junctions i and j are matched, and if the match is successful the pose is computed. As before, only the upper half or the lower half of the grid along any of the major diagonals is effectively utilized.

9.3.5   Pose Clustering

Pose clustering in the six-dimensional parameter space of rigid-body motion is carried out by histogramming independently the translation and rotation parameters. A three-dimensional accumulator array is needed to compute the histogram for the rotational parameters ξ, η, and θ, as well as the translational parameters x, y, and z. As discussed earlier, the Connection Machine software allows the processors to be configured in an n-dimensional grid [Ramamoorthy et al. 1989]. Limited memory considerations necessitated a coarse initial quantization. After the initial histogramming, the contents of the accumulator are thresholded to identify the cells containing at least a certain number of votes. These cells are tested recursively for peaks. Finer quantizations enabled a more accurate localization of peaks in parameter space.

9.4   Object Recognition on the Hypercube

Interpretation tree search for three-dimensional object recognition and localization was discussed in Chapters 5 and 6. The control structure of the interpretation tree search is *hypothesize-and-test* with *backtracking*. The interpretation tree search is found to have quadratic complexity in the number of scene and model features in single-object scenes. In multiple-object scenes with occlusion and clutter, however, the combinatorial explosion of the search space of possible scene interpretations causes a severe degradation in the performance of the interpretation tree search. The interpretation tree search has exponential complexity in the number of scene and model features in such cases. The degradation of the interpretation tree search is manifested as loss of accuracy in recognition and localization, and as increased recognition and localization time. Parallel implementation of the interpretation tree search on a suitable parallel architecture is therefore highly desirable in order to achieve a speedup of the search process.

In this section, we present a parallel interpretation tree search algorithm on the Intel iPSC/2 hypercube. The Intel iPSC/2 hypercube is an MIMD architecture with distributed memory and is based on the message-passing paradigm. The iPSC/2 used for our experiment consists of 32 nodes connected to a host machine. In our implementation, we consider only limited cases of two-dimensional polygonal objects in both single- and multiple-object scenes. We consider three strategies for mapping the interpretation tree search process on the hypercube and examine the performance of the algorithm for each of these mapping strategies in terms of parameters such as speed-up, processor utilization, inter-processor communication overhead, and load sharing between processors. It is shown that the requirement for uniform load sharing leads to increased inter-processor communication.

9.4.1 Scene Description

The input sensory data is assumed to be sparse range data, as is typical of tactile or spot range sensors. The object(s) in the scene are recognized and localized by matching sensory data with prestored models of the objects in the memory of the computer.

The two-dimensional objects considered here are modeled as N-sided polygons. Each sensory measurement is in the form of a 4-tuple (x, y, n_x, n_y), where the coordinates (x, y) denote the sensor location, and the coordinates (n_x, n_y) denote the sensed surface or side normal at point (x, y). Sensory measurements are in the scene coordinate frame of reference. The interpretation tree search process determines if a given sensory measurement is consistent with a given side (face) of the object model, i.e., it pairs a sensory measurement with a given side (face) of the object model. Angle and distance measurements are used to discard inconsistent matches. Given N sensory measurements numbered from 0 to $N-1$, the interpretation tree for an object model with M sides numbered from 0 to $M-1$ is generated by matching a sensor measurement $s_i, 0 \le i \le N-1$ with each of the model sides $m_j, 0 \le j \le M-1$. Each match (s_i, m_j) is represented by a node in the interpretation tree (Figure 9.2).

The branching factor of the tree is M, where the children of a node (s_i, m_j) are the nodes $(s_{i+1}, m_0), (s_{i+1}, m_1), ... (s_{i+1}, m_{M-1})$. If the root node is at level 0, then the resultant interpretation tree has N levels and M^N leaf nodes. A con-

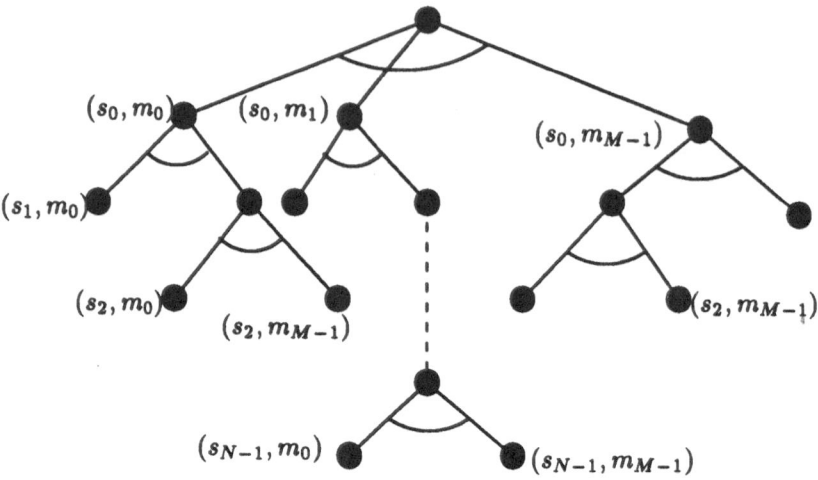

Figure 9.2: An interpretation tree for 2-D polygonal object recognition.

sistent set of pairings of sensory measurements with object model sides is called a *valid scene interpretation* and is represented by a path in the interpretation tree from the root node to one of the leaf nodes. A valid scene interpretation is also used to compute the global pose of the object which would place the model in registration with the object in the scene.

9.4.2   Model Data

The data structures for the representation of object models are:

1. A two-dimensional array dist[ ][ ] of size $M * M$ is used to store the maximum and the minimum distances between each side in the object model. For $i < j$, dist[i][j] contains the minimum distance between sides i and j in the object model. For $i > j$, dist[i][j] contains the maximum distance between sides i and j in the object model; dist[i][i] contains the length of side i.

2. A two-dimensional array angle[ ][ ] stores the angle between two sides in the object model. For $i < j$, angle[i][j] contains the angle between sides i and j in the object model. The other entries in the array are zero.

3. The one-dimensional arrays x0[ ] and x1[ ] contain the x coordinates of the endpoints of the sides of the object model. For example, x0[i] and x1[i] are the x coordinates of the endpoints of side i in the object model. Similarly, the one-dimensional arrays y0[ ] and y1[ ] contain the y coordinates of the endpoints of the sides of the object model.

4. The one-dimensional arrays nx[ ] and ny[ ] contain the x and y coordinates of the normal vector to the sides (faces) of the object model. For example, nx[i] and ny[i] contain the x and y coordinates of the normal to side (face) i in the object model.

A side (face) m_i in the object model is specified by the 6-tuple (x0[i], y0[i], x1[i], y1[i], nx[i], ny[i]) in the model coordinate frame of reference.

9.4.3 Scene Feature Data

The data structures used to represent the sensory data are:

1. The two-dimensional array initdist[ ][ ] contains the distance between two sensory measurements. For $i < j$, initdist[i][j] represents the distance between sensory measurement s_i and s_j.

2. The two-dimensional array initangle[ ][ ] contains the angle between two sensory measurements. For $i < j$, initangle[i][j] represents the angle between sensory measurement s_i and s_j.

3. The one-dimensional arrays sx[ ] and sy[ ] denote the x and y coordinates of the sensory measurement (sensor position). For example, sx[i] and sy[i] denote the x and y coordinates of the ith sensory measurement s_i.

4. The one-dimensional arrays nsx[ ] and nsy[ ] denote the x and y coordinates of the side (face) normal as sensed by the sensor. For example, nsx[i] and nsy[i] denote the x and y coordinates of the normal sensed by the sensory measurement s_i.

The sensory measurement s_i is specified by the 4-tuple (sx[i], sy[i], nsx[i], nsy[i]) in the scene coordinate frame of reference.

9.4.4 Pruning Constraints

At each stage in the interpretation tree search process a sensory measurement is matched with a side (face) in the object model. An *interpretation* is a set of sensory measurement-object model side (face) pairs $\{(s_i, m_j)\}$ where $0 \leq i \leq N - 1$ and $0 \leq j \leq M - 1$. An interpretation is said to be *valid* if any two pairs (s_i, m_k) and (s_j, m_l) within the interpretation satisfy the following three constraints:

1. *Unique interpretation constraint.* The two pairs (s_i, m_k) and (s_j, m_l) are said to satisfy the unique interpretation constraint if $i \neq j$. That is to say, a sensory measurement cannot be assigned to more than one side in a single interpretation, although more than one sensory measurement can be assigned to a single side.

2. *Distance constraint.* Given two pairs (s_i, m_k) and (s_j, m_l) within an interpretation, if $d(s_i, s_j)$ denotes the distance between the sensors, then $d_{min}(m_k, m_l) \leq d(s_i, s_j) \leq d_{max}(m_k, m_l)$, where $d_{min}(m_k, m_l)$ and $d_{max}(m_k, m_l)$ denote the maximum and minimum distances, respectively, between the sides m_k and m_l on the object model.

3. *Angle constraint.* Given two pairs (s_i, m_k) and (s_j, m_l) within an interpretation, if $\theta(s_i, s_j)$ is the angle between the surface normals sensed by the sensors s_i and s_j, and $\theta(m_k, m_l)$ the angle between the normals to the side m_k and m_l on the object model, then $\theta(s_i, s_j) = \theta(m_k, m_l)$ within the bounds of sensing error.

A *partial* interpretation is a set of valid sensor-side pairs $\{(s_i, m_j) | 0 \leq i \leq L, L < N - 1, 0 \leq j \leq M - 1\}$. A *complete* interpretation is a set of valid sensor-side pairs $\{(s_i, m_j) | 0 \leq i \leq N - 1, 0 \leq j \leq M - 1\}$ and wherein there exists a pair (s_{N-1}, m_j) for some value of j. At level L where $L < N$ in the interpretation tree, a partial interpretation $\{(s_i, m_j) | 0 \leq i \leq L-1, 0 \leq j \leq M-1\}$ is extended by the pair (s_L, m_k) for some value of k such that $0 < k \leq M - 1$. If the result of extending the partial interpretation at level L is a partial interpretation at level $L + 1$ $\{(s_i, m_j) | 0 \leq i \leq L, 0 \leq j \leq M - 1\}$ that satisfies all the aforementioned constraints, then the corresponding path in the interpretation tree is explored further, else it is pruned. If the partial interpretation at level $L+1$ $\{(s_i, m_j) | 0 \leq i \leq L, 0 \leq j \leq M - 1\}$ is such that it satisfies all the aforementioned constraints and if, furthermore, $L + 1 = N$, then a leaf node in the interpretation tree has been encountered, which makes the partial interpretation at level $L + 1$ a complete interpretation. All the complete interpretations in an interpretation tree can be determined using a *hypothesize-and-test* with backtracking search procedure on a conventional uniprocessor architecture.

9.4.5   Localization

Given a complete scene interpretation at the end of the interpretation tree search, the next step is to determine the transformation from the model coordinate frame of reference to the scene coordinate frame of reference, which will place the object model in registration with the object in the scene. This process of determining the exact location and orientation of the object in the scene is referred to as localization. Given two sensory measurement-object model side pairs (s_i, m_k) and (s_j, m_l), the exact location of each sensory measurement on corresponding model sides (in the model coordinate frame of reference) is determined using the distance constraint. Let (m_x, m_y, n_x, n_y) be the position of the sensory measurement s_i on the model side m_k in the model coordinate frame of reference. Let (s_x, s_y, n'_x, n'_y) be the position of s_i in the scene coordinate frame of reference. The angle of rotation θ is determined by

$$cos\theta \quad = \quad n_x \cdot n'_x + n_y \cdot n'_y \tag{9.1}$$

The translation parameters t_x and t_y are determined by

$$s_x \quad = \quad R_\theta m_x + t_x \tag{9.2}$$

$$s_y = R_\theta m_y + t_y \qquad (9.3)$$

where R_θ is the two-dimensional rotation matrix corresponding to the angle θ. Thus (t_x, t_y, θ) are the localization parameters corresponding to the pair (s_i, m_k). A complete scene interpretation is deemed to be *globally* consistent if each pair (s_i, m_j), where $0 \le i \le N-1, 0 \le j \le M-1$ in the complete interpretation yields identical localization parameters.

9.5 Mapping the Interpretation Tree on the Hypercube

In order to parallelize the interpretation tree search on the hypercube it is necessary to map the interpretation tree structure on the underlying hypercube architecture. The mapping strategy has a great impact on how the original task is subdivided into subtasks and on how concurrency is exploited among subtasks. The process of mapping is thus essentially a task-decomposition process. We consider in this section three strategies for mapping the interpretation tree on the hypercube architecture.

9.5.1 Breadth-First Mapping of the Interpretation Tree

Each side of the object model is mapped onto a single node processor in the iPSC/2 hypercube. Thus if the object model has M sides, there must be at least M processors available in the hypercube. The current interpretation is stored in a structure called **interptype** that contains an array **it[ ]**. A pointer type **interpptr** points to a structure of the type **interptype**. If the variable **interp** is declared to be of the type **interpptr**, then the current interpretation is represented by the array **interp->it[ ]** of length N (total number of sensors). The model and the scene data is made available to each node processor. At level L in the interpretation tree, the kth node in the hypercube would try to extend each of the current partial interpretations $\{(s_i, m_j) \mid 0 \le i \le L-1, L < N-1, 0 \le j \le M-1\}$ by the pair (s_L, m_k). This is done by the assignment **interp->it[L] = k**. The extended partial interpretation is checked for consistency by using the previously mentioned constraints. If the extended partial interpretation is found to be consistent, then it is broadcast to all node processors in the hypercube using the **gsendx()** facility. If a leaf node in the interpretation tree is encountered (i.e., $L = N - 1$), then the extended partial interpretation (if consistent) is deemed complete and it is conveyed to the host. If an extended partial interpretation is found to be inconsistent, then it is not broadcast, corresponding to pruning.

The traversal of the interpretation tree is terminated when every path in the interpretation tree from the root node to a leaf node has been either traversed or pruned. The host keeps track of the number of leaf nodes visited or pruned during the interpretation tree search process by using a counter. If a node processor visits a leaf node, then it instructs the host to increment the counter by 1. If the node processor prunes the interpretation tree at level k, then it

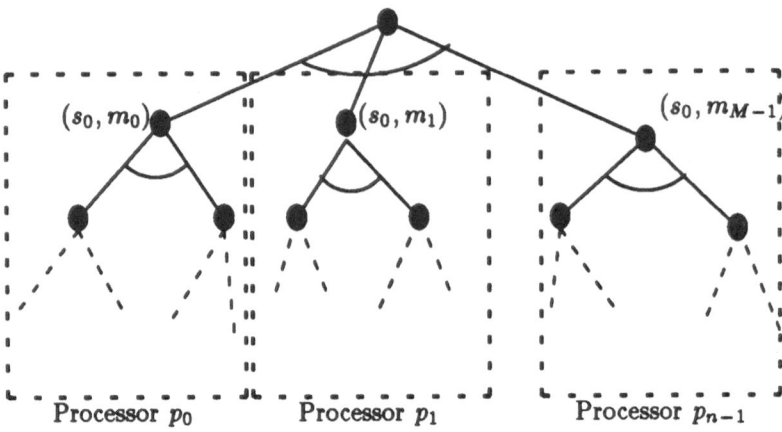

Figure 9.3: Depth-first mapping of an interpretation tree on a hypercube.

instructs the host to increment the counter by M^{N-k}. The host terminates the interpretation tree search process when the contents of the counter equal M^N.

Each node in the interpretation tree performs the same task—extending an existing partial interpretation, constraint checking, pruning, and message processing. The breadth-first mapping achieves perfect load-balancing since each node processor visits the same number of interpretation tree nodes. The cost in terms of inter-processor communication, however, is excessive. Also, there is a limitation in that the number of sides (faces) in the object model cannot be greater than the number of node processors in the hypercube.

9.5.2 Depth-First Mapping of the Interpretation Tree

The entire interpretation tree at the first level is decomposed into groups of subtrees (Figure 9.3). A group may contain a single subtree or a block of adjacent subtrees. Each processor explores its group of subtrees using the *hypothesize-and-test* with backtracking search procedure. In the present implementation, the search procedure has been implemented as a recursion. The unique interpretation constraint, the distance constraint, and the angle constraint are used to prune inconsistent paths in the interpretation tree. When a complete interpretation is found, the node processor conveys it to the host via a message. When a node processor has finished exploring its group of subtrees, it sends an appropriate message to the host. The host terminates the interpretation tree search when all the node processors are finished and proceeds with the pose determination.

The depth-first mapping of the interpretation tree involves no inter-processor communication. The only communication is between the host and the individual node processors. However, because of the unpredictable nature of the search process, some subtrees could be pruned earlier than others. This causes load imbalance among the node processors. Some nodes may finish exploring their group of subtrees and stay idle while other nodes are still exploring theirs. The depth-first mapping has the advantage that more than one subtree can be handled by a single node processor. This is a considerable improvement over the breadth-first mapping that requires that the number of sides (faces) in the object model not exceed the number of available node processors in the hypercube.

9.5.3 Depth-First Mapping of the Interpretation Tree with Load Sharing

The interpretation tree is decomposed into groups of subtrees just as in the case of the simple depth-first mapping. A single subtree or a block of adjacent subtrees is assigned to each node processor. Each node processor proceeds to explore its group of subtrees using the hypothesize-and-test with backtracking search procedure as in the case of the simple depth-first mapping. As mentioned previously, due to the unpredictable nature of the search process some node processors may explore their assigned group of subtrees earlier than others. Thus it is virtually impossible to distribute the subtrees *a priori* between the processors so as to ensure perfect load sharing. In the depth-first mapping with load sharing, the host keeps a record of the status of each node processor. The host associates a *flag* with each node processor. The flag indicates whether the processor is *busy* or *idle*. When the interpretation tree search process is initiated, the status flag of all the processors set to *busy*. When a particular node processor completes exploring its group of subtrees, it conveys the result to the host and also signals the host to change its status flag from *busy* to *idle*. The host checks to determine the closest *busy* processor to the now *idle* processor in terms of the Hamming distance in the hypercube. The host interrupts the busy processor and signals it to transfer part of its workload to the idle processor. The busy processor transfers half of its present workload to the idle processor via a message. The idle processor on receipt of the message from the busy processor sends a message to the busy processor acknowledging the receipt of the workload and asking it to resume its task. Simultaneously, the idle processor sends a message to the host requesting the host to change its status flag from *idle* to *busy*. The communication sequence is depicted in Figure 9.4.

The depth-first mapping with load sharing manages to achieve load balancing without excessive inter-processor communication. The communication between the host and the node processors is limited to transfer of the result of the search process from the node processor to the host. The inter-processor communication is limited to the extent of load-sharing. Other than that, the individual node processors explore their respective subtrees independently of each other.

9.5.4 Experimental Results

The parallel interpretation tree search algorithm is implemented and tested on synthetic tactile data from two-dimensional scenes. Both single-object and multiple-object scenes are used. The interpretation tree search algorithm for

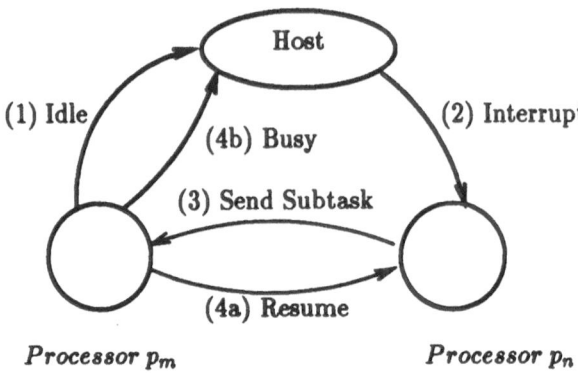

Figure 9.4: Communication sequence necessary for load sharing.

a single-object scene is modified slightly in order for it to be able to handle multiple-object scenes. This is done by addition of a *null* side (face) to each object model. The assignment of a sensory measurement to the null side (face) of an object model is equivalent to saying that the particular scene feature is not matched to any side (face) of the object model. The assignment of a sensory measurement to the null side (face) of an object model is not checked for constraint satisfaction.

Figure 9.5 shows an input scene containing a single object, whereas Figure 9.6 shows an input scene containing two objects. Table 9.1 summarizes the results of the parallel interpretation tree search using breadth-first mapping (BFM), depth-first mapping(DFM), and depth-first mapping with load sharing (DFMWLS), respectively, for the input scene shown in Figure 9.5. Table 9.2 summarizes the results of the parallel interpretation tree search using breadth-first mapping (BFM), depth-first mapping(DFM), and depth-first mapping with load sharing (DFMWLS), respectively, for the input scene shown in Figure 9.6. For each mapping technique the run time of the interpretation tree search process for different number of sensory measurements (N) is noted.

As can be seen from Tables 9.1 and 9.2, interpretation tree search with BFM was the most extensive in terms of running time for the interpretation tree search process. This could be attributed to the fact that the BFM entails constant broadcasting of information by each of the individual processors and also communication between the host and the node processors. Interpretation tree search with DFM was seen to be the fastest, since there was no inter-processor communication. However, the fact that DFM does not ensure a balanced load among the node processors is reflected in the different running times for the interpretation tree search at different node processors. In Tables 9.1 and 9.2 this fact has been noted by entering the maximum and minimum running times for the node processors. Interpretation tree search with DFMWLS is seen to

Figure 9.5: An input scene containing a single object.

Figure 9.6: An input scene containing multiple objects.

Table 9.1: Performance of the parallel interpretation tree search on a single object scene.

Search Technique		Number of sensory measurements		
		3	5	7
BFM		2410	3113	3140
DFM	max	3	5	5
	min	1	1	1
DFMWLS		214	216	194

Table 9.2: Performance of the parallel interpretation tree search on a multiple object scene.

Obj. No.	Search Technique		Number of sensory measurements		
			3	5	7
1	BFM		33128	34112	35186
	DFM	max	56	68	83
		min	14	17	26
	DFMWLS		887	1017	1218
2	BFM		21540	23115	24124
	DFM	max	47	58	74
		min	11	16	25
	DFMWLS		807	1004	1057

be a good compromise between the BFM and the DFM. The running time of interpretation tree search with DFMWLS is higher than that of interpretation tree search with DFM, which is the price we pay for load balancing. At the same time, the running time of interpretation tree search with DFMWLS is lower than that of interpretation tree search with BFM since the former avoids redundant inter-processor communication. Similar results are observed in the case of other input scenes.

Bibliography

[1] Acampora, A. S., and Winters, J. H. [1989] Three-dimensional ultrasonic vision for robotic applications. *IEEE Trans. Pattern Analysis and Machine Intelligence*, PAMI-11, Vol. 11, No. 3, (March), 291–303.

[2] Agin, G. J., and Binford, T. O. [1976] Computer description of curved objects. *IEEE Trans. Computers*, C-25, No. 4, (April), 439–449.

[3] Ahola, R., Heikkinen, T., and Manninen, M. [1985] 3-D image acquisition by scanning time-of-flight measurements. *Proc. Intl. Conf. on Advances in Image Processing and Pattern Recognition* (Pisa, Italy, Dec. 10-12), 447–453.

[4] Allen, P. K. [1988] Integrating vision and touch for object recognition tasks. *Intl. Journal Robotics Research*, Vol. 7, No. 6, (December), 15-33.

[5] Allen, P. K., and Michelman, P. [1990] Acquisition and interpretation of 3-D sensor data from touch. *IEEE Trans. Robotics and Automation*, Vol. 6, No. 4, (August), 397–404.

[6] Almasi, G. S., and Gottilieb, A. [1989] *Highly Parallel Computing*. Benjamin/Cummings Publishing Company, New York.

[7] Annaratone, M., Arnould, E., Gross, T., Kung, H. T., Lam, M. S., Mezilcioglu, O., Sarocky, K., and Webb, J. A. [1986] Warp architecture and implementation. *Proc. 13th Int. Sym. Computer Architecture*, Computer Science Press, 346–356.

[8] Asada, M., Ichikarva, H., and Tsuyi, S. [1988] Determining the surface orientation by projecting a stripe pattern. *IEEE Trans. Pattern Analysis Machine Intelligence*, PAMI-10, Vol. 10, No. 5, 749–754.

[9] Bajcsy, R., and Solina, F. [1987] Three dimensional object representation revisited. *Proc. Intl. Conf. Computer Vision* (London, U.K.), 231–240.

[10] Baker, H. H., and Bolles, R. [1985] Epipolar-plane image analysis: a technique for analyzing motion sequences. *Proc. IEEE Workshop on Computer Vision-Representation and Control* (Bellaire, MI, Oct. 13-16), 168–178.

[11] Ballard, D. H., and Brown, C. M. [1982] *Computer Vision*, Prentice-Hall Inc., New Jersey.

[12] Barnard, S. [1986] A stochastic approach to stereo vision. *Proc. 5th Natl. Conf. Artificial Intelligence* (Philadelphia, PA, Aug. 11-15), 676–680.

[13] Barnard, S. T., and Fischler, M. A. [1982] Computational stereo. *ACM Computing Surveys*, Vol. 14, No. 4, (December), 553–572.

[14] Barnard, S., and Thompson, W. B. [1980] Disparity analysis of images. *IEEE Trans. Pattern Analysis and Machine Intelligence*, PAMI-2, Vol. 2, No. 4, (July), 333–340.

[15] Barnes, G. H., Brown, R. M., Kato, M., Kuck, D. J., Slotnick, D. L., and Stokes, R. A. [1968] The ILLIAC IV computer. *IEEE Trans. Computers*, TC-17, Vol. 17, No. 8, (August), 746–757.

[16] Barr, A. H. [1981] Superquadrics and angle preserving transformations. *IEEE Computer Graphics and Applications*, Vol. 1, No. 1, (January), 11–23.

[17] Barr, A. H. [1984] Global and local deformation of solid primitives. *Computer graphics*, Vol. 18, No. 3, (July), 21–30.

[18] Barshan, B., and Kue, R. [1990] Differentiating sonar reflections from corners and planes by employing an intelligent sensor. *IEEE Trans. Pattern Analysis and Machine Intelligence*, PAMI-12, Vol. 12, No. 6, (June), 560–569.

[19] Batcher, K. [1980] Design of a massively parallel processor. *IEEE Trans. Computers*, TC-29, Vol. 29, No. 9, (September), 836–840.

[20] Beheim, G., and Fritsch, K. [1986] Range finding using frequency-modulated laser diode. *Applied Optics*, Vol 25, No. 9, (May), 1439–1442.

[21] Bergen, J. R., and Julesz B. [1983] Textons, the fundamental elements in preattentive vision and perception of textures. *Bell System Technical Journal*, Vol. 62, No. 6, (July-August), 1619–1644.

[22] Bergevin, R., and Levine, M. D. [1989] Generic object recognition: building coarse 3D descriptions from line drawings. *Proc. IEEE Workshop on Interpretation of 3D Scenes* (Austin, TX, November), 68–74.

[23] Besag, J. [1974] Spatial interaction and the statistical analysis of lattice systems. *Jour. Royal Statist. Soc.*, Series B, Vol. 36, 192–326.

[24] Besl, P. J. [1988a] Active optical range imaging sensors. *Machine Vision and Applications*, Vol. 1, 127–152.

[25] Besl, P. J. [1988b] Geometric modeling and computer vision. *Proc. IEEE*, Vol. 76, No. 8, (August), 936–958.

[26] Besl, P. J. [1990] Geometric signal processing. *Analysis and Interpretation of Range Images*, R. C. Jain and A. K. Jain (Eds.), Springer-Verlag, 141–387.

[27] Besl, P. J., and Jain, R. C. [1985] Three-dimensional object recognition. *ACM Comput. Surveys*, Vol. 17, No. 1,(March), 75–145.

[28] Besl, P. J., and Jain, R. C. [1986] Invariant surface characteristics for 3-D object recognition in range images. *Computer Vision, Graphics and Image Processing*, Vol. 33, 33–80.

[29] Besl, P. J., and Jain, R. C. [1988] Segmentation through variable order surface fitting. *IEEE Trans. Pattern Analysis and Machine Intelligence*, PAMI-10, Vol. 10, No. 2, (March), 167–192.

[30] Bhandarkar, S. M., and Siebert, A. [1992] Integrating edge and surface information for range image segmentation. *Pattern Recognition* (in press).

[31] Bhandarkar, S. M., and Suk, M. [1988] Hough clustering technique for surface matching. *Proc. IAPR Workshop on Computer Vision* (Tokyo, Japan, Oct. 12-14), 82–85.

[32] Bhandarkar, S. M., and Suk, M. [1991a] Pose verification as an optimal assignment problem. *Pattern Recognition Letters*, Vol. 12, 45–53.

[33] Bhandarkar, S. M., and Suk, M. [1991b] Sensitivity analysis for matching and pose computation using dihedral junctions. *Pattern Recognition*, Vol. 24, No. 6, (June), 505–513.

[34] Bhandarkar, S. M., Shankar, R. V., and Suk, M. [1991c] Exploiting parallelism in 3-D object recognition using the Connection Machine. *Robotics and Autonomous Systems*, Vol. 8, 291–309.

[35] Bierderman, I. [1985] Human image understanding: recent research and a theory. *Computer Vision, Graphics and Image Processing*, Vol. 32, 29–73.

[36] Biederman, I. [1987] Recognition-by-components: a theory of human image understanding. *Psychological Review*, Vol. 94, No. 2, 115–147.

[37] Binford, T. O. [1971] Visual perception by computer. *Proc. IEEE Conf. on Systems and Controls* (Miami, Florida, Dec.), 292–301.

[38] Binger, N., and Harris, S. J. [1987] Applications of laser radar technology. *Sensors*, Vol. 4, No. 4, 42–44.

[39] Bolles, R. C., and Horaud, P. [1986] 3DPO-a three-dimensional part orientation system. *Int. Journal Robotics Research*, Vol. 5, No. 3, (Fall), 3–26.

[40] Boult, T. E., and Gross, A. D. [1987] Recovery of superquadrics from depth information. *Proc. Spatial Reasoning and Multisensor Fusion Workshop*, (St. Charles, Illinois), 128–137.

[41] Boult, T. E., and Gross, A. D. [1988] Error of fit measures for recovering parametric solids. *Proc. Intl. Conf. Computer Vision*, 690–694.

[42] Bourdon, O., and Medioni, G. [1989] Object recognition using geometric hashing on the Connection Machine. Technical Report, Institute for Robotics and Intelligent Systems, University of Southern California, Los Angeles, California.

[43] Boyter, B. A., and Aggarwal, J. K. [1986] Recognition of polyhedra from range data. *IEEE Expert*, (Spring), 47–59.

[44] Boyer, K. L., and Kak, A. C. [1987] Color-encoded structured light for rapid active ranging. *IEEE Trans. Pattern Analysis Machine Intelligence*, PAMI-9, Vol. 9, No. 1, (January), 14–28.

[45] Brady, M., and Ponce, J. [1985] Toward a surface primal sketch. *Proc. IEEE Conf. Computer Vision and Pattern Recognition*, 420–425.

[46] Brooks, R. A. [1981] Symbolic reasoning among 3-D models and 2-D images. *Artificial Intelligence*, Vol. 17, 285–348.

[47] Brou, P. [1983] Using the gaussian image to find the orientation of an object. *Intl. Journal Robotics Research*, Vol. 3, No. 4, 89–125.

[48] Brown, C. M. [1981] Some mathematical and representational aspects of solid modeling. *IEEE Transactions on Pattern Analysis and Machine Intelligence*, PAMI-3, Vol. 3, No. 4, (July), 444–453.

[49] Campbell, D. [1986] Ultrasonic non-contact dimensional measurement. *Sensors*, (July), 37–43.

[50] Capocelli, R. M., and DeLuca, A. [1973] Fuzzy sets and decision theory. *Information and Control*, Vol. 23, 446–473.

[51] Chakravarty, I., and Freeman, H. [1982] Characteristic views as a basis for three-dimensional object recognition. *Proc. SPIE Conf. Robot Vision*, Vol. 336, 37–45.

[52] Chaudhary, V., and Aggarwal, J. K. [1990] Parallelism in computer vision: a review. *Parallel Algorithms for Machine Intelligence and Vision*, V. Kumar, P. S. Gopalakrishnan and L. N. Kanal (Eds.), Springer-Verlag, 271–309.

[53] Chavel, P., and Strand, T. C. [1984] Range measurement using Talbot diffraction imaging of gratings. *Applied Optics*, Vol. 23, No. 6, 862–871.

[54] Chen, H. H., and Huang, T. S. [1988] A survey of construction and manipulation of octrees. *Computer Vision Graphics Image Processing*, Vol. 43, 409–431.

[55] Chen, C., and Kak, A. C. [1989] A robot vision system for recognizing 3-D objects in low-order polynomial time. *IEEE Trans. Systems, Man, Cybernetics*, SMC-19, Vol. 19, No. 6, (November/December), 1535–1563.

[56] Chien, C. H., and Aggarwal, J. K. [1985] Recognition and matching of 3-D objects using quadtrees/octrees. *Proc. Third Workshop on Computer Vision*, (Bellaire, Michigan, October), 49–54.

[57] Chien, C. H., Sim, Y. B., and Aggarwal, J. K. [1988] Generation of volume/surface octree from range data. *Proc. IEEE Conf. Computer Vision Pattern Recognition*, 254–260.

[58] Chou, P., Brown, C., and Raman, R. [1987] A confidence based approach to the labeling problem. *Proc. IEEE Workshop on Computer Vision*, (Miami Beach, Florida), 51–56.

[59] Clemens, D. T., and Jacobs, D. W. [1991] Space and time bounds on indexing 3-D models from 2-D images. *IEEE Trans. Pattern Analysis Machine Intelligence*, PAMI-13, Vol. 13, No. 10, (October), 1007–1017.

[60] Cline, A. K. [1981] Surface smoothing by splines under tension. Technical Report CNA-170, Dept. of Computer Science, University of Texas, Austin, Texas.

[61] Clowes, M. [1971] On seeing things. *Artificial Intelligence*, Vol. 2, No. 1, 79–116.

[62] Connell, J. H. [1985] Learning shape descriptions: generating and generalizing models of visual objects. Technical Report AI-TR-853, MIT, Cambridge, MA.

[63] Crisman, J. D., and Webb, J. A. [1991] The Warp machine on Navlab. *IEEE Trans. Pattern Analysis and Machine Intelligence*, PAMI-13, Vol. 13, No. 5, (May), 451–465.

[64] Crowley, J. [1985] Dynamic world modeling for an intelligent mobile robot using a rotating ultra-sonic ranging device. *Proc. IEEE Conf. Robotics and Automation*, (St. Louis, MO, March), 735–741.

[65] Crowther, W., Goodhue, J., Gurwitz, R., Rettberg, R., and Thomas, R. [1985] The Butterfly parallel processor. *IEEE Computer Architecture Technical Committee Newsletter*, (September-December), 18–45.

[66] Cypher, R., and Sanz, J. L. C. [1989] SIMD architectures and algorithms for image processing and computer vision. *IEEE Trans. Acoustics, Speech and Signal processing*, ASSP-37, Vol. 37, No. 12, (December), 2158–2174.

[67] Cypher, R., Sanz, J. L. C., and Synder, L. [1987] Hypercube and shuffle-exchange algorithms for image component labeling. *Proc. 1987 Workshop on Computer Architecture for Pattern Analysis and Machine Intelligence*, (October), 5–10.

[68] Dario, P., Bergamasco, M., Ferni, D., Fiorillo, A., and Vaccarelli, A. [1987] Tactile perception in unstructured environments: a case study for rehabilitative robots application. *Proc. IEEE Intl. Conf. Robotics and Automation*, (Washington, DC), 2047–2054.

[69] Dario, P., and De Rossi, D. [1985] Tactile sensors and the gripping challenge. *IEEE Spectrum*, (August), 46–52.

[70] Dhome, M., and Kasvand, T. [1987] Polyhedra recognition by hypothesis accumulation. *IEEE Trans. Pattern Analysis and Machine Intelligence*, PAMI-9, Vol. 9, No. 3, (May), 429–438.

[71] Dubois, D., and Prade, H. [1980] *Fuzzy Sets and Systems: Theory and Applications.* Academic Press Inc., New York.

[72] Duff, M. J. B. [1978] Review of the CLIP image processing system. *Proc. AFIPS Nat. Comp. Conf.*, 1055–1060.

[73] Duff, M. J. B. (ed.) [1986] *Intermediate-level Image Processing.* Academic Press Inc., New York.

[74] Duff, M. J. B. and Levialdi, S. (Eds.) [1981] *Languages and Architectures for Image Processing.* Academic Press Inc., New York.

[75] Eggert, D., and Bowyer, K. [1989] Computing the orthographic projection aspect graph of solids of revolution, *Proc. IEEE Workshop on Interpretation of 3-D Scenes*, (Austin, TX, November), 102–108.

[76] Electro-Optical Information Systems [1990] Product Information. EOIS, Santa Monica, CA.

[77] Eshera, M. A., and Fu, K. S. [1984] A graph matching distance measure for image analysis. *IEEE Trans. Systems, Man and Cybernetics*, SMC-14, Vol. 14, No. 3, (May/June), 398–408.

[78] Eshera, M. A., and Fu, K. S. [1988] An image understanding system using attributed symbolic representation and inexact graph matching. *IEEE Trans. Pattern Analysis and Machine Intelligence*, PAMI-8, Vol. 8, No. 5, (September), 604–617.

[79] Ettinger, G. J. [1987] Hierarchical object recognition using libraries of parameterized model subparts. Technical Report AI-TR-963, MIT, Cambridge, MA.

[80] Fan, T. J., Medioni, G., and Nevatia, R. [1987] Segmented descriptions of 3-D surfaces. *IEEE Journal on Robotics and Automation*, RA-3, Vol. 3, No. 6, (December), 527–538.

[81] Fan, T. J., Medioni, G., and Nevatia, R. [1989] Recognizing 3-D objects using surface descriptions. *IEEE Trans. Pattern Analysis and Machine Intelligence*, PAMI-11, Vol. 11, No. 11, (November), 1140–1157.

[82] Faugeras, O. D., and Herbert, M. [1986] The representation, recognition and locating of 3-D objects. *The Int. Journal of Robotics Research*, Vol. 5, No. 3, (Fall), 27–52.

[83] Faux, I. D., and Pratt, M. J. [1979] *Computational geometry for design and manufacture*. John Wiley and Sons, New York.

[84] Fearing, R. S. [1990] Tactile sensing mechanisms. *Intl. Journal of Robotics Research*, Vol. 9, No. 3, (June), 3–23

[85] Flynn, M. J. [1972] Some computer organizations and their effectiveness. *IEEE Trans. Computers*, Vol. C-21, 1972, 948–960.

[86] Flynn, P. J., and Jain, A. K. [1988] Surface classification : hypothesis testing and estimation. *Proc. IEEE Conf. Computer Vision and Pattern Recognition*, (June), 261–267.

[87] Flynn, P. J., and Jain, A. K. [1989] On reliable curvature estimation. *Proc. IEEE Conf. Computer Vision and Pattern Recognition*, (June) 1989, 110–116.

[88] Flynn, P. J., and Jain, A. K. [1991a] CAD-based computer vision: from CAD models to relational graphs. *IEEE Trans. Pattern Analysis Machine Intelligence*, PAMI-13, Vol. 13, No. 2, (February), 114–132.

[89] Flynn, P. J., and Jain, A. K. [1991b] BONSAI: 3-D object recognition using constrained search. *IEEE Trans. Pattern Analysis and Machine Intelligence*, PAMI-13, Vol. 13, No. 10, (October), 1066–1074.

[90] Foley, J. D., Van Dam, A., Feiner, S. K., and Hughes, J. F. [1990] *Computer Graphics, Principles and Practice*, Second Edition. Addison-Wesley Publishing Company, New York.

[91] Ganapathy, S. [1975] Reconstruction of scenes containing polyhedra from a stereo pair of views. Stanford AI Lab Memo, AIM-272, Stanford University, Stanford, CA.

[92] Gargantini, I. [1982] Linear octrees for fast processing of three-dimensional objects. *Computer Graphics Image Processing*, Vol. 20, 356–374.

[93] Gasvik, K. J. [1983] Moire technique by means of digital image processing. *Applied Optics*, Vol. 22, No. 23, 3543–3548.

[94] Geman, S., and Geman, D. [1984] Stochastic relaxation, Gibbs distributions and the Bayesian restoration of images. *IEEE Trans. Pattern Analysis and Machine Intelligence*, PAMI-6, Vol. 6, (December), 721–441.

[95] Gigus, Z., and Malik, J. [1990] Computing the aspect graph for line drawings of polyhedral objects. *IEEE Trans. Pattern Analysis and Machine Intelligence*, PAMI-12, Vol. 12, No. 2, (February), 113–122.

[96] Goad, C., [1983] Special purpose automatic programming for 3-D model-based vision. *Proc. DARPA Image Understanding Workshop*, (Arlington, VA), 94–104.

[97] Grimson, W. E. L. [1985] Computational experiments with a feature-based stereo algorithm. *IEEE Trans. Pattern Analysis and Machine Intelligence*, PAMI-7, Vol. 7, No. 1, (January), 17–34.

[98] Grimson, W. E. L. [1986] The combinatorics of local constraints in model-based recognition and localization from sparse data. *Journal ACM*, Vol. 33, No. 4, (October), 658–686.

[99] Grimson, W. E. L. [1990] The combinatorics of object recognition in cluttered environments using constrained search. *Artificial Intelligence*, Vol. 44, 121–165.

[100] Grimson, W. E. L., and Huttenlocher, D. P. [1990a] On the sensitivity of the Hough transform for object recognition. *IEEE Trans. Pattern Analysis and Machine Intelligence*, PAMI-12, Vol. 12, No. 3, (March), 255–274.

[101] Grimson, W. E. L., and Huttenlocher, D. P. [1990b] On the sensitivity of geometric hashing. *Proc. IEEE International Conference on Computer Vision*, (Osaka, Japan), 334–338.

[102] Grimson, W. E. L, and Lozano-Perez, T. [1984] Model-based recognition and localization from sparse range or tactile data. *The International Journal of Robotics Research*, Vol. 3, No. 3, (Fall), 3–35.

[103] Grimson, W. E. L, and Lozano-Perez, T. [1987] Localizing overlapping parts by searching the interpretation tree. *IEEE Trans. Pattern Analysis and Machine Intelligence*, PAMI-9, Vol. 9, No. 4, (July), 469–482.

[104] Grossman, P.,[1987] Depth from focus. *Pattern Recognition Letters*, Vol. 5, No. 1, (January), 63–69.

[105] Gupta, A., Bogoni, L., and Bajcsy, R. [1989] Quantitative and qualitative measures for the evaluation of superquadric models. *Proc. IEEE Workshop Interpretation of 3-D Scenes*, (Austin, Texas), 162–169.

[106] Guzman, A. [1968] Computer Recognition of Three-Dimensional Objects in a Visual Scene. Ph.D. Thesis, MAC-TR-59, Project MAC, MIT, Cambridge, MA.

[107] Hackwood, S., Beni, G., and Nelson, T. J. [1986] Torque sensitive tactile array for robotics. *Robot Sensors Vol. 2: Tactile and Non-Vision*, A. Pugh (Ed.), Springer-Verlag, New York, 123–131.

[108] Haralick, R. M. [1984] Digital step edges from zero crossing of second directional derivatives. *IEEE Trans. Pattern Analysis and Machine Intelligence*, PAMI-6, Vol. 6, No. 1, (January), 58–68.

[109] Haralick, R. M., Watson, L. T., and Laffey, T. J. [1983] The topographic primal sketch. *Int. Journal of Robotics Research*, Vol. 2, No. 1, (Spring), 50–72.

[110] Harrison, D. D., and Weir, M. P. [1990] High speed triangulation-based 3-D imaging with orthonormal projections and error detection. *IEEE Trans. Pattern Analysis Machine Intelligence*, PAMI-12, Vol. 12, No. 4, (April) 1990, 409–416.

[111] Heikkinen, T., Ahola, R., Manninen, M., and Myllyla, R. [1986] Recent results of the performance analysis of a 3D sensor based on time-of-flight. *Proc. SPIE Intl. Symposium on Optical and Optoelectronic Applied Sciences and Engineering*, (Quebec, Canada), 427–433.

[112] Hersman, M., Goodwin, F., Kenyon, S., and Slotwinski, A. [1987] Coherent laser radar application to 3D vision and metrology. *Proc. Vision-87 Conference*, (Detroit, MI, June 8-11), 3.1-3.12.

[113] Hillis, W. D., [1985] *The Connection Machine*. MIT Press, Cambridge, MA.

[114] Hoffman, C. M. [1989] *Geometric and Solid Modeling: An Introduction*. Morgan Kaufman, Los Altos, CA.

[115] Hoffman, R., and Jain, A. K.[1987] Segmentation and classification of range images. *IEEE Transactions Pattern Analysis and Machine Intelligence*, PAMI-9, Vol. 9, No. 5, (September), 608–620.

[116] Hoffman, D., and Richards, W. [1985] Parts of recognition. *Cognition*, Vol. 18, 65–96.

[117] Horn, B. K. P. [1977] Understanding image intensities. *Artificial Intelligence*, Vol. 8, No. 2, 201–231.

[118] Horn, B. K. P. [1984] Extended Gaussian images. *Proc. IEEE*, Vol. 72, No. 12, (December), 1671–1686.

[119] Horn, B. K. P., and Ikeuchi, K. [1984] The mechanical manipulation of randomly oriented parts. *Scientific American*, Vol. 251, No. 2, 100–111.

[120] Hough, P. V. C, [1962] A method and means for recognizing complex patterns. U.S. Patent 3,069,654.

[121] Hu, G., and Stockman, G., [1989] 3-D surface solution using structured light and constraint propagation. *IEEE Trans. Pattern Analysis Machine Intelligence*, PAMI-11, Vol. 11, No. 4, (April), 390–402.

[122] Huffman, D. A. [1971] Impossible objects as nonsense sentences. *Machine Intelligence 6*, B. Meltzer and D. Michie (Eds.), Edinburgh University Press, Edinburgh, Scotland.

[123] Hwang, K., and Briggs, F. A. [1984] *Computer Architecture and Parallel Processing*. McGraw-Hill, New York.

[124] Ikeuchi, K. [1981] Recognition of 3-D objects using the extended Gaussian image. *Proc. 7th Intl. Conf. Artificial Intelligence*, 595–600.

[125] Ikeuchi, K. [1987] Generating an interpretation tree from a CAD model for 3-D object recognition in bin-picking tasks. *The International Journal of Computer Vision*, Vol. 1, No. 2, 145–165.

[126] Ikeuchi, K., and Hong, K. S. [1991] Determining linear shape change: toward automatic generation of object recognition programs. *CVGIP: Image Understanding*, Vol. 53, No. 2, (March), 154–170.

[127] Ikeuchi, K., and Horn, B. K. P. [1981] Numerical shape from shading and occluding boundaries. *Artificial Intelligence*, Vol. 17, Nos. 1-3, (August), 141–184.

[128] Ikeuchi, K., and Kanade, T. [1988] Automatic generation of object recognition programs. *Proceedings of the IEEE*, Vol. 76, No. 8, (August), 1016–1035.

[129] Inokuchi, S., Nita, T., Matsuda F., and Sakurai, Y. [1982] A three-dimensional edge-region operator for range images. *Proc. 6th International Conference on Pattern Recognition*, 918–920.

[130] Inokuchi, S., Sato, K., and Matsuda, F. [1984] Range imaging system for 3-D object recognition. *Proc. Seventh Intl. Conf. Pattern Recognition*, (Montreal, Canada, July 30 - Aug. 2), 806–809.

[131] Jackins, C., and Tanimoto, S. L. [1980] Oct-trees and their use in presenting 3-D objects. *Computer Graphics and Image Processing*, Vol. 14, 249–270.

[132] Jain, A. K., and Dubes, R. C. [1988] *Algorithms for Clustering Data*. Prentice Hall, New York.

[133] Jain, A. K., and Hoffman, R. L. [1988] Evidence-based recognition of 3-D objects. *IEEE Trans. Pattern Analysis and Machine Intelligence*, PAMI-10, Vol. 10, No. 6, (November), 783–802.

[134] Jain, A. K., and Nadabar, S. G. [1990] MRF model-based segmentation of range images. *Proc. Int. Conf. Computer Vision*, (December), 667–671.

[135] Jain, R. C., Bartlett, S. L., and O'Brien, N. [1987] Motion stereo using ego-motion complex logarithmic mapping, *IEEE Trans. Pattern Analysis Machine Intelligence*, PAMI-9, Vol. 9, No. 3, (May), 356–369.

[136] Jain, R. C., and Jain, A. K. [1989] Report on range image understanding workshop, East Lansing, Michigan, March 21-23, 1988. *Machine Vision and Applications*, Vol. 2, 45–60.

[137] Jarvis, R. A. [1983a] A perspective on range finding techniques for computer vision, *IEEE Trans. Pattern Analysis Machine Intelligence*, PAMI-5, Vol. 5, No. 2, (March), 122–139.

[138] Jarvis, R. A. [1983b] A laser time-of-flight range scanner for robotic vision. *IEEE Trans. Pattern Analysis Machine Intelligence*, PAMI-5, Vol. 5, (September), 505–512.

[139] Julesz, B., and Bergen, J. R. [1983] Textons - the fundamental elements in preattentive vision and the perception of textures. *Bell Systems Technical Journal*, Vol. 62, No. 6, (July-August), 1619–1644.

[140] Kak, A. C. [1985] Depth perception for robot vision. *Handbook of Industrial Robotics*, Wiley, New York, 272–319.

[141] Kandel, A. [1978] Fuzzy sets, fuzzy algebra and fuzzy statistics. *Proc. IEEE*, Vol. 66, No. 12, (December), 1619–1630.

[142] Kaufmann, A. [1975] *Introduction to the Theory of Fuzzy Subsets*. Vol. 1, Academic Press Inc., New York.

[143] Kaufmann, A., and Gupta, M. M. [1985] *Introduction to Fuzzy Arithmetic*. Van Nostrand Reinhold Company, New York.

[144] Kim, W. Y., and Kak, A. C. [1991] 3-D object recognition using bipartite matching in discrete relaxation. *IEEE Trans. Pattern Analysis and Machine Intelligence*, PAMI-13, Vol. 13, No. 3, (March), 224–251.

[145] King, A. A., and White, R. M [1985] Tactile sensing array based on forming and detecting an optical image, *Sensors and Actuators*, Vol. 8, 49–63.

[146] Klir, G. J., and Folger, T. A. [1988] *Fuzzy Sets, Uncertainty and Information*, Prentice Hall, New Jersey.

[147] Knoll, T. F., and Jain, R. C. [1985] Recognizing partially visible objects using feature indexed hypotheses. Technical Report RSD-TR-10-85, Robot Systems Division, Center for Research on Integrated Manufacturing, University of Michigan, Ann Arbor, Michigan.

[148] Koenderink, J. J., and Van Doorn, A. J. [1979] Internal representation of solid shape with respect to vision. *Biological Cybernetics*, Vol. 32, No. 4, 211–216.

[149] Korn, M. R., and Dyer, C. R. [1987] 3-D multiview object representations for model-based object recognition. *Pattern Recognition*, Vol. 20, No. 1, (January), 91–103.

[150] Korn, G. A., and Korn, T. M. [1972] *Mathematical Handbook for Scientists and Engineers*, McGraw Hill, New York.

[151] Kowalik, J. S. (Ed.) [1986] *Coupling Symbolic and Numerical Computing in Expert Systems*. North Holland, Amsterdam, Netherlands.

[152] Kowalik, J. S., and Kitzmiller, C. T. (Eds.) [1988] *Coupling Symbolic and Numerical Computing in Expert Systems, II*. North Holland, Amsterdam, Netherlands.

[153] Kriegman, D. J., and Ponce, J. [1990] Computing exact aspect graphs of curved objects: solids of revolution. *Intl. Journal Computer Vision*, Vol. 5, No. 2, 119–136.

[154] Krishnapuram, R., and Casasent, D. [1989] Determination of three-dimensional object location and orientation from range images. *IEEE Trans. Pattern Analysis and Machine Intelligence*, PAMI-11, Vol. 11, No. 11, (November), 1158–1167.

[155] Krotov, E., and Martin, J. P. [1986] Range from focus. *Proc. IEEE Intl. Conf. Robotics and Automation*, (San Francisco, CA, April 7-10), 1093–1098.

[156] Kuipers, B. J., and Byun, Y. T. [1988] A robust qualitative method for robot spatial learning. *Proc. Seventh National Congress on Artificial Intelligence*, (Saint Paul, MN, August), 774–779.

[157] Kung, H. T. [1982] Why Systolic Architectures?. *IEEE Computer*, Vol. 15, (January), 37–46.

[158] Lamdan, Y., and Wolfson, H. J. [1988] Geometric hashing: a general and efficient model-based recognition scheme. *Proc. IEEE International Conference on Computer Vision*, (London, U.K.), 238–249.

[159] Langridge, D. J. [1984] Detection of discontinuities in the first derivatives of surfaces. *Computer Vision Graphics and Image Processing*, Vol. 27, 291–308.

[160] Lee, Y. T., and Requicha, A. A. [1982] Algorithms for computing the volume and other integral properties of solids II. *Comm. ACM*, Vol. 25, 642–650.

[161] Leger, J. R., and Snyder, L. A. [1984] Real-time depth measurement and display using Fresnel diffraction and white-light processing. *Applied Optics*, Vol. 23, No. 10, 1655–1670.

[162] Leighton, F. T., [1982] Parallel computations using mesh of trees. Technical Report, MIT, Cambridge, MA.

[163] Levialdi, S., (Ed.) [1985] *Integrated Technology for Parallel Image Processing*. Academic Press Inc., New York.

[164] Levitt, T. S., and Lawton, D. T. [1990] Qualitative navigation for mobile robots. *Artificial Intelligence*, Vol. 44, 305–360.

[165] Lewis, R. A., and Johnston, A. R. [1977] A scanning laser range finder for a robotic vehicle. *Proc. 5th Intl. Joint Conf. Artificial Intelligence*, (Cambridge, MA, Aug. 22-25), 762–768.

[166] Li, H., and Maresca, M. [1989] Polymorphic-torus architectures for computer vision. *IEEE Trans. Pattern Analysis Machine Intelligence*, PAMI-11, Vol. 11, No. 3, (March), 244–257.

[167] Lin, W. C., and Chen, T. W. [1988] CSG-based object recognition using range images. *Proc. 9th Int. Conf. Pattern Recognition*, (November), 99–103.

[168] Little, J. J. [1985] Determining object attitude from extended Gaussian images. *Proc. 9th Intl. Conf. Artificial Intelligence*, 960–963.

[169] Little, J. J., Blelloch, G. E., and Cass, T. A. [1989] Algorithmic techniques for computer vision on a fine-grained parallel architecture, *IEEE Trans. Pattern Analysis and Machine Intelligence*, PAMI-11, Vol. 11, No. 3, (March), 244–257.

[170] Lowe, D. G. [1985] *Perceptual Organization and Visual Recognition.* Kluwer Academic Publishers, Boston, MA.

[171] Lowe, D. G. [1987] Three-dimensional object recognition from single two-dimensional images. *Artificial Intelligence*, Vol. 31, 355–395.

[172] Mader, D. L. [1985] Holographic interferometry of pipes: precision interpretation by least square fitting. *Applied Optics*, Vol. 24, No. 22, 3784–3790.

[173] Malik, J. [1987] Interpreting line drawings of curved objects. *International Journal of Computer Vision*, Vol. 1, No. 1, 17–37.

[174] Malik, J. [1989] Recovering three-dimensional shape from a single image of a curved object. *IEEE Trans. Pattern Analysis and Machine Intelligence*, Vol. 11, No. 6, (June), 555–566.

[175] Marr, D. [1982] *Vision.* Freeman, San Francisco, CA.

[176] Marr, D., and Nishihara, H. K. [1978] Representation and recognition of the spatial organization of three-dimensional shapes. *Proc. Royal Society of London*, Vol. B:200, 269–294.

[177] Marr, D., and Poggio, T. [1976] Cooperative computation of stereo disparity. *Science*, Vol. 194, 283–287.

[178] Marroquin, J., Mitter, S., and Poggio, T. [1987] Probabilistic solution of ill-posed problems in computational vision. *Journal of American Statistical Association*, Vol. 82, 76–89.

[179] Martin, W. N., and Aggarwal, J. K. [1983] Volumetric descriptions of objects from multiple views. *IEEE Trans. Pattern Analysis Machine Intelligence*, PAMI-5, Vol. 5, No. 2, (March), 150–158.

[180] Meagher, D. [1982a] Geometrical modeling using octree encoding. *Computer Graphics and Image Processing*, Vol. 19, 129–147.

[181] Meagher, D. [1982b] Efficient synthetic image generation of arbitrary 3-D objects. *Proc. Intl. Conf. Pattern Recognition and Image Processing*, (Las Vegas, Nevada, June), 473–478.

[182] Miller, R., and Stout, Q. [1985] Geometric algorithms for digitized pictures on a mesh connected computer. *IEEE Trans. Pattern Analysis Machine Intelligence*, PAMI-7, Vol. 7, No. 2, (March), 216–218.

[183] Miller, R., and Stout, Q. [1987] Data movement techniques for the pyramidal machine. *SIAM Journal of Comp.*, Vol. 16, No. 1, (February), 38–60.

[184] Mitiche, A., and Aggarwal, J. K. [1983] Detection of edges using range information. *IEEE Trans. Pattern Analysis and Machine Intelligence*, PAMI-5, Vol. 5, No. 2, (March), 174–178.

[185] Mott, D. H., Lee, M. H., and Nicholls, H. R. [1986] An experimental very high resolution tactile sensor array. *Robot Sensors Vol. 2: Tactile and Non-vision*, A. Pugh (Ed.), Springer-Verlag, New York, 179–188.

[186] Munkres, J. [1957] Algorithms for the assignment and transportation problems. *Journal SIAM*, Vol. 5, No. 1, (March), 32–38.

[187] Nackman, L. R. [1984] Two dimensional critical point configuration graphs. *IEEE Trans. Pattern Analysis and Machine Intelligence*, PAMI-6, Vol. 6, No. 4, (July), 442–449.

[188] Nagata, T., and Jha, H. B. [1988] Determining orientation, location and size of primitive surfaces by a modified Hough transformation technique. *Pattern Recognition*, Vol. 21, No. 5, (May), 481–491.

[189] Naik, S. M., and Jain, R. C. [1988] Spline-based surface fitting on range images for CAD applications. *Proc. IEEE Conf. on Computer Vision and Pattern Recognition*, 249–253.

[190] Nevatia, R., and Binford, T. O. [1977] Description and recognition of curved objects. *Artificial Intelligence*, Vol. 8, 77–98.

[191] Newport Corporation [1990] Product information, design and testing with holography. *Machine Vision Component*, Fountain Valley, CA.

[192] Nicholls, H. R., and Lee, M. H. [1989] A survey of robot tactile sensing technology. *Intl. Journal Robotics Research*, Vol. 8, No. 3, (June), 3–30.

[193] Nitzan, D. [1988] Three dimensional vision structure for robot applications. *IEEE Trans. Pattern Analysis Machine Intelligence*, PAMI-10, Vol. 10, No. 3, (May), 291–309.

[194] Papoulis, A. [1984] *Probability, Random Variables and Stochastic Processes*, McGraw Hill Book Co., New York.

[195] Paul, R. P. [1981] *Robot Manipulators: Mathematics, Programming and Control*. MIT Press, Cambridge, MA.

[196] Pentland, A. P. [1986] Perceptual organization and representation of natural form. *Artificial Intelligence*, Vol. 28, No. 2, 293–331.

[197] Pentland, A. P. [1987] A new sense of depth of field. *IEEE Trans. Pattern Analysis Machine Intelligence*, PAMI-9, Vol. 9, No. 4, (July), 523–531.

[198] Pentland, A. P. [1990] Automatic extraction of deformable part models. *Intl. Journal of Computer Vision*, Vol. 4, 107–126.

[199] Pirodda, L. [1982] Shadow and projection Moire techniques for absolute and relative mapping of surface shapes. *Optical Engineering*, Vol. 21, 640–682.

[200] Plantinga, W. H., and Dyer, C. R. [1986] An algorithm for constructing the aspect graph. *Proc. 27th IEEE Symposium on the Foundation of Computer Science*, (New York), 123–131.

[201] Plantinga, W. H., and Dyer, C. R. [1990] Visibility, occlusion and the aspect graph. *Intl. Journal Computer Vision*, Vol. 5, No. 2, 137–160.

[202] Ponce, J. [1990] Straight homogeneous generalized cylinders: differential geometry and uniqueness results. *International Journal of Computer Vision*, Vol. 4, 79–100.

[203] Ponce, J., and Brady, M. [1985] Toward a surface primal sketch. *Proc. IEEE Intl. Conf. Robotics and Automation*, (St. Louis, MO, March), 420–425.

[204] Ponce, J., Chelberg, D., and Mann, W. [1989] Invariant properties of straight homogeneous generalized cylinders and their contours. *IEEE Trans. Pattern Analysis Machine Intelligence*, PAMI-11, Vol. 11, No. 9, 951–966.

[205] Preston Jr., K., and Uhr, L. (Eds.) [1982] *Multicomputers and Image Processing: Algorithms and Programs*. Academic Press Inc., New York.

[206] Raibert, M. H. [1984] An all digital VLSI tactile sensor array. *Proc. Intl. Conf. Robotics*, (Washington, DC), 314–319.

[207] Ramamoorthy, C. V., and Sheu, P. C. [1988] Object-oriented systems. *IEEE Expert*, (Fall), 9–15.

[208] Ramamoorthy, G. [1991] *Model-based tracking using motion from motion.* Ph.D. Dissertation, Syracuse University, Syracuse, New York.

[209] Ramamoorthy, G., Shankar, R. V., and Suk, M. [1989] Pose determination using model-vertex pairs on the Connection Machine. *Proc. IEEE Int. Workshop for Tools on AI*, 1145–1150.

[210] Rao, K., and Nevatia, R. [1988] Generalized cone descriptions from sparse 3-D data. *International Journal of Computer Vision*, Vol. 2, No. 1, 22–40.

[211] Reeves, A. P. [1984] Parallel computer architectures for image processing. *Computer Vision Graphics Image Processing*, Vol. 25, 68–88.

[212] Reid, G. T. [1986] Automatic fringe pattern analysis: a review. *Optics and Lasers in Engineering*, Vol. 7, 37–68.

[213] Requicha, A. A. [1980] Representation for rigid solids : theory, methods and systems. *ACM Comput. Surveys*, Vol. 12, No. 4, 437–464.

[214] Requicha, A. A., and Voelcker, H. [1982] Solid modeling: a historical summary and contemporary assessment. *IEEE Computer Graphics and Applications*, Vol. 2, No. 2, (March), 9–24.

[215] Requicha, A. A., and Voelcker, H. [1983] Solid modeling: current status and research directions. *IEEE Computer Graphics and Applications*, Vol. 3, No. 7, (October), 25–37.

[216] Rieger, J. H. [1987] On the classification of views of piecewise smooth objects. *Image and Vision Computing*, Vol. 5, No. 2, (May), 91–97.

[217] Rioux, M. [1984] Laser range finder based upon synchronized scanners. *Applied Optics*, Vol. 23, No. 21, 3837–3844.

[218] Rioux, M., and Blais, F. [1986] Compact 3-D camera for robotic applications. *Journal Optical Society of America*, Vol. 3, No. 9, (September), 1518–1521.

[219] Robertson, B. E., and Walkden, A. J. [1986] Tactile sensor system for robotics. *Robot Sensors, Vol. 2: Tactile and Non-Vision*, A. Pugh (Ed.), Springer-Verlag, New York, 89–97.

[220] Rosenfeld, A., and Kak, A. C. [1982] *Digital Picture Processing.* 2nd Edition, Vols. 1 and 2, Academic Press Inc., New York.

[221] Russell, R. A. [1985] Object recognition using articulated whisker probes. *Proc. 15th Intl. Symposium Industrial Robots*, (U.K.), 605–612.

[222] Sadjadi, F. A., and Hall, E. L. [1980] Three dimensional moment invariants. *IEEE Trans. Pattern Analysis and Machine Intelligence*, PAMI-2, Vol. 2, No. 3, (March), 127–136.

[223] Samet, H. [1980] Region representation: quadtrees from binary arrays. *Computer Graphics and Image Processing*, Vol. 13, 88–93.

[224] Samet, H. [1990] *The Design and Analysis of Spatial Data Structures.* Addison-Wesley Publishing Company, Reading, Massachussetts.

[225] Sampson, R. E. [1987] 3D range sensor via phase shift detection. *IEEE Computer*, Vol. 20, No. 8, (August), 23–24.

[226] Sasaki, O. and Okazaki, H. [1986a] Sinusoidal phase modulating interferometry for surface profile measurement. *Applied Optics*, Vol. 25, No. 18, 3137–3140.

[227] Sasaki, O., and Okazaki, H. [1986b] Analysis of measurement in sinusoidal phase modulating interferometry. *Applied Optics*, Vol. 25, No. 18, 3152–3158.

[228] Sato, N., Heginbotham, H., and Pugh, A. [1986] A method for 3D part identification by tactile transducer. *Robot Sensors Vol. 2: Tactile and Non-Vision*, A. Pugh (Ed.), Springer-Verlag, New York, 133–143.

[229] Sato, K., and Inokuchi, S. [1985] 3D surface measurement by space encoding range imaging. *Journal Robotic Systems*, Vol. 2, No. 1, 27–39.

[230] Seitz, C. L. [1985] The Cosmic Cube. *Communications of the ACM*, Vol. 28, No. 1, (January), 22–33.

[231] Shafer, S. A. [1985] *Shadows and Silhouettes in Computer Vision.* Kluwer Academic Publishers, Boston, Massachussetts.

[232] Shaw, D. E. [1984] SIMD and MSIMD variants of the NON-VON supercomputer. *Proc. IEEE COMPCON '84*, (March), 360–363.

[233] Shrikhande, N., and Stockman, G. [1989] Surface orientation from a projected grid. *IEEE Trans. Pattern Analysis Machine Intelligence*, PAMI-11, Vol. 11, No. 6, (June), 650–655.

[234] Siegel, H. J. [1981] PASM: A reconfigurable multimicrocomputer for image processing. *Languages and Architectures for Image Processing*, M. J. B. Duff and S. Levialdi, (Eds.), Academic Press Inc., New York.

[235] Siegel, D. M., Drucker S. M., and Garabicta, I. [1987] Performance analysis of a tactile sensor. *Proc. IEEE Intl. Conf. Robotics and Automation*, (Washington, DC), 1493–1499.

[236] Skolnick, M. I. [1962] *Introduction to Radar Systems.* McGraw Hill, New York.

[237] Smith, D. R., and Kanade, T. [1986] Autonomous scene description with range imagery. *Computer Vision, Graphics and Image Processing*, Vol. 31, 322–334.

[238] Solina, F., and Bajcsy, R. [1990] Recovery of parametric models from range images: the case for superquadrics with global deformations. *IEEE Trans. Pattern Analysis Machine Intelligence*, PAMI-12, Vol. 12, No. 2, (February), 131–147.

[239] Srinivasan, Y., and Lumia, R. [1989] A pseudo interferometric laser range finder for robot applications. *IEEE Trans. Robotics and Automation*, RA-5, Vol. 5, No. 1, (February), 98–105.

[240] Sripadisvarakul, T., and Jain, R. C. [1989] Generating aspect graphs for curved objects. *Proc. IEEE Workshop Interpretation of 3-D Scenes*, (Austin, TX, December), 109–115.

[241] Stein, F., and Medioni, G. [1992] Structural indexing: efficient 3-D object recognition. *IEEE Trans. Pattern Analysis Machine Intelligence*, PAMI-14, Vol. 14, No. 2, (February), 125–145.

[242] Stockman, G. [1987] Object recognition and localization via pose clustering, *Computer Vision, Graphics and Image Processing*, Vol. 40, 361–387.

[243] Stolfo, S. J., and Miranker, D. P. [1986] The DADO production system machine. *Jour. Parallel and Distributed Computing*, Vol. 3, 269–296.

[244] Svetkoff, D. J. [1986] Towards a high resolution video rate, 3D sensor for machine vision. *Proc. SPIE Conf. Optics, Illumination and Image Sensing for Machine Vision*, Vol. 728, (Cambridge, MA, Oct. 30-31), 302–309.

[245] Talbot, H. [1836] Facts relating to optical sciences, *Philosophy Magazine*, Vol. 9, No. 4, 401–407.

[246] Tamminen, M., Karnonen, O., and Mantyla, M. [1984] Ray-casting and block model conversion using a spatial index. *Computer Aided Design*, Vol. 16, 203–208.

[247] Tanimoto, S. L., Ligocki, T. J., and Ling, R. [1987] A prototype pyramid machine for hierarchical cellular logic. *Parallel Hierarchical Computer Vision*, L. Uhr (Ed.), Academic Press Inc., New York.

[248] Technical Arts Corp. [1990] Product literature. Redmond, WA.

[249] Thinking Machines Inc. [1987] *Connection Machine model CM-2 technical summary*. Thinking Machines Technical Report HA87-4, Thinking Machines Corp., Cambridge, MA.

[250] Thinking Machines Inc. [1988] **Lisp reference manual*. Thinking Machines Corp., Cambridge, MA.

[251] Tou, J. T., and Gonzalez, R. C. [1974] *Pattern Recognition Principles*. Addison Wesley Publishing Company, Reading, MA.

[252] Tozer, B. A., Glannville, R., Gordon, A. L., Little, M. J., Webster, J. M., and Wright, D. G. [1985] Holography applied to inspection and measurement in an industrial environment. *Optical Engineering*, Vol. 24, No. 5, (September-October), 746–753.

[253] Tucker, L. W., and Robertson, G. G. [1988] Architecture and applications of the Connection Machine. *IEEE Computer*, (August), 26–38.

[254] Turney, J. L., Mudge, T. N., and Volz, R. A. [1985] Recognizing partially occluded parts. *IEEE Trans. Pattern Analysis Machine Intelligence*, PAMI-7, Vol. 7, No. 4, (July), 410–421.

[255] Uhr, L. [1984] Algorithm-structured computer arrays and networks. *Architectures and Processes for Images, Percepts, Models and Information*, Academic Press Inc., New York.

[256] Uhr, L. (Ed.) [1987a] *Parallel Computer Vision*. Academic Press Inc., New York.

[257] Uhr, L. [1987b] *Multicomputer Architectures For Artificial Intelligence: Toward Fast, Robust, Parallel Systems*. Wiley-Interscience, New York.

[258] Ullman, S. [1979] *The Interpretation of Visual Motion*. MIT Press, Cambridge, MA.

[259] Umeyama, S., Kasvand, T., and Hospital, M. [1988] Recognition and positioning of three-dimensional objects by combining matchings of primitive local patterns. *Computer Vision, Graphics and Image Processing*, Vol. 44, 58–76.

[260] Veenstra, J., and Ahuja, N. [1986] Efficient oct-tree generation from silhouettes. *Proc. Intl. Conf. Computer Vision and Pattern Recognition*, (Miami, Florida, June), 537–542.

[261] Vemuri, B. C., and Aggarwal, J. K. [1986] Curvature-based representation of objects from range data. *Image and Vision Computing*, Vol. 4, No. 2, (May), 107–114.

[262] Vemuri, B. C., and Aggarwal, J. K. [1987] Representation and recognition of objects from dense range maps. *IEEE Trans. Circuits and Systems*, Vol. CAS-34, No. 11, (November), 1351–1363.

[263] Verri, A., and Poggio, T. [1989] Motion field and optical flow; qualitative properties. *IEEE Trans. Pattern Analysis and Machine Intelligence*, PAMI-11, Vol. 11, No. 5, (May), 490–498.

[264] Vranish, J. M. [1986a] Magnetoresistive skin for robots. *Robot Sensors Vol. 2: Tactile and Non-Vision*, A. Pugh (Ed.), Springer-Verlag, New York, 559–631.

[265] Vranish, J. M. [1986b] Magnetoinductive skin for robots. *Proc. 16th Intl. Symposium Industrial Robots*, (Kempston, Bedford, U.K.), 559–631.

[266] Vuylsteke, P., and Oosterlinck, A. [1990] Range image acquisition with a single binary-encoded light pattern. *IEEE Trans. Pattern Analysis Machine Intelligence*, Vol. 12, No. 2, (February), 148–164.

[267] Wah, B., and Li, G. J. (Eds.) [1985] *Computers for Artificial Intelligence Applications*. IEEE Computer Society Press, Los Alamitos, CA.

[268] Wallace, R. S., and Howard, M. D. [1989] HBA vision architecture : built and benchmarked. *IEEE Trans. Pattern Analysis and Machine Intelligence*, Vol. 11, No. 3, (March), 227–232.

[269] Walters, D. [1987] Selection of image primitives for general purpose visual processing. *Computer Vision, Graphics and Image Processing*, Vol. 37, 261–298.

[270] Waltz, D. [1975] Understanding line drawings of scenes with shadows. *Psychology of Computer Vision*, P. H. Winston (Ed.), McGraw Hill, New York.

[271] Wang, Y. F., Mitichie, A., and Aggarwal, J. K. [1987] Computation of surface orientation and structure of objects using grid coding. *IEEE Trans. Pattern Analysis and Machine Intelligence*, Vol. 9, No. 1, (January), 129–137.

[272] Weinshall, D. [1987] Qualitative depth and shape from stereo in agreement with psychological evidence. MIT AI Lab. Memo 1007, (December), MIT, Cambridge, MA.

[273] Weinshall, D. [1990] Qualitative depth from stereo with applications. *Computer Vision, Graphics and Image Processing*, Vol. 49, No. 2, (February), 222–241.

[274] Will, P. M., and Pennington, K. S. [1971] Grid coding: a preprocessing technique for robot and machine vision. *Artificial Intelligence*, Vol. 2, 319–329.

[275] Will, P. M., and Pennington, K. S. [1972] Grid coding: a novel technique for image processing. *Proc. IEEE*, Vol. 60, No. 6, (June), 669–680.

[276] Witkin, A. P. [1981] Recovering shape from texture. *Artificial Intelligence*, Vol. 17, Nos. 1-3, (August), 17–45.

[277] Wolfson, H. J. [1990] Model-based object recognition by geometric hashing. *Proc. European Conference Computer Vision*, 526–536.

[278] Wong, A. K. C., Lu, S. W., and Rioux, M. [1989] Recognition and shape synthesis of 3-D objects based on attributed hypergraphs. *IEEE Trans. Pattern Analysis and Machine Intelligence*, PAMI-11, Vol. 11, No. 3, (March), 279–290.

[279] Yalamanchili, S., Palem, K. V., Davis, L. S., Welch, A. J., and Aggarwal, J. K. [1985] Image processing architectures: a taxonomy and survey. *Progress in Pattern Recognition 2*, L. N. Kanal and A. Rosenfeld, (Eds.), Elsevier Science Publishers, Amsterdam, Netherlands.

[280] Yamaguchi, K. Y., Kunii, T. L., and Fujimura, K. [1984] Octree-related data structures and algorithms. *IEEE Computer Graphics and Applications*, Vol. 4, 53–59.

[281] Yamamoto, H., Sato, K., and Inokuchi, S. [1986] Range imaging system based on binary image accumulation. *Proc. Intl. Conf. Pattern Recognition*, (Paris, France, October), 229–255.

[282] Yang, H. S., and Kak, A. C. [1986] Determination of the identity, position, and orientation of the topmost object in a pile. *Computer Vision, Graphics, Image Processing*, Vol. 36, Nos. 2-3, (Nov.-Dec.), 229–255.

[283] Yau, M. M. [1984] Generating quadtrees of cross sections from octrees. *Computer Vision Graphics and Image Processing*, Vol. 27, 211–238.

[284] Yokoya, N. and Levine, M. D. [1989] Range image segmentation based on differential geometry - a hybrid approach. *IEEE Trans. Pattern Analysis and Machine Intelligence*, PAMI-11, Vol. 11, No. 6, (June), 643–649.

[285] Zadeh, L. A. [1965] Fuzzy sets. *Inform. Control*, Vol. 8, 338–353.

[286] Zadeh, L. A. [1968] Probability measures of fuzzy events, *Jour. Math. Analysis and Appl.*, Vol. 23, 421–427.

Index

ACRONYM 3, 8, 10, 93
active triangulation 28
angle constraint 161, 170, 270
area constraint 161
aspect graph 84
aspects 84, 109
attribute constraints 108
attribute pair 117
attribute set 117
attributed edge 117
attributed hypergraph 122
attributed relational graph 116
attributed vertex 117
axis of rotation 189, 213
axis of symmetry 184, 195, 205
azimuthal angle 18
backtracking 161, 267, 270, 272, 273
basis features 125
bending deformation 97, 127
BFM 271, 274, 277
biharmonic operator 51
bilaplacian operator 51
binary constraints 107, 132, 167, 207,
        209, 210
binocular stereo 25
binomial distribution 240, 244, 246
biorthogonal Chebychev polynomial
        59
biorthogonal polynomial 58
bipartite graph 119, 122
biquartic polynomial 51, 62
BONSAI 62, 108
Boolean hypercube 264, 265
breadth-first mapping 271
Butterfly 258
C* 263
Caltech Hypercube 258

Cellular Logic Information Proces-
        sor 4 258
centralized search 105
characteristic view 84, 85, 109, 116,
        119
class hierarchy 136
class-subclass hierarchy 138
class-subclass object hierarchies 136
CLIP 258
CLIP 4 258
CLIP 7 258
clique potential function 71
clustering
        in parameter space 148
clustering algorithm
        iterative 148
clutter 145, 180, 183, 235, 267
CM 257, 258, 264
CM-2 258, 260, 262, 263
CM-FORTRAN 263
coarse-to-fine strategy 116
combinatorial complexity 145, 159,
        160
combinatorial explosion 12, 183, 214
communications network 260
complex curved objects 184, 206
computational paradigm 3
computer vision 1, 3, 4, 257
        computational paradigm 3
concave edge pixels 151
conical surface 184, 192, 193, 197,
        198, 200, 210, 205, 206, 207,
        214, 265
        apex of 201
        localization of 201
        parameter space for 205
        recognition of 207

Connection Machine 205, 257, 258, 260, 263, 264, 265, 266
consistent labeling 103
constraint propagation 9, 74, 103, 135, 136, 139, 151, 157, 159, 165, 167, 168, 183, 206, 214
    graph-theoretic 7
constraint-directed search 104
constructive solid geometry 80
contour classification 150
contour detection 147
contour extraction 150
contour generators 94
contour lines 150, 157
contour pixels 151, 152, 154
control strategies 1, 7, 9, 10, 12, 135
    flexibility 11
convex edge pixels 151
convolution 259
Coons patch 37
correspondence problem 27
Cosmic Cube 258
coupled systems 135, 136
coupling of symbolic and numerical methods 11
crease edges 50, 118
crease likelihood ratio 71
curvature
    average 68
    Gaussian 68
    maximum 68
    mean 68
    minimum 68
    ratio 68
curvature edges 50
curved objects 183
    recognition of 183
curved surfaces 183, 214
    localization of 265
    recognition of 190
    representation of 184
cylindrical surface 184, 192, 193, 197, 198, 200, 205, 206, 207, 214, 265
    axis of 197
    centroid of 220

    localization of 200
    parameter space for 205
    recognition of 207
DADO 258
DADO2 258
data abstraction 137
data processors 260
data-directed search 107
data-driven search 104
data-parallel algorithm 258, 259
data-parallel computing 260
data-parallel operation 260, 263
data-parallel program 260
data-parallelism 258, 264
decomposed Hough clustering 114
degree constraint 166
depth edges 199
depth-first mapping 272
    with load sharing 273
descriptions
    surface 8
    distinctive 8
    generic 8
    global 8
    local 8
    volumetric 8
DFM 272, 274, 277
DFMWLS 273, 274, 277
differential geometry 41
diffraction blurring 33
Digital Optronics 23
dihedral feature junction pairs 207
dihedral feature junctions 174, 184, 206, 207, 210, 213, 214, 220, 224, 234, 266
    matching of 207
    pose determination of 210
    types of 207
dihedral junctions 160, 169, 170, 171, 173, 174, 207, 223, 224, 227, 234, 249, 250
    matching of 224, 227, 249
distance constraint 167, 270
distinctive feature 110
distributed search 105
edge attribute set 117

edge constraint 167
edge detection 259
edge likelihood ratio 73
edge operators
    Canny 50
    Kirsch 50
    Laplacian-of-Gaussian 50
    Sobel 50
edge parameters 151
    computation of 151
edge-linking 259
elastomer 35
Electro-Optical Information Systems
    32
elementary area attributed graph 122
elevation angle 18
Environmental Research Institute of
    Michigan 23
epipolar line 26
equiangular 18
Euler angle 98, 107, 112, 127
existence and uniqueness theorem 43
extended Gaussian image 8, 86
extrinsic attributes 120
extrinsic property 43
false hypotheses 184, 195
false interpretations 192
false matches 184
false peak 235
feature clustering 58
feature extraction 1, 13, 77, 79, 139,
    145, 157, 185, 196, 198, 205,
    223, 265,
feature matching 170
feature sphere 109
feature-indexed-hypothesis method 8
features
    model 223, 235, 236, 237, 239,
      240, 241, 242, 243, 250
    scene 223, 235, 236, 237, 239,
      240, 241, 242, 243, 248, 250
focus of expansion 28
focusing techniques 32
frame buffer 260, 262, 263
Frenet frame 45
Fresnel diffraction 33

front-end computers 260, 262, 263
fundamental forms of the surface 187
    first 187, 199
    second 187
fuzzy event 244, 245, 247, 249
fuzzy match 245
fuzzy numbers 245
fuzzy relation 243
fuzzy set 235, 242
fuzzy-probabilistic model 223, 235
Gauss-Newton technique 128
Gaussian curvature 40, 49, 56, 58,
    60, 69, 87, 183, 184, 185,
    187, 188, 192, 196, 197, 199,
    206, 214
Gaussian image 86
Gaussian map 132
Gaussian mask 55
Gaussian random variable 246, 247
Gaussian sphere 86, 87, 109, 110,
    114, 197, 198, 202,
generalized cylinders 8, 89
    axis of 89
    bilinear 91
    circular 91
    cross section of 89
    curved 90
    homogeneous 91
    linear 91
    oblique 91
    open 91
    plane of cross section of 89
    polygonal 91
    right 91
    straight 90
    sweeping rule of 89
    toroidal 91
    uniform 91
generalized Hough transform 112, 116,
    126, 145, 157, 160, 169, 174,
    180, 181, 183, 184, 188, 190,
    192, 223, 224, 235, 236, 237,
    239, 240, 241, 242, 243, 244,
    248, 249, 251, 264
    evaluation of 192
    hierarchical 116

limitations of 193
shortcomings of 184
steps of 192
with qualitative features 196
generalized images 3
generate-and-test 108
geodesic circle 132
geodesic tessellation 89
geometric hashing 124, 126
geometric primitives 39
geometric reasoning 3
geons 83
Gestalt clustering 132
Gibbs process 70
global shape descriptor 145, 183
global transformation 162
globally valid scene interpretation 106
graph monomorphism 118
graph-theoretic description 103
hash table 124
HCL Pyramid 258
Hessian matrix 61
HGF 159
hierarchical matching 123
high- level vision 3, 4, 258, 259
highest-confidence-first algorithm 70
histogram 266
histogramming 265, 266
holographic interferometry 32
Hough accumulator 111, 173, 179
Hough array 111, 179, 238, 249
Hough bucket 237, 238, 239, 241,
        242, 243, 245, 247, 251
Hough clustering 9, 12, 110, 151, 157,
        169, 179, 180, 193, 195, 196,
        198, 205, 206, 214
    iterative 154
    limitations of 193, 195
    two-dimensional 154
Hough space 111, 112, 115, 157, 173,
        184, 192, 193, 213
    false peaks in 184
    maxima detection 192
    six-dimensional 190, 192, 196
    spurious hypotheses 193, 214
    spurious peaks 206

Hough transform 110
    three-dimensional 114, 116
    two-dimensional 74, 147
Hungarian marriage problem 167, 174
hypercube 257, 258, 265, 266, 267,
        271, 272, 273
hypergraph 122
hypergraph monomorphism 124
hypothesis generating feature 108
hypothesis generating feature set 159,
        160
hypothesis generation phase 108
hypothesis verification 147, 153, 174
hypothesis verification phase 108
hypothesize-and-test 9, 105, 109, 161,
        267, 272, 273
I/O controller 260
ill-posed problem 3
Illiac-IV 258
image processing 1, 257, 258
    satellite 258
included angle 223, 227, 250, 252
    uncertainty in 250
index 130
index space 130
index table 132
indexing 8, 130
inertia matrices 100
inheritance 137
inside-out function 127
interest features 125
interpretation tree 9, 105, 106, 206,
        235, 266, 267, 268, 269, 270,
        271, 272, 273, 274, 277
    parallelization of 271
    paths in 161
    pruning of 161, 168
interpretation tree search 105, 130,
        145, 159, 160, 168, 174, 179,
        180, 181
    parallel 273, 274
interpretive control 109
interpretive search 105
intrinsic attributes 120
intrinsic characteristic 42
intrinsic images 3

intrinsic properties 183
invalid objects 78
invalid pixels 150
invariant surface curvatures 183
invariant surface features 44
inverse mapping 3
iPSC 258
iPSC/2 267, 271
iterative conditional modes 70
iterative model fitting 127, 129
jump edges 50, 118
jump likelihood ratio 71
junction labeling 133
junction matching 165, 173, 224
junction-labeling 12
K-means clustering 192
knowledge 1, 10
    common sense 3
    control 10
    domain-specific 3, 4
    in low-level vision 3
    meta 3
    qualitative nature 11
    use of 3
knowledge-based systems 135
Laplacian operator 151
least-squares plane fitting 67
length constraint 166, 170
Levenberg-Marquardt technique 128
limb edges 118
local shape descriptors 183
localization 1, 7, 10, 11, 13, 103, 270
    accuracy of 192, 193, 195, 205
locally valid scene interpretation 106
low-level vision 3, 4, 258, 259
Markov random field 69
Massively Parallel Processor (MPP)
    258
match quality 119, 174
maximal clique 206
maximal clique detection 103
maximum a posteriori estimate 70
Maxwell-Boltzmann statistics 240, 244,
    245
mean curvatures 40, 49, 56, 58, 60,
    69, 183, 184, 185, 187, 188,

192, 196, 197, 199, 206, 214
membership function 235, 242, 243,
    244, 245, 248
merging criteria 149
message-passing 136
methods 138
MIMD 257, 258, 259, 267
model ARG 117, 119
model facet pair 113
model-directed search 107
model-driven search 104
Moire interference pattern 31
Moire interferometry 31
moment invariants 101
Monge patch 18, 49
monomorphism 118, 119, 120, 123
motion 259
motion stereo 27
    axial 27
multiple instruction stream-multiple
    data stream 257
Navlab 259
NCUBE/ten 258
needle map 87, 197, 198, 201
neighborhood constraint 161
Newport Corporation 32
NEWS grid 262
node consistency 107
non-maxima suppression 55
non-planar facets 160, 185, 188, 189
non-spherical point 188
non-umbilic point 185, 189
NON-VON 258
nonsense objects 78
normal curvature 47
null model feature 108
object 136
    class 137
    composite 137
    constraint 137
    matched 138
    primitive 137
object attributed hypergraph 123
object consistency constraint 166
object-oriented framework 136

object-oriented representation 136, 137

object recognition 264

occluded scene facets 161, 162, 179

occluding boundaries 94

occluding contour 128

occlusion 145, 157, 159, 161, 162, 171, 174, 179, 180, 183, 184, 185, 192, 195, 196, 200, 201, 202, 206, 214, 220, 235, 236, 237, 241, 243, 248, 249, 267

oct-tree 8, 98, 99

Odetics, Inc. 23

omega interconnection network 258

optical interferometry 30

optimal assignment problem 167, 174

orientation axis 113

orientation constraint 166

orientation histogram 87

orthogonal Chebyshev polynomial 61

orthographic 18

oversegmentation 153, 168

parallel algorithms 259

parallel architectures 257, 259

parallel computers 257, 259
   reconfigurable 259

parallel computing
   in vision 257

parallel constructs 263

parallel divide-and-conquer 266

parallel floating point accelerator 260

parallel implementation 257

parallel processing 259, 260
   in computer vision 257

parallel processing unit 260, 262

parallelism 135, 140
   data 140
   functional 140

parameter space 112, 234, 235, 236, 237, 238, 241, 244, 248, 250, 251

part-subpart hierarchy 136

part-subpart object hierarchies 136

PASM 259

perceptual grouping 11

perceptual organization 39

pinhole camera 26

planar facets 145, 151, 152, 153, 157, 161, 166, 168

planar patches 149, 150

planar surface patches 145

plane fitting 147

Platonic solids 89

point-wise curvature 184, 188, 190, 192, 205

Poisson approximation 240, 242, 247

Poisson distribution 244, 246, 248

polyhedral object 145, 147, 156, 157, 174, 180

polyhedral object recognition 145

pose 184, 189, 213, 214
   global 184
   global 206, 268
   globally consistent 183
   globally consistent 213

pose clustering 173, 213, 266

pose computation 207, 223, 249, 266

pose determination 162, 192, 210, 213, 224

pose hypothesis 114, 173, 184
   verification of 173

pose parameters
   errors in 223

post processing
   of clustering results 149

precompiled search 105

preprocessing 145

primitive block attributed graph 122

principal curvature 40, 58, 183, 185, 187, 188, 189, 190, 192, 195, 199, 201, 206
   maximum 183, 185
   minimum 183, 185

principal projections 100

principal surface curvatures 47

probabilistic occupancy model 240, 241, 244

problem graph 140

projection geometry 147, 152

proximity constraint 165

pyramid computer 258

quadric curve 94

qualitative attributes 132, 159, 161, 166, 174, 179, 180
qualitative features 1, 7, 11, 12, 13, 83, 130, 134, 145, 159, 160, 170, 174, 179, 180, 181, 183, 184, 196, 223, 235, 241, 242, 243
    advantages of 202
    in recognition 198, 202
    the role of 12
qualitative topology 84
radar sensors 20
    amplitude modulated 21
    frequency modulated 23
    time-of-flight 21
radius function 92
random peaks 244
range image 17
    xyz form 17
    forms 17
    sensors 17
range sensors
    active 20
    classification of 20
    contact 20
    non-contact 20
    passive 20
    tactile 34
ray-tracing 77, 80, 100
Rayleigh criterion 21
recognition 103
    using qualitative features 196
recognition-followed-by-localization 7, 103
recognition-via-localization 7, 103, 105
reconfigurable network 258
redundancy factor 239, 241
region growing 58, 69, 147, 150
region label 41
regression 62
regularization 3, 259
relational constraints 108
relational description 103
relational structures 116
    matching of 116
relaxation 259

representation 8, 77, 136
    aspect graph-based 84
    constructive solid geometry 80
    distinctive 79
    feature-level 77
    generic 79
    geometric 77
    geon-based 83
    global 79
    local 79
    multiple-view 84
    qualitative 83
    superquadric-based 94
    surface-based 79
    unambiguity of 78
    uniqueness of 78
    using extended Gaussian image 86
    using generalized cylinders 89
    using octree 98
    volumetric 79
    wire-frame 79
representation modeling 77
representation scheme 7, 78, 135
representational granularity 157
rigid-body motion 125, 185, 188, 192, 205, 206, 266
rigid-body transform 107, 119
roof edge 50, 147, 151, 152, 153, 166, 199, 200,
rotation 185, 188, 189, 195, 205, 214
rotation matrix 164, 195
rotation parameters 214, 223, 227, 234
rotational transformation 162
scene ARG 117, 119
scene facet pair 113
scene interpretation hypothesis 165
    verification of 165
search strategy
    bottom-up or data-driven 10
    centralized 10
    distributed 10
    interpretive 10
    precompiled 10
    top-down or model-driven 9

segmentation 4, 50, 145, 156, 159, 161, 166, 168, 174, 223, 242, 243
    edge-based 50
    hybrid 69
    numerical 67
    region-based 58
    the role of 39
segmentation algorithms 139, 145
segmentation problem 41
segmentation schemes
    edge-based 147
    region-based 147
sensitivity analysis 223, 224, 227, 235, 249
sensors
    based on focusing techniques 32
    based on Fresnel diffraction 33
    based on optical interferometry 30
    proximity 34
sequencer 260, 262, 263
shadow pixels 150
shape descriptions
    global 7
shape function 92
shape parameter 94, 98, 127
shape-from-shading 3, 12, 133
shape-from-stereo 12, 133
shape-from-texture 12, 133
SIMD 257
    fine-grained 258, 259
    mesh-connected 258
SIMD/MIMD 259
simulated annealing 70
single instruction stream-multiple data stream 257
site-labeling 69
sonar sensors 23
space curve 44
    curvature function 44
    speed function 44
    unit binomial vector function 45
    unit normal vector function 45
    unit tangent vector function 44
specialization 137

spherical product 95
spherical surface 190, 192, 197, 202, 205, 207, 214
    localization of 201, 202, 207
splashes 131
splines
    B 62, 186
    bicubic 62
    cubic B 63
    tension 64
spurious hypotheses 184
    number of 214
spurious interpretation 183
spurious peak 12, 116, 184, 195
    in generalized Hough transform 239
spurious scene hypotheses 235
*Lisp 263
step edge 147, 151, 152, 155, 169
step edge parameters
    computation of 154
stereo 259
structural indexing 131, 132
subgraph isomorphism 103, 118, 206
superellipse 94
superellipsoid 96
superquadratic model fitting 128
superquadric 94
superquadric curve 94
superquadric representation 127
superquadrics 8
surface curvature 44, 185, 186, 195, 205, 206
surface curvature features 186
surface discontinuities 39, 147, 157, 199, 200
surface feature extraction 192
surface-fitting 58, 186, 192, 198, 205
surface fundamental forms 41
    first 41, 60
    second 42, 60
surface matching 192, 214
surface normal 67, 186, 188, 189, 192, 197, 199, 201, 205, 206
surface patches 39
surface reconstruction 259

surface types 184, 185, 192, 197, 205,
        206, 220
    elliptic 67
    hillside 61
    hyperbolic 67
    parabolic 67
    peak 61
    pit 61
    planar umbilic 67
    qualitative 184, 196, 199, 207,
        214
    ravine 61
    ridge 61
    saddle 61
    umbilic 67
symbolic reasoning 10
system graph 140
systolic array 259
    programmable 259
tactel 34
tactile 267
tapering 96, 127
Technical Arts Corporation 29
terminator boundaries 94
tessellation 89
textons 11
textons 133
TGF 160, 184, 188
thinning 259
three-dimensional object recognition
        1, 4, 7, 9, 11
    common goals 10
    model-based 10
3-DPO vision system 8
3D-POLY 108, 109
torsion function 45
transducers
    capacitive 35
    conductive 35
    magnetic 36
    mechanical 36
    optical 36
    piezoelectric 35
    pyroelectric 35
    resistive 35

transformation generating feature 112,
        160, 169, 184
transformational constraint 132
translation parameters 98, 127, 223,
        227
translation vector 113, 189
translational transformation 162
triangulation sensors 25
umbilic surface 195
unary constraint 106, 207, 209
unique interpretation constraint 134,
        162, 242, 269
unoccluded scene facets 174, 179, 181
vertex attribute set 117
vertex compatibility table 122
vertex refinement
    for roof edges 153
    for step edges 154
view axis 113
view-sphere 84, 86
viewpoint sampling 110
virtual processors 262, 264
visual event 84
WARP 259
weighted generalized Hough trans-
        form 235, 242, 244, 248, 249,
        251, 252
wire-frame 79
wrap-around mesh 264, 265
z-buffer 77, 100